10⁰⁰

LETTERS OF HORATIO GREENOUGH

AMERICAN SCULPTOR

LETTERS OF

HORATIO GREENOUGH

AMERICAN SCULPTOR

EDITED BY

NATHALIA WRIGHT

The University of Wisconsin Press

Published 1972
The University of Wisconsin Press
Box 1379, Madison, Wisconsin 53701

The University of Wisconsin Press, Ltd.
70 Great Russell Street, London

First printing

Printed in the United States of America
Kingsport Press, Inc., Kingsport, Tennessee

ISBN 0–299–06070–5; LC 77–176417

To

Richard Beale and Lois Davis

and

Rolando and Gloria Anzilotti

of

America and Italy

CONTENTS

The Correspondence

ILLUSTRATIONS

Frontispiece

Horatio Greenough, ca. 1839
From editor's collection

Following page 210

ACKNOWLEDGMENTS

I wish to thank the following owners of letters by Greenough and authorities in charge of collections containing letters by Greenough for allowing copies of these manuscripts to be made and, when it was within their jurisdiction, for granting permission to publish them: Accademia di Belle Arti, Florence; The Adams Manuscript Trust, c/o Massachusetts Historical Society; The American Academy of Arts and Letters, New York City; Archives of American Art, Smithsonian Institution; Archivio del Stato, Florence; Professor James F. Beard, Clark University, literary executor of James Fenimore Cooper; The Beinecke Rare Book and Manuscript Library, Yale University; Biblioteca e Archivio del Risorgimento, Florence; Biblioteca Nazionale Centrale, Florence; Professor E. Maurice Bloch, University of California, Los Angeles; The Boston Athenaeum; Boston Public Library; Brown University Library; L. W. Butterfield, Editor-in-Chief of the Adams Papers; The Carl and Lily Pforzheimer Foundation, New York City; Duke University Library; The Emerson Memorial Association; the Fenimore Cooper family; Haverford College Library; The Henry Francis Du Pont Winterthur Museum, Winterthur, Delaware; The Historical Society of Pennsylvania, Philadelphia; The Houghton Library, Harvard University; Isaac Mendoza Book Store, New York City; The Library of Congress; The Trustees of the Longfellow Trust, Boston, Massachusetts; Maine Historical Society; Massachusetts Historical Society; Morristown National Historical Park, Morristown, New Jersey; National Academy of Design, New York City; The National Archives; The New-York Historical Society; The New York Public Library; The New York State Library, Albany; Henry G. Nickerson, Dedham, Massachusetts; David Richardson, Washington, D. C.; Mrs. Nina Howell Starr, Gainesville, Florida; Wellesley College Library; William L. Clements Library, University of Michigan; Yale University Library.

I wish further to thank the following owners of copyrighted material for permission to quote passages from this material: The Belknap Press of Harvard University Press, Trustees of the Boston Public Library, *Harvard Library Bulletin,* Yale University Press.

I am also grateful to the following persons for assistance in obtaining information used in the annotations: Mr. John Alden, Keeper of Rare Books, Boston Public Library; Professor James F. Beard, Clark University; Mrs. Clara L. Dentler, Florence; Mr. David McKibbin, Art Librarian, The Boston Athenaeum; Dr. Harold Orton, Emeritus Professor, University of Leeds; Baron Giuseppe Rapisardi di S. Antonio, Florence; and the directors, curators, secretaries, or reference librarians of the following institutions: Accademia Nazionale di San Luca, Rome; Baker Library, Harvard University; Boston Public Library; Bostonian Society; The City Library Association, Springfield, Massachusetts; Columbiana Collection, Columbia University; Dartmouth College Library; Harvard University Archives; General Reference and Bibliography Department, The Library of Congress; Diplomatic, Legal, and Fiscal Records Division, National Archives; The New Haven Colony Historical Society; Orsz. Szépmuveszeti Muzeum, Budapest; The Pilgrim Society, Plymouth, Massachusetts; The South Carolina Historical Society, Charleston; Thomas Crane Public Library, Quincy, Massachusetts; Touring Club Italiano, Milan; Universitatsbibliothek Wien, Vienna; University College, Dublin.

To Professor Rolando Anzilotti, University of Pisa, I acknowledge a particular debt for his assistance in the transcription and translation of Greenough's Italian, as well as in many other projects involving American-Italian relationships, and wish to express my deep gratitude for his guidance and hospitality in Italy over the years this volume has been in preparation.

NATHALIA WRIGHT

Knoxville, Tennessee
October 1971

INTRODUCTION

THIRTY-FIVE years after the death of Horatio Greenough in 1852 at the age of 47, his sister-in-law Frances Boott Greenough, wife of his brother Henry, published *Letters of Horatio Greenough to his Brother, Henry Greenough* (Boston, 1887). This volume contains seventy of Horatio's letters to Henry and one each to his father and his fellow Bostonians Samuel A. Eliot and Robert C. Winthrop. It also contains an introductory biographical sketch, several short biographical passages, and connecting groups of letters written by Frances, as well as a few letters from Greenough's relatives and friends. The book was thus not only a collection of Greenough's letters—the only one before the present collection—but in effect a biography, fuller in many respects than Henry T. Tuckerman's *A Memorial of Horatio Greenough* (1853), the only other separately published account to appear for over a century.

During this period Greenough, the first American to enter the profession of sculpture, shared critical neglect with most other American sculptors of the nineteenth century. As a group they are, indeed, less distinguished for their artistic achievement than for their historical significance. Yet, in view of his unique prominence as the sculptor of two works for the United States Capitol, as well as his lifelong association with many American writers and his own accomplishments as a writer, this virtual oblivion for so long calls for special explanation.

Greenough's reputation, once highest among his professional American contemporaries, was at the time of his death uncertain, largely because neither of his works for the Capitol won popular approval. His *Washington* for the Capitol Rotunda, a major attempt to carry out his conception of art as an expression of the ideal, represented the subject half-draped and in the pose of Phidias's *Zeus* and was generally condemned for both indecency and evidence of foreign influence.

His group *The Rescue,* for a blocking on the steps of the east front of the Capitol, was a partial concession to the current vogue of realism —it depicted a pioneer man restraining an Indian from killing a pioneer woman and child—but was judged too tame by most of those who commented on it at all. His one book, *The Travels, Observations, and Experience of a Yankee Stonecutter,* printed a few months before he died, contained the fullest expression of his functional theory of architecture, the first explicit annunciation of such a theory by an American. But apparently only a few copies were distributed, and his ideas not being understood, it was hardly noticed. The fact that he died deranged, moreover, further blurred his claims to achievement.

In the middle of the present century, however, Greenough has been rated as one of the two or three best among the first generation of American sculptors. More significantly, he has been recognized as an architectural theorist who contributed directly to the emergence of the functional school of American architecture headed by Louis Sullivan. He was also a highly individualistic American intellectual, the often influential friend of many others of his day. It is chiefly in the last of these roles that he is revealed by the letters in this collection.

Greenough's letters deserve to be collected for several reasons. Stylistically they are almost always interesting, often memorable. He wrote with fluency and a flair for turning phrases, while at the same time observing certain conventions of the epistolary genre which link him with a long line of letter writers. Perhaps partly because he spent most of his life abroad yet was eager to be known among his countrymen, he usually took occasion to report his activities in detail and volunteered his opinions on a variety of subjects. To his intimates he freely expressed his drastically fluctuating moods. His letters are thus of the greatest biographical importance, evincing not only the multiplicity of his projects and his distinctive views—particularly on art, politics, literature, and national character—but also his ambition and nationalism, his warmth yet formality, his sensitivity and intensity. Above all, Greenough's letters are a contribution to American cultural history. He seemed instinctively to compare American and European political and social institutions, artists, and works of art; and he seldom failed to claim an American distinction and superiority.

This collection of letters represents Greenough's entire career, with its several interruptions and changes of interest. It includes most of, if not all, those in the outstanding series of letters which he is known to have written to Washington Allston, Cooper, Emerson, Robert Gilmor, Jr., Samuel F. B. Morse, Hiram Powers, and representatives of the U.S. government. The only conspicuous absence is that of the dozen or more which he wrote Edward Everett.

The first two letters in this volume were written in 1825, the year in which Greenough graduated from Harvard, won the judges' decision for the best design in the competition for the Bunker Hill Monument, and went to Rome to study sculpture. For the next two years (during which period he became ill and returned to America), there are only three. The number increases from three in 1828 to twenty-three in 1832, the year in which he received his first government commission, averages nine during the next six years, rises to twenty-one in 1839, and averages eleven from 1840 through 1843. During his remaining eight years abroad (he visited America in 1842–43), the letters average only three or four a year. Throughout this period he had few private commissions, was increasingly disturbed by the government's failure to pay the installment due on his second commission for the Capitol, and was frustrated by the delay in obtaining marble to complete it. After the summer of 1845, when his first child was born, he had new domestic interests. Most of the letters for 1845 and 1846 describe the hydropathic treatment from which his wife benefited at this time. From the fall of 1845 to the spring of 1850 his brother Henry (to whom he was closer than to anyone else) and Henry's family were in Europe, most of the time living near Horatio and his family. With his final return to America in the fall of 1851, Greenough's interests and projects proliferated as never before; during the twelve months from November 1851 to November 1852 there are thirty-one letters, more than for any other period of the same length.

These 241 letters of Greenough's are addressed to some eighty persons. The largest group of recipients, to whom about half the letters were written, were patrons or represented patrons of his works. Twelve—John Quincy Adams, William Cullen Bryant, Samuel Cabot, Gino Capponi, Cooper, Gilmor, David Hoffman, Thomas H. Perkins, Josiah Quincy, James I. Roosevelt, E. E. Salisbury, and John C. Warren—were his private patrons, though not all his letters to them were concerned with their orders. The thirty-one to Cooper, who was one of his most valued friends, are more than twice the number to any other person. Besides chronicling the execution of the group which Cooper ordered—*The Chanting Cherubs*—they reveal the young sculp-

tor in a particularly ingratiating light. To Gilmor, his first major patron, there are twelve letters, reporting work on Gilmor's orders for a
bust of Mrs. Gilmor and a statue, the *Medora,* as well as purchases of
items for Gilmor's art collection. In connection with his works for the
government, there are about thirty letters to various officials, including Adams, George Bancroft, and several secretaries of State, the
Treasury, and the Navy. About a dozen other letters concern projects
which Greenough never carried out: the Bunker Hill monument, an
equestrian *Washington,* statues of Benedict Arnold, John André, and
Nathan Hale, a monument to Cooper, and new designs for U.S. coins.

Of the other half of these letters, nearly a fourth were written to
artists and about the same number to writers and editors of periodicals. To Washington Allston, whom Greenough considered his artistic
master and intellectual father, he wrote at greater length and more
personally than to anyone else outside his family. The most prominent
writer among his correspondents, besides Bryant and Cooper, was
Ralph Waldo Emerson, to whom Greenough wrote seven letters.
Among the other writers with whom he corresponded were Lady
Bulwer, Richard Henry Dana, William Dunlap, Abner Dumont Jones,
G. W. Greene, Walter Savage Landor, Henry Wadsworth Longfellow,
R. H. Wilde, James Kirke Paulding, and Henry T. Tuckerman.

The eighteen remaining letters are mostly short, conventional, and
miscellaneous in content. They deal with the issuance and acceptance
of invitations, the introduction and recommendation of friends, reports on purchases of art objects, the transmission of books and
articles, negotiations with bankers, and acknowledgments of election
to honorary societies. There are a few to old personal and family
friends, like his Harvard classmate Francis J. Higginson and Robert
C. Watterson, with whose wife Greenough's wife had been brought
up; and there are three to his mother and his brothers John and
Henry.

It is perhaps noteworthy, considering Greenough's long residence
abroad and wide circle of European acquaintances, that few of his
letters are to Europeans, and that most of these are of little significance. Altogether, only seventeen have come to light: to Robert Balmanno, Lady Bulwer, Gino Capponi, Emanuele Fenzi, Walter Savage
Landor, G. B. Niccolini, G. W. Poussin, and John Ward [?]. For all
his cosmopolitanism, Greenough's longest and deepest associations
were with Americans.

Chronological Table, 1805–1852

1805   6 September, born in Boston.

1825   *ca.* March, entered competition for design of Bunker Hill Monument; graduated from Harvard College; May, went to Rome to study sculpture, arriving in the fall.

1827   March, sailed for Boston because of illness, arriving in May.

1828   January–May, visited New York, Philadelphia, Washington, and Baltimore; May, sailed for Italy; September–*ca.* November, in Carrara; *ca.* November, settled in Florence.

1831   September–November, in Paris to model bust of Lafayette.

1832   Commissioned by Congress to execute statue of Washington for rotunda of the Capitol.

1834   August–September, in Paris to obtain authorities for *Washington.*

1836   May, sailed for New York, arriving in June; June–July, in Washington to examine site for *Washington;* July–September, in Boston; September, with sister Louisa, sailed for England; November–December, in London; December, went to Paris.

1837   January, went from Paris to Florence; July, received congressional commission for a group for blocking of steps on east portico of the Capitol; 14 October, married Louisa Ingersoll Gore.

1841   June–September, in Paris; September, sailed for New York; September–November, in Boston; November, went to Washington.

1843   January–July, arranged for removal of *Washington* to Capitol grounds; April, moved to Wilmington, Delaware; May–July, visited Philadelphia, Boston, and New York; July, sailed for Liverpool; July, August, essays "Remarks on American Art" and "American Architecture" published in the *United States Magazine and Democratic Review;* July–September, in England; September–October, went from London to Florence by way of Paris, Strasbourg, Munich, and Milan.

1844   April, went to Gräfenberg, Silesia, for the water cure for his wife.

1845   11 May, birth of son Henry (later, Horatio) Saltonstall Greenough; September, returned to Florence.

1846   May–September, in Freiwaldau, Silesia.

1848   Built studio on Piazza Maria Antonia (now Independenza), Florence.

1851   July, completed *The Rescue,* left Florence with family; July–August, in Switzerland; September, in England; October, sailed for Boston;

November, went to Washington; December, *Æsthetics at Washington* published.

1852   January, in Washington and New York; January–*ca.* March, in Boston; *ca.* April, established studio in Brooklyn; May, took family to Newport, Rhode Island; *ca.* 1 September, *The Travels, Observations, and Experience of a Yankee Stonecutter* published; September, in Washington; 4 December, hospitalized; 18 December, died.

TEXTS AND EDITORIAL POLICY

THE present edition of Greenough's letters consists of all that have been located except three addressed to the editors of the *Home Journal*, printed there in June 1852 and reprinted in his *Travels*, and those in Frances B. Greenough's *Letters*. The 241 letters in this collection come from widely scattered sources.[1] The originals have been found for 213 letters, of which 188 are here printed in their entirety for the first time. As for the remaining twenty-eight, four are available only as quoted in letters by others, one as a typed copy of a letter manuscript, and the rest in previously printed versions. The 217 manuscripts are located in some twenty-seven depositories here and abroad.

Greenough customarily wrote with care, forming letters precisely, sloping words to the right, and producing even and flowing lines from margin to margin. In the most important of his letters he elaborated capitals and spaced salutations and closings on separate lines. He seldom failed to punctuate at the ends of sentences, close parentheses and quotation marks, and capitalize properly. Like many of his contemporaries, however, he preferred the dash to the period and rarely used the semicolon. His paragraphs were usually deeply indented, although, especially in his early letters, he tended to leave unduly long spaces between words when shifting subjects, as if to indicate new paragraphs. At least in early years he made drafts of some letters. Several later ones, however, suggest by the cramped hand, the obvious errors in spelling, and the omission or repetition of words that they were composed under pressure and not read over. Only occasionally did he cancel or insert passages. His chief deficiency was his misspelling, which he blamed on his study of foreign lan-

1. The source for each letter and place of previous publication (if any) are given in the general note at the end of the letter.

guages—Greek in his youth and Italian and French later. He seemed, in fact, self-conscious about his epistolary form. "My orthography is my own," he wrote Lady Lytton, "and I punctuate by the grace of God as the Kings say which means in a graceless manner." To Charles G. Loring he alleged that he would never have been aware of either his spelling or his grammatical weaknesses but for his wife, "who not having received a *liberal education* is pretty well versed in her mother tongue —." In any case, he often had his letters written by either his wife or his brother Henry.

In the present volume, Greenough's letters are reproduced with a minimum of editorial alteration. Superscript letters have been brought down to the line, and apostrophes have been added to contractions, abbreviations, and possessives where necessary, but Greenough's habit of omitting periods after "Mr.," "Mrs.," and the like has been preserved. Words inadvertently repeated, cancellations, and false starts have not been reproduced. Obvious misspellings and those archaic or peculiar spellings likely to give pause to the modern reader have been silently corrected. Certain technical terms, which occur infrequently, have been corrected as indicated in the notes. When it is uncertain whether the mark of punctuation at the end of a sentence is a dash or a period, a period has been used, and sentences and fragments without punctuation have been properly closed. Sentences and fragments preceded by terminal punctuation are begun with capital letters. Parentheses and quotation marks have been completed when necessary, and elongated dashes filling out lines have been omitted. Undue space between words, apparently used by Greenough to indicate a new paragraph, is not noted, but a new paragraph is begun where the space occurs. Editorial additions are enclosed in brackets, and doubtful readings and dates are indicated by bracketed question marks. Postmarks have been omitted.

The letters have been numbered consecutively and are presented chronologically. Full identification of each correspondent is given in a general note following the first letter addressed to him.

Citations have been kept to a minimum. Most of the information in the notes, when undocumented, comes from the editor's *Horatio Greenough: The First American Sculptor* (Philadelphia, 1963) and from general encyclopedias and biographical dictionaries. The following works in particular have been employed without credit:

Allgemeines Lexikon der Bildenden Künstler. Edited by Ulrich
Thieme and Felix Becker. Leipzig, 1907–50.

Biographical Directory of the American Congress, 1774–1927. Washington, 1928.

L. R. Hamersly. *List of Officers of the U.S. Navy and of the Marine
Corps, 1775–1900.* New York, 1901.

Sources other than these, and other than those listed under "Abbreviations and Short Titles," are given in full upon their first citation in
every letter.

Abbreviations and Short Titles

Beinecke	Beinecke Rare Book and Manuscript Library, Yale University
Biblioteca Nazionale	Biblioteca Nazionale Centrale, Florence
BPL	Boston Public Library
Cooper	James Fenimore Cooper. *The Letters and Journals of James Fenimore Cooper.* Edited by James Franklin Beard. 6 vols. Cambridge, Mass., 1960–66.
Flagg	Jared Flagg. *The Life and Letters of Washington Allston.* New York, 1892.
Greenough	Hamilton Perkins Greenough. *Some Descendants of Captain William Greenough of Boston, Massachusetts.* Santa Barbara, 1969.
Houghton	Houghton Library, Harvard University
HSP	Historical Society of Pennsylvania
LC	Library of Congress
Letters	Horatio Greenough. *The Letters of Horatio Greenough to his Brother, Henry Greenough.* Edited by Frances Boott Greenough. Boston, 1887.
MHS	Massachusetts Historical Society
NA	National Archives
NEHGR	*New England Historical and Genealogical Register*
NYHS	New-York Historical Society
NYPL	New York Public Library
ProcMHS	*Proceedings of the Massachusetts Historical Society*

LETTERS OF HORATIO GREENOUGH

AMERICAN SCULPTOR

1. To the Bunker Hill Monument Association
   [March?] 1825

To the committee of the Bunker-Hill monument Association

Gentlemen

Having designed an obelisk instead of a column, and presented a model rather than a perspective drawing for the purpose of illustration — it has seemed to me proper to explain, what might be interpreted a willful or negligent disregard to the published proposals of your committee.[1]

I have given you my design in a model — because — as it may be examined from every quarter, it may be said to *contain* in itself a perspective of the object, as seen from *every point* instead of *one only,* and is on that account more easily and perfectly understood.

I have made choice of the obelisk as the most purely *monumental* form of structure. The column grand and beautiful as it is *in its place* (where it stands beneath the weight of a pediment & supports a long line of heavy entablature) considered as a monument seems liable to unanswerable objections. It steps forth from that *body* of which it has been made a harmonious *part* to take a situation which of all others requires *unity* of form — hence — the more completely it has been *fitted* to a situation so different — the greater must be the number of *useless* appendages and *unmeaning* parts when it assumes its new place and office — in fact — that increase in the upper part of the shaft of the column in each of the Greek orders as plainly implies a *weight above* to be supported as the base implies a *ground* on which to *stand.*

The proportions of this obelisk are taken from one at ancient Thebes.[2] The height from the ground to the top of the plinth is twenty feet — from the plinth to the apex of the shaft one hundred feet.

A circular staircase, lighted by narrow windows of glazed loop holes which could not be seen at a short distance, might be carried as high as the base of the pyramid in which the structure terminates. This staircase might be entered at one of the sides of the plinth by a door, of the same colour as the rest of the building, and made without any

3

projecting parts about it — so that the lines would not be cut up, or the masses of light and shadow broken.

The entrance would be reached by ascending a flight of twenty steps — which are to be seen on each side of the lower base in the model — The four blocks at the angles are designed to receive four groups of monumental or allegorical sculpture[3] — These are indicated by the pieces of clay seen on those parts of the model. But should any circumstance prevent or delay the erection of these, four large field pieces would form noble and appropriate ornaments, and would contrast pleasingly with the general form of the other parts of the structure.

The scale in the drawing of the section is reduced to one half that of the model. — No 12

Addressed: To Nathaniel P Russell Esqr[4] / Treasurer of the Bunker-Hill monument association / Boston / with N 12 — / Plan & Model

NOTES

The Bunker Hill Monument Association announced in January 1825 a competition, to end 1 April, for the design of a monument to be erected on the site of the Battle of Bunker Hill. A premium of $100 was offered.

Manuscript: Bunker Hill Monument Association Papers, MHS. Previous publication: G. W. Warren, *The History of the Bunker Hill Monument Association* (Boston, 1877), p. 159.

1. The Standing Committee of the Association, which announced the competition, called specifically for a plan and a perspective drawing of a 220-foot column. The judges recommended that Greenough receive the prize, but none was awarded; and although an obelisk was built, it was not from Greenough's design.

   The model has apparently been destroyed, but Greenough sent a drawing of his design to Samuel F. B. Morse (see Letter 43 to Morse and Plate V). Another drawing of it is reproduced in Samuel Swett, "Horatio Greenough, the Designer of the Bunker Hill Monument," *NEHGR* 18 (1864): 60, and in Warren, *History of the Bunker Hill Monument Association*, p. 160.

2. Presumably that erected by Queen Hatshepsut of the Eighteenth Dynasty (*ca.* 1580 B.C.) before the temple of Ammon, estimated to be 97½ feet high.

3. Drawings which Greenough made for these groups depicted a nude male figure being held down by a lion, then forcing the lion down, next seeming to embrace the lion, and last looking upward, his hands clasped, a sword resting on his leg, an eagle and a scroll on the ground before him. The first three were entitled "Subjection of the Colonies," "Resistance of the Colonies," and "Discomfiture of the British Forces"; the fourth was apparently untitled. Tracings of the drawings, made by one of Henry Greenough's daughters, are

in the editor's collection. Her tracing of the drawing for the second group is reproduced in Swett, "Horatio Greenough," p. 60.
4. Nathaniel Pope Russell (1779–1848) was a Boston merchant, Massachusetts state legislator (1822), and state senator (1826–27).

2.   To Henry Alexander Scammell Dearborn [April?] 1825

Boston — Monday —

Dear Sir

The inclosed is the estimate which I promised should be sent you as soon as finished — I regret that I have been unable to furnish it sooner —.

Yours with respect —
Horatio Greenough

May 25. Estimate of erecting an obelisk on Bunkers Hill Charlestown.[1]

1818.	perch stone[2] — @ 27v		$.	8181	
58160.	feet cube rough stone — 2v			19387.	
37108.	feet super. Labor & Sett[3] ⅙.			9279.	
	Cramps.[4] &c			200.	37045.[5]
1200	feet. Rim Supr & Sett	⅞		1500. —	
945.	Do. Steps to inside of Obelisk	⅞		1181. —	2681.
40110.	Feet cube to obelisk.	2/		13370.	
16440.	Do. Super. Labor &c	⅙.		4110.	
	Irons Cramps. &c			750.	18230.
				Dolls.	57956.

Height of the monument. 220 feet.

Addressed: For / H. A. S. Dearborn Esqr / *Boston*
Endorsed: Horatio Greenough's / Estimate of / the cost of / an obelisk / 97.400[6]

NOTES

Henry Scammell Dearborn (1783–1851) was a director of the Bunker Hill
Monument Association.

This letter was probably written in April 1825; early in May 1825, Greenough sailed from Boston for Italy, to study sculpture.

Manuscript: Mellen Chamberlain Autograph Collection, BPL.

1. The enclosure is in Henry Greenough's hand. In another hand, sideways on
   the left margin alongside the first three items: "Foundation and Base / pre-
   liminary."
2. A perch is commonly 24¾ cubic feet, but here it was apparently reckoned
   27 cubic feet (or volume).
3. Apparently "super" means square feet and "sett" the process of lowering into
   place and fixing the stone.
4. Devices to hold blocks together.
5. The total should be 37,047.
6. The source of this figure is not clear. The final cost of the monument was
   $101,963.

3.   To George Parkman
   1 May 1826

[Rome]

I shall deliver your parcel to Madam M.[1]

NOTES

George Parkman (1791–1849), Boston physician, assisted Greenough in his study
of anatomy while he was a student at Harvard.

Source: George Parkman to Lady Margaret Mount Cashell 1 November 1826,
The Carl and Lily Pforzheimer Library, New York City. Parkman's letter gives
the date and place of Greenough's letter. Greenough reached Rome in the fall of
1825.

1. Lady Margaret (King) Mount Cashell (1773–1835) was known as Mrs.
   Mason after she left her husband to live with George William Tighe. In 1804
   she and Tighe settled in Pisa, Italy. Possibly the parcel contained books on
   medicine, a subject in which she was long interested. See Edward C. McAleer,
   The Sensitive Plant: A Life of Lady Mount Cashell (Chapel Hill, 1958).

4.　To Washington Allston
　9 May 1826

Rome May 9th 1826

My Dear Sir

I had in my letter to Mr Edmund[1] given a hasty outline of my plans and my progress in order that I might have the benefit of both your remarks for I feared I should not have time to write you — but a circumstance has delayed the departure of my friend, and I seize the interim to express myself more fully — I shall tell my opinions and open my heart to you sir with confidence and with pleasure — sure — that what is true will please you & that where I mistake you will correct me —

When I first came to Rome I was engrossed with the *means* of our art. Happening to fall in with men whose chief merit is in *execution*[2] and hearing nothing but their opinions on art I was led for a few weeks to think more of the mechanical than the truly intellectual part of the art & though I had a strong notion that *something more* than mere drawing and composition was necessary yet my notion was vague. I applied myself with eagerness to my work however — soon mastered all that seemed so wonderful in execution and obtained some notion of form — But the acquaintance of Thorwaldsen[3] made the greatest change in my views — By a *few words* which he said in expressing his opinion on my work — he learned me to think for myself in my art — This I have done — of course imperfectly yet industriously and faithfully. My object now is to obtain in *execution* — a truth of eye and hand & a command over my material which will enable me to model the figure in all its ages from infancy to decrepitude — under any circumstances naked — draped — etc at rest, in action — By means of this power I hope to embody my *composition* of which I wish to make myself completely a master from the mere management of line as in Architecture & single statues up to the true poetry of telling a story with truth and grace. I hope also to pay much attention to *character* a beauty in a work of art perhaps the most gratifying of all to the intellect & which has been always most neglected — in fact none but the very first minds have seized it or discovered its principles.

I would not convey an idea that I think the above powers are to be acquired separately — I have made it a point to study them all together. The only separate studies I follow are those of parts — as the extremities for instance and of drapery which I carry on at my leisure hours.

I have become fond of *portrait*. I have found it a difficult but a very interesting study — to seize the character of an individual — & then there is always so much beautiful & characteristic detail in a face that much of execution & form may be learned from modelling it —

The Italians generally have a *narrow* idea of art — They look merely at execution — there are one or two very honourable exceptions however in my art and there are in yours Camuccini and Benvenuti[4] who are thoroughly *studied* in the *academical* departments but in whose work, except a pleasing management of line, I never saw one jot of what is dear to me in a picture — The English again though they rather *neglect* all that the Italians aim at produce delightful works. Their principal sculptor — Mr Gibson[5] was a pupil and is a disciple of Canova[6] an artist of whom I think less every day — He was clever. But he was superficial & sensual in his style — & a most barefaced misrepresenter of Nature — He I am convinced will fall *very low very shortly* — It is astonishing to me that an artist ever attempts to imitate another in what *characterises* his style as *individual*. After all the sad examples before our eyes — yet still desirous of doing something *like* what is established in reputation they *ape* instead of truly *imitating*. They *study* the *Greeks* for examples *altogether* instead of studying as the Greeks *did*.

The Germans[7] are in my opinion a most respectable band of artists. Though their second rate men not *comprehending* fully the principles on which their superiours study the old masters fall into *manner* — yet it is not a manner of ignorant knack or facility. It is laborious & has much that is valuab[le in] [*page torn*] it. But their first men are wonderful — A laborious investiga[tion] [*page torn*] of Nature and industrious study of the means of art is with them made to bear in telling the most beautiful poetical stories & in rendering the most delicate & deep sentiment. I shall be much disappointed if they do not found a school of pure & solid art — Something as a Scotch proverb says "that the wind will not pass under" —

I have already finished a figure which occupied me several months and some busts.[8] Whenever I see a fine cast from Nature I purchase it and from these parts I model at my leisure — I find that I see the

Antique with a different eye after it — The figure at which I am at present employed is a David — "Thou comest to me with a spear and shield etc."[9] I am getting every day more and more in love with the subject as a study of form and character. I hope hereafter to attempt composition in groups and bas relief — Should I be able I think of remaining here several years more — for to leave Rome not master of my art and that too without any hopes of employment at home would be blasting all I am sure — We have all been delighted here with the news of the sale of your picture[10] — The English all think of having you yet in London — they think you will certainly return — There are several artists here who were here with you — the Rippenhousens — Thorwaldsen — Alvarez[11] — etc —

Should I please myself in my David — I think of sending a drawing of it to Boston — These have been here — Mr Fisher & Mr McLellan of New York[12] — a young painter who has a good notion of colour —. Mr Weir[13] of N Y is my present companion — we live together. He is studying historical painting — With every wish for your happiness

Sir am Yours — Horatio Greenough

Addressed: Mr Washington Alston Esqr / *Boston Mass*

NOTES

Washington Allston (1779–1843), landscape and portrait painter, who spent many of his earlier years abroad, lived at this time in Boston. Greenough first met him in 1823, as a junior at Harvard, and often acknowledged him as a spiritual father.
Manuscript: Dana Papers, MHS.
1. Edmund Trowbridge Dana (1779–1859), an intimate friend of Allston's, spent most of his life as a man of leisure (H. W. L. Dana, "The Dana Saga," *Cambridge Historical Society's Publications* 26 [1940]: 95–100). In his junior year in college Greenough often visited Dana's house in Cambridge and in his senior year had rooms there.
2. Probably followers of the Italian sculptor Antonio Canova (see n. 6).
3. Albert Bertel Thorwaldsen (1770–1844), Danish sculptor, at this time the head of the neoclassical school of sculpture, lived in Rome after 1797. Greenough carried letters of introduction to him.
4. Vincenzo Camuccini (1771–1844) was the chief Italian painter of the neoclassical school, living in Rome. Pietro Benvenuti (1769–1844), the best Tuscan painter of this school, living in Florence, later was known personally by Greenough.
5. John Gibson, English sculptor, lived in Rome (see note to Letter 85).

6. Antonio Canova (1757–1822), Italian sculptor, was the founder of the neo-classical school of sculpture.
7. Presumably Greenough refers to the group of German painters in Rome called the Nazarenes, consisting chiefly of Johann Friedrich Overbeck (1789–1862), Peter von Cornelius (1783–1867), and Julius Schnorr von Carolsfeld (1794–1872). They opposed neoclassicism and tried to revive the treatment of Christian subjects in art.
8. Greenough's statue *The Dead Abel* was not put in marble and presumably has been destroyed. Among the busts which he executed at this time was a self-portrait; apparently it too was not put in marble and has been destroyed.
9. This statue was not finished, Greenough's work being interrupted shortly after this time by illness and his consequent return to America.
10. Possibly Greenough refers to the subscription to Allston's painting *Belshazzar's Feast* made by ten persons, each contributing $1000, during the 1820's (Flagg, p. 210; Edgar P. Richardson, *Washington Allston* [Chicago, 1948], p. 126). No record seems to exist of an individual purchase of a work by Allston early in 1826.
11. The brothers Franz (1786–1831) and Johann (1789–1860) Riepenhausen, German engravers and painters, lived in Rome from 1807 until their deaths. Don Jose Alverez de Pereira y Cubero (1768–1827), Spanish sculptor, settled in Rome in 1804. Allston was in Rome from 1804 to 1808.
12. Alvan Fisher (1792–1863), genre and portrait painter, had a studio at this time in Boston. "McLellan" is presumably Thomas McCleland, or McClelland, who was painting portraits in New York in the early 1820's. See George C. Groce and David H. Wallace, eds., *The New-York Historical Society's Dictionary of Artists in America, 1564–1860* (New Haven, 1957); William Dunlap, *History of the Rise and Progress of the Arts of Design in the United States* (New York, 1834), 2:471.
13. Robert Weir (1803–89), landscape and historical painter, went abroad to study late in 1824. He shared rooms with Greenough in Rome from the end of 1825 to the summer of 1826, helped care for him during his illness in 1826–27, and accompanied him to America in 1827.

5. To Josiah Quincy
4 September 1827

Dear Sir.

Having paid considerable attention to portrait sculpture, during the short time that I have been studying my art, I am anxious to leave behind me, in case of another visit to Europe, several busts which may serve as specimens of my workmanship.[1] And as I have always heard you spoken of as one who wished well to the Fine arts, I take the liberty to ask of you the favour of sitting for a bust.[2]

I should perhaps require a greater number of sittings than a painter would, on account of my inexperience and the necessity of giving the whole finish of nature, instead of confining myself to a single view of the head; but any hour of the day might be chosen which would best suit you and the length of the sittings might be regulated by your own convenience.

I am, Sir, with due respect,
Your most obedient Servant,
Horatio Greenough.

Hon'le Josiah Quincy
Sept. 4th 1827.

NOTES

Josiah Quincy (1772–1864), lawyer, politician, and college president, was at this time mayor of Boston.
    This letter is in Henry Greenough's hand.
    Manuscript: Josiah Quincy II Papers, MHS.
1. Greenough returned home because of illness in the spring of 1827 and remained about a year.
2. The bust was apparently modeled in the fall of 1827 and put in marble in 1828–29. It is now in the Boston Athenaeum.

6.   To Samuel F. B. Morse
15 May 1828

My Dear Sir
    I shall probably embark shortly for Italy and as a very favourable opportunity offers of sailing from this port, I shall not have the pleasure of seeing you again in N. Y. as I intended in case of my sailing to Havre.[1] I have been much gratified, by the honour done me by your Academy.[2] I am grateful too, Sir, to the source from whence it originated. In my letter to Mr Morton,[3] I did not mention the copy of the Apollo, which I formerly told you I thought might be useful in your gallery[4] — it is entirely at your service, whenever you may think it worth the while to have it transported.

I have been delighted with Mr I Hone's picture, which is now at the Ath'm Gallery[5] — Tis like Lawrence.[6] I am sorry that we have not more pictures from your city. The little miss with her puss was another confirmation to me of what Alston always said, that the gifts of colour and chiaro scuro go hand in hand. Our exhibition[7] will probably be more profitable this season even than the last. 1500$ have been received in less than a fortnight. I beg that when you see Mr Vanderlyn,[8] you would ask him if he has received the vermilion and ivory addressed to him and left by me in the care of Mr McLellan; Twas for a Mr Trott.[9] Will you express to him my regret at not having seen the author of the "Marius" and the "Ariadne"? Tell him that it would have been a great pleasure, to have carried his remembrance to Thorwaldsen, whom I have heard speak of him with great regard.

Will you remember me to Mr Bryant and to Dr Greenhow.[10] I hope to enjoy Mr Cole's[11] company in Italy — As for Weir (who has I trust taken the mustard seed) I shall meet him erelong in Florence. I regret that the circumstance of meeting Mr Perkins[12] hurried me so rapidly from N. Y. I hoped, that in case Mr Convers[13] had occasion for my portrait, that it would have been of your hand. As it is, I can but offer a bust which I modelled at Rome, two years since, — Perhaps one engraving from a bust would give a variety to the book,[14] besides being in harmony with my profession. I must request you to watch the draw-ing, as much of the detail may be absolutely too bad for the purpose. Mr Alston, with whom I passed the last evening, is well and fuller of the art (if possible) than ever. Mr Stuart,[15] I fear, is going — With the highest esteem and the best wishes for your success in the great cause in which you are engaged, I remain, Yours sincerely,

Horatio Greenough
May 15th 1828

S F B Morse Esqr / P.N.A.[16] — N. Y

PS   I request that you will command my utmost exertions in any form connected with yourself or your friends which my residence in Italy will give me the opportunity to make — I need not tell you who have been a traveller and know what it is to recognise the handwriting of a friend, how much I shall be gratified by a communication from you during my absence.

Addressed: Samuel F. B. Morse Esqr / New York.

NOTES

Samuel Finley Breese Morse (1791–1872), best known for his invention of the electric telegraph, was at this time a historical and portrait painter. Greenough, furnished with a letter of introduction from Allston, met him in New York in February 1828. During Morse's sojourn in Europe a few years later, he and Greenough were intimate friends, but after that they had little in common.
Manuscript: Morse Papers, LC.

1. Greenough had just returned to Boston from a trip to Washington, made for the purpose of modeling the bust of President John Quincy Adams. En route both ways he had stopped in New York.

2. The National Academy of Design was founded in 1825 by several artists, including Morse, who at this time was serving as its first president (Thomas Seir Cummings, *Historic Annals of the National Academy of Design* [Philadelphia, 1865]; Eliot Candee Clark, *History of the National Academy of Design, 1825–1953* [New York, 1954]). At its annual meeting in May 1828 Greenough was elected an honorary member (his diploma is in the editor's collection). From the following year until 1838 he was designated Professor of Sculpture. He showed works at the annual May exhibitions from 1832 to 1835, in 1841, and in 1848 (Mary Bartlett Cowdrey, comp., *National Academy of Design Exhibition Record, 1826–1860* [New York, 1943], 1:196–97).

3. John Ludlow Morton was at this time secretary of the National Academy of Design (see note to Letter 44).

4. Presumably Greenough refers to a copy of the head of the *Apollo di Belvedere* in the Vatican Museum which he acquired in Rome and brought with him to the United States in 1827, and which he offered to give the National Academy of Design. Nothing further seems to be known about it.

5. In 1824 Morse painted a portrait of five-year-old Elizabeth Kent Hone, daughter of Isaac S. Hone of New York (Edward L. Morse, ed., *Samuel F. B. Morse: His Letters and Journals* [New York, 1914], 1:257; photostatic copy of Ms. family records in the Bible of James Kent, Hone's father-in-law, Kent Family Papers, NYHS). The painting, which shows the child holding a cat, was shown at the Boston Athenaeum Gallery in 1828. It is now in the M. and M. Karolik Collection in the Museum of Fine Arts, Boston.

6. Sir Thomas Lawrence (1769–1830) was the most fashionable English portrait painter of his day.

7. The public loan exhibition of paintings at the Boston Athenaeum Gallery.

8. John Vanderlyn (1775–1852), portrait and historical painter, who had been in Rome with Allston, was living at this time in New York. His *Marius Amidst the Ruins of Carthage* is now in the M. H. de Young Memorial Museum, San Francisco; his *Ariadne* is now in the Pennsylvania Academy of Fine Arts, Philadelphia.

9. Benjamin Trott (*ca.* 1770–1843), miniature and portrait painter, was living at this time in Newark, New Jersey.

10. William Cullen Bryant had become assistant editor of the *New York Evening Post* in 1826 (see note to Letter 210). Robert Greenhow (1800–1854), physician, translator for the U.S. State Department, and historian, was practicing medicine at this time in New York City.

11. Thomas Cole, painter, had a studio at this time in New York (see note to Letter 46).
12. Probably either Thomas Handasyd Perkins, Jr. (1796–1850), or James Perkins, Jr. (d. 1828), son and nephew respectively of Thomas Handasyd Perkins, of whose shipping firm they were members (Augustus Thorndike Perkins, *A Private Proof Printed in Order to Preserve Certain Matters Connected with the Boston Branch of the Perkins Family* [Boston, 1890], pp. 35, 112; William H. Whitmore, "Memoir of Augustus Thorndike Perkins, A.M.," *ProcMHS*, 2d ser., 7 [1892]: 429). The elder Perkins gave Greenough passage to Europe a few days later on one of the firm's vessels (see Letter 7).
13. Presumably Sherman Converse (1790–1873), editor and publisher, at this time living in New York (Franklin Bowditch Dexter, *Biographical Sketches of the Graduates of Yale College* [New Haven, 1912], 6:536–37).
14. No such book seems to have been published.
15. Gilbert Stuart (1755–1828), celebrated American portraitist, painted portraits of Greenough's parents. That of David Greenough and one of Elizabeth Bender Greenough are reproduced in Lawrence Park, *Gilbert Stuart: An Illustrated Descriptive List of His Works* [New York, 1926], 1:371–72, where they are erroneously identified as David Stoddard Greenough, Jr., and his wife. Another portrait of Elizabeth Bender Greenough attributed to Stuart is in the possession of David Richardson, Washington, D.C.
16. Painter of the National Academy.

7. To Robert Gilmor, Jr.
17 May 1828

My Dear Sir

Were I with you, I know that you would not hear one word of my gratitude, one acknowledgement of obligation. You would tell me how happy you were that you had been instrumental in serving me. I know you are sir, and I am the more obliged to you on that account. — I ought to tell you, however, as [you] may not yet know it, that an offer has been made me, through Mr. Wm. H. Elliott, of a loan of $1000,[1] which will give me the opportunity of executing in Italy the works already ordered of my hand[2] and put me in a condition to receive commissions. Who all the gentlemen are, who have done me this signal kindness, I, as yet, know not; but I am sure, that if they could know how the hope of once more entering the arena of art cheers and nerves me, they would feel some pleasure at the change they have wrought.

Let me turn to the author of all this, let me say, I thank you with my whole heart.

It is quite probable that I may embark in a few days, for Gibraltar. Col Perkins has generously offered me a passage in a ship of his, which is about to sail.[3] You are of course aware of the facility of embarking there, for Leghorn. I may therefore hope to be established in Florence[4] in eight or ten weeks from the time of sailing. I shall remain in Florence untill I have completed my engagements. Mess Grant, Pillans and Com'y.[5] will be my bankers. Any communications to me will reach me readily through their hands. The bust of your lady[6] (should you continue disposed to have it executed in marble) can be sent addressed to their care. Should it crack (as General Sullivan[7] mentioned to me you feared) it can be strengthened by the same material inside and, by closing the seam externally it will be as strong as before. I shall endeavour to send you, by Mr Wm. Gillmore, whom I had the pleasure of meeting at Gen. Sullivan's the Arabesques of the Loggia of Raphael — the engravings are the best that have been made from that work.[8]

As for the length of my absence, it must depend on the success I may meet with in obtaining commissions. I hope that the work which I may send to this country will induce some of the patrons of art to add a statue to their collections. I shall have great pleasure in communicating to you, from time to time, what I think may interest you. Please remember me to Mrs Gilmor. I am, Sir, with sincere respect

Your Obliged Servant
Horatio Greenough
May. 17. 1828.

Robert Gilmor, Esq. / Baltimore

P. S.   Inclosed are sketches of a shepherd boy. of Sappho. of Jacob and Rebecca. They were first thoughts made after dinner with the cigar. If either should please you as a subject for a statue, I shall be glad — if not & you should still wish me to model something for you, I beg you will choose the subject and (with you Sir I shall have no fear) mention how you would have the important points as drapery etc managed —

Addressed: Robert. Gilmore. Esq. / Baltimore
Endorsed, in Gilmor's hand: May 17, 1828 / Horatio Greenough / ans'd 27 Oct. 1828 / with remittance on Leghorn for / 100 D.

NOTES

Robert Gilmor, Jr. (1774–1848), Baltimore shipping merchant, was a generous patron of artists and owner of one of the best American art collections of the early nineteenth century. In March 1828 he commissioned Greenough to do a bust of his wife and a statue. Greenough spent the last of March and the early part of April of that year at Gilmor's home, modeling the bust. After the summer of 1833, when their last account was settled, the two had little association. See Anna Wells Rutledge, "Robert Gilmor, Jr., Baltimore Collector," *Journal of the Walters Art Gallery* 12 (1949): 19–39; Nathalia Wright, "Horatio Greenough, Boston Sculptor, and Robert Gilmor, Jr., his Baltimore Patron," *Maryland Historical Magazine* 51 (1956): 1–13.

This letter, except for the postscript, is in Henry Greenough's hand.
Manuscript: Gratz Collection, American Painters, Sculptors, Engravers, HSP.

1. William Harvard Eliot (1795–1831) was prominent in the cultural, business, and political life of Boston ("Brief Memoirs and Notices of Prince's Subscribers," *NEHGR* 23 [1869]: 339). Apparently Gilmor had called the attention of one or more of his Boston friends to Greenough's eagerness to return to Italy and lack of funds to do so, with the result that this loan was advanced.

2. These certainly included busts of Josiah Quincy, John Adams, and Mrs. Gilmor, the statue for Gilmor, and probably the ideal bust entitled *The Genius of Love*. During his visit to America Greenough had modeled, in addition to those mentioned above, busts of Washington, John Quincy Adams, and John Marshall, but there seems to be no evidence that he had received orders for them in marble. Other commissions he may have had at this time were for a bust of Professor Andrews Norton of Harvard and one for a Philadelphian.

3. Thomas Handasyd Perkins, Boston shipping merchant, was at this time lieutenant colonel of the Massachusetts governor's guard (see note to Letter 104). Apparently Greenough sailed the day after writing this letter in the brig *Bashaw*, belonging to Perkins' firm, bound for Gibraltar and Canton.

4. Probably the temperate climate of Florence induced Greenough to choose this city rather than Rome as his destination. He had not, however, made his final decision about where to settle in Italy (see Letter 8).

5. In Leghorn (see Letter 26).

6. Sarah Reeve Ladson (1790–1866) was Gilmor's second wife (records in the Charleston Historical Society; Elizabeth Heyward Jervey, comp., "Marriage and Death Notices from the City-Gazette and Daily Advertiser," *South Carolina Historical and Genealogical Magazine* 30 [1929]: 254).

7. William Sullivan (1774–1839), Boston lawyer, was brigadier general of the Boston brigade of state militia.

8. William Gilmor (1775–1829) was a brother of Robert Gilmor, Jr. (chart of the Gilmor family made by Mrs. Ellen Gilmor Buchanan, Robert Gilmor Memoirs (Ms. 1729), Maryland Historical Society). The designs by Raphael to which Greenough refers are the purely decorative parts of the Loggie of the Vatican, ornamented chiefly by Raphael's frescoes of Biblical subjects. Presumably the engravings to which Greenough refers are those by Giovanni Ottaviani and Giovanni Volptao in *Le Loggie di Raffaele, incise da Giovanni Ottaviani e Giovanni Volptao nell' anno 1770*, new ed. [Rome? n.d.].

8.   To Washington Allston
   10, 16, 17 October 1828

Carrara — October 10th, [16, 17] — 1828.

My Dear Sir —

I will seize this moment of leisure (being on the eve of going to Florence for a few days) to give you some idea of my present situation and prospects. I was induced by several considerations to spend a few months here[1] before settling at Florence or Rome — The marble for my busts was to be had here for about ¼ what it would cost in either of those cities[2] — The preparatory labour was less expensive — A boaster[3] gets from 12 to 15$ in Rome, here he's contented with 6 or 7 — So that in case spots veins or other blemishes appear, as the work advances, it can be recommenced at a much greater advantage. My personal expences here are about ½ what they would be at Florence even. So that were it not for their magnificent academy, galleries, and the chance of finding some commissions at Florence I could find it in my heart to remain all winter here, for the climate is fine and the country beautiful. The object of my trip to Florence ('tis only a day's ride) is to ascertain whether the statues for the Theatre[4] can be had of the size required — After all the enquiries I have made I doubt it — if they can be found twill be at Florence for Trentanove[5] whom I saw at Leghorn thought there were none of that size & character in Rome. While there I shall have opportunity of availing myself of the experience of some of the first artists and I shall write Mr Brimmer[6] a particular account of my proceedings — You will oblige me by communicating this to him — So much Sir for Business —

The Florentine yearly exhibition[7] is now open and I shall visit that city so dear to my imagination with double interest — I enjoy Sir highly even the anticipation of sitting in that noble square with the capi d'opera of the cinque cento around and before me[8] — smoking a cigar which I brought from Boston — Ultimus Romanorum[9] the sole remaining one of a hundred of Mr Callender's[10] best "Flints" — It is thought the pictures will be uncommonly fine this year at the exhibition — I will keep this sheet open untill I have seen them — some slight account of them might interest you. I have seen several sculptors, old acquaint-

ances at Rome — Nothing new has appeared as yet among them —
Mr Lough[11] was expected from London — I have it directly from persons capable of judging and who have known him that he is a remarkable man — full of enthusiasm and spirit — ignorant as yet of drawing
but an able modeller and gifted with a power of composing — Thorwaldsen is expected here — his Christ is nearly finished in the marble
by one of the Carrarese sculptors — he will retouch it here himself —
He has since I was in Rome modelled the figure of Poniatowski for the
Equestrian statue, a Releiquoi for the tomb of Pius VII.,[12] and several
smaller works. Gibson is where he was — Wyatt[13] is growing in reputation — From Severn[14] I have not heard though I wrote him immediately
on my arrival in Leghorn.

Florence — 16. Oct. I will not try to tell you my feelings at finding
myself again in this city which seems and always seemed to me the
most inspiring place in the world[15] — I went on Sunday to the crowded
exhibition — The Academy is I suppose the finest establishment of the
kind[16] — I passed through a gallery containing casts of all the finest
sculpture in Europe and entered the Exhibition hall — In painting I
found almost nothing to like — admiration out of the question — The
right path once lost — the talent of Italy has led Italy astray — so that
in spite of all this princely encouragement, their works bear no comparison with the first struggles of the cinque cento neither for Expression nor colour nor drawing, rightly so called. The downright proof of
the badness of their system is that they do *nothing* well in portrait, in
landskape, in history they are the same and so like one another that it's
evident that some one vice of art has crushed or is crushing in them
every feeling of individual mind. Nature (with the mass) is to them
what virtue is to the mass of men a very fine thing to talk about of a
good sun shiny day — They believe that they see her come nightly and
daily into their hall of the nudo, throw off her clothes — take any
character the professor pleases — nay they find her so excessively true
that they must dilute a little the *reality* of her character to bring it into
the circle of the bello — This they do not in the form only but in composition in colour in chiaro scuro and thus they turn out works cousins
german of the opera, the ballet — and all the family of belle cose of
their country and age.

Now it seems to me that the early works of Lionardo of Raph — and
Michel Angelo[17] point out as directly the road to excellence as one
could wish. I look upon the Gallery and the Palazzo Pitti[18] as two great

instructors — One learns to think there Sir — And when that's said I believe all is said.

17th — After What I have said of the young men of Italy generally twould be wrong not to do justice to Bartolini whose works I see with an eye alltogether different from that of 3 years since when I visited him for the first time.[19] I was much struck with the figure of a boy treading grapes which I saw at Carrara which was full of nature. I have visited him since and have found his study and his conversation equally instructive — Let me give you a short account of the man — He is by birth a Florentine[20] who has studied by himself with this maxim as I had it from himself Che' la Natura a bellezza e benedetto e quello che le va un' po' vicino.[21] He was at Paris where [he] bore away the palm from the Frenchmen themselves in drawing with the point.[22] Under Napoleon he was professor of the Academy of Carrara and executed many magnificent works for the Emperor — He fell with his patron and was thrown on English patronage and bust making for his bread[23] — As a composer he's behind Thorwaldsen for he wants his fertile mind and his poetic imagination but in carrying out his conceptions and making every thing he represents keep its place though singly [?] studied he's perhaps before any of them — for he works the marble like a Greek[24] — And now I would say one word on that subject — I have examined the works of Mich Ang of the Greeks of Canova and Thorwaldsen and the result has been that I have determined to master this part of the art for I'm now sure that no workman can do more than boast, (and finish the ornamental parts) of a work of excellence as it should be done. That the Greeks did so is proved by the small number of works from the same hand. That Mich Ang did it is safe for no man in his day could help him — the art of taking points[25] was not known — Canova without his exquisite chiselling would have been nobody. Tis rather his surface than his sentiment or science which has charmed this age. Thorwaldsen getting commissions late could only think in clay — he trusted to the exactness of modern method to render him in marble what he entrusted to it [in] clay — He has found more than one man of real merit in the art (as a modeller too) who has been capable of feeling what he wanted and of doin[g] [*page torn*] but not always — The Christ — which I think the finest wo[rk] ou[r] [*page torn*] art has given the world since the golden time of Leo[26] is executing by men unworthy of it (sub rosa some future artist will see the marble in Copenhagen and ask did this figure ever bring tears of admiration into an artist's eyes? Yet in truth it has) — Let any man ask me where the beauty, the glory of the Venus and Apollo[27] lie — I say in answer that I'll not define it but I'll say that it lies within the thickness of [a] dollar in every part of their bodies and I will engage by reducing it that much in one part and increasing it in another to make them ordinary figures —

I requested Bartolini as I was coming to Florence to spend the winter to be my adviser and instructor in drawing and modelling — (being of the opinion of Raffaelo who did not form himself under one sole artist but learned drawing of one perspective of another — colour of a third — travelling over his beautiful country as a bee hums through a garden — now settling upon Titian and now rising to MA)[28] — Bartolini told me it would be a pleasure to him to have me near him offered me an apartment frankly in his own elegant studio.[29] Encouraging me by many flattering things which I might repeat were we smoking together Sir as I have perhaps done before sufficiently to make me suspected vain — I shall profit by his politeness and generosity — the coming winter —

With regard to the casts of the ear from life — I have ransacked the collections of that kind in vain as yet, and I have searched among the models with as little success — I shall be obliged to examine among my acquaintance and as soon as possible I will send them to you — Ultramarine is made here but by one individual who supplies Benvenuti and it is so much dearer than that of Rome that I'm sure I shall be doing as you would wish in sending you but a small quantity of the 2nd quality and waiting untill an opportunity offers of procuring the first from Rome — There it is 16 dollars the ounce here it is 30 —

I am in excellent health and spirits quite pleased with the appearance of my marble work thus far and in hopes that something will turn up that will call me to the execution of a figure — Pray Sir don't forget to send me such a picture as you spoke of — I have many acquaintance among the first conversaziones of artists and dillettanti[30] and long to shew them how nobly *we American apples swim.*

> I remain Sir with all
> affection Yours
> and the Master's[31]
> Hor. Greenough

I send you ¼ of an ounce of Ultramarine at 16 dollars the ounce.

Addressed: Washington Allston Esq. / Boston — Mass.

NOTES

Manuscript: Dana Papers, MHS.
1. Greenough arrived in Carrara about September 1828.
2. Apparently a piece of marble large enough for a bust cost about eighty dollars in Florence and Rome at this time (see Letters 12 and 13).
3. A man who boasts, or roughly hews, the sculptor's model in marble. Greenough always omitted the *a* in the noun and the verb.
4. Probably the Tremont Theater in Boston, which was opened in 1827. The façade, containing two niches for statuary, was designed by George Watson Brimmer (see n. 6). The statues, which are depicted in Philip Harry's painting *Tremont Street, Boston* (*ca.* 1843), were added not long before 1843 (*M. and M. Karolik Collection of American Paintings 1815–1865* [Cambridge, 1949], p. 291). The building was destroyed by fire in 1852 (Samuel Adams Drake, *Old Landmarks and Historic Personages of Boston* [Boston, 1906], pp. 291–93).
5. Raimon Trentanove (1792–1832), Italian sculptor, enjoyed considerable popularity among Americans at this time (R. D. W. Connor, *Canova's Statue of Washington,* Publications of the North Carolina Historical Commission Bulletin no. 8 [Raleigh, 1910], pp. 46, 48, 58–60; Cooper, 1:412). The Boston Athenaeum had a bust of Washington by him, of which Greenough made a sketch, probably as a study for the bust of Washington which he modeled in Boston in 1827 (Greenough's sketchbook, begun in Rome in 1826, in the editor's collection).
6. Presumably George Watson Brimmer (d. 1838), Boston merchant turned architect and designer, and connoisseur of painting (William Reed Deane, "Watson Genealogy," *NEHGR* 18 [1864]: 366; Rose T. Briggs, *Plymouth Rock: Its History and Its Significance* [Plymouth, 1956], p. 8).
7. The annual exhibition of the Academy of Fine Arts.
8. Presumably Greenough refers not to the relatively uninteresting Piazza San Marco, which the academy adjoins, but to the Piazza a block east — that of the SS. Annunziata, one of the most symmetrical and beautiful in Florence, with its fifteenth- and sixteenth-century buildings and, in the center, the equestrian statue of the Granduke Ferdinand I by Giambologna, erected in 1605.
9. "The last of the Romans." The term was applied to several Romans— including Marcus Junius Brutus, Caius Cassius Longinus, and Stilicho—and to several later persons as well, notably Congreve (by Pope) and Horace Walpole.
10. Probably Richard B. Callender, listed in the *Boston Directory* for 1827 as a dealer in West Indian goods.
11. John Graham Lough (1806–76), an English sculptor of humble origin who studied chiefly from the Elgin Marbles in the British Museum.

12. Thorvaldsen did statues of Christ and his disciples for the Frue Kirke (the Church of Our Lady) in Copenhagen; a bronze statue of the Polish prince Józef Poniatowski for Warsaw, which was not erected there until 1919; and a mausoleum for Pius VII, who is buried in the Clementine Chapel of St. Peter's (Eugene Plon, *Thorvaldsen: His Life and Works*, trans. I. M. Luyster [Boston, 1873], pp. 77–81, 89–95, 146, 219–22, 254–55). Thorvaldsen confined his work largely to modeling, allowing his students and assistants to put the models into marble.

13. James Richard Wyatt (1795–1850), English sculptor, went to Rome in 1822 at the encouragement of Canova.

14. Joseph Severn (1793–1879), English painter, who accompanied John Keats to Rome in 1820 and cared for him in his last illness, spent most of the rest of his life there.

15. Greenough stopped briefly in Florence on his way to Rome in the fall of 1825 and also en route from Rome to Leghorn early in 1827.

16. The Accademia di Belle Arti in Florence was established in 1562 by Cosimo I. In 1784 it was enlarged and moved to its present location in the Via Ricasoli, where it houses a valuable collection, offers instruction in the arts, and sponsors exhibitions.

17. These artists, as well as others of the Renaissance, were not popular with the neoclassical school, but Allston admired them all, particularly Michelangelo.

18. The Galleria degli Uffizi and the Galleria Palatino in the Palazzo Pitti house the chief art collections in Florence.

19. Lorenzo Bartolini (1777–1850) was the leading Tuscan sculptor of the early naturalistic movement. Radical in theory, he held that nature was beautiful in all her forms (once bringing in a hunchback for his students to draw), but in practice he was more conservative, notably in draping his figures rather than clothing them in the dress of their time. (See Mario Tinti, *Lorenzo Bartolini* [Rome, 1936], vol. 1.) Greenough had met him en route to Rome in 1825. One letter from him to Greenough, dated 17 March 1839, has been preserved.

    Bartolini's nude *L'Ammostatore*, "the grape-treader," is considered a landmark in the development of naturalism in sculpture in the nineteenth century. It is now in the Pinacoteca Tosi-Martinengo, Brescia.

20. Bartolini was born at Savignano, near Bologna (Tinti, *Bartolini*, 1:26).

21. "That nature is beauty and blessed is he who goes a little near her."

22. Bartolini was in Paris from 1799 to 1808, at first studying in the atelier of the painter Jacques Louis David (Tinti, *Bartolini*, 1:41–55). "Drawing with the point" means drawing with an etching needle or chisel.

23. Bartolini was appointed director of the School of Sculpture at the Academy of Fine Arts in Carrara in 1807, through the influence of Napoleon, who had been the subject of some of Bartolini's work in Paris and whose sister Eliza Baciocchi, ruler of the principality including Carrara, wished to improve that institution. Most of the works which Bartolini executed at this time were busts and statues of the Bonaparte family, notably a group of Napoleon I, Marie Louise, and their son, "the King of Rome" (Tinti, *Bartolini*, 1:53, 58, 59, 63).

    After the abdication of Napoleon in 1814, mobs broke into Bartolini's studio in Carrara, and he was forced to leave the city. He settled in Florence in 1815. His English patrons at this time included Mary Berry and William George Spencer, sixth duke of Devonshire (Tinti, *Bartolini*, 1:65, 74.)

24. Most nineteenth-century sculptors did little more than model in clay, delegating the marble work to assistants.
25. This process consisted of marking points on the marble block corresponding to points of various depths on the model and drilling to these depths in preparation for the rough cutting of the marble. See the account in Richard Westmacott, *Handbook of Sculpture* (Edinburgh, 1864), pp. 368–69.
26. Pope Leo X, Giovanni dei Medici (1475–1521), is noted for his patronage of Raphael, his continuation of the construction of St. Peter's, and his literary circle.
27. Presumably the *Venus dei Medici,* in the Uffizi Gallery in Florence, and the *Apollo di Belvedere.*
28. Raphael studied with Perugino in Perugia and with Pinturicchio in Siena, and in Florence became acquainted with such different talents as those of Botticelli, Ghirlandaio, Filippino Lippi, Leonardo, and Michelangelo (Giorgio Vasari, *Lives of Seventy of the Most Eminent Painters, Sculptors and Architects,* ed. E. H. and E. W. Blashfield and A. A. Hopkins [New York, 1897], 3:127–36).
29. Presumably that in Borgo San Frediano, which Bartolini had constructed about this time (Tinti, *Bartolini,* 1:83).
30. Bartolini—who belonged to the group of artists, writers, and intellectuals in Florence largely responsible for the Tuscan *risorgimento*—had presumably introduced Greenough to other members of this group. Notable among them were the historian Gino Capponi, the poet Giuseppe Giusti, and the Swiss littérateur Jean Pierre Viesseux (see Mario Tabarrini, *Gino Capponi* [Florence, 1879]; Susan Horner, *The Tuscan Poet Giuseppe Giusti, and His Times* [London, 1864]; Paolo Prunas, *L'Antologia di Gian Pietro Vieusseux* [Rome-Milan, 1906]).
31. Edmund T. Dana, so called by Greenough and his classmate at Harvard John Howard "on account of his serene wisdom and fine perception in art and letters" (Henry T. Tuckerman, *A Memorial of Horatio Greenough* [New York, 1853], p. 16).

9. To Robert Gilmor, Jr.
25 February 1829

Florence — Feb'y 25, 1829.

Dear Sir

My silence has been a longer one than I had hoped. The reason is that I have been waiting till I might have something pleasant to tell you for there [has] been nothing new in the world of art since my arrival in Italy. I landed at Leghorn in August after a detention of somewhat more than a month at Marseilles. — The small pox prevailed there and a quarantine of 25 days was in consequence laid on vessels thence in the ports of Italy while a cordon sanitaire cut all communication with the Sardinian territory — Immediately on the removal of the latter I proceeded to Genoa where I embarked for Leghorn.

I was induced by several considerations to make some stay in Carrara — I had several busts to execute.[1] I could there have my choice of marble at a low rate. I wished to become acquainted with the different qualities of marble yielded by the quarries — their prices and the value of labour in the town — There was nothing like being on the spot. So I concluded to regain my practise in working marble and go to Florence in the winter. My journey to Florence was hastened by the arrival in that city of Mr Cooper[2] who at the suggestion of my friend Mr Ombrosi[3] did me the honour to consent that I should model his bust. I completed the model about a month since and have commenced the marble.[4]

I am already considerably advanced in a group which I have undertaken for Mr Cooper. Tis a copy of a passage in a picture of Raphael at the Pitti palace representing two cherub boys chaunting[5] — they stand isolated in the picture and form of themselves a sweet composition. Should I succeed in transferring to them a portion of that angel beauty and infantile form which are so charmingly combined in the original I shall execute them in marble. Those who have seen them have been surprised that they have never been so copied before — The suggestion was Mr Cooper's.

Thorwaldsen's last work is the monument of Pius VII. Tis highly spoken of. The King of Bavaria visited the study the other day and on the sight of this work immediately decorated the artist with the insignia of an order of merit.[6] Benvenuti is employed in painting the ceiling of the Medicean Chapel for which he is to receive 35,000 Francesconi.[7] Bartolini is bringing to a close his copy of Titian's venus in marble for Lord Londonderry[8] a work which has occupied him for a long time and which I think the most exquisite piece of *finish* I have seen of a modern. A monument to Dante on a great scale is executing by Ricci a professor of the Florentine Academy[9] — The idea of Dante who sits in a melancholy musing is not amiss. The execution is quite mediocre.

With regard to myself Sir though I am every day more and more confirmed in the sense I have always entertained of the dignity and glory of my art yet its immense difficulty and the combinations of rare qualities requisite for great success in it are such as to induce me to be very modest in my expectations. Should I be fortunate enough however to be employed in a way which while it should pay for my bread would keep me in the study which I require and thus enable me to persevere I think I may hope to become ultimately a respectable artist. But I am sensible that it will require the whole force, the utmost strain of the faculties given me to effect it. I am the pioneer of a band which I doubt not will hereafter enrich and beautify the cities of the Republic. I am warmed with the thought that if I seize on the right path they will do me the honour of having begun well.

As for patronage I [am] more afraid of not deserving than of not finding it. I do my countrymen the justice to believe that I have but to place myself on a level with the sculptors of Europe and I shall be preferred to them.

I have received the bust of Mrs Gilmore.[10] I shall execute it with as little delay as the nature of my present engagements will allow. I shall work with zeal, with gratitude, and if it were what I would fain make it for your sake I should indeed be an artist.

I have thought of you often in examining the collections of old pictures for sale here — The peace[11] has been so long a one and the number of wealthy travellers so great that this has become a regular trade and I have yet seen nothing in the way of a work of art which could be purchased to advantage — In my reading I have met with a very interesting and valuable book intitled "Lettere sulla Pittura, Scultura ed Architettura."[12] The work consists of letters of artists or relating to the arts from the dates of the age of Michelangelo down to that of Poussin[13] — These letters contain much good sense and good criticism — They interest also by the clear view they give of the private characters of the old masters — They let the light in upon all the manouvreings and intrigue which influenced the employment of artists the execution of works etc. They form seven volumes and may [be] had for less than two doll's a volume though rare books — Begging you will remember my respectful regards to Mrs Gilmore I remain Dear Sir

Your Obliged Friend and Serv't
Horatio Greenough

Robert Gilmore Esqr Baltimore

Addressed: Robert Gilmore Esqre / Baltimore.

NOTES

Manuscript: John S. H. Fogg Collection, Maine Historical Society.

1. He certainly had those of Josiah Quincy, John Adams, John Quincy Adams, and Mrs. Gilmor, and possibly the ideal *Genius of Love* and portraits of Washington, John Marshall, and Andrews Norton.

2. James Fenimore Cooper arrived in Florence with his family on 22 or 23 October 1828 (Cooper, 1:345; see Letter 16).

3. James Ombrosi (*ca.* 1777–1852) was commissioned the first U.S. Counsul in Florence, but the office was not recognized by the Tuscan government, and he acted chiefly as a commercial agent for Americans. He was notoriously unreliable (RG 59, General Records of the Department of State, Dispatches of and Instructions to U.S. Consuls, Florence, NA; Leo Francis Stock, *Consular Relations between the United States and the Papal States* [Washington, 1945], 2:9).

4. Greenough subsequently made another model, Cooper having gained so much weight that the first was no longer a good likeness and used the block of marble first intended for the Cooper bust for his bust of Morse (see Letters 14 and 41).

5. *The Chanting Cherubs,* a group of two singing angels, was copied from a detail in Raphael's painting the *Madonna del Baldacchino* in the Palazzo Pitti. Its fate after Cooper sold it in 1848 is unknown. For an account of its execution and exhibition, see Nathalia Wright, "*The Chanting Cherubs:* Horatio Greenough's Marble Group for James Fenimore Cooper," *New York History* 38 (1957): 177–97.

6. Louis I (1786–1868), king of Bavaria, presented Thorvaldsen with the Cross of the Commander of the Crown of Bavaria in recognition of his artistic achievement (Eugene Plon, *Thorvaldsen: His Life and Works*, trans. I. M. Luyster [Boston, 1873], pp. 86, 110).

7. The chapel referred to is the Capella dei Principi, added to the church of San Lorenzo in Florence as a mausoleum for the Medici rulers of the city. The ceiling is decorated with frescoes of scenes from the Old and New Testaments, painted by Benvenuti.

   An Italian francescone was equal to about $1.10 in American currency at this time.

8. Bartolini copied in marble Titian's *Venere di Urbino,* in the Uffizi Gallery, for Charles William Stewart (later, Vane), third marquis of Londonderry (1778–1859). The statue is now in the Fabre Museum, Montpellier.

9. Stefano Ricci (1767–1837), pupil of Canova and rigid neoclassicist, was professor of sculpture at the Academy of Fine Arts in Florence from 1825 until his death. He is chiefly known for this cenotaph, which consists of a seated statue of Dante, contemplating the *Divine Comedy* open on his knees, and two female figures representing Italy and Poetry.

10. The cast, made in America.

11. After the defeat of Napoleon at Waterloo in 1815.

12. Giovanni Bottari, *Raccolta di Lettere sulla Pittura Scultura, e Architettura, scritte dai piu celebri Professori, che in dette Arti fiorirono dal Secolo XV:° al XVII.°* 7 vols. in 4 (Rome, 1754).

13. The French classical painter Nicholas Poussin (1594–1665) spent most of his life after 1624 in Rome.

10. To Thomas Aspinwall
1 April 1829

Florence — April 1st, 1829.

To Thomas Aspinwall Esqr
Sir

I have received your favor of the 17th Ult'o in which you inform me that you have agreeably to my request advanced my brother[1] the sum of 6£ — I thank you heartily for it. Enclosed is a bill of exchange on my bankers for that amount.

Will you when you see my brother tell him that my prospects are cheering — that I have modelled for Mr Cooper the novelist a group of cherubs which I am to execute in the marble and that I have made the portrait in marble of the same gentleman? Assure him that any good fortune which may befall me shall be good fortune to him also and that if he finds himself cruelly embarrassed he but shares the fate of his brother. Regretting that my brother and myself must be known to you only by our calls on your politeness and your generosity and again begging you will accept my sincere thanks I remain kind Sir

Your Obliged Serv't
Horatio Greenough

Addressed: To Thomas Aspinwall Esqre / U.S. Consul — / London.

NOTES

Thomas Aspinwall (1786–1876) of Brookline, Massachusetts, a lawyer by train-ing, was U.S. Consul in London from 1815 to 1853 (Charles C. Smith, "Memoir of Col. Thomas Aspinwall, A.M.," *ProcMHS*, 2d ser., 8 [1892]: 32–38).
    Manuscript: Dreer Collection, Architects and Sculptors, HSP.
  1. John Greenough was living at this time in London, where he had gone to study painting (see note to Letter 133).

11. To Washington Allston
   18 April 1829

Florence — April 18th 1829.

My Dear Sir

An Accident reminded me last evening how long it had been since I had written to you — I was in a coffee house near the bridge of the Trinity with young Cooper[1] when an English gentleman to whom I had been hastily introduced the evening before entered and seating himself near us commenced a conversation — The topic was the high degree of civilization common among the peasants of Tuscany and he spoke of his own countrymen pretty freely I assure you — At a pause in the conversation he asked me suddenly if I knew Mr Alston — Yes very well — Do you indeed how is he? — We were in Rome a long time together and we have enjoyed a great deal in each other's company. I asked his name — twas Wallis![2] Was not that droll? I had often heard this gentleman's name but it never had occurred to me that it might be the same you had mentioned as the England-hater — He has been long settled in Florence — has a fine large palace in S. Gaetano, and is still painting and educating his son.[3] He invited me forthwith to call on him and promised me the sight of a large picture which he has lately finished. Before I close this I shall probably be able to tell you something more of him.

Mr Cooper who has passed the winter here and will remain for some months to come always asks with much interest after you and Mr Dana[4] when I receive a letter. I have found in him a man who understands perfectly what my aim is and who seems to have gradually become thoroughly interested in my success. Mason[5] has probably mentioned to you the group which I am doing for him. He has since it has been advanced been highly pleased with it — This little work has brought me some visitors among others Lord Normanby[6] a man of much taste and great elegance of manners etc who seemed quite pleased with what I had done. I believe I am beginning to find again the thread which fell from my hands in Rome so suddenly and so fearfully[7] but it sometimes seems to me that art is a true Will o' the Wisp. The grand aim of my studies since my return to Italy has been the formation of a *method* both in drawing and modelling which shall enable me to pay in the future my whole attention to form and expression without continual interruption and mortification from doing that first which should be done last — The grand defect of all self taught artists. I am the more resolute on this point because I see it effected every day by the most ordinary minds in every department of the art. Mr Cooper thinks I ought now to try to get some commission from Government which will enable me to take a stand as an American sculptor — I shall certainly be most happy whenever my country gives me an opportunity of shewing how strongly I feel the glorious character of her institutions — by embodying in my art the great principles on which she has founded them — but I have in the mean time no fear — I am sure that if I do myself justice in the works which go from my hand from time to time that tis impossible I can fail of meeting with a fair proportion of encouragement.

I have lately received a letter from Mr Brimmer[8] in which he asks the expence of having copies made from the old masters here — I mentioned to him the prices stating at the same time my opinion that any copies made by the "craft" of Florence or Rome would in point of colour be no better perhaps worse (for they would mislead young artists) than prints while in drawing etc they would hardly equal — I said thus much because I felt it my duty. You will agree with me in thinking it impossible that the youthful painters can study or the dillettanti stare with much profit at such caricatures of Titian & Paul[9] as come from the dead palettes of the Italians of today.

I was in the study of Benvenuti the other day while he was at work. He was making a cartoon for the dome of the Medicean chapel which is to be painted in fresco by him[10] — The figure on which he was employed was that of Cain rushing *out* of the picture from the body of his brother while the deity above appears calling upon him — The style is French — though there is much knowledge and fine drawing.

I found my way the other day into a chamber in the gallery which seemed to me worth all I had yet seen, twas filled with Venetians — Titian — Paul Bassan Giorgione[11] etc — What brilliancy is there! what music of colour — what grandeur of masses! I know not how it is but tis only when I see a picture of one of those men that I forget my own art and long to be a painter — How is it that the present school who seem to feel breadth and simplicity in form should be so insensible to the beauty of the same qualities in light and shade? The truth is they are ruined by the study of statues — They get all their first impressions in the plaster gallery —

I sent you 3 months since some Ultramarine fearing that you might [have] calculated on me [to] [*page torn*] neglect procuring it elsewhere. Tis not to be had here on so favourable terms [as] [*page torn*] at Rome — which is the reason why I sent you so little and sent Mr Fis[her][12] [*page torn*] none — Will you mention this to Mr F? Whenever I have an opportunity of employing a friend who understands the matter I shall provide for you both — A little new year's book has arrived here in which is an engraving from Mr F——'s prairie on fire.[13] Mr Cooper said twas the best — the only good illustration he had seen from his books.

You will have seen before this some of my busts[14] — I sigh while I write it — I pray you to remember the difficulties I have had in my way my long frequent interuptions — my sickness — But why should I ask? I know you will be but too disposed to think favourably of them — Believe me I am sensible of many of their defects and though I can *do* no better now yet I can I think see my way clear to much better things — I have great courage and great hunger after glory. I would fain be one of the small band of American "Old Masters." I beg you will remember me to Mr R Dana and to the Master — I am Dear Sir Yrs Affec'y

H Greenough

P. S.   Mr Wallis and Mr Cooper desire to be remembered kindly to you — *I do hope* that you remember the picture which you thought it possible you might send me[15] —

Addressed: To / Washington Allston Esqr / Boston. Mass.

NOTES

Manuscript: Dana Papers, MHS.
1. The Ponte Santa Trinità crosses the Arno River. Presumably Greenough was with William Yeardly Cooper (1809–31), son of J. F. Cooper's brother William, who was traveling with the J. F. Cooper family (Cooper, 1:153).
2. George Augustus Wallis (1770–1847), Scottish landscape painter and picture

dealer, spent most of his career in Europe, particularly after 1818, in Florence. He was notorious for his mendacity. See *Letters*, pp. 102–3.

3. Wallis lived in the Piazza San Gaetano (now degli Antinori). His son Trajan, also a painter, studied briefly in Stuttgart.

4. Probably Richard Henry Dana, writer and editor, and brother of Edmund Dana (see note to Letter 183).

5. Possibly Jonathan Mason, Jr. (1795–1884), Boston portrait and figure painter (Harvard University Archives). He was probably a friend of Henry and Alfred Greenough at this time (*Letters*, p. 55). The group referred to in this sentence is *The Chanting Cherbus* for Cooper.

6. Constantine Henry Phipps (1797–1863) was created first marquis of Normanby in 1838. At this time he was attached to the British legation in Florence, and he and his wife were prominent in the social life of the expatriate elite in the city (Michael Sadlier, *Blessington-D'Orsay* [London, 1933], pp. 106–8; Willard Connely, *Count D'Orsay: The Dandy of Dandies* [London, 1952], p. 99).

7. Greenough became seriously ill, beginning with an attack of malaria, in Rome in the summer of 1827 and consequently returned to America early the next year.

8. Presumably George Watson Brimmer.

9. Paolo Cagliari, called Veronese (1528–88), is noted in the Venetian school of painters for his cool, clear colors.

10. See Letter 9, n. 7.

11. Titian, Paolo Cagliari, Jacopo Bassan (1510–92), and Giorgone (*ca.* 1478–1510) were the greatest of the Venetian colorists. Allston admired this school of painters above all others and devised a method of his own to achieve an effect of luminousness comparable to theirs (Flagg, pp. 181–203).

12. Alvan Fisher.

13. N. P. Willis, ed., *The Token: A Christmas and New Year's Present* (Boston, 1829), contains, opposite page 215, an engraving by Elisha Gallaudet of Alvan Fisher's painting *The Prairie on Fire*, illustrating the sentence in chapter 23 of Cooper's *The Prairie* (1827) in which Leatherstocking proposes to fight the prairie fire with a fire of his own. The painting was exhibited at the Boston Athenaeum Gallery in 1829.

14. Those of Josiah Quincy, John Quincy Adams, and John Adams apparently were shipped to America early in 1829. The first and second are in the Museum of Fine Arts in Boston; the third in the First Church in Quincy, Massachusetts. Another *John Quincy Adams* and another *John Adams* are in the Museum of Fine Arts in Boston, and a third *John Quincy Adams* is in the New-York Historical Society.

15. Nothing further seems to be known of any such picture.

12. To Robert Gilmor, Jr.
16 May 1829

Florence May 16th — 1829 —

My Dear Sir

I should feel guilty of insensibility to the many proofs you have given of the kind interest you take in my concerns, were I not to hasten to communicate to you my pleasant news respecting myself. I have just compleated the model of my group for J. F. Cooper Esqr in which I have been fortunate enough to please my employer and to receive as great a portion of praise at the hands of my brother artists, as one so inexperienced has a right to hope for. Bartolini in particular, whose name as one of the first Italian sculptors must be familiar to you, expressed much pleasure and did me the honor to offer me the advantages of a pupil, i.e. the use of his studies, the loan of instruments and workmen and the sight of his pensioned models, in a way which will save me much money.

Mr Cooper has very generously offered to exhibit my group in N.Y. for my benefit, — he thinks that besides the assistance and profit of the proceeds, I may hope to become more known by means of it & thus open the door to other employment of a similar kind. And here I would do justice to the liberality and national spirit of this distinguished gentleman, who with no other proof of my ability than such as could be afforded him by the sight of a bust[1] which I executed on my arrival here, and with the certainty that I was an untried student in the higher walks of this difficult art, entrusted to me the execution of a group and encouraged and excited me by praise and flattering attentions throughout the work. I have found in him my Dear Sir another Mr Gilmore and I would to God that my power & my talent were equal to my love of my art that I might the better do honour to the favourable opinions of both of you.

In the meanwhile my health though even is delicate and requires much attention — yet as I have perceived in my constitution for the past year a tendency to confirmation, I nourish the hope that prudent diet and the exercise of the chisel will harden and strengthen me for the most laborious processes and the closest study.

Your bust[2] will, unless some accident intervenes, be in N.Y. by the month of August. I shall be obliged to draw on you for 50 Dolls on account of the expence of marble and preparation — for I have made it one of my rules that nothing shall go from my study with which I have not done my utmost to please the employer — the consequence of the adoption of this maxim has been that I have spent on one or two of my first busts rather more than the stipulated price,[3] but I'm so convinced of the good policy of this rule that I don't regret it.

I send you in company with this letter a salver and vase cast in Scagliola[4] from a piece of plate by Cellini, the greatest genius that ever devoted itself to that class of sculpture. I fell in with it in an obscure shop and it cost a mere trifle. You will I believe find a description of it in his biography written by himself and translated by one of the Roscoes.[5]

A peasant in digging a short time since at Fiesole fell in with a vase containing about $500 value in silver coins of the epoch of the triumvirate with several consular and other pieces[6] — He was observed trying to pass them in the market of Florence, was arrested and confessed the fact — He had already sold many to the silversmiths at a very mean price — In [co]nsequence [*page torn*] of the notoriety of this thing the coins are in great request, yet I hope to be able to obtain one or more of them before I close the case in which the salver is to be packed. Begging you will remember me kindly to Mrs Gilmore I remain

Dear Sir Your Obliged Friend and Serv't
H Greenough

Addressed: To / Robert Gilmor Esqe / Baltimore.
Endorsed, in Gilmor's hand: Feb'y 25. May 16. 1829 / Horatio Greenough / ans'd 10 Nov. by / his brother

NOTES

Manuscript: Gratz Collection, American Painters, Sculptors, Engravers, HSP.
1. That of Cooper.
2. That of Mrs. Gilmor.
3. At this period Greenough customarily charged $100 for a bust.

4. An imitation of ornamental stone, consisting of powdered gypsum mixed with glue, whose surface is variegated while soft with mineral dust and finally polished. None of the works purchased by Greenough for Gilmor has been located.

5. *Memoirs of Benvenuto Cellini,* trans. Thomas Roscoe, 2 vols. (London, 1822). Cellini described several vases which he made, but it does not seem possible to identify that to which Greenough refers.

6. Probably Greenough refers to the Second Triumvirate of Rome, formed in 43 B.C. The term "consular" was commonly used in the past to designate coins of the Roman Republic.

13. To Henry Greenough
16 September 1829

[Florence]

You will oblige me by informing Mr Gilmore, by letter, of the following circumstances: His bust[1] arrived in Leghorn in the month of January. I sent it to my agent in Carrara ordering him not to commence boasting the marble for it untill I should come. For though I was satisfied that the head was better than anything I had done in America I was not content with the drapery which surrounds the shoulders and determined to spare no pains to make the merit of the whole equal to that of the head. This agent, having quarrelled with Bartolini, suspected that I might have been persuaded by B to dismiss him from my service; and being a man famous for his avarice, began immediately to boast, hoping by the excellence of his work to reconcile me to his disobedience. On arriving at Carrara & finding all hopes of altering the bust cut off, I explained to him the mischief he had done and told him I would consult my friends among the artists and inform him of my conclusion — The artists all agreed I should do well to make the alteration. Therefore I wrote to Carrara, offering to pay half price for boasting, as my work had been ruined. The fellow flew into a violent passion swore I should pay 25 Francesconi and did me several ill turns which it would only disgust you to hear. At length in his exasperation he wrote me an insulting letter in which he spoke disrespectfully of the Americans as a nation. Knowing that from the law I had little hopes of saving money I placed his letter in the hands of our consul calling upon him to exercise his authority in settling the matter. The consul wrote him a letter in which official threats, reproof and persuasion were happily mingled and the result was that the fellow became frightened, answered humbly and finally made the consul his plenepotentiary in the affair, sending him the bust and cast. After paying 12 Francesconi I received my property in a state to fulfill my engagements with Mr Gilmore. I might finish it and send it on its way home in two months time full as good as Mr G expects it. But I feel it my duty to do more. Of this marble I shall make a simple head & neck omitting the drapery and send it to Mr G. as a specimen of my work which if he pleases he may present to some friend. I shall accompany it with sketches of the other design which I intend to execute for him, with a large portion of the person covered with drapery which we all think will make a much richer and finer bust. The former will be done in about two months; the latter will depend on the nature of my engagements and the degree of good faith fortune may grant me in my workmen.[2]

NOTES

Henry Greenough (1807–83), architect and occasional painter and writer. He and Horatio were closer to each other than to any other member of the family. At this time Henry was teaching school in Jamaica Plain, a Boston suburb.

Source: Henry Greenough to Robert Gilmor, Jr., 29 October 1829, Miscellaneous Manuscripts, G, NYHS. Henry's letter gives the place and date of Horatio's letter.

1. That of Mrs. Gilmor.
2. Apparently Greenough made only one bust, from the original design. It was finished by mid-November 1829 and shipped to Baltimore in February 1830. It is now in the possession of Mrs. Grover Cleveland Edwards, Inman, South Carolina.

14. To Washington Allston
19, 20 September 1829

Florence, Sept'r. 19, [20] 1829

My Dear Sir

This is saturday evening and allowing for the difference of longi-
tude you will be about to take your seat in the Cam Hourly —
Would that I were in the saddle trotting the uneven Brooklyn road
to meet you there at the masters,[1] for since Mr Cooper left Florence,
I have scarse had a moment's talk (in my mother tongue) except
such as enters one ear and goes out at the other. I have begun
several letters to you out of pure longing to get vent — But have
not finished any — I know not why — I believe I'm losing that gift
of the G^2 which used to carry me without effort through 5 or 6 pages.
I've set down now however in good earnest and I trust in the
interest of the moment for excitement and material — For tomorrow
morning the annual Exhibition of the Academy opens and there
are several works of peculiar pretension to be seen — Our Friend
Mr Wallis has 17 historical landskapes there one of which has already been sold to an English nobleman who saw the rooms while
the hangmen were at work — Mr Peale exhibits the Washington
and a portrait of myself[3] — of the other pictures I will speak afterward —

A Monument to Dante is now erecting in S. Croce by the side of
that of M. Ang. It is the production of Ricci who presides over the
Sculptural department of the Academy. The ashes of the banished
bard you are aware are at Ravenna and sticklers for delicate propriety have insisted on the absurdity of erecting any other than an
honorary monument. Gov't however probably from an unwillingness
to do things by halves, have ordered a regular Sepulchral one — thus
opening to the sculptor those convenient stores of common place
and convention — the Sarcophagus, the emblematic mourners and the
figure of the poet. The work is soon described. Dante sits aloft, half
naked — while the figures of Italy and Poesy weep over the Sarcophagus below. To my imagination there is an inconsistency in represent-

ing the living figure of a person on the *tomb* raised to his memory. The prostrate figures of Donatello and the earlier sculptors are hard and they are uniform, but they are true to the thought which they are intended to convey and their uniformity rather helps than hinders their effect.[4] The critics are displaying their acumen by tracing resemblances between the Italy and Poesy of Mr Ricci and similar figures of Canova and other sculptors — for my part I should give them more credit could they point out one essential *difference* between any two members of the stupid family, from its first appearance to the present moment.

I confess that I see the works of the sculptors of the age with a different eye from that which I brought home when I left Italy before. Being more familiarized with the mechanical part of the art and with those expedients (not to say tricks) which are become common property in it, I look for thought, for imagination, for feeling — and believe me I am seldom much excited by any *fresh* marbles — Thorwaldsen has my respect always sometimes my admiration — But Flaxman poor Flaxman![5] I hold to be a first rate man — He has given us on a few sheets of paper more to be grateful for than all the brass and marble which art has appropriated at such immense cost for many a year. Were F's outlines from the poets[6] his only works I could account for the neglect of his countrymen — I could excuse the British Gov't for heaping commissions on Westmacott[7] and others even where Flaxman competed for them. But the first artists here still speak with enthusiasm of the colossal group of Saturn and Ops — They tell me that the form was twin to the composition and the detail of the naked was worthy of the time of Pericles. This group was detained at Leghorn by the breaking out of the French war and came into the hands of Bartolini, who had a few years since the satisfaction of restoring it to the original proprietor[8] — The fact is, I believe, from what I have seen with my own eyes of the British nobility and gentry, that they have no real feeling or love of art as a mass — I may be mistaken —

I believe I have spoken to you before of Bartolini — He is my present instructor and friend and had it not been for the facilities which he has afforded me in regard to study, workmen etc, I had long since spent my last dollar — Though I do not go all his lengths in certain opinions on art, yet I do think them the very ones calculated to make him the best of instructors — Nature is his idol and

to imitate her exactly his whole desire — To accomplish this end he
has formed the most exact mechanical process — He has made the
deepest researches into the nature of his materials of any master of
the day — He is the P Perugino[9] of modern Sculptors and counts more
able men among his pupils than Canova or Thorwaldsen — "Where
there is a beautiful model" said he to me when I was introduced
to him — "there is Rome" — When I mentioned to him my intention
of making a statue — Have you found your model? No Sir — "Look
for one. Don't think at your age of beau idealizing and squeezing
4 ugly men into one handsome one — I see by your busts that you are
capable of what you intend. If you find a model you will do yourself
honour in your statue. Otherwise you will never content yourself."
Bartolini's story is romantic — Let me give you an outline of it — Poor
in his boyhood of course — few in Italy in these days enter the arena
of art with stuffed pockets. At 6 yrs old behold him singing ballads
in the Granduke's square[10] — at 7 in an Alabaster shop — where he
determined to go to Volterra[11] — the fountain head of the trade
where hundreds manage by means of it to — starve — Defrauded by
his master at Volterra,[12] he enters the private study by night — traces
the prints which had taken his fancy and decamps to Florence and
begins to work in the old shop[13] — and to look about him — Is fancied
by a French officer who takes him barefooted and with peeping
knees into his train, dresses him gives him wages and sets out for
France — At Genoa forced to quit his master who is ordered into
active service — but persists in going to Paris, takes letters of introduction — Stopped at the Frontier of the Var for want of passport
and held in durance vile — Recognized by a friend the ab'e men'd
officer and set at liberty — goes to Marseilles — to Lyons — is hoaxed
of his cash by another old acquaintance — Drags on to Paris half
starved. Presents his letters — they were addressed to a person of importance and were his whole hope. Great man didn't know the gent
who had thus honoured him was surprised nevertheless would think
of him — might call another day. Began to Study at the School of
F. Arts — Half starved — called many times on the great man but
was put off from day to day — Carried the prize at the Academy —
great glee — went to receive the honourary reward presented with a
bronze medal.[14] Being very hungry — was enraged — Jerked the medal
into the Seine — Worked away the best he could — Walked the street
after some time and recognized his friend the officer in a splendid

coach — Off. had been promoted — B was so thin and ragged that off didn't recognize him ran up and shouted, was known and taken in by the off. clad, put in a way to study with comfort. Off. leaves Paris — consigns him to a new benefactor[15] begins to make a noise with his works and to have pupils to talk very loud and long against the School of David[16] — Daughter and Sister of his host both in love with him — Turned out of doors — never mind! — works away — Dispute with David in presence of many artists — as to the merits of Raph and Poussin — asks David which he would prefer an eighth of a Raph or of a Poussin. David put in a great rage — Gets commissions — Makes the acquaintance of Denon — employed by Gov't[17] — Well situated — Desirous of forming a school — gets permission to go to Carrara as Director of the Imp Works for 3 years. Forms a school and brings forward many promising boys[18] — Executes many works of importance. Downfall of Buonap — Cry raised against the *too liberal* Bartolini by the Mob of Carrara — escapes like a dog and repairs to Leghorn with intention of going to the U States — Repairs to Mr App who had before advised the step[19] — discouraged — Mr McCall[20] comes to Leghorn comm. to find artists to adorn the Capitol — Goes to Carrara and takes a dozen dunderheads whose ignorance and presumption has ruined that building[21] — B. comes to Florence and settles — The English pour in upon Italy — Commissions — busts statues — Vases — bas-reliefs — Monuments up to this hour.

Sunday Sept 20 — I made one this morning of a crowd which thronged the Acad door waiting untill the Grand Duke[22] had satisfied his curiosity — a task which he accomplished in 2½ hours — Well Sir! There's not much to talk about after all — A large pict. by Bezzuoli of the Entry of Charles V into Florence[23] — An Ajax saving himself from the tempest and blaspheming against the gods[24] — and a Mary Queen of Scotts listening to the Italian music of David R.[25] form the whole of the remarkable matter — in this exhibition. Bezzuoli has taken a stride in this picture — one too which has gratified many impatient *subjects* of the Benvenuti and Cammuccini dynasty — The pict. is composed with sentiment rather than Science — drawn with a great love and a great Study of Nature — very well coloured — there is throughout a feeling for the picturesque which quality alone would make it a novelty as coming from an Italian of today — The scene is a broad street just inside the gate which forms the greater part of the back ground — A body [of] deputed magistrates with some of the chief citizens of Florence fill the right hand of the canvass and present a fine dramatic bit — in the various feelings produced among them by the tone [of] usurpation taken by Ch — as soon as he found himself within the Walls. The left space is occupied by the crowd and by the characters of the church etc which made part of the ceremony — I said it was well coloured — Let us understand that *well* is only of the first degree of comparison — There is a picture in the Philadelphia Academy[26] which would in [a] trice turn his pearl to lead his brown to earth were it [to] be hung by the side of him — Much merit is due to Bezzuoli — he loves the art and has painted this picture for 1000$ which of course has scarsely covered his expences to say the utmost — The Ajax was the last work of young Sabatelli[27] — whose late death has put us all in mourning — He was so young — yet had such a union of natural and acquired powers that all Italy looked to him as one who would give a new impulse to the art. He had not his equal in drawing or in colour perhaps in the country — in learning as an artist he was behind none — He was as remarkable for his amiable and modest conduct among the artists as for his superiority over them — He was tall and powerful in body — fond of athletic exercises and feats of strength — He fell like Raphael a victim to imprudencies which have robbed the world of many great minds.[28] — The picture of Mary was by Cavalleri a portrait painter much in vogue with the English[29] — It was an attempt to imitate that effect of chiaro Scuro and colour for which some of the Eng. are remarkable. It excited the attention of all the Italians the admiration of many — Twas something new for them — They cannot believe that The old masters coloured differently from themselves — they attribute the tone of Titian to time — Such is the slavery of education — I know many very clever It[alians] — 3 or 4 who want but a beck from a hand which they venerate to become fine painters — I doubt if destiny will accord it them in this age in this country — On the whole this was a clever imitative work — I don't understand why the artist adopted along with the excellencies of his prototypes that slovenly manner of drawing hands and feet and hiding them as much as possible — perhaps he thought it belonged to the *secret.* Many have spoken to me quite *patronizingly* of Mr Peale's Washington — and I have gnashed my teeth to think I had not one sample of what we are proud of that I might hold it up and say — See!

what rank does the man whom you thus acknowledge worthy of your praise hold with us?

And now Sir I shall give you in as few words as possible a bird's eye view of my state and hopes — I have in progress the bust of Mrs Gilmore and the Cherubs of Mr Cooper both in marble. When these are done I shall have finished all orders — For the bust of Mrs G I have rec'd 100$ and shall when tis dispatched see 50 more. For the cherubs I have rec'd 50$ and shall when they are done see 150 more a sum which will do little more than cover the expences if so much. Cooper however does not suspect this — He intends exhibiting the work for my benefit at N York — In the meanwhile I have closed my accounts with my banker[30] and find myself 200$ in pocket — of this 108 will be exhausted by board and lodging for the coming year — Yet Sir do I intend nay I have already made preparatory expences to the execution of a model of a Statue[31] — If I am not to risk something for the art now while my blood is warm and my hopes are high and I have the health and the courage to abide the consequencies when shall I do it — Any thing rather than floundering in lazy hopes! In the mean while should not something unusual take place 1 year, perhaps less will have turned my pocket wrong side out — the Demon Want will seize it and drag me on ship board — There the fiend's power ends — for a short voyage will bring me again into the light of eyes — within sound of voices — and touch of hands of which I often dream and for which in my *fits* my heart yearns as if it would break — Yours truly HG

P.S.   I have rec'd a letter from Mr Cooper dated Sept 15 Sorrento the following extract will describe his situation and employments. "I think we shall stay here untill Dec. I am getting fat and I hardly think you would find the bust a likeness — This is a delightful spot — sea breezes — sea bath fruits — and we literally overhang the bay the water washing the foot of the cliffs on which our house may be said to be suspended — I work every day and am in the middle chap of the 'Water Witch.'[32] This is doing well for a month you will say — I had however 5 chapters written at St Illario.[33] — I am glad you have undertaken a Washington. Go on boldly with the work — Make the figure as severe and simple as possible — for these qualities contain the essence of the imaginative in such a man. It will suit our ideas of his character and of our own. Aim rather at the *natural* than the classica[l] [*page torn*] take care always to preserve the dignity of the man and of his st[ation]" [*page torn*].[34]

I had intended to try to get 1500$ to execute my f[igure] [*page torn*] in marble — it could be done for that sum and would no doubt get me wherewithal to pay all my debts — but Mr Gore[35] who is just arrived here paints the *state of pockets* in Boston with so sombre a pencil that I am fearful they already repent the money they have before trusted me with — Master Edmund God bless you —

PPS   I sent you nearly a year since some Ultramarine and ashes — consigned to the care of Mr Morse of N Y — but have heard nothing of its arrival — there was also a cast of an ear.

Addressed: To Washington Alston Esqre / Care of / David Green-ough[36] Esqre / Boston. Mass.

NOTES

Manuscript: Dana Papers, MHS.
1. For years Allston customarily spent Saturday nights at the home of Ed-mund T. Dana, presiding over a small coterie of which Greenough was a member during his junior and senior years at Harvard. Presumably the "Cam Hourly" was the stage which ran hourly from Cambridge to Cam-bridgeport and Lechmere Point, at the north end of Boston, and the "Brooklyn road" was the old road to Cambridge from Boston through the town of Brookline (*Historical Map of the Town of Brookline, Massachusetts* [1945]).
2. Gab.
3. Rembrandt Peale, painter, was in Florence from July 1829 to April 1830 (see note to Letter 35). The *Washington* which he exhibited at the Academy of Fine Arts in Florence was his famous composite "Port-Hole" portrait (so-called because of the effect of a frame around the head); it is now in the vice-president's room of the Capitol. His portrait of Greenough, painted in Florence, is now in the Wadsworth Athenaeum, Hartford, Connecticut.
4. Examples of such figures are Donatello's Baldassarre Coscia in the Bap-tistery in Florence and Giovanni Crivelli in the church of Santa Maria in Aracoeli in Rome; Desiderio da Settignano's Carlo Marsuppini in the church of Santa Croce in Florence; and Bernardo Rossellino's Leonardo Bruni, also in the church of Santa Croce.
5. John Flaxman (1755–1826), English sculptor and draftsman, did not excel at the most lucrative type of sculpture — portrait busts and statues — but he had a wide patronage, and his drawings of scenes from classical literary works and from Dante were especially popular. Bartolini admired him very much.

6. Flaxman's most famous drawings, chiefly simply designed and emotionally restrained outlines, were those for the *Iliad* and the *Odyssey* (Rome, 1793), the tragedies of Aeschylus (London, 1795), the *Divine Comedy* (London, 1817), and Hesiod's *Works and Days* and *Theogony* (London, 1817).

7. Richard Westmacott (1775–1856), English sculptor, who studied under Canova in Rome and early achieved considerable fame, had by this time executed many statues of public figures for St. Paul's and Westminster Abbey in London and for public sites in several other cities.

8. No figures of these subjects (a mythical king of Italy and his wife) by Flaxman seem to be known. Probably the allusion is to his reconstruction, during his stay in Rome from 1789 to 1794, of the *Torso di Belvedere* in the Vatican Museum, which consisted of a male and a female figure. This work, however, was rather generally criticized (the chief objection being that the male was too ponderous for the female figure), and he eventually destroyed it (Allan Cunningham, *The Lives of the Most Eminent British Painters and Sculptors* [New York, 1854], 3:262). A plaster cast of it is in University College, London.

   By the "French war" Greenough apparently means the war declared by France on England and Holland in 1793.

9. Pietro di Cristoforo Vannucci, called Perugino (*ca.* 1445–1523?), Umbrian painter, whose pupils included the young Raphael.

10. The Piazza Signoria in Florence was also called the Piazza Granduca. Bartolini moved with his family from Savignano to Florence when he was six (Mario Tinti, *Lorenzo Bartolini* [Rome, 1936], 1:27).

11. The alabaster shop in which Bartolini worked was that of one Boccini, in Borgo Ognissanti, but according to Tinti, he decided to go to Volterra in 1795, at the age of eighteen (Tinti, *Bartolini,* 1:30–37 *passim*).

12. The master was a Frenchman named Corneil, who promised Bartolini, as a reward for ornamenting a large alabaster vase, that he might make tracings of Corneil's copies of Flaxman's designs for the *Iliad,* the *Odyssey,* and Aeschylus' tragedies (Tinti, *Bartolini,* 1:38).

13. According to Tinti, Bartolini worked in the sculpture shop of Francesco Schianta on his return to Florence in 1798.

14. In 1802 the first prize — a gold medal — in the *prix de Rome* contest sponsored by the Académie des Beaux Arts of the Institut de France was awarded to the Swiss Pancrace Egensviller. Since the work submitted by Bartolini was widely considered superior, he was subsequently awarded the second prize, a bronze medal (Tinti, *Bartolini,* 1:48–49).

15. Presumably Count Michel Louis Étienne Regnault de Saint-Jean-d'-Angely (1762–1819), French politician, who held several high offices under Napoleon (Tinti, *Bartolini,* 1:49).

16. Jacques Louis David (1748–1825), leading French painter of the neoclassical school, exerted an enormous influence on the art of Europe at this time. Bartolini, together with the painters Jean Auguste Dominique Ingres and François Marius Granet, rebelled against the conventions which David fostered, particularly that respecting the *beau ideal* arrived at from the study of Greek statues (Tinti, *Bartolini,* 1:44, 45, 168–71).

17. Dominique Vivant Denon (1747–1825), chief art advisor to Louis XV and to Napoleon I, and Director General of the Museums of Paris, commissioned Bartolini to execute a colossal bust of Napoleon and one of the bas reliefs

on the column commemorating the Napoleonic campaign of 1805, erected in 1810 in what is now the Place Vendome. Bartolini may also have been officially employed in Paris to restore an antique statue of Aesculapius (Tinti, *Bartolini,* 1:52).

18. Presumably Greenough refers to Bartolini's directorship of the artistic program of the Banca Elisiana in Carrara, an institute housed in the Academy of Fine Arts, which was formed for the purpose of exporting marble and training sculptors. It was under the immediate authority of Napoleon's government in Paris (Tinti, *Bartolini,* 1:57–59, 61–62).

19. Thomas Appleton (1763–1840) of Boston was U.S. consul in Leghorn from 1798 until his death (Isaac Appleton Jewett, *Memorial of Samuel Appleton, of Ipswich, Massachusetts* [Boston, 1850], p. 36). Presumably Bartolini consulted him in 1814, and Appleton probably discouraged him because the War of 1812 had made the completion of the Capitol uncertain. There was, moreover, some dissatisfaction with the two Italian sculptors already employed, chiefly because they worked very slowly (Charles E. Fairman, *Art and Artists of the Capitol of the United States of America* [Washington, 1927], pp. 5, 21, 25).

20. Richard McCall was U.S. consul at Barcelona from 1816 to 1825 and acting consul, or Navy Agent, of the U.S. there earlier. In August 1815 he was asked to help Giovanni Andrei, one of the Italian sculptors employed in Washington, get to Italy to have the columns for the Capitol and White House executed and also to engage three other sculptors to work on the Capitol. Apparently McCall went to Leghorn to expedite matters (Commissioners of Public Buildings and Grounds of the District of Columbia John P. Van Ness and Richard Bland Lee to Giovanni Andrei, 8 August 1815; to the secretary of the navy, 12 August 1815; to McCall, 15 August 1815, RG 42, Records of the Office of Public Buildings and Grounds, NA).

21. Greenough's account is somewhat inaccurate. Andrei and two other Italians who returned with him to Washington in 1816 were all from Carrara, but two were decorative sculptors only, of creditable performance. Most of the statuary in the Capitol, chiefly the four reliefs in the rotunda, was done by three Italians from other cities—Antonio Capellano, Enrico Causici, and Giuseppe Valaperti—all of whom came to the United States independently (Charles E. Fairman, "Art of the Italian Artists in the United States Capitol," *Congressional Record,* 1930, 62, pt. 3:2630–34).

22. Leopold II (1797–1870), Austrian grand duke, ruled Tuscany from 1824 to 1859.

23. Giuseppe Bezzuoli (1784–1855) was a Florentine painter in oil, watercolor, and fresco. His *Entry of Charles VIII into Florence* is now in the Academy of Fine Arts in Florence.

24. This painting, by Francesco Sabatelli (1803–29), is now in the Gallery of Modern Art in the Palazzo Pitti, Florence.

25. Mary Stuart employed as her secretary the Piedmontese musician David Rizzio (1535?–66). The present location of the painting is unknown. It was done by Ferdinando Cavalleri (1794–1865), a professor at the Academy of St. Luke in Rome.

26. Allston's *Dead Man Revived by Touching the Bones of the Prophet Elisha* (Flagg, p. 118).

27. See n. 24 above.

28. According to Vasari, Raphael died of a fever contracted when returning from

a visit to his mistress. Later authorities agree that his death was hastened by overwork, not only painting but excavating Roman ruins (Giorgio Vasari, *Lives of Seventy of the Most Eminent Painters, Sculptors, and Architects,* ed. E. H. and E. W. Blashfield and A. A. Hopkins [New York, 1897], 3: 121–22).

29. See n. 25 above.
30. Presumably Grant, Pillans and Company, Leghorn. By the next February Greenough was apparently banking with Emanuele Fenzi (*Letters,* p. 45), with whom he kept his account during most of the rest of his residence in Florence.
31. Presumably of Washington, as indicated in Cooper's letter to Greenough, 15 September 1829, quoted in Greenough's postscript to this letter.
32. *The Water-Witch,* which contains descriptions of the Bay of Naples and its environs, was published a year later.
33. The Coopers lived in a villa of this name from the first of May until the end of July 1830 (Cooper, 1:346).
34. Greenough's quotation is not entirely accurate (Cooper, 1:389–90).
35. John Christopher Gore (*ca.* 1806–60), Boston landscape painter, was in Florence as an art student from 1829 to 1832 (William Brewer, *Up and Down California* [New Haven, 1930], p. 105; Writers' Program, Northern California, *Monterey Peninsula* [Stanford, 1941], pp. 167–68). Greenough married Gore's sister.
36. David Greenough (1774–1836), Horatio's father, was a builder and real estate dealer in Boston (Greenough, pp. 37, 39).

15. To Washington Allston
17 November 1829

Florence, Nov'r 17th 1829.

My Dear Sir

As I pass, from time to time, one of those hills which lie so frequent across the road I am travelling, my first wish after my curiosity has been slaked, is always to communicate to you what I have seen and what I think, confident that your wishes for my advancement will prompt you [to] correct my errors to which my inexperience and the nature of the company in which I travel, make me liable. I have I believe arrived at that point in execution without the attainment of which I think no one can give the object of art his whole mind — I copy what I see before me with tolerable readiness and accuracy — whatever the object be whether the naked drapery — hair or even animals and vegetables tis soon rendered by a hand schooled to obey

an eye practiced in scanning geometrically its outline and dissecting
its variety of surface from light and shade — This security of method
I owe to the study of drawing — Twas drawing that taught me the
necessity of a scrupulous outline — twas drawing that taught me
that the planes[1] of a form are shaded in proportion to their obliquity
to the source of light. The foundation of my system of modelling lies
in this fact — For fear my language may be obscure I'll try to explain.
We will suppose[2] a square mass of modelling earth of which we
see only one side which is opposite the source of light. With a flat
spattel we cut down the earth on each side at an angle of 45°
we have[3] the two sides aa being inclined to the source of light
become partially shaded — now it's clear that if these planes were
followed by others less and less oblique to the source of light we
should at length get the side of a cylinder thus.[4] Performing a similar
operation at the top and bottom at the angles etc we should at
length get a semisphere and we should in the course of the work
have produced every variety of tint to be found in the naked for
the naked is composed we know entirely of plane convex and sometimes though rare by concave surfaces. To carry any method of
execution however simple in its principles to a high degree of finish
— requires much time and a delicate eye and hand — which we know
require years of practice to obtain them — Here modelling has repaid
again what drawing had lent her for with this system I plant my
shadows and conduct half tints after having settled my outline with
the greatest security — so much so that I find the pen a very agreeable
instrument to draw with —

Sublimity — Majesty — beauty truth — seem to me the only true
elements of my art either in conception — composition or form —
Perhaps I might have said truth supposing it to contain beauty — but
truth is not always beauty — therefore I have mentioned both yet I
still contend that beauty is always truth nor can I admit as genuine in
form a single plane or curve not belonging to the organization nor can
I pardon except in colossal works or others where a certain effect is the
legitimate object of the work any ommission of the parts above mentioned a point in which Canova sinned terribly against my theory who
provided the chief muscles were in their place thought of nothing but
making sweet gradations of shadow — To take up the thread I dropped
— truth is not always beauty and though I can bring myself to allow
it's sometimes necessary to make a work merely true — I consider such

a work the lowest in the order of works of sculpture — Still I prefer it to the half way attempt to reconcile and mix a grand whole with mean detail — Still truth I think necessary in a work but tis possible truth I mean not reality — I love reality dearly and when I want to enjoy it I go to the market place — the church the wharf and I get at a glimpse more of it than is to be found in all the works of Chantrey.[5] Nor can I help thinking as I see the peasant standing or moving how feeble my art is in imitation and how improper an object reality is for a medium so abstract so refined so poetical as sculpture — I think therefore that instead of attempting to convey trivial detail we should seek to ennoble our works by putting into them all that we can conceive to move the mind — all that's dear in beauty all that's moving in passion all that's grand in thought. I would not go so far as M Ang whose drapery is often unlike any kind of cloth in its planes and foldings — For the eye is disgusted at the impossible — Such is my notion of my art — I am sensible how necessary repeated efforts are [to] enable me to embody them. I know that twould require very different commissions from those which fall daily into my hands at present[6] and which though they feed my body starve my soul by keeping me constantly busy on trifles.

Cooper is the noblest patron I have yet found — has the broadest ideas on the subject of art and wishes me well personally I've reason to think. We talk much of you when we are together — He is a true American and is therefore proud of you. I rec'd a letter from him last Sunday in which he insists on my coming to Rome to spend a few weeks with him there[7] — I feel such a longing to get a sight of old friends and old sights there that I may be tempted to go — I have tried the receipt you gave me for a palette and I hope one day to arrive at proficiency enough in painting to paint a portrait for my amusement now and then — but let me protest that of all the subjects which I have ever attempted to understand colour is the most subtle — unaccountable incomprehensible — by long examination I think I have found that comparatively few *pictures* are *coloured* — Even of those of name — Some are drawn in a chiaroscuro with paint somewhat approximating in its general tint to flesh. Others are painted in downright light and shade with a little tinge of colour glazed into them — Almost all seem to have had a conventional palette which is too partially or generally reasoned to embrace the variety of nature or render her delicate distinctions — Titian, Titian is my man and some of the Dutchmen too please me quite as much — There's a picture in the Flemish room by Giordeans of Venus on a car with Love by her side and several marine deities about her[8] which is one of the most luxurious bursts of light and colour that ever feasted eye — Such a union of brilliance warmth and harmony as really I think surpasses every thing Italian I have seen — I fear from the silence with which my work has been rec'd in Boston that they [think] I am not their man[9] — In the mean while unless they send me work or I should find it here — (not probable for travelling Jonathan is very philosophical) I shall in the course of 8 months get aground — Nothing not even my love of my art shall tempt me to stay here one moment at the risk of incumbering my personal friends here — I have been looked on since I have been here by the respectable artists as a man whose game is tolerably sure and pride will send me straight to Leghorn when I find *soundings* growing shallow There is a roof in Boston which covers 12 heads[10] on which I had hopes to pour oil of comfort — if I fail I know they'll pour it on mine — if I didn't think this I should be truly miserable — In the meanwhile my group advances — my bust of Mrs Gilmore is finished — I'm pressing on from the boy to the man — Not one solid blow struck for a name — at an age when M. Angelo — had nearly finished his colossal David[11] — The grandest piece of the naked that the Christian world has seen done — I knock under. God bless you Sir — Love to Mr Richard — and the Master

Hor Greenough

I hope when I go to Rome to be able to send you some more Ultramarine.

Addressed: To / Washington Allston Esqre / Care of David Greenough Esqre / Boston. Mass.

NOTES

Manuscript: Dana Papers, MHS. Previous publication (in part): Flagg, pp. 223–24.
1. This word occurs five times in this letter; each time Greenough wrote "plain."
2. Here Greenough drew a square.
3. Here Greenough drew a rectangle with shaded ends labeled *a* and *a.*
4. Here Greenough drew a rectangle shaded so as to represent a cylinder.
5. Sir Francis Legatt Chantrey (1781–1842), the leading English sculptor of his day, was noted for his portrait busts and statues. His statue of Washington for the State House in Boston was unveiled in October 1827, at which time Greenough was in the city.

6. Greenough was exaggerating. The only commission he is known to have received in the fall of 1829 was for the bust of Cornelius Bradford, a friend of Cooper's who was visiting in Florence.

7. In his letter to Greenough, 5 November 1829, Cooper urged him to bring *The Chanting Cherubs* to Rome, suggesting "we might do something with them perhaps," presumably meaning that the work might be publicly exhibited (Cooper, 1:395). Greenough did not go, however.

8. This work, by Jakob Jordeans (1593–1678), is in the Uffizi Gallery.

9. Greenough's busts of John Adams, John Quincy Adams and, presumably, Josiah Quincy reached Boston about 1 July 1829 (Diary of John Quincy Adams, 2, 3 July 1829, Adams Papers, MHS). The *John Adams* was set up in the First Church in Quincy on 22 October 1829. The *John Quincy Adams* and the *Josiah Quincy,* which were shown at the Boston Athenaeum exhibition the following spring, were praised by a reviewer in the *North American Review* for October 1830, but there was apparently objection in some quarters to the fact that the Adamses were undraped (U.S. Congress, Senate, *Memorial of Horatio Greenough, Praying The removal of the Statue of Washington from its present position in the Rotundo, to the grounds in front of the western façade of the Capitol,* 27th Cong., 3d sess., 1843, S. Doc. no. 57, p. 5).

10. Greenough's parents and all his brothers and sisters except John were living at this time at 7 Chestnut Street, Boston. The children were Henry, Alfred (1809–51), Louisa (1809–92), Laura (1815–51), Ellen (1814–93), Charlotte (1815–59), and Richard Saltonstall (1819–1904) (Greenough, pp. 41–42). Presumably the other three members of the household were servants (*Letters,* p. 64).

11. Michelangelo executed this work during the period from his twenty-sixth to his twenty-ninth year. At this time it was still standing before the entrance to the Palazzo Vecchio, for which place it had been ordered.

16. To James Fenimore Cooper
7 January 1830

Florence — Jan'y 7th 1830 —

My Dear Sir — I have just left Molini[1] whom I found very ready to accept the business mentioned in your letter of the 30th Ult'o — His answers were as follows — He can put but two sheets in type at once for want of compositors — The same reason puts the division of the task between two offices out of the question — 2 sheets a week are the utmost he can *engage to finish* and the delay as well as expense of sending them to Rome, he presumes you are as able to calculate as himself. With regard to price (taking it for granted that the work is of the same bulk with the last)² he will do it for the same price, each volume being delivered to your agent and paid for when compleated — but he afterward added the condition — "the handwriting being equally distinct as that of the former manuscript." He assured me that he fully believed that no objection would be made by the Censor³ to the printing the answer to the Ed — Rev'w — of which you make mention⁴— He promised to mention the thing to him and I shall probably in the course of 3 or 4 days be able to write you a favourable answer on this head —

This answer will reach you somewhat later than you had a right to expect — The reason is this — Your letter found me convalescent from an attack of fever brought on by some exposure and a little imprudence. I went out the day before yest'y for the first time — Molini I found was engaged at the Pitti P — untill 5 *PM* which was too late for me — Yest'y was Epiphany — so that though tardy you will I hope find me innocent — I would have transferred the commission to the Consul but he took a severe cold at my house in assisting at the operation of letting my blood and has not since left his lodgings though quite recov'd. Tell Mr Cooper said he that there has been a great alarm at Pisa — 3 individuals of the family of Pozzo di Borgo⁵ lately arrived in that city having died in a sudden manner and a fourth having been attacked with the same alarming symptoms — the usual precautions against the Plague were resorted to — The disorder was pronounced to be the Bubonic fever of the Levant — The faculty⁶ however have examined the affair and have decided that no great danger is to be apprehended — that the complaint is a violent febrile attack of a typhoid character — There said the Consul (turning under the bed clothes and thrusting his nightcapped pate through the curtains) in a voice of thunder That's authentic! The Consul and Mr Molini desire to be remembered respectfully to yourself and family — May I ask how your expectations are answered in the sight of the treasures of the Vatican and Capitol?

Yours with respect
Horatio Greenough

J. Fenimore Cooper Esqre / Rome

PS   The Consul thinks that if complaints were entered against Luigi by your Swiss servant — two desirable objects might be effected — the recovery of damages for the poor creature and the decision of the judges against Luigi in the other affair⁷ —

Addressed: To / James Fenimore Cooper Esqre / Care of / F C Cicognani Esqre[8] / U.S. Consul / Rome.

NOTES

James Fenimore Cooper (1789–1851) was in Europe from 1826 to 1833, with his wife and their five children; his nephew William was with them for the first five years, until his death. Greenough met Cooper in Florence soon after his arrival in late October 1828 and saw a great deal of him during his sojourn there, until the end of the following July (see Letter 9 and subsequent letters). Though they had little contact after Cooper's return to America, Greenough remained one of Cooper's most loyal friends.

Manuscript: Cooper Collection, Beinecke.

1. Giuseppe Molini was a Florentine printer, proprietor of the Dante's Head Press there. In his letter to Greenough of 30 December 1829, Cooper asked him to consult Molini about printing Cooper's recently completed novel *The Water-Witch* (Cooper, 1:398–99). Learning that Molini could not do the work rapidly enough, Cooper, in his reply to Greenough's letter, dated 28 January 1830, reported that he had decided to send his manuscript to Paris to be printed (Cooper, 1:402–3).

2. In the spring of 1829 Molini made a printing of Cooper's *The Wept of Wish-ton-Wish* (Cooper, 1:367).

3. A Roman Catholic priest responsible for granting or denying a license for publication; see Letters 17 and 18.

4. In his letter of 30 December 1829 Cooper also asked Greenough to see if someone in Florence could print a reply which Cooper had written to an article by William Empson in the *Edinburgh Review* for June 1829, comparing Cooper's *Notions of the Americans* (1828) unfavorably to Basil Hall's *Travels in North America in the Years 1827 and 1828* (1829). Although Cooper's reply was printed at least in part by Molini, it was never published, and the manuscript has apparently not been preserved (see Letters 17–19).

5. Count Carlo Andrea Pózzo di Bórgo (1764–1842), Corsica-born diplomat with strong republican leanings, was from 1815 to 1835 the Russian ambassador in Paris, where Cooper met him in 1827 (Cooper, 1:203).

6. The medical faculty of the University of Pisa.

7. Luigi, one of the Coopers' servants in Florence, had seduced their Swiss cook, Lucie (Cooper, 1:399, 404). By "the other affair" Greenough refers to the aftermath of a suit which Luigi, after being discharged for unreliability, had brought against Cooper for ten dollars in wages. Before Cooper left Florence this suit was settled, he paying the lawyer the dollar due Luigi and the costs. Afterwards, attempts were made by Ombrosi, apparently in collusion with Luigi and the lawyer, to obtain more money from Cooper on the grounds of the case's being continued and even of a new one's being instituted (Cooper, 1:413; 2:44–45).

8. Felice C. Cicognani, a Roman advocate previously in the service of the Pope, served as U.S. consul in Rome from 1823 to 1837 (Leo Francis Stock, ed., *Consular Relations between the United States and the Papal States* [Washington, 1945], 1:xxv).

17.   To James Fenimore Cooper
5 March 1830

Florence — March 5th 1830

My Dear Sir

I am so intoxicated by the arrival in Florence of my younger brother,[1] in better health than I have seen him for years, that I fear I shall make but sad work, in attempting to give account of my negotiations with Mollini — But I will gird up my loins and try to be coherent — On the rec't of your last[2] I hasten'd to Mollini, who assured me that he would willingly engage to have the copies struck off in a month, but for the circumstance of the proofs going to Rome before printing, which operation alone would occupy more than that space of time — Now as it seemed to me highly probable, that you would be willing to give up seeing the proofs, for the sake of dispatch — I allowed the manuscript to be put into the hands of the Censor — for he will not have finished reading untill Wednesday next; so that you will have time to countermand me or give Mollini his own time, before the license shall have been given. The Censor has had an attack of gout from which he has not fully recovered — otherwise his decision would have been already given — I have been to visit him this evening and he has had the complaisance to promise to hear me read the article early in the coming week, should he not be able to leave his bed by that time — He asked if there was any allusion to the Jesuits in the work, to which I answered that as far as I had read I had met with nothing of the kind — Mollini has no doubt of obtaining the permission and I own I am of his opinion —

I have rec'd a letter from Mr Gilmor[3] in which he expresses the greatest pleasure at having rec'd the casts from Cellini's vase and Urn — He gives me an order which is just what I wanted — viz a female figure from 3 to 4 ft high, draped in part at least — leaving to me the subject and even the liberty of making a male figure should I have on hand any favourite invention —

You cannot imagine how pleased I was at the news you gave with regard to the intentions of Mr Shemmerhorn[4] — I found I was still remembered at a moment when I began to fear that people had forgotten me entirely — I found I had the prospect of working another group in Italy, when I had begun to fear that I should return to America this summer — I recognised your agency in my behalf and believe me my obligations to you are rather a pleasure than otherwise to me.

My Brother's arrival has given the finishing touch to my good-fortune — I have the prospect of his company as long as I remain abroad, of being [able] to contribute to his instruction in the art — of receiving assistance from him in such of my studies as have hithertoo entirely occupied him[5] — I have by me a poem delivered by Richard Dana before some society,[6] which I shall endeavour to send you — Mr Gilmor admires your choice of a subject for a groupe and regrets that he had not thought of the same. He has searched among the engravings from the old masters to find something similarly calculated for effect in marble —

The Boys[7] are far advanced — I am thoroughly interested in them — and I hope yet to be proud of them — Begging to be respectfully remembered to Mrs Cooper and the family[8] I remain Dr S[ir] [*page torn*]

Sincerely Yours
Horatio Greenough

To / James F Cooper Esqre / Rome

Addressed: To / James F Cooper Esqre / care of / F C Cicognani Esqre / U.S. Consul / Rome

NOTES

Manuscript: Cooper Collection, Beinecke.
1. Henry Greenough went to Florence in the hope that his health would im-improve there, but since it did not, he returned home in the summer of 1833 (*Letters,* pp. 44–45).
2. In his letter to Greenough of 17 February 1830, Cooper asked him to ar-range to have Molini print Cooper's letter to the *Edinburgh Review,* which at the same time he sent Greenough (Cooper, 1:403–4).
3. This letter was dated 9 October 1829. For other matters in it, see Greenough's Letter 21 to Gilmor.
4. Peter Schermerhorn (1781–1852), wealthy New York merchant and banker, was in Rome at this time (Richard Schermerhorn, Jr., *Schermerhorn Geneal-ogy and Family Chronicles* [New York, 1914], pp. 163–65). In his letter to Greenough of 26 February, Cooper said that Schermerhorn wished to give

Greenough an order for a group. When he was in Florence a few weeks
later, however, Schermerhorn ordered nothing, possibly because of the interference of Ombrosi (Cooper, 1:404, 412).

5. Probably Greenough refers to Henry's drawing during the years from 1824
   to 1826, when he was employed in making building plans for his father
   (*Letters,* p. 44).
6. Probably *A Poem Delivered before the Porter Rhetorical Society, in the
   Theological Seminary, Andover, September 22, 1829* (Boston, 1829). Entitled "Thoughts on the Soul," it appears in Dana's *Poems and Prose Writings* (New York, 1850), 1:85–96.
7. *The Chanting Cherubs.*
8. Cooper's wife was the former Susan Augusta De Lancey. Their children
   were Susan Augusta, Carolina Martha, Anne Charlotte, Maria Frances, and
   Paul.

18.   To James Fenimore Cooper
15 March 1830

Florence March 15 — 1830

My Dear Sir

I have just put your letter[1] into the hands of Mr Molini with the
approval of the censor — I have been obliged to read the whole work
into Italian for him for the sake of expedition. Otherwise I know not
when he would have made an end of it.

In the sentence "The finger of Providence pointed to a place where
the *most* devoted of his worshippers might erect their altars" — He
erased the word "most" as conveying an idea derogatory to the Catholic
forms of [wor]ship[2] [*page torn*] —

Also the passage — "I am old enough to remember its language"
(where you speak of the English press) to Alexander who "was yesterday a Saint and today a Debauchee a patriot or a tyrant etc" stuck in
the throat of the good father. I talked hard to him however and he
concluded to change merely the word Debauchee for "any thing
else" — The sentence "We have seen his successor within a 12 month
represented now as a cormorant now as a butterfly — hero or dastard
as his battalions approached or receded from the Balkan." he thought
himself not at liberty to license[3] — The notes remain to be read. I shall

expect your advice with regard to the above passages – in the mean while the printing will go on.

I am Dr Sir Yours Sincere[ly] H Greenough

Addressed: To / James F Cooper Esqre / Care of / F. C. Cicognani Esqre / U.S. Consul. / *Rome*

NOTES

Manuscript: Cooper Collection, Beinecke. Previous publication: James Fenimore Cooper, *Correspondence of James Fenimore-Cooper,* ed. James F. Cooper (New Haven, 1922), 1:178–79.

1. Cooper's letter to the *Edinburgh Review.*
2. Presumably Cooper's sentence referred to the discovery and settlement of the United States by predominantly Protestant groups.
3. Alexander I (1777–1825), czar of Russia, was liberal in his early policies but in later years became tyrannical and unbalanced on the subject of religion. Czar Nicholas I (1796–1855), brother of Alexander I and his successor, undertook in 1828 an invasion of the Balkan penisula, which proved unsuccessful. Presumably the censor objected to both sentences because they might have offended the Austrian rulers of Tuscany, Austria being a member with Russia and Prussia of the Holy Alliance.

19. To James Fenimore Cooper
10 April 1830

Florence – April 10th 1830 –

My Dear Sir.

I have written to Mr Molini your directions with regard to the bill and the sheets already printed[1] – An engagement has prevented my seeing him untill this evening. My regret at the turn this affair has taken arose solely from my wish that you should be served as I feel myself bound to serve you – faithfully. I have had more than one twinge about your law suit and I was ambitious to shew you that I was influenced in giving my little aid to you by a pure wish to further your designs – In speaking of the law suit I do not mean in the least to reflect upon Ombrosi – I refer to the laywer and gentry of that stamp – depend on it Sir they make persons in your situation their prey.

Your "conditions" to the bargain of the groupe[2] are marked by the same liberality which I have found in all your treatment of me – I shall subscribe to them with all my heart – The groupe begins to make quite a figure – The Marchesa-Riccardi[3] called there the other day – by chance I believe and expressed much pleasure at the sight of them. She begged I would inform her when they were finished as she wished to bring some friends to see them. I am (under the rose) modelling the bust of Giulia Grisi – whom I think the loveliest woman I ever set eye upon – You perhaps remember her as having made her debut last year at the Pergola[4] – Thereby hangs a long tale of Ombrosi's Machiavelian subtlety – I will take an opportunity of telling you all about it – It is characteristic – I will inclose in a letter to you while at Venice the profile of Washington[5] which Mrs Cooper was so kind as to lend me – Will you remember my thankful regards to her – my respects to the family. I remain Dear Sir

Yours with Respect
Horatio Greenough

J Fenimore Cooper Esqre / Rome

Addressed: To / J Fenimore Cooper Esqre / care of / F. C. Cicognani / U.S. Consul Rome

NOTES

Manuscript: Cooper Collection, Beinecke.
1. In his letter to Greenough of 6 April 1830, Cooper said he would not agree to publishing his letter to the *Edinburgh Review* without seeing the proofs. He asked Greenough to send him a copy of what Molini had already printed, together with the bill for it, thus terminating his work (Cooper, 1:406–7).
2. In his letter to Greenough of 6 April 1830, Cooper proposed that Greenough send *The Chanting Cherubs* to America as Greenough's property (thus duty would not have to be paid on it) and exhibit it for three months in New York; afterwards, when Cooper had paid the balance of the cost and the transportation, it would be transferred to his order. As an alternative, Cooper suggested that for a certain sum, including the transportation, Greenough deliver the group to Cooper in America and Cooper take on the arrangement for the exhibition (Cooper, 1:407). Greenough accepted the first proposal in this letter.
3. In his letter to Cooper of 7 March 1831, Greenough calls her the Marchesa

Strozzi Riccardi. Possibly she was Anna Strozzi, who married the Marchese Vincenzo Riccardi in 1795 (Pompeo Litta, *Famiglie Celebri Italiane* [Milan, 1839], vol. 4, pt. 2, plate xxii).

4. Giulia Grisi (1811–69), Italian operatic soprana, was a leading prima donna in Europe for some thirty years. Nothing further seems to be known about Greenough's bust of her. The Pergola Theatre in Florence was used chiefly for musical performances. Grisi made her debut there on 26 December 1829, in *L'Ezio* by Philippe Celli, but the performance was not as well received as was expected (*Giornale di Commercio* [Florence], 30 December 1829).

5. Greenough sent Cooper a letter and the profile, which he received in Venice on 5 May 1830 (Cooper, 1:412). Neither has been located, and the profile has not been identified.

20. To Robert Gilmor, Jr.
25 April 1830

Florence. April 25th. 1830.

My dear Sir.

I Seize my first moment of leisure to inform you of what my prospects are with relation to the objects you desire me to send you.[1] I have in my eye a good picture or two which I may, I think, make a good bargain of, but I am obliged to be extremely cautious. You know enough of picture-dealers to understand why I am so, and, if I am somewhat slower than you could wish, will, I doubt not, attribute it to my regard for your true interest.

I have by me a fine copy of a celebrated landscape of Salvator's which was made by a nephew of the famous Sabatelli.[2] I gave only $10 for this picture and was yesterday offered double my money by an American gentleman — Mr Peale borrowed it of me to finish a copy which he had commenced, of the same picture — I shall enclose it to you and if on the sight of it you overcome your aversion to copies far enough to pay me what I gave for it, it shall be yours — I bought it with an eye to your drawing-room before I received your last letter — Should you not care to have it I will thank you to send it to Boston, with a note of directions to my brother[3] which note will be enclosed in the package.

With regard to the statue you honour me by ordering I have thought best to make a figure of a girl, about nine years of age, for

adult forms on a small scale produce but a mean effect unless de-
cidedly in miniature — I have made several sketches but have not yet
entirely pleased myself in the combination of the qualities I wish to
unite in it. It shall be my care to transmit to you a small drawing of
what I fix on as soon as I shall have established the composition — I
have written to Mr Grant[4] that I shall draw on him for $250 when the
clay is put up and for $300 when the marble is consigned to him —
making the price rather below than above the ordinary cost of similar
works by artists of a respectable standing — Should this sum, however, exceed what you thought of laying out, I shall beg you to reduce
it to $400 by subtracting $150 from the receipts of the exhibition — I
know that in America the value of statues is often underrated and I
fear being thought to exact too high prices — Hithertoo I have scarcely
supported my own shop and have once or twice been rather anxious
on account of the state of my funds but, all that is past. Mr Cooper's
group will be in New York in the course of four months. I have six
or seven other commissions on hand[5] and am in the best health — I
have succeeded so well in a bust of Washington in pleasing my
countrymen[6] that I think of getting up a statue of him which I could
finish by degrees and which when done would I doubt not, pay my
debt[7] in America and give me assistance in my art besides — Do not
imagine, my dear sir, that I am uneasy under the obligation which I
feel toward the gentlemen who assisted me, no sir; I shall carry that
to my grave with pleasure, but the debt, I confess, I think daily of and
the brightest day I have long seen will be that when I shall be able
to refund what has been advanced me. In the mean while I trust
that generous treatment of me was not thrown away. I hope, sir, and
I believe, that I shall become useful to my nation as an artist and that
the day will arrive when young Americans, devoting themselves to
the art, will find in my study that instruction in the rudiments of
Sculpture, to obtain which I have travelled so far, & have spent so much
time and money. Begging to be remembered to Mrs Gilmor and her
sister[8]

I remain dear Sir

Yours.

Horatio Greenough —

Addressed: To / Robert Gilmor Esqre / Baltimore.
Endorsed, in Gilmor's hand: H. Greenough — ans'd 27 [?] Oct

NOTES

This letter, except for the signature and address, is in Henry Greenough's hand.
Manuscript: Mellen Chamberlain Autograph Collection, BPL. Previous publication: Nathalia Wright, ed., "Letters by Horatio Greenough in the Library," *Boston Public Library Quarterly* 11 (1959): 77–78.

1. In his letter to Greenough of 9 October 1829, Gilmor gave him an order for a statue of a female figure three or four feet high (see Letter 17 and the third paragraph of this letter). He also asked him to look for a picture which Gilmor might add to his collection, and stated that he had authorized Grant, Pillans, and Co., Leghorn, to give Greenough credit to carry out these commissions. Greenough's reply to this letter, written about February 1830, was evidently lost en route. For its contents, see Letter 21.

2. Salvator Rosa (1615–73), Italian landscape painter, poet, muscian, actor, and revolutionary, was in great vogue during the early Romantic period. The copyist has not been identified. His uncle was presumably Luigi Sabatelli (1772–1850), Florentine painter, who was a professor at the Academy of Fine Arts in Milan from 1808 until his death.

3. Alfred Greenough, a Boston merchant. Letters by him appear in *Letters*, pp. 54–58, 61–69, 72–76.

4. Of Grant, Pillans, and Co., Leghorn.

5. The only other works Greenough is known to have been working on about this time were the busts of Cornelius Bradford, Cooper, John T. Kirkland, and Giulia Grisi, but Cooper's and probably Grisi's were not commissions. Presumably he had orders for one or more busts of Washington, but from whom is not known.

6. One of these busts was purchased by James I. Roosevelt and another, from a new model, by Commodore James Biddle (see Letter 37). The only bust of Washington by Greenough which has been located, presumably from one of these models, is in the Museum of Fine Arts, Boston.

7. The $1000 lent him at the instigation of Gilmor in May 1828.

8. Possibly Mrs. Chiffelle, whose daughter Charlotte and son-in-law Charles Carroll Harper Greenough knew. Mrs. Gilmor had four other sisters, however: Mesdames Baron, Bee, Gregorie, and Grimke ("The Diary of Robert Gilmor," *Maryland Historical Magazine* 17 [1922]: 258).

21.   To Robert Gilmor, Jr.
7 September 1830

Florence — Sept 7th. 1830.

My Dear Sir

I beg you will be under no uneasiness with regard to the miscarriage of your letter of credit — at least on my account. It is true that had your orders reached me without delay I had long before this despatched them one and all — I perceive that you also have never rec'd one or two of my last letters from your date of June 12th 1830 which I rec'd from Mess Grant and Pillans this morning — On the rec't of your first letter (Oct 9 1829 date) I wrote to Mr Grant asking if he had had no notice of the letters sent me or the credit given me — he answered in the negative authorising me to draw for $100 immediately and very properly requesting to see the letter in which you mention the credit — He had never before had any intimation of the thing and in fact I believe it was not untill very lately that he rec'd your instructions owing doubtless to miscarriage of one of your letters and delay at Gibraltar of the other. After reading your first letter I answered you mentioning the having sent the bust — my having rec'd your orders — and proposing as a subject for a statue for you the dead figure of Medora from Byron's Corsair.[1] I stated that I could do the figure for 500$ and I mentioned to you the difficulty of procuring authenticated works of the good masters at any thing like a reasonable price — I delayed setting up the figure of Medora lest you might not wish to spend so much money and I looked around very diligently for a picture worthy of you — I have found a portrait of Salvator Rosa which needs no authentication for the price of 100$ and a Van der Werf[2] representing cupids bringing the wild boar bound — to Venus for 250$. Neither of these pictures did I dare to purchase, the first because as a portrait I feared you might think it dear and the second because the price really seemed to myself exorbitant — I would if I had the money have bought both these pictures on my own account — In fact with a small capital here nothing would be easier than to spend a thousand or two of Dollars to great profit — I am not sanguine in my hopes of obtaining any thing original of Cellini's for you — I had 2 small silver bas reliefs offered me the other day for little more than their weight of bullion one of which was struck with a die the other wrought with the hammer and then chased but — as they were interesting merely as shewing the method and as they were of the ignorant manner and bad taste of the last century I neglected them — I shall search diligently for the boy you mention in one of the Madonnas and should I not be able to find it I shall compose one my- self with the same view viz — to be useful in bearing a lamp or vase of flowers. I have drawn on you for the sum of 250$. — If I can get your statue through for that amount I shall be most happy if not I shall draw for the remainder of the sum to which you have limited my credit — I carry on a great many undertakings unassisted — alone — I live with the greatest economy and I only seek the opportunity of employment and honour and a decent livelihood — I have lived a very active life since I have been here yet so expensive are the opera- tions of my art that I have sunk 1000$ in these 2 years together with all the prices of my works — In some instances the price given me has barely paid the marble and clay and moulding — and yet have the gentlemen who ordered seemed to think I made them pay dearly — Yet I am not discouraged or disheartened. My strength has in- creased with the increasing demand for it — my health is excellent and I yet hope to repay in some sort the debt of gratitude to yourself and some other friends in America — With regard to the pedestals — unless you wish to have them richly ornamented which I presume from your silence about it you do not they may be made in Philadelphia or Baltimore even quite as well as at Carrara and come to you much cheaper — the only difficulty is the form — which they will execute to the order and draught of an Architect without any difficulty — I prefer myself the truncated tuscan column with the torus of the base orna- mented to any other pedestal for busts or small light statues — lest I should not be clear I will make a slight sketch and enclose it.[3] Begging that in case I may have made too high a charge for your statue you will inform me of it I assure you that you may do so without any risk of wounding or creating any unpleasant feeling on my part — I know you too well to attribute to any other than the justest and soundest reasons any such rem[onstra]nce [*page torn*] from you — I remain Dear Sir

> With compliments to Mrs Gilmor and family
> > Yours Sincerely
> > Horatio Greenough

P.S I have despatched through Mess Grant Pillans & co a case containing the copy of Salvator which I before mentioned and a small
painting on marble which I bought for $2–50 cts and which was part
of the Torregiani collection.[4] I thought it had considerable spirit and
as such curiosities are to be found in all the collections I thought you
might like it.

Addressed: To / Rob't Gilmore Esqre / Baltimore / Care of / G G & S
Howland[5] / *New York*

NOTES

Manuscript: Mellen Chamberlain Autograph Collection, BPL. Previous publication: Nathalia Wright, ed., "Letters by Horatio Greenough in the Library,"
Boston Public Library Quarterly 11 (1959): 78–80.
1. *The Corsair* was published in 1814.
2. Probably Adriann Van der Werff (1659–1722), historical, genre, and portrait painter.
3. This sketch has apparently not survived.
4. The Torrigiani family of Florence had a large art collection, most of it
   housed in the larger of the two Torrigiani palaces on the Piazza Mozzi (E.
   Grifi, *Saunterings in Florence* [Florence, 1930–31], pp. 399–400).
5. Gardiner Greene and Samuel Shaw Howland were New York shipping agents
   at 49–50 South Street (*Longworth's American Almanac, New-York Register
   and City Directory* [1830–31]).

22.   To Samuel F. B. Morse
27 November 1830

Florence – Nov 27th 1830

To S. F. B. Morse Esqre
My Dear Sir
    Allow me to introduce to you my friend Mr Benjamin Field of Bos-
ton who is about to visit Rome for a few days[1] – As my friend's stay
in your city will be limited he will naturally wish to examine objects of
the most prominent interest – Any assistance which you can give him
in accomplishing this object will truly oblige My Dear Sir

Your Friend and Serv't
Horatio Greenough

Addressed: S. F. B. Morse Esqre / P.N.A. / Benj Field Esqre / Rome

NOTES

> Manuscript: Morse Papers, LC.
>
> 1. Presumably Greenough refers to Benjamin Faxon Field (1806–93), a Boston merchant (Frederick Clifton Pierce, *Field Genealogy* [Chicago, 1901], 2: 748).
>
> Morse, who was in Europe from 1829 to 1832, reached Rome on 20 February 1830, having passed through Florence about the middle of that month (Samuel Irenaeus Prime, *The Life of Samuel F. B. Morse, LL.D.* [New York, 1875], pp. 173, 187; Edward L. Morse, ed., *Samuel F. B. Morse: His Letters and Journals* [Boston, 1914], 1:337).

23. To George Stillman Hillard?
November 1830

[Florence]

[to C]

With regard to the manner in which young artists are supported in Italy, and the source from whence they derive encouragement, they are the same with all the different nations of Europe. All the academies of the capital cities have pension funds to support the cleverest of their young men in Italy, some for three, some for four, some for five, and even six years. The English have, I believe, about $2000 a year. The Russians $700. The Austrians 1000 francs for their journey to Rome, 1000 for their return to Vienna, and 2000 per annum during the three years they remain there. The French have a national academy at Rome, in what was formerly the villa of the Medici family;[1] there they are lodged and boarded, in the most comfortable manner, and have an allowance per diem, for their current expenses. . . .

You inquire, whence comes my encouragement? I work for *less* than any other artist of any standing will, and that is the secret of my commissions. Do you ask how I am able to do it? by denying myself every indulgence that costs money. . . .

If I cannot make some sacrifices to fame while I am young and have
hope, when shall I do it?

NOTES

"C.," who quotes extracts from Greenough's letter in his article, was possibly
George Stillman Hillard (1808–79), Boston lawyer and man of letters, who was
a fellow student of Greenough's at Harvard. Hillard's article entitled "Mr.
Greenough's New Group of Statuary" (about Greenough's *Angel and Child*), in
the *New England Magazine* for January 1835, sounds as though its author was
the same as that of the two articles signed "C." about Greenough's *Chanting
Cherubs* and *Medora* in the *Boston Courier* in 1831 and 1833. Hillard visited
Greenough in Florence in 1847 and wrote an account of him in *Six Months in
Italy* (1853).
    Source: "Sculpture. To the Editor of the *Courier*" [signed "C."], *Boston
Courier*, 6 May 1831. The place and date are given by "C."
    1. The Académie de France à Rome, founded in 1725, was moved in 1801 to
    the Villa Medici on the Viale del Pincio.

24.   To James Fenimore Cooper
        6 December 1830

My Dear Sir —
    The present is in substance a duplicate of a letter which I ad-
dressed to you about six weeks since and which I presume miscarried
with many others at the time that the Austrian arrangement[1] first took
place. In the last letter which I wrote you before the above mentioned
one[2] I stated that I would willingly agree to deliver the boys to your order in the U.S. as you had proposed — I did not reflect when I said so
that I was insuring the groupe a safe passage across the water and I
dare say you did not yourself mean it so — I am willing in case the work
miscarries to give up all claim upon you hereafter but I must beg to
be exc[used] [*page torn*] from being responsible for the voyage[3] —
and that because I cannot pay to that amount — You see how small
my fortune is — I assure you the groupe pleases generally — I mean
that John Bull shall see it if possible while I await your answer[4] —
Could and would Gen Lafayette give me sittings for his head if I

were to make a jaunt to Paris? His portrait would be worth a fortune to me hereafter — Will you if you think he has the time to spare ask him to sit? I only ask 6 sittings of an hour — I have rather more facility than when I made your bust — We are as usual in this town except that the Consul and I do not exactly agree. I charge him with double dealing with me — I beg you will remember me respectfully to Mrs Cooper and the family.

Your Obliged Serv't Horatio Greenough

Florence Dec 6 — 1830 —

Addressed: Rue St Florentin No 13 / To / J. Fenemore Cooper Esqre / Paris.

N O T E S

This letter does not seem to have passed through the mails and was probably carried to Paris by a friend of Greenough's.
    Manuscript: Cooper Collection, Beinecke.
1. Greenough probably refers to the movement of Austrian troops into the Papal States in October 1830, ostensibly to forestall revolutionary outbursts prompted by the July Revolution of 1830 in Paris.
2. Presumably that of *ca.* 5 May 1830, which is unlocated. In his Letter 19 to Cooper, Greenough had agreed to deliver *The Chanting Cherubs* to Cooper's order in America.
3. In his reply to this letter of Greenough's dated [4?] February 1831, Cooper said he would assume the risk of *The Chanting Cherubs'* arrival in America and of all accidents during the time it was in Greenough's hands (Cooper, 2:53).
4. Greenough meant he wanted to show *The Chanting Cherubs* to English residents in Florence, in hopes they might give him commissions (see Letter 26).

25. To James Fenimore Cooper
     20 December 1830

Florence Decem. 20th 1830.

My Dear Sir.

I received your letter of the tenth this morning.[1] I fear that my request, that you would procure me sittings from the General has
caused you some inconvenience. To find a fit moment to talk with him
about busts must, at present, be no easy matter. From what you say,
I perceive that you are fully aware, how usefull this portrait may be
to me. I have thought about the matter and made up my mind to put
my works in such a state that I can leave them by the end of February,
when I will come to Paris and if the Gen'l is willing to sit I am not
without hopes to persuade the artist that he has extorted an un-
reasonable bargain from the old gentleman to the violation of my
birthright.

The group is not in Boston, as you hoped, but remains still in my
study where it has untill now awaited your answer. You wish me to
say something of it. The marble though excessively hard, has turned
out exquisite both for texture and for tint. In the form I am confident
of having far surpassed the model. The face of the little fellow is
thought to resemble your son Paul. The wings are wrought so light &
thin that they are quite as transparent as drawing paper. The difficulty
of the mechanical execution is acknowledged to be immense. In order
to indicate the subject I have written on the plinth, in front "Gloria in
excelsis Deo" & behind "sculptured in Florence for James Fenimore
Cooper, 1830." The work if I may trust appearances pleases generally
& that, highly. I myself am far better satisfied than I ever hoped in the
most sanguine moments that I passed in your company. Bartolini when
last in my study amongst other flattering assurances, said that you had
every reason to be fully contented. He has gone so far as to say to
American gentlemen who have visited him that his conscience would
never permit him to accept a commission from our government untill
my hands were full. He congratulates me on my prospects in going to
Paris and offers me a warm reception from some of the best artists
there.[2] It is my intention to offer proposals to the public for erecting a

momument in commemoration of the revolution to be erected in front
of the Capitol at Washington which I will pledge myself shall cost
very little more at all events and probably less than the plaster figure
of America which is perched on the entablature of the house of Representatives to the great apparent danger of the Speaker's head.[3]
May I ask you, Sir, to give them thirty lines from your pen to point
out to them the bad taste and the bad policy of giving the children's
bread to dogs? Do not imagine, however, that I refer to Persico.[4]
Though not a great artist he did his work diligently and as far as I
know unpretendingly. They have rewarded him nobly and I am glad
of it.

I have written for arrangements to be made for the exhibition of the
groupe. It will be placed on a pedestal high enough to raise it to the
level of the eye with a dark crimson curtain behind.[5] I look confidently
to a handsome profit from this exhibition. If disappointed I shall be
embarrassed and that seriously. Come what will, I will never run to
brood under the wings of home. I came abroad to make myself known
and respected in my own country. If I succeed, I will return and form
a school, if not I will have at least the honour of laying my bones in a
land so fraught with genius that even her starved out mediocrity com-
mands a respect which I cannot earn.

I heartily sympathize with your perplexity about the lawsuit.[6] I
have found Mr Ombrosi's ideas of the reciprocal duties between him
and myself widely different from mine. Ever since his disappointment
at not finding your money ready for him as soon as I had looked at
the lawyer's papers and confessed that all seemed *square* to me, he
has been coming out with occasional demonstrations of ill will which
have induced me to drop from intimacy to civility, from civility to
wary caution which last feeling actuates my every action where he is
concerned. If you wrote to stop the lawsuit no charges can be made
for services done posterior [to] [*page torn*] the receipt of your letter.
If Ombrosi told you that all was over he was either mistaken or worse.
He assured me when the question about paying first arose, that unless
you forwarded the money he should pay it himself; he has been importuned by the lawyer ever since yet he has not paid it. It's clear he
meant that this speech should reach you and touch a delicate point
of your pride. You ask me what I would do. If his call was on myself
I would pay him, for he must either be satisfied or have his mouth
stopt but both your character and your interest are out of his reach.

Were I in your case I would order him to keep quiet[7] and in case I were disregarded I would give him something that would sit heavier on his stomach than the want of an "*Exaequator.*"

I remain Dear Sir
Yours Sincerely Hor. Greenough
To James Fennimore Cooper, Esq.

Addressed: Rue St Florentin No 13 / To / J Fenimore Cooper Esqre / Paris

NOTES

All but the complimentary close, signature, and address is in Henry Greenough's hand.

A letter book copy of this letter is in the editor's collection. It differs from the letter sent in several particulars, the most important being Greenough's reference to and sketch of a pair of alabaster leaves which he thought of preparing for *The Chanting Cherubs* (see n. 5).

Manuscript: Cooper Collection, Beinecke.

1. In this letter Cooper reported that Lafayette was too busy with political matters to sit for his portrait at that time (a few days later the trial of the ex-ministers of Charles X began, at which Lafayette exerted his influence to keep death sentences from being issued them); that he had promised the sculptor David d'Angers, who had recently executed a bust of him, not to sit for another sculptor; but that he would consider Greenough's request if Greenough came to Paris in the spring. Cooper encouraged Greenough to do so, pointing out, "You may have a statue to make some day, and the object is worth the risk" (Cooper, 2:44–45).

2. It was probably at Bartolini's suggestion that Greenough called on Ingres in Paris in September 1831 (*Letters,* p. 86). Ingres and Bartolini were intimate friends during Bartolini's stay in the city in his early years (Mario Tinti, *Lorenzo Bartolini* [Rome, 1936], 1:43, 45–46, 50–51).

3. This figure was executed by the Italian sculptor Enrico Causici, who was active in the United States from about 1823 to 1832 (Charles E. Fairman, *Art and Artists of the Capitol of the United States of America* [Washington, 1927], pp. 30, 50–52). Greenough met him in Baltimore in 1828, where he was executing the statue of Washington to top the column of the Washington memorial in that city.

4. Luigi Persico (1791–1860), a native of Naples, came to Lancaster, Pennsylvania, as a portrait painter in 1819 (W. U. Hensel, "An Italian Artist in Old Lancaster," *Papers Read Before the Lancaster County Historical Society* 16, no. 3 [1912]: 74). In Washington in 1828, Greenough may have seen his designs for the figures in the pediment of the east front of the Capitol. In 1829 he was commissioned to execute the statues of War and Peace on the east portico. He worked on them at Naples, from where Cooper sent Green-

ough word of him late that year (Cooper, 1:395). See also Fairman, *Art and Artists of the Capitol*, pp. 47–48, 76–78, 109.

5. At this point in the letter book copy Greenough wrote: "I have some idea of preparing fig leaves of alabaster to be attached to them by means of a thin white ribbon *in case of necessity* — it can be easily done by forming the leaf into a ring at the stem." Following this are sketches of the statue and of the fig leaves. See Plate II.

6. In his letter to Greenough of 10 December 1830, Cooper asked advice about what to reply to Ombrosi's request for money to pay the costs of Luigi's suit against Cooper (see Letter 16, n. 7).

7. About 4 February 1831, Cooper wrote Ombrosi a letter intended to "silence him," which apparently did so (Cooper, 2:53).

26. To Grant, Pillans, and Co.
8 January 1831

Florence — January 8th 1831 —

To Mess Grant Pillans & Co — Leghorn —
Gentlemen

I have rec'd from Mr Robert Gilmore of Baltimore a letter[1] which I presume from the postmark and superscription has passed through your hands — explaining the manner in which that gentleman wishes me to act for him and relieving me from the somewhat oppressive idea that he expected me to make a statue and buy sundry pictures and other works of art for the sum of 500\$ — which amount I had mentioned to him would probably be my charge for the statue only. In the above mentioned letter he agrees to pay the 500\$ for the statue and moreover authorises me to draw on him for the sums necessary through Mr Truman[2] or the Mess Barings Broth's[3] — Mr Gilmor's words are these "Indeed at all times when you meet with any thing you *know* I would like to possess and not extravagantly dear you have my permission nay my request to send it to me and Mess Grant and Pillans will reimburse you for your expenses on my account by shewing them this letter."

I have just completed a group in marble for my countryman Mr Cooper and am about to send it to Boston. The circumstance of being an American and seeing little or nothing of that class of society who take interest in works of taste has prevented my study having been visited but by occasional American travellers — I am ambitious that Mr Grant[4] of Florence should see this groupe before it goes and if you think he would be pleased also to see it may I ask of you the favour of facilitating my object — I remain Gentlemen Your Obliged Serv't

H Greenough

NOTES

Grant, Pillans, and Co. was an English shipping and exchange firm in Leghorn. (See *Grosses Adressbuch der Kaufleute, Fabrikanten und Handelnden Gewerbsleute von Europa und den Hauptpläzen der Fremden Welttheile,* vol. 4, no. 20 [Nurnberg, 1845], p. 76.)
   Manuscript: Editor's collection, letter book copy.
1. Presumably that of 24 October 1830. See Letters 20 and 21.
2. Evidently connected with Grant, Pillans, and Co.
3. Baring Brothers was an eminent English banking house founded by Sir Francis Baring (1740–1810). His son Alexander (1774–1848), first Baron Ashburton, was its head at this time.
4. Probably John Grant, presumably a member of the same family as the Grant in business with Pillans in Leghorn. After the last sentence in the paragraph above Greenough wrote and then canceled: "I should be much pleased if the shewing the letter above ment'd to Mr John Grant."

27. To James Fenimore Cooper
17 February 1831

Florence. 17. Feb'y. 1831.

My Dear Sir.
   Your letter in which you so kindly offer me the balance of the price of the boys reached me the very day after I had despatched a letter begging you to advance it to me.[1] Had I imagined you had thought of it you may suppose I should willingly have spared you that part of my letter which speaks of the affairs of my family.[2] I have been not a little chagrinned at it. In asking a favour of the sort, however, I felt

it my duty to explain my situation and I doubt not you will forgive me. —

I dare say you are right in your opinion of the Boston critics; but they have hitherto been so kind to me that I felt a confidence in trying my virgin statues with them;[3] though I confess that while the chisel was in my hand I thought neither of them nor any critics und[er] [*page torn*] the sun.

You ask me how I am situated with regard to the Consul. I had all along adopted the non-intervention system, — but it would not do. He drove up so sharply one morning that he got my opinion of the law affair[4] in as downright English as my dabbling in Foreign languages will allow me to utter. You know his style of innuendo. He no doubt injures my trade in a small way but my prospects can hardly be seriously affected by him either one way or the other and even if they were, I could not pay the price he sets on his *protection* though he would insure me both fame & fortune.

I regret much that in the present posture of my affairs my duty chains me here — yet I hope Gen Lafayette will remember your recommendation in my behalf should I have it in my power to visit Paris in the course of the Year — I remain Dear Sir Yours respectfully

Horatio Greenough

Addressed: To / J. Fenemore Cooper Esqre / Care of Messrs Wells & Co.[5] / Paris — / Rue St Florentin No 13

NOTES

All but the last paragraph, complimentary close, signature, and street address is in Henry Greenough's hand.
    Manuscript: Cooper Collection, Beinecke.
1. In his letter of [4?] February 1831 to Greenough, Cooper offered to have him draw on his account or to pay him in Paris (Cooper, 2 : 53–54). The balance of the price of the group was evidently $150 (see Letter 14 to Allston). Greenough's letter to Cooper, written about 9 February 1831, has not been located.
2. Possibly John Greenough was in financial difficulties and Horatio was preparing to lend him money again, their father being unable to do so; see Letter 10.
3. Cooper had written: "You will be covered with twaddling criticism in Boston, which is no better, with all due reverence to your nativity . . . than a gossiping country town, though it has so many clever people. The tone of criti-

cism in Boston is essentially narrow and vulgar — so narrow and vulgar as scarce to conceal the parochial sort of venom which engenders it. . . . There is . . . five times the real taste and twenty times the breeding in either of the three other Cities than in Boston . . ." (Cooper, 2:53–54).
4. That involving Luigi (see Letter 16, n. 7).
5. Welles and Co. was a Boston banking firm, founded by Samuel Welles (1778–1841), which had branches in Paris and London. Welles was head of the Paris branch at this time (Albert Welles, *History of the Welles Family in England and Normandy with* . . . *Some of the Descendants in the United States* [New York, 1876], p. 123).

28.   To James Fenimore Cooper
7 March 1831

Florence — March 7th 1831

My Dear Sir

I received your kind letter of the 22nd Ultimo[1] this morning and thank you most heartily for the prompt attention you gave to my need — I would thank you moreover for the generosity with which you have treated me on this occasion but I have always thought words poor answers to real obligation — When I look back upon the many such instances of kindness in my friends I feel a longing to be worthy of them a longing which I can't express — The Groupe went to Boston in the Brig Magnet[2] — Had I rec'd your letter a little earlier I would have sent it to N York — At all events I have ordered it to be exhibited there if the Boston folk treat it well — Those who saw it there in its finished state expressed much pleasure. One Italian Lady (the Marchesa Strozzi Riccardi) who saw it by chance interested herself so far in it as to send me one of her dependants who had a fine boy, for a model — I intended to have requested Lord Normanby to look at it again as he had taken the trouble to see it in its imperfect state but he went to Milan about the time it was finished and has but just returned — The Groupe gained for me the acquaintance and friendship of a Mr Adami[3] who was formerly a sculptor and whose house I dare say you remember — It is next to Scheiderff's Hotel[4] and is built with an Egyptian facade and ornamented by many works of the old gentleman's own hand. He went so far as to offer me the use of some fine rooms on his ground floor — I assure you I find great comfort in visiting this old gentleman occasionally who has an agreeable family a fine library and many interesting objects of art — The more so because I have been so long living in a complete desert for the heart — The time you spent here spoiled me for living abroad—I never had expected to find that sort of intercourse out of my own country and to fall so suddenly from it to the regular artist's life here where one is met at every turn by interested or ill willed actions was chilling —

We are expecting Mr Morse here daily from Rome.[5] Mr Chapman was on his way to Paris but finding the difficulty and the annoyances to which he should subject himself in a journey through Venice etc at present he has made up his mind to remain with us for some time to come[6] —

We buried a countryman here a week since — a Mr Dwight[7] — he had [an] attack very like the one which prostrated me 4 years since[8] but he fell into the hands of very different physicians — I don't remember any violent remedies in my case — He was blistered and bled and purged — and died in short on the 2nd or 3rd day — The physician said he despaired of saving his life from the first — Mine did likewise — but how different were the consequences of his despair — Thinking he could do nothing for me he let me alone and the Great Mother took care of me — Mr Dwight's Dr thought he could do nothing to save his patient, but he was determined nevertheless to do all he could —

I believe from the silence of the late new acquaintances of Mr Ombrosi on the subject of the law suit that he has lulled as the sailors say — formerly it was one of the first claims he urged for the sympathy of his protegee's. Montesquieu says — Il y a des mechants qui seroient moins dangereux s'ils n'avoisent aucune bonté[9] — There is his portrait to the life — After all what we blame in the man has its origin in what we should pity if we could see its operation. It must be resolved into one of these two — want of knowledge — want of mind of the faculty to see consequences — I ask pardon for this garrulity and will close this before it gets worse by a sketch and explanation of my plan for a National Monument — The ground plan is thus[10] The white spaces at the corners are the foundations of the Dies a, b which are 4 — on the Eastern one I design Columbus seated pondering on the globe — on the north a Mother clasping her infants while an Indian steals behind her — on the west King Philip[11] seated amid the bones of his fallen brethren — on the south civilization as a Female seated with

the implements of industry in her hands while a boy is represented
at her side as reading. On the side c and on the other corresponding
sides — I should de[sign] [*page torn*] four points of the history of
the   Rev — oppression — Remonstrance — Resistance — Independence.
These I should represent in the form of historic bas reliefs — The
whole I would surmount with a statue of Washington in the act of
resigning his authority as General in chief — I have designed this
monument not so much from any hope I have of ever being so respectably employed as from a thirst to get vent in something large —
I like to think about great works though my stars have forbidden their
execution. I beg you will remember my respectful regards to Mrs
Cooper and the family — I remain Dear Sir

Yours sincerely
Horatio Greenough

PS   On the rec't of your letter authorising my drawing for the balance
etc I took up the sum of 50 Francesconi at Fenzis[12] and shall avail
myself of your last for the drawing for the remainder.

Addressed: To / James Fenemore Cooper Esqre / Care of Messrs
Wells & Co / Paris

NOTES

Manuscript: Cooper Collection, Beinecke.
1. In this letter, which was evidently written in reply to Greenough's letter of *ca.*
   9 February 1831 and which seems not to have been preserved, Cooper
   evidently told Greenough to draw on him for the balance of the price of *The
   Chanting Cherubs* and the cost of its transportation to America (Cooper, 2:
   62; 1:407).
2. It left Leghorn on 18 February 1831 (*New-England Palladium and Commercial Advertiser,* 12 April 1831).
3. Lorenzo Adami had assembled a sizable library, chiefly of books related to
   the fine arts, and also had a good many paintings in his house on Fondaccio
   San Spirito (Pietro Thouar, *Notizie e Guida di Firenze e de' suoi Contorni*
   [Florence, 1841], pp. 179, 412–13).
4. The Albergo di Schneiderff, on the Lungarno near the Ponte alla Carraja, was
   one of the chief hotels in Florence (Federigo Fantozzi, *Pianta Geometrica
   della Citta di Firenze* [Florence, 1843], p. 262).
5. Morse arrived in Florence on 9 March and left on 16 May 1831 (Edward L.
   Morse, ed., *Samuel F. B. Morse: His Letters and Journals* [New York, 1914],

1:385; Dairy of Samuel F. B. Morse, 16 May 1831, Samuel F. B. Morse Papers, LC).

6. John Gadsby Chapman, painter, was in Florence for six months, from late February or early March. During that time he painted Greenough's portrait; it is now in the Boston Athenaeum. See note to Letter 200.

   The revolutionary outbreaks at Bologna and Parma in February 1831, though put down by Austrian soldiers, had unsettled the peace throughout northern Italy at this time.

7. James S. Dwight (1799–1831), of Springfield, Massachusetts, died on 24 February 1831, according to one record (Thomas B. Warren, comp., "Springfield Families," Ms. in the Public Library, Springfield), on 1 March, according to another (*Boston Columbian Centinel,* 20 April 1831).

8. Reportedly of malaria; see Letter 11, n. 7.

9. "There are wicked persons who would be less dangerous if they did not have any good quality." This statement has not been located in Montesquieu's writing.

10. See Plate III.

11. Metacomet (d. 1676), chief of the Wamponoag Indians, called King Philip. In King Philip's War (1675–76), a colonial victory, Philip was betrayed and killed by an Indian. Cooper's *Wept of Wish-ton-Wish,* which treats an episode in the war, contains one of the many literary pictures of him.

12. Greenough was now using the banking firm of Emanuele Fenzi e Compagnia in Florence (see note to Letter 77). About 1 March Greenough had drawn on Cooper to pay part of the expense of transporting the work (see Letter 29).

29. To James Fenimore Cooper
26 March 1831

Florence — March 26th 1831 —

My Dear Sir —

I hasten to inform you of having availed myself of your order to obtain the balance of 500 Francs — I had before drawn for 282.22. I drew March 18, 1831 for 217.18 which I was told at Fenzis would be the sum of 500 francs less the expenses etc — Mr Morse is living here in the same house with me as likewise Mr Cranch of Washington[1] — I have rec'd another order for my bust of Washington from a Mr Rooseveldt[2] of N.Y. — We are living very quietly amid such a hurry of reports — etc that I for my part have given up all idea of learning the truth with regard either to Poland or France[3] — I write in great haste as you will observe — I Beg you will present my respectful compliments to Mrs Cooper and the family — Mr Morse has just stepped in requests that I will join his respects *to all.*

> I remain Dear Sir
> Yours most sincerely
> Horatio Greenough

To J Fenimore Cooper Esqre / Paris

Addressed: To / J Fenemore Cooper Esqr / Care of / Mess Welles & Co / Paris.

NOTES

Manuscript: Cooper Collection, Beinecke.
1. Greenough was living at this time at No. 4488 Via Valfonda. John Cranch (1807–1901), portrait painter, was in Italy from 1830 to 1834. Greenough met him in 1828 in Washington, where his father, William Cranch, was chief judge of the U.S. Circuit Court of the District of Columbia.
2. James I. Roosevelt was evidently in Florence this month (Roosevelt to S. F. B. Morse, 11 March 1831, Samuel F. B. Morse Papers, LC). See note to Letter 36.
3. Both Poland and France were unsettled following revolutions—that of July 1830 in Paris and that of November 1830 in Warsaw.

30. To Robert Gilmor, Jr.
12 April 1831

Florence — April 12th 1831 —

To Robert Gilmor Esqre / Baltimore
My Dear Sir —

I have delayed answering your kind letter of Oct 24th 1830 — because I have had hopes from day to day of being able to announce to you the having procured something for your collection — I learned with pain that you had suffered from so long and so severe an indisposition and though you seem to write in good health if I were allowed to prescribe I would recommend to you another visit to this beautiful but unhappy country[1] — The change of air and scenery — the diversion of the thoughts from one's ailments by agreeable objects has never in my experience failed to produce a favourable effect on the impaired health of such as really enjoy art — Mr Morse (who is now here under the same roof with me) has been uncommonly happy in this his tour of Italy — He has learned much at an age when the many cease to learn and has become a boy in health by the same process that has rendered [him] more than ever sage in art — I thank you most heartily for your kind advice with regard to my own health —I am and have been for many months perfectly well — Regularity of habits in a young person soon gives a regular state of health and with such exercise as the marble gives me cannot fail in a few years to render me robust — I fear I must disappoint you with regard to the cameo of Mrs Gilmor[2] — They who profess that branch of art live at Rome altogether and to send the bust there for the purpose of being copied would be productive of an expence ill proportioned to the chance of success. I think those workmen are feebler in portrait than in ideal heads —

On the 9th inst I had the satisfaction of despatching to Mr Grant a picture for you which I am confident will give you the highest satisfaction. It is one of the sweetest morceaux of Albano[3] — a Repose in Egypt — The picture from its size its subject its treatment is every way adapted to your apartments — It made part of a choice collection of the Count Lozzi[4] of this city a travelled connoisseur — at his decease his widow sold the collection at a great sacrifice — The person into whose hands this picture fell wanted 150 Francesconi for it. After much chaffing I made him listen to the price of 112 Fi in hopes that by leaving the frame with him I might have the picture for 100 — but was unwilling to subtract more than 4 Fri in case I left the frame. I thought therefore I was acting for your best interests by taking both. The secret of my getting this picture so cheap is that the prospect of war[5] was beginning to disperse the English families whose presence in this country operates wonderfully in keeping up the prices of works of art. In fact should events force the English to abandon Italy the occupation of the greater picture dealers is gone and their already invested capital must suffer — Mr Morse assured me he thought the picture would have been cheap at 500$ and he congratulates you on its possession — An Italian Engraver was about to have engraved it but was deterred by the possibility of its leaving

the country before he could compleat his drawing — I hope it may be
a means of shewing the talent of some of our American Engravers in
the higher walks of that art — We expect Mr Harper[6] here on his return from Rome in the course of the week. During his former visit to
Florence as he went to Rome he saw the figure which I had commenced for you — I was pleased with it myself as possessing nature
and a pleasing expression but I shall be candid with you in saying
that the being obliged to make it serve to bear a vase of flowers
cramped very much that latitude in composition so dear to the imagination — Determined however not to allow such a feeling to interfere
with the fulfilment of your wishes I carefully and diligently finished
the model and shewed it to my friends. Mr Morse as well as the other
Americans who saw it will I dare say bear witness to the thoroughness
of the trial — Many were highly pleased [by] it — But I remembered
how different was the sensation produced from that of Mr Cooper's
group and I was determined that your figure should be my best work
up to the date of its production at all events, and reading over your
letter of Oct 24 in which you give the desired liberty, I determined to
make another trial and have accordingly begun the study of a figure
which I before mentioned to you the Medora as described by Byron
in the corsair[7] — Here I can unite beauty to touching interest and a
convenient form for your house to novelty — I can make it rich in
drapery and can do what has not been done in Italy for many years
— attempt to interest and charm the eye and mind with a female form
without appealing to the baser passions — The subordination of which
is one [of] the great blessings which make ours the best of countries
— and the want of which, if not a cause is surely one of the most re-
volting accompaniments of Italian degradation — Our great men have
shewn the world that liberty and quiet and civilization are not incompatible. It belongs to our artists to shew that the arts of the imagination may charm without seducing and refine without corrupting a
great people. Before I close I will only say if I ever should meet with
such a Venus as that of Mr Derby's[8] I will not fail to do my utmost
to put it in your possession — Begging you will remember my most
respectful compliments to Mrs Gilmor

> I remain Dear Sir
> Your Obliged Friend and Serv't
> Horatio Greenough

Addressed: Robert Gilmor Esqre — / Baltimore —
Endorsed, in Gilmore's hand: Horatio Greenough / ans'd 16 Nov

NOTES

Manuscript: John S. H. Fogg Collection, Maine Historical Society.

1. Gilmor had visited Italy in 1800–1801, in the course of his Grand Tour of Europe in 1799–1801. His journal, covering the entire tour, is in the Maryland Historical Society.
2. Gilmor wanted one designed from Greenough's bust of her.
3. Francesco Albani (1578–1660) was a Bolognese painter.
4. The German Count Palatine Charles de Lootz, or Lozzi, as he called himself in Italy, in his late years was in difficulty with the Tuscan government for evasion of taxes and had a reputation for unreliability (R. H. Super, *Walter Savage Landor* [New York, 1954], p. 157).
5. That is, of more revolutionary outbreaks such as had occurred in Bologna and Parma.
6. Charles Carroll Harper (1802–37), grandson of Charles Carroll of Carrollton, Maryland, who married a niece of Mrs. Gilmor's, was secretary of the American legation in Paris at the time of his death ("The Diary of Robert Gilmor," *Maryland Historical Magazine* 17 [1922]: 236). See also Letter 50.
7. Greenough completed this work in 1833. It is now in the possession of Mrs. Sumner Parker, The Cloisters, Brooklandville, Maryland.
8. Probably Elias Hasket Derby (1739–99), merchant and shipowner of Salem, Massachusetts. He owned a good many art objects and valuable household wares, and in 1797, built an elaborate dwelling designed by Samuel McIntire. Gilmor visited him there in 1797 (Robert Gilmor, Jr., "Memorandums Made in a Tour to the Eastern States in the Year 1797," *Bulletin of the Boston Public Library* 11 [1892]: 85).

31. To James Fenimore Cooper
21 June 1831

Florence — June 21st 1831 —

My Dear Sir —

I have this morning rec'd accounts of the opening of the exhibition of the group[1] — The receipts of the first week at the close of which the letter was despatched were 140 Dolls — My brother tells me that Alston walked into town from Cambridge to see the work before its being advertized[2] — He sent me word that he had expected much but that his anticipations had been surpassed. He pointed out to gentlemen who were present certain anatomical details in the knees etc, which he said proved an intelligent use of the living model — They speak very encouragingly of hopes of other orders — The newspapers did their part manfully[3] — I don't know if you have the Boston prints in Paris — if so you will observe that they have understood remarkably well the *intention* of the figures. They have found in them just what we wished they should contain & much more than I dared to hope that I had embodied — I transcribe a few verses written by Dana upon them and printed in one of the papers, I transcribe them because I know that you will be pleased to see such a confirmation of your own kind hopes in my behalf — and as for the vanity of so doing — you know how much of that feeling the contemplation of my own works has afforded me hitherto — I own that I am delighted with *sympathy* wherever I find it —

> Whence come ye Cherubs? from the moon?
> Or from a shining star?
> Ye sure are sent a blessed boon,
> From some kind world afar:
> For while I look my heart is all delight;
> Earth has no creatures half so fair and bright.
>
> From moon nor stars we hither flew;
> The moon doth wane away;
> The stars they pale at morning dew;
> We're children of the day.
> Nor change nor night was ever ours to bear:
> Eternal love and light and joy we share —
>
> 3.
> Then sons of light from Heaven above
>   Some blessed news ye bring!
> Come ye to chant eternal love
>   And tell how seraphs sing?
> And in your breathing, conscious forms, to shew
> How finer forms above live, breathe & glow?

4.
Our parent is a human mind,
    His winged thoughts are we:
To sun nor stars are we confined,
    We pierce the deepest sea.
Moved by a brother's call, our father bade
Us light on Earth & here our flight is stayed.[4]

Since writing the above I have rec'd accounts of the third week of the exhibition. The amount was then $300 — My brother tells me that a letter of yours has appeared in one of the New York papers and has been of the greatest service in *awaking* the discerning public[5] — My brother will superintend the transportation to N.Y. and the exhibition there[6] and I have reason to hope for a very well timed relief from it — And now Sir let me thank you again for the friendly eye with which you saw hopes in me as an artist and for the generous hand you stretched out to me and which has not wearied during the long interval between the ordering and the delivery of my work — I know how much I owe you Sir but believe me the obligation is dear to me — That group will always be most pleasingly associated in my mind — It was ordered at a moment which was a crisis in my life — when wearied with bust making I began to think that there was no hope for one of my turn of thought in America — It was commenced in ill health and melancholy — It was chiselled amid some difficulties — I found both health and spirits in the task and am likely to be much assisted by its being seen, in many ways direct and indirect —

I have heard lately that you have taken a house in Paris for a year[7] and of course presume that you have given up the thoughts of your Italian excursion this summer — John Bull seems to have commenced skimming what Voltaire called the froth of his beer[8] — Florence wears very much the same aspect as ever — I get the Tuscan news through Galignani[9] generally —

Begging you will present my respects to Mrs Cooper and the family I remain Dear Sir

                                        Yours with respect
                                        Horatio — Greenough —

Addressed: To / James Fenemore Cooper Esqre / Paris —

NOTES

Manuscript: Cooper Collection, Beinecke.

1. *The Chanting Cherubs* was exhibited in Boston from 18 April to 1 June 1831 under the supervision of Alfred Greenough. For an account of this exhibition and that in New York, see Nathalia Wright, "The Chanting Cherubs: Horatio Greenough's Marble Group for James Fenimore Cooper," *New York History* 38 (1957): 177–97.

2. Both Alfred and Mrs. Greenough reported Allston's approval of the figures. In her letter to Henry of 4 May 1831, Mrs. Greenough wrote: "Mr. Allston told me he thought them admirably well done. 'He had no idea Horatio could do anything like this, though he expected something very fine'" (*Letters*, p. 70).

3. The chief notice of *The Chanting Cherubs* which had appeared in the Boston papers by the end of the first week of the exhibition was that in the *Advertiser* for 22 April, which consisted of Richard Dana's poem (quoted in this letter) and a flattering prose description. Brief notices also appeared in the *New-England Palladium and Commercial Advertiser*, 12, 19 April; the *Independent Chronicle & Boston Patriot*, 13 April; and the *Transcript*, 18 April and succeeding days. Subsequently there were several other favorable notices, notably another poem in the *Advertiser* for 30 April; an account in "The Editor's Table" in the *American Monthly Magazine* 3 (1831): 66–67; and "Tyro's" article, "Letter on the Chanting Cherubs," *New-England Magazine* 1 (1831): 20–26.

4. Stanzas three and four are in Henry's hand. The poem, entitled "The Chanting Cherubs," appears with minor alterations in Richard Dana, *Poems and Prose Writings* (Boston, 1833), 1:120.

5. Cooper's letter to Charles King of 29 July 1830 (Cooper, 1:431–33), giving an account of *The Chanting Cherubs*, was published in part in the *New-York American* on 30 April 1831. It was quoted by Boston's *Columbian Centinel*, *Advertiser*, and *New-England Palladium and Commercial Advertiser* on 3 May, and by the *Independent Chronicle & Boston Patriot* on 4 May.

6. Under Alfred's supervision, *The Chanting Cherubs* was transported to New York in the summer and stored with Cooper's friend Peter Jay until its exhibition in the fall.

7. About the middle of March Cooper leased the greater part of the Hotel St. Susanne, 59 rue St. Dominique, Faubourg St. Germain, for a year. Here he and his family lived until they left Paris permanently on 16 August 1832 (Cooper, 2:47, 405).

8. Greenough refers to a description of the English which has been erroneously ascribed to Voltaire by several authorities. The earliest of these ascriptions which has been located is that in John Moore, *A View of Society and Manners in France, Switzerland, and Germany*, 3rd ed. (London, 1780, [1st ed., London, 1779]), 1:271: "He [Voltaire] compared the British nation to a hogshead of their own strong beer; the top of which is froth, the bottom dregs, the middle excellent." Presumably Greenough's reference is to the first and second English reform bills, presented in the House of Commons in March and June 1831; both were defeated.

9. *Galignani's Messenger* was the daily English language newspaper founded by Giovanni Antonio Galignani, a bookseller and publisher, in Paris in 1814.

32. To William Rollins
[August?] 1831

I have this day dispatched to Leghorn the marble bust of Doctor Kirkland.[1] You will find the marble free from spots to an unusual degree, but will observe some few yellowish stains which were not visible untill after the surface was uncovered by a sharp chisel. I mention this, lest these stains should be mistaken for soiled spots & washed; an operation which I should avoid as long, & repeat as seldom as possible with statuary.

Should this bust be placed in the Athenaeum, as I learned was intended, I beg you will do me the favor to request that it may have a descending & if possible a northern light. Unless a bust be placed in nearly the same light in which it was wrought, its modulations of surface, its character, its flesh, evapourate. It becomes sheer stone.

Excuse my importunity on a point which I deem so essential. You will find the best effect produced by turning the right shoulder of the bust a little towards the source of light, so that the shadow of the nose may nearly reach the left corner of the mouth.[2]

NOTES

William Rollins, of Boston, was possibly a member of the firm of Atkinson and Rollins, which engaged in the India trade (*Boston Directory* [1831]). He and his wife were in Florence in the fall of 1829 (Joseph Grinnell, Benjamin A. Gould, and William Rollins to the trustees of the Boston Athenaeum, 17 January 1832, Boston Athenaeum).

The bust discussed in this letter was presumably dispatched about August 1831; it reached Boston in January 1832 (Grinnell, Gould, and Rollins to the Trustees of the Boston Athenaeum, 17 January 1832).

Source: William Rollins to Seth Bass (Librarian of the Boston Athenaeum), 3 February 1832, Boston Athenaeum. Previous publication: Mabel Munson Swan, *The Athenaeum Gallery, 1827–1873* (Boston, 1940), p. 142.

1. John Thornton Kirkland (1770–1840), Unitarian minister and president of Harvard when Greenough was a student there, was in Florence with his wife in the fall of 1829. When Greenough asked permission to model his bust, Kirkland at first refused, saying that he could not afford to pay for one, but finally agreed to sit for Greenough without obligation ("Letters by Mrs. John T. Kirkland," *ProcMHS*, 2d ser., 19 [1905]: 448). In the course of the winter

several Americans traveling in Italy engaged Greenough to put the cast in marble for presentation to the Boston Athenaeum, where it remains. The committee for the donors consisted of Rollins; Joseph Grinnell, a merchant in Salem; and Benjamin A. Gould, a teacher in the Boston Latin School (Grinnell, Gould, and Rollins to the trustees of the Boston Athenaeum, 17 January 1832). Another donor may have been the wealthy New York merchant Rufus Prime ("Letters by Mrs. John T. Kirkland," p. 446).

2. The printed version of this letter includes, after this paragraph, a sentence not in the manuscript: "A pedestal three feet high is recommended."

33. To Robert Gilmor, Jr.
10 October 1831

Paris[1] Oct'r 10th 1831 —

To Robert Gilmor Esqre / Baltimore
My Dear Sir —

My situation at the present moment is such as to scarse allow of my taking up the pen — but I cannot permit such an opportunity to pass without saying a few words particularly as I think several letters both of yours and mine must have miscarried — I have seized the moment of leisure afforded me by the taking of the points of the statue I have modelled for you[2] to make this journey to Paris — My health has been benefitted by it and I shall have attained another object of professional importance at least as I understand it. I mean the modelling a portrait of General Lafayette — I have also remodelled the bust of Mr Cooper on account of the remarkable change for the better in his appearance since I last made his portrait — I cannot allow this opportunity to pass without congratulating you on the success of Mr Cole the landskape painter in whom I know you have always taken the deepest interest[3] — He has wonderfully improved since I saw him in N York — My letters from Florence this morning inform me that he has commenced the first of a series of historical or rather poetic landskapes[4] — of which the plan as he detailed it to me struck me forcibly — My Medora is thought to be my best work thus far — I mean the marble shall be as nearly worthy of you as I can make it —

My kind friend Mr Cooper says he has hopes that Government will shortly employ me on some work which shall give me an opportunity

of coming before the nation as a national artist — I am confident that
you will be pleased to know it — I only have to ask that you will speak
in my favour should your conscience permit it and I remain dear Sir

With respects to Mrs Gilmor

Yours truly

Horatio Greenough

Addressed: To / Robert Gilmor Esqre / Baltimore.

Endorsed, in Gilmor's hand, recto: Horatio Greenough / ans'd 29;
verso: Mr Greenough is an American Sculptor at Florence engaged to
execute the Statue of Washington for the Capitol — He made the
fine statue of Medora in my possession — RG

NOTES

This letter does not seem to have passed through the mails and was probably
carried to Gilmor by a friend of Greenough's.

    Manuscript: Miscellaneous Papers, The William L. Clements Library, University of Michigan.

1. Greenough left Florence about 20 August and reached Paris on 6 September
   (*Letters,* pp. 77–90).
2. *Medora.*
3. Thomas Cole was first patronized by Gilmor, who owned at least three landscapes by him, in 1825 (William Dunlap, *History of the Rise and Progress of
   the Arts of Design in the United States* [New York, 1834], 2:461). Cole was
   in Florence from about 1 June 1831 to February 1832, living first at No.
   4488 Via Valfonda with Greenough, Cranch, and Morse (Thomas Cole, *The
   Course of Empire, Voyage of Life, and Other Pictures of Thomas Cole . . . ,*
   ed. Louis L. Noble [New York, 1853], pp. 92, 129, 145).
4. This work was originally intended to be the first in a series of four pictures
   entitled *The Course of Empire.* Cole spent most of his first seven months in
   Florence painting it and sent it to Gilmor in return for money which Gilmor
   had advanced for his trip abroad (Cole, *The Course of Empire,* pp. 141,
   143). The painting's present location is unknown.

34. To Washington Allston
October 1831

Paris — Oct'r 1831.

To Washington Alston Esqre —
My Dear Sir —

The intention I have had for several months of making this journey and the preparation for it must be my excuse for not having written you in the interim — Since my arrival here I have had leisure in abundance, still I was unwilling to write untill I had given a glance at the treasures of Art for which Paris is noted —

I came to Genova in the Columbus steamer and after looking again at my favourite Vandykes and the street of Palaces,[1] took the Diligence to Turin, where in 2 days I succeeded in finding nothing whatever in the shape of Art, if I except their *barocco* brick palaces, which are rather paltry to an eye that comes from farther south — I passed the Alps at Mont Cenis; don't think that I'm going to inflict a description — One may as well be silent about them unless one could employ their own language of waterfall and avalanche and thunder — I will only say that as I walked among the higher hills with each of the four seasons in sight, under a quick succession of shadow and sun light it seemed as if God had spoken his last word to this world and all was hurrying back to Chaos[2] — The ocean's self never produced on my imagination any thing like the effect of those first born of creation — Perhaps it was the reaction that made me so dead to all that there may be of beauty between Chamberi and Paris — at all events I thought I had seldom passed through a more uninteresting country — On arriving in Paris I was again forcibly struck — by the size of the city — its magnificence and luxurious gayness — (for there is less of what I call elegance here than in Italy) its vast pleasure grounds — its numerous bridges and their beautiful and scientific construction — I confess I was prejudiced against Paris — who would not be that had been (as I) in the habit of reading every morning a few pages of Alfieri's autobiography — where this fine city is qualified as a *fetida cloaca* etc etc at every other paragraph[3] — I was eager to see the statues of the great Frenchmen on the Pont de Louis XVI[4] — I re-

membered the insulting tone assumed in speaking of Italian sculpture
in the chamber of Deputies, at the period of their creation — I find
in these figures no cause for exultation on the part of this school — Let
them be confronted with the statues of Arnolfo and Brunelleschi by
Pampaloni[5] and I believe the whole world artists or not will find them
inferiour — You remember the Colossi of Monte Cavallo[6] — and the
intelligence with which their skeletons are so moved that the eye
recognizes the human form at the greatest distance — Well these
artists have done just the reverse — Their figures are so upright — so
cloaked and scarfed and robed — so clumsily supported and so loaded
with accessories that from the Pont Royal[7] they have little more meaning than the blocks from which they have been carved — As you come
near to them it's true you see figures well proportioned — sculptured
with more or less of spirit — and one or two of them have dignity and
expression — Still as collossi for their situation they must be considered as failures —

I have found a great deal to delight me at the Louvre. Paolo was
surely one of the grandest fellows that ever breathed — It's useless to
tell me that the figures are heterogeneous etc etc, in short to criticise
the magician of Venice by rules drawn from Raphael — He that has
eyes to see and can feel, will love Paolo too well to dissect him in
that cool manner. He held his broad mirror up and a world is there
with gleams of exquisite feeling and truth that would seem out of the
reach of art — things Sir not dreamt of in the philosophy of the Roman
School — He reminds me of Shakespeare — he must be felt — I would
give more for one impression than for 3 unanswerable arguments on
a question of art for words are clumsy things after all. I have been
less disgusted at the modern french pictures than I had anticipated —
perhaps I'm grown callous — As a frenchman addressing himself to
frenchmen I think we must allow David great cleverness at least. The
french-greek physiog of his ideal figures is nauseous — I felt however
that the cold, grey ground-glass atmosphere in his pictures prevented
my allowing them their full merit — One feels the want of a great
coat and a cigar in looking at them — I didn't know Poussin until
now — He felt the Italians to the core as well as the greek — Le Sieur[8]
rather disappointed me — still even he shews that the modern vices
are acquired not inherent — I think Le Brun[9] gains nothing in colour.
I liked him better in the prints — Art seems at a pretty low ebb here
just now. The number of clever men employed in twiddle-twaddle,

caricature, indecent pictures etc is quite surprising — The statue gallery has been shorn of its beams since you were here. Tis but so so
after Italy — The Parisians strike me agreeably as to physique — You
see a finer animal health generally than in Italy — but the physiog'
is inferiour — One is struck by female faces at every step but the eye
is seldom won; there's a want of that harmony of lines which so often
pleases in an Italian head of even the 2nd or 3rd order — In manner
they seem to me to have more of *façon*[10] than the Italians but less
politeness — they are quicker but not so intelligent — honester perhaps but still more selfish and that's droll — I have on the whole been
so well pleased with Paris that I propose residing here a few months
at some future period, before returning to America —

Since I have been here I have remodelled Mr Cooper's bust[11] — I
have also modelled a bust of a young N Yorker who is here[12] — one
of the Princess Belgoioso of Milan[13] a very pretty and a very clever
woman — and have commenced one of Gen'l Lafayette. Mr. Morse[14]
who sits here by my side (having just finished his cigar) thinks it
the strongest likeness I've made — I hope to send you a lithographic
print of it before long[15] —

In the many conversations we had on Art when I was last in
America though you expressed much pleasure at the efforts that were
making in Architecture among us, yet I remember you fully agreed
with me that broader principles of art and a more intelligent imitation were necessary to the formation of a pure and masculine style
of building — This remembrance of your sympathy induces me to
communicate to you a few thoughts of this art, as I have had opportunity to observe it, my impressions with regard to its present state
among us and what it strikes me may be done to improve it — I will
give you briefly my opinion of what I have seen and in suggesting
any thing I beg to have it understood that I do it with my hat in my
hand, — with a deep sense of the merit of those who have modelled
our later buildings and a wish that it may be reciprocated by a frank
expression of the views taken of my art of its capabilities among us
and the hopes of its advancement.[16]

Architecture seems to me to have been enthralled ever since a claim
to *universal* and *indiscriminate* admiration has been established for the
Greek school — I shall join you of course in excepting the Gothic
which by throwing out the greek canons and recurring to nature to
express a new sentiment got a new style, at once grand and pathetic

as a whole and harmoniously rich in detail — The Gothic embodied the poetry of religion and triumphed over matter to deify spirit — The Greek adored matter and instead of sending towers high into the blue as twere to seek a heaven or to shew it when found it kept every member of its temples where the eye might taste their beauty and so proportioned and posed that it should be not only safe but strong — The Gothic by a mysterious combination of lines seems to lift the spirit from earth and shew her her home — The Greek woos the eye and lulls us into content below while its horizontal lines seem to measure the steps the mind may take beyond which all is dark. The uses for which the Greek temple were made were one — the form was unity itself — its parts harmonized with the whole —

The attempts in Italy to graft the christian sentiment on the greek stock — to expand the Pantheon to hold the Hebrew God, to recombine the greek elements into a new form for a new worship seem to me to have produced but a bastard result — No one is readier than myself to admit how much there is for the heart as well as for the imagination and the eye in the Italian church — I love their vast hushed interiour, their mild air and their mellow light — Their historic and poetic shadowings of art which seem as the incense rises and the chant peals, to take life and join in the worship — But these churches — this worship are the product of times in which a corrupt priesthood had engrossed government religion arts, sciences and even society and each of these institutions was promoted or sacrificed as the interests of that priesthood required — Our religion not only does not ask these sacrifices but forbids them — Our church is but an oratory a lecture room — We do not make it too large to be filled by one human voice — it possesses but two important features — the pulpit whence issues the word of God to man — The organ loft whence earth answers to heaven — Here is great simplicity of worship yet do I think these elements capable of very grand combinations —

In America we have since we began to look for art in buildings, made several attempts more or less successful, to place our Architecture on a footing with that of other nations — We have built combinations, Italian in intention at least if not in feeling — but they seem not to have satisfied any one — We have made pointed windows and clustered columns, but the small proportion of our means devoted to this end, have not allowed us either the vastness or the rich detail of the gothic — so that our happiest efforts in this way are as far from their models as is a horseshed from the temple of Venus — In our despair we have recurred to ancient Greece the mother of art — We have warmed at the praises bestowed on her buildings and have resolved to take to ourselves by a *coup de main* both the style and the praise — We have done with her temples what modern Europe has so often tried with every department of her literature and with no better success. The Dram's Personae may indeed be reduced to the classic 3 or 4, the chorus may be introduced and the lyric entre actes divided into strophe and antistrophe but a pale and insipid imitation is the only fruit — These spirits in the vasty deep of past epochs *will not come when we do call for them*[17] — The parthenon in Philadelphia,[18] shoved in between the common buildings of a street — shorn of its lateral colonnades and pierced every where for light reminds us of a noble captive stripped alike of arms and ornaments and set at work with the other drudges of his conqueror. If his grand air be not quite gone, if some vestige of his former comeliness or some badge of office be still visible about him they only serve to render his present degradation more apparent —

In a letter which I wrote to the committee of the Bunker Hill monument, I endeavoured to shew that by taking a member — a dependent part and making of it a monument, an inconsequent and unmeaning whole would result — for if that member be fitted for its situation all those features which connect it with the surrounding parts become absurd when it stands alone — T'is a limb without a body, a sentence without a verb, a tune broken off in the middle — As a column was in Greece organized to pose upon the earth and to support an entablature; so was the whole fabric constructed with an eye to its exposure and the worship for which it was intended — if well adapted to that exposure and that worship how shall it be fitted for a climate and a service so different?

Let us turn now to Nature the only true school of art — Has she ever been the slave of any one idea of beauty or of grandeur? Her sublimity is manifest alike in the sailing eagle, the bounding lion and the rolling whale — Her beauty asks no sacrifice of the existence or even of the comfort of its wearer — There's scarse a member which may not be found enlarged or annihilated by turns in the animal creation, as the wants of the creature demand. She always organizes the frame for its exposure and its work yet always leaves it beautiful — We propose then that she be imitated in this important respect more compleatly than has been done, we would recommend the use of the combinations we have inherited from preceding schools when-ever they will serve our turn and harmonize with the plan of our work — Nor do we mean merely that the object for which a building is constructed shall be nowise sacrificed to an abstract idea of form — we would that the shell of each fabric be as it were, moulded on the wants and conveniences desired — Such has been the case with naval architecture — and he who has seen a ship at sea will confess that in that work man has approached nearest his maker — Our fleets alone can shew that the world is not retrograde —

In a bank for instance where the business transacted requires light we propose to get it not by stealth as if we were ashamed of it, but as openly as tis given by the creator to our own brain and that without fear of consequences — Where the business done within is so much connected with what is abroad as in a Bank we propose to render ingress and egress as convenient as possible to numbers, and so on with every want that those employed in such buildings may have experienc'd — And we shall receive all condemnation of such art as we would the complaint that the greyhound is too light for beauty, the horse too heavy — that horns are monstrous, or the necks of grazing cattle too long for proportion — We can at least shew that he who condemns us condemns with us the principles of creation — nor shall we be mortified at not having pleased men whom God him-self has not been fastidious to satisfy — It is true that this style of art asks for much in feeling of which we have but the germ but why should we be discouraged — In our political institutions we have dared to be new — Can we not shew that art too has a reason as well as government? and that no model of past times when science was less and superstition reigned has a prescriptive right to cramp our convenience or to repress our invention?

That no one individual can accomplish the task we have thus planned is clear at a glance — It requires all the knowledge among us — all the light which can be thrown on the requisites of a building by those who are to occupy it, all the science of our engineers and mathematicians to find the most direct rout to their attainment, all the feeling and the imiation of our architects and painters to give a harmonious connection to the parts thus assembled — that these different bodies of men are equal to it is shewn by what they have already achieved in their various departments, for as we are [we] have no reason to decline a comparison with the present nations of Europe as far as *taste* in Architecture is concerned —

As for what painting and Sculpture are to do among us it seems to me that they will depend entirely on our love for our institutions — If we continue to stand tip-toe along the Atlantic shore endeavouring to catch the last word from Europe nothing great will surely be done — But if we will turn our eyes inward a little, calculate results and embody principles then art becomes important and we shall have it for we seldom long feel the want of any thing in America.

I see by some of the papers that some well intentioned persons have been shocked by the nudity of my cherub-boys[19] — I had thought the country beyond that — There is a nudity which is not impure — there is an impurity which pierces the most cumbrous costume — Let my group be compared with hundreds of prints which are to be seen in the English french and american annuals and which are put into the hands of our sisters and wives and I leave it to any conscientious man to say whether I have gone to the full length of the letter with which modern delicacy has measured the range of art — With love to Master Edmund and Richard and respectful compliments to Mrs Alston[20] I remain Dear Sir Yours truly —

Horatio Greenough —

NOTES

This letter must have been written after October 13; Greenough had his first sitting from Lafayette, which he mentions in this letter, on that date (*Letters*, p. 87).

   Manuscript: Dana Papers, MHS. A draft of a portion of this letter, containing a number of miscellaneous sketches, is in the editor's collection. See Plate IV. Among the sketches, the profile of the man bearing the notation "expects to be lathered" is of Morse; that next to it may be of Ombrosi, who had a large nose; that bearing the notation "a promising lad" is probably of Paul Cooper; and the small profile with protruding chin is of Brisbane.

   1. Van Dyck spent five years in Italy, during which time he painted a series of portraits of Genoese nobility.
      The Strada Nuova, now Via Garibaldi, was celebrated for its thirteen palaces, all but two built by Galeazzo Alessi, a pupil of Michelangelo.
   2. Some of the same images as those in this description of the Alps occur in Greenough's letter to his brother Henry, 9 September 1831 (*Letters*, p. 84).
   3. Count Vittorio Alfieri (1749–1803), Italian dramatist, heartily disliked France and the French. He called Paris a *fetènte cloáca* ("stinking sewer") in his *Vita di Vittorio Alfieri da Asti Scritta da esso* (1806), pt. 1, ep. 3, ch. 5.

4. This bridge, now the Pont de la Concorde, over the Seine was built between 1787 and 1790. Several years later twelve statues were erected on it, each by a different sculptor, representing various French warriors and statesmen.

5. The statues of Arnolfo di Cambio (*ca.* 1232–1312), Italian sculptor and architect, and of Filippo Brunelleschi (1377–1446), the first great architect of the Renaissance, by Luigi Pampaloni (1791–1847), the chief nineteenth-century Tuscan sculptor after Bartolini, occupy niches in the Palazzo dei Canonici in the Piazza del Duomo in Florence.

6. The two colossal marble statues of young men in the act of taming horses, one on each side of the obelisk in the Piazza di Monte Cavallo on the top of the Quirinal Hill in Rome, are thought to be Roman copies of a Greek bronze group representing Castor and Pollux.

7. The second bridge up the Seine from the Pont de la Louis XVI, built in 1685.

8. Eustache Le Sieur (1616–55) was a French painter, chiefly of religious subjects.

9. Charles Le Brun (1619–90), French painter, was artistic arbiter to Louis XIV.

10. "Affectation."

11. It was put in marble in 1832–33. It is now in the Boston Public Library.

12. Albert Brisbane (1809–90), social philosopher and Fourierite. Greenough's bust of him has apparently been destroyed.

13. Princess Christina Belgiojoso-Trivulzio (1808–71) was a disciple of Mazzini and an ardent supporter of the Italian Revolutionary movement (see H. Ramsen Whitehouse, *A Revolutionary Princess: Christina Belgiojoso-Trivulzio* [London, 1906]). Greenough's bust of her was probably not put in marble, since about this time her fortune was confiscated by the Austrian government. The bust has apparently been destroyed.

14. Morse arrived in Paris from Germany shortly after Greenough, and the two took rooms at 25 rue de Surène.

15. No such print seems to have been made. The bust was put in marble probably in 1833 and 1834. It is now in the Pennsylvania Academy of Fine Arts, Philadelphia; two other busts from the same model are in the Museum of Fine Arts and the Senate Chamber of the State House, Boston. An engraving of the work was made in 1834.

16. Essentially the same ideas and some of the same phrases contained in the rest of this letter occur in Greenough's essay "American Architecture," in the *United States Magazine and Democratic Review* 13 (1843): 206–10.

17. See *Henry IV*, III, i, 53–55.

18. The Second Bank of the United States in Philadelphia, erected between 1818 and 1824, was designed by William Strickland to resemble the Parthenon. Presumably Greenough saw it in 1828.

19. During the third week of the Boston exhibition of *The Chanting Cherubs,* the figures were outfitted with dimity aprons. Correspondents in the *Boston Courier* for 9 and 11 May, the *New York Evening Post* for 17 and 24 May, and *Niles' Weekly Register* for 18 June 1831 protested vigorously, and the aprons were subsequently removed.

20. Martha Remington Dana (1784–1862), Allston's second wife, married him 1 June 1830. She was a sister of Edmund T. and R. H. Dana, and first cousin of Allston's first wife. (Edgar P. Richardson, *Washington Allston* [Chicago, 1948], pp. 97, 134.)

35. To Rembrandt Peale
     8 November 1831

Paris. Nov'r 8th 1831.

To Rembrandt Peale Esqre
My Dear Sir —

I am taking breath for the first time since I parted with you[1] — I have heard of you indirectly through the papers several times. Though I am not sure whither to direct this or whether it will ever reach you — yet I feel it a pleasing duty to inform you of my operations and I hope you will favour me with a few words on your own prospects of benefitting the country — I arrived in this truly magnificent city on the 6th of Sept'r and commenced modelling almost immediately. I have remodelled Cooper's head — made a bust of General Lafayette — one of the Princess Belgoioso a Milanese lady — one of another Italian lady[2] and one of a Mr Brisbane of the state of New York — When I tell you that circumstances required that I should be on the alert for more than a fortnight to seize each pitiful quarter of an hour afforded by the pressure of Gen Lafayette's affairs — you will sympathise with me — for you well know what it is to come into contact with great political *notables* — I have finished however and they say it's like him — thanks to Cooper who pinned the old gentleman to his chair one morning for two whole hours with stories and *bons mots* — I believe that was the saving of my bust — for I had become out of humour with it and you know how fatal *that* often proves —

I hear you have been publishing and that your book[3] is doing good — We are all obliged to you — You can take in consequence of your experience and your acquaintance with European art a higher tone in instructing our countrymen than perhaps any other living artist — Pray Sir — convince them that one American Work is of more value to the U.S. than 3 foreign ones even of superiour merit — If they mean that all their pictures shall be painted by strangers — they are in the wrong both as regards economy and praiseworthiness — If they do not — then let them employ us manfully and not tell us to learn to swim before we venture into the water — I have not seen your book.

I doubt if it be here — Will you when you see Mr Sully[4] do me the favour of presenting my respectful regards to him? Mr Cooper told me this morning that he had heard you talked of returning to Europe — this grieved me in spite of the pleasure I promise myself in your company should you return to Florence, because I fear you are not satisfied with the state of the public feeling on art — and I had been hoping that we had made some progress since I left America — Cooper's new book the Bravo is taking wonderfully here — If you could transfuse a little of that man's love of country and national pride into the leading members of our high society I think it would leaven them all and leave them quite as good men and surely much better patrons — Mr Peale the scholars of America have looked so much abroad for salvation in letters arts and manners that they have not only overlooked home but have unfitted all under their influence for judging impartially of any thing American — They have carted sand in upon a fine soil and nothing but a flood of satire can remove it and bring to light the fertile bottom which they have encumbered — How does Angelo?[5] Let him draw — draw — and model — if possible for painting I think he has more than his share of readiness in — Mr Wallis used often to ask after you — I remain Dear Sir Yours with respect

Hor. Greenough

Addressed: To / Rembrandt Peale Esqre / Philadelphia / Care of / David Greenough Esqre / Boston. Mass.

NOTES

Rembrandt Peale (1778–1860), portrait, miniature, and historical painter, was in Italy from the end of 1828 to the summer of 1830. He wrote an account of his visit in *Notes on Italy* (Philadelphia, 1831).
    Manuscript: Miscellaneous Manuscripts, G, NYHS. Previous publication (with a few excisions and alterations): *New-York Mirror,* 3 March 1832, pp. 278–79.
    1. That is, since Peale left Florence in April 1830.
    2. Nothing further seems to be known about this bust.
    3. *Notes on Italy.*
    4. Thomas Sully (1783–1872), English-born American portrait painter, spent most of his mature life in Philadelphia. Greenough probably met him there in 1828.
    5. Michael Angelo Peale (1814–31), Peale's son, was a painter.

_36._   To James I. Roosevelt
8 December 1831

Marseilles — Nov'r [December] 8th 1831.

My Dear Sir.

I have just arrived here on my way to Florence from Paris where I have been making several busts (among others one of General Lafayette) in plaster which I am to carve in marble on my arrival in Italy. I had the pleasure of finding your letter introducing Mrs Payson[1] though I have been so unfortunate as to be a few days too late to see that lady — She went by the last steamboat — I write this in much haste to allay any anxiety you may feel about your bust. The marble is spotless and the work I believe an improvement on the former one[2] — When I left Florence there was something to be done to the back part and a pedestal to be made. I chose to see it after those parts were wrought as the underworkmen take advantage sometimes of one's absence to slight their work — The bust will be shipped immediately. I have rec'd an order from Com'e Biddle[3] for another in consequence of the officers of one of our ships having seen yours — I congratulate you my dear Sir on your marriage — Whatever may be a man's situation I have always thought he has but one half of happiness until he has a domestic establishment. If I can be of any service to yourself or any friends of yours in Florence I beg you will command me — Will you present my respectful compliments to Mrs Roosevelt and believe

me Dear Sir
Yours truly
Horatio Greenough

James I Roosevelt Esqre / New York —

NOTES

James I. Roosevelt (1795–1875) was a New York lawyer, judge, and congressman (Charles B. Whittlesey, _The Roosevelt Genealogy, 1649–1902_ [Hartford, Conn., 1902], p. 51).

Greenough dated this letter 8 November, but it is obvious, from the places and dates of Letters 35 and 38, and from the postmark of Letter 37 (which he also wrote from Marseilles and also dated November), that it was written on 8 December.

Manuscript: Editor's collection.

1. Roosevelt's letter to Greenough of 4 October 1831 (collection of David Richardson, Washington, D.C.) was carried from New York by Frances Lithgow Payson (1800–1877), whose husband, John Larkin Payson, was U.S. consul in Messina from 1827 to 1845 (William Dawson Bridge, ed., *Genealogy of the John Bridge Family in America, 1632–1924* [Cambridge, 1924], pp. 431–33). In his letter, Roosevelt inquired about the bust of Washington which he had ordered from Greenough the preceding March, and authorized Greenough to draw on him for its price.

2. Presumably the last Washington bust which Greenough had made; for whom is not known.

3. James Biddle (1783–1845), U.S. naval officer, was at this time commodore of the American squadron in the Mediterranean.

37. To James Fenimore Cooper
8 December 1831

Marseilles. Nov'r [December] 8th 1831.

My Dear Sir —

I left Paris at just the right moment.[1] Had I remained another day I should have missed the steam-boat at Lyons for Avignon — As it was I came without interruption (excepting one night's rest at Lyons) to this city where I found the Francesco 1mo about to sail,[2] giving me time however to repose and to look about me —

I arrived yest'y morn'g and found three letters waiting for me — one from Mr Rosevelldt authorising me to *draw* — one from my Brother[3] and one from Mr McMurtrie[4] containing an order of a bust of Washington from Com Biddle — Mr McM informs me that the Com intends ordering two other busts, and assures me that he hopes to effect a subscription for a statue among the officers of the squadron at Mahon this winter.[5]

How delightful is this balmy air of Provence after the sleet and snows of the north — Here am I writing without a fire in an atmosphere only inferiour to the sea coal summer of your house. The sight of the Mediterranean as we came over the hills yesterday just after sunrise did my heart good — The rocks here and there along the coast were swathed in vapour but it was sweeping away and the water sparkl'd and looked fairly happy — It seemed as Brisbane would say to have a pleasing *individual consciousness*.

Marseilles is certainly a very fine town though I have never been so struck before by the greedy bustle of trade — They've an off hand way of being civil too which would chill but for its heartiness — However I believe I'm a little dainty in that respect just now.

I'm very happy in the prospect of being soon at work upon my third statue. I go to it with a strength and a motive which I have never felt before — Hithertoo I have been obliged to spur myself to the task, in modelling the Medora I had but to laisser aller[6]— I trust it will be the same with the marble — Now that you are become Italian I beg you will read the sonnet of Petrarch which contains the passage — "Non comme fiamma che per forza è spenta — ma che per se medesma si consume"[7] — etc. You will find there the soul of my figure — or what I wish should be such.

You are aware that I enjoyed myself too much at Paris to leave it without regret. I had been so long living secluded amid those who cared not for me that I was prepared to relish every comfort of intercourse and of kindness — Do come to Italy — It were worth your while to cross Mt Cenis were it but to see those bright billiard cloths the plains of Piedmont lighted by the sun — if you but heard that happy la! la sull la! carolled among the vines — but come to Tuscany and weave us a rich story from the stuff which the Guelphs and Ghibellines have made ready for you — That's the classic ground of the middle age — Will you remember me most kindly to Mrs Cooper and your lovely family — I congratulate you most warmly on the possession of such a store of satisfaction — If I can serve any friends of yours who come to Italy I know you will afford me that pleasure. I shall be most happy at the reception now and then of one of those snug little notes of yours. Love to friend Morse if you please.

Yours affectionately

Horatio Greenough

size of the grapes[8] — here which are as firm as in September.

Addressed: J Fenimore Cooper Esqre / Care of Mess Welles & Co / Paris.

NOTES

This letter is postmarked "8 Dec 1831." Like Letter 36, it was written in December, though Greenough dated it November.

Manuscript: Cooper Collection, Beinecke.

1. About 30 November 1831.
2. The steamship *Francesco Primo* plied between Marseilles and Leghorn (Thomas Cole, *The Course of Empire, Voyage of Life, and Other Pictures of Thomas Cole* . . . , ed. Louis L. Noble [New York, 1853], p. 127).
3. Probably Henry.
4. James McMurtrie was a broker and art patron in Philadelphia.
5. Nothing seems to have come of any of these plans.
6. "To let go."
7. "Not as a flame which by force is spent / But which by itself consumes itself" (*Trionfo della Morte*, I, 160–61).
8. Preceding this phrase, Greenough drew a cluster of grapes.

38. To James Fenimore Cooper
17 December 1831

Florence Dec'r 17. 1831. Via S. Sebastiano
Casa dei Frati[1] —

My Dear Sir —

I arrived here without accident on the 14th inst, and had the pleasure of finding my brother well and fairly established in my new lodgings. The last letters of my brother in N—— York informs me that he had succeeded in obtaining Col Trumbull's new rooms for exhibition[2] — He thought all would be ready by the 28th of October — I think I wrote you from Marseilles that I had rec'd a commission for a bust of Washington from Com'e Biddle — That gentleman's agents in Marseilles had however rec'd no instructions from him on the subject; he was probably not aware that it is usual to pay the half price on giving an order — The money paid by Mr Roseveldt goes to cover expenses of my *household* incurred during my absence. Of a commission from Col. Perkins,[3] the report of which came directly from one of his own family, I have as yet heard nothing directly — I have but 2 napoleons[4] in my purse — I shall wait until the next post day and if I get no letters, I see no alternative but to have recourse again to you — I don't know if Fenzi will cash my draft — I think he will — He has known me several years — What will you think of my eagerness to pay you the 500 fr you before lent me?[5] You will be amused at my expence — Yet I assure you I firmly hoped at that time never to have occasion to ask assistance from any one again. — I shall not conceal from you that should the exhibition yield nothing I see no immediate prospect of being able to pay you — What shall I say? I will speak of something else — I learned yesterday that an artist was here from Rome with a copy of the Transfiguration — They pronounce his name Chatelain[6] — I'm confident it's the individual you mentioned. I have taken steps to see his picture and learn his price — The copy was exhibited here this autumn and was much esteemed — You will hear from me again on the subject. I shall make no bargain untill I again receive your order unless the artist is about to leave Florence which I hear is not the case — I went to see Maria Fleetwood[7] yesterday — she is much more comfortably lodged than when my brother saw her before — She at that time occupied a house known throughout the suburb as *la Casaccia*[8] — I found her on a 2nd floor and in a decent neighbourhood — Her husband came to the door when I knocked — one glance at him convinced me that he was the cause of all her troubles — He's one of the stupidest men I've seen and that's a bold word. The woman seems healthy and has a very prepossessing face — She told me she depended on her daily work for her daily bread and that work was not always to be had — *This touched me home* and I told her I had occasion for a person who could cook and do chamber-work and if she could devote half a day to my *menage* I should take her in preference to another. Her dolt of a spouse made difficulties and shook his head saying that "Il mondo parlerebbe"[9] — a good one truly — Unless I'm mistaken however he doesn't count much in the administration — She has been here this morning while I have been writing and desires me to present her thankful remembrance to you. I give her words[:] Fattemi la grazia quando scivete Signore di dire alla Signora Cooper quanto le son obbligata — alle signorine auche tanto buone che io piango quando si penso — fattemi il piacere Signore — non lo dimenticate vi prego[10] —

Cole has painted a glorious landskape during my absence 6 feet by 4[11] — He makes quite a figure here — The Grand Duke expressed himself highly pleased with a small picture of his view of the Arno down the stream from the Pont' Alla Carraia[12] — He is studying the figure with astonishing success and is now painting a composition of the Angel appearing to the shepherds in which the figures are principal[13] — He's going to be a great artist — I shall always be very proud of having induced him to study the figure — I knew by his pale face and eternal sighing that mere landskape of any class was too small a ball for his calibre. An artist of my acquaintance here has found a new fault in his countrymen the Florentines — He made a composition of Leda receiving the embraces of the Swan — he satisfied himself with what he calls the movement but was compelled to give up the plan by the strictures of his [page torn][14]

[No signature]

NOTES

Manuscript: Cooper Collection, Beinecke.
1. This edifice, located at the rear of the church of the SS. Annunziata, was owned by the Frati dei Servi Maria and for years partly rented to artists.
2. Alfred Greenough arranged to have *The Chanting Cherubs* exhibited in the new quarters of the American Academy of the Fine Arts, Barclay Street, New York; the president of the Academy was the painter John Trumbull (1756–1843).
3. Nothing further seems to be known about this commission.
4. A napoleon was worth about $8 at this time.
5. In February and March 1831.
6. Cooper and Peter Schermerhorn had tried earlier to purchase a copy of Raphael's *Transfiguration* by a foreign artist, but the artist had refused their offer (Cooper, 2:77). The artist whom Greenough names was possibly Cavaliere Augusto Chatelain (Octavian Blewitt, *A Hand-Book for Travellers in Central Italy,* 2d ed. [London, 1850], p. 292).
7. This woman, formerly in the employ of the Coopers, had written Mrs. Cooper that she was destitute and asked that Mrs. Cooper recommend her for employment in Florence (Cooper, 2:168). Greenough evidently had his brother Henry call on her soon afterward.
8. "Unpleasant affair."
9. "The world would talk."
10. "Do me the favor when you write the Signor [Cooper] to say to Mrs. Cooper how much I am obliged to her — to the young ladies also so good that I weep when I think of them — do me the favor Signor — do not forget it I pray you."
11. This was the painting to which Greenough referred in Letter 33.
12. Cole's *Sunset on the Arno.* Its present location is unknown.
13. Cole's *Angels Appearing to Shepherds* is now in the Boston Athenaeum.
14. The remainder of the manuscript contains only the beginnings of the last eight lines of the letter.

39. To Samuel F. B. Morse
5 January 1832

Florence. Jan'y 5th 1831. [1832]
Via S. Sebastiano —

S F B Morse Esqre
My Dear Sir

Your letter of the 17 Dec'r has just been rec'd and read — I sit down to answer it forthwith for several reasons. I regret most sincerely that my group has been exhibited in New-York in a manner directly or indirectly unfavourable to the N—— Academy.[1] You will I am sure do me the justice to believe that had I been aware of it I should have countermanded the arrangement — My brother had the entire arrangement of the thing — It did not occur to me that my work could be made a party tool of — I had therefore given him no farther instructions on the subject than that he should find a decent room in a central situation. If those gen[tleme]n imagine that I am to be bamboozled into an approval of their association for the discouragement of art they will soon find their error — The review of Cuningham[2] of which I read you a portion remains still with me — I found it rather crude and resolved to file it a little before I sent it — On my arrival here I found several numbers of the N.A. Review in which were articles on the fine arts — one by Edward Everett on Statuary — superficial pretending — insolent — abounding in blunders but very learned withal. The other by Alexander Everett on the Atheneum Exhibition — anything than what it should be[3] — I propose then to work into my review a few remarks on the style of criticism on art among us — and some by hits at associations for the discouragement and humiliation of artists — I shall make it clear that I'm no kneeling or compromising man in an affair where the dignity of our professions are concerned — Under whatever form we are to exist — we must be respected as men and reverenced (at least in art and what relates to it) as artists.

I am under the necessity of saying that if that part of my letter which you did not comprehend gave you pain — it gave me also the greatest pain to think that I had written it.[4] I am trying to extract the

arrow "in vacuo quae vulnera pectore fecit" as Apollo said of his[5] —
You perceived that I was unhappy and you feared I was not at ease
within — ie in the sanctum sanctorum my opinion of my own motives
— Now when a man is poor very poor — stung by ambition — overwhelmed by obligations — encumbered with duties that tax him to
the utmost — should he be capable in the midst of all this of finding
a corner in his heavy heart wherein to enshrine an image of loveliness
and purity which should be at once a blessing and scourge to him —
Yet all hopeless — all mere brain-work — can you not find in that
man's *circumstances* my dear Morse a cause for his misery without
going to search for it in his conscience? and that man your friend
too? — Let it go — I'm sure that as long as we differ so much on a
grand point so long all my ills will seem to you to spring from that
difference — You say I shall not relish that part of your letter — I
relish any thing which shews your regard for me — What you say
about *well directed* etc makes me think you do me the honour to
think with Mr Gore[6] that I'm in Love with an opera singer the
hackneyed mistress of God knows how many innamorati — I've pilot
enough aboard to save me from all that — I assure you though I don't
navigate with exactly your chart. I have been in some distress since
my arrival here — and am at this moment *waiting* and *hoping* but
thank God hard at work and therefore easy through the day — I pass
some nights a little poetically to be sure,[7] but hope all will soon go
well — Nothing shall ever force me to regret my choice of profession
though I starve for it. Will you say to Dr Niles[8] that I will undertake a colossal head of Washington of the proportions of the Braschi
Antinöus[9] for 500$ provided the committents will pay all charges of
carriage and packing which may amount to 20 or 30 more and furnish
me with a credit for the half price on giving the order — When you
consider that I must remodel the head for effect — You will agree
that I can't make much money by it. Will you remember me to the
Coopers and believe me your heterodox but true friend

H. G.

Cole is here and well. He is just finishing a very fine landskape[10] has
made astonishing progress in the figure and has the best possible
spirit as to art and a due sense of what must be done — They are
all very industrious — and have made great progress — My brother
sends his love —

Addressed: Samuel F. B. Morse Esqre P.N.A. / Poste Restante[11] — / Paris.

NOTES

This letter is dated 1832, rather than Greenough's "1831," on the basis of internal evidence: *The Chanting Cherubs* (see n. 1, below) was exhibited in New York in November and December 1831.

   Manuscript: Morse Papers, LC.

1. Morse, as president of the National Academy of Design, took offense at the exhibition of *The Chanting Cherubs* in the American Academy of the Fine Arts (see Letter 41). He and others had founded the National Academy to protest the way Trumbull administered the American Academy, allowing artists little voice in its affairs (Thomas Seir Cummings, *Historic Annals of the National Academy of Design* [Philadelphia, 1865], pp. 18–21; Eliot Candee Clark, *History of the National Academy of Design, 1825–1953* [New York, 1954], pp. 5–13).

2. Probably of Allan Cunningham, *The Lives of the Most Eminent British Painters and Sculptors,* 3 vols. (New York, 1831). No such review as Greenough refers to seems to have been published.

3. Edward Everett (1794–1865), teacher and statesman, and Alexander Hill Everett (1790–1847), editor and diplomat, were brothers. Edward was professor of Greek at Harvard when Greenough was a student there. The articles —reviews respectively of Francesco Milizia's *Del' arte di vedere nelle belle arte del designo . . .* (Venice, 1798) and *Catalogue of the Pictures Exhibited at the Fourth Exhibition in the Gallery of the Boston Athenaeum* (Boston, 1830)—appeared in the *North American Review,* 32 (1831): 1–21, 31 (1830) : 309–37.

4. Evidently Greenough's preceding letter to Morse, written early in December 1831, reflected a good deal of discouragement about his career at this time. It may also have contained an allusion to Giulia Grisi, whose bust Greenough modeled in 1830 and whom he thought very beautiful (see Letter 19, n. 4), which may account for his reference to an opera singer later in this letter. Morse, rather Calvinistic in outlook, apparently thought he detected the expression of a guilty conscience in Greenough's earlier letter.

5. The quotation ("[which] made this wound in my disengaged heart") is part of a speech delivered by Apollo to the nymph Daphne in Ovid, *Metamorphoses* 1. 520.

6. John C. Gore.

7. Greenough probably means he occasionally suffered from insomnia, as he had in Rome in 1827 and 1828.

8. Nathaniel Niles, formerly a physician, was at this time secretary of the American legation in Paris (see note to Letter 51). Nothing came of the project.

9. The statue of Antinuoüs, the youth loved by Hadrian, so called because after its discovery in 1795 it was first taken to the Palazzo Bracchi in Rome; it is now in the Vatican Museum.

10. Presumably the same painting mentioned in Letter 33.

11. General delivery.

40. To Robert Gilmor, Jr.
       13 January 1832

Florence. 13.th Jan'y. 1832.

To R. Gilmor Esqr / Baltimore.
My Dear Sir.

Your letter of the date 16th Novem. 1831. reached me a few days since and gratified me more than I can express. I had felt anxious from the moment I had purchased the Albano;[1] for I know how many requisites a picture must have to find favour with one who has a feast of varied styles continually before him. Your letter has removed that anxiety — You are pleased — and I am easy. I assure you that I shall hereafter follow your advice of consulting some more experienced judge, for I confess I saw no trace of restoration upon the work nor did Mr Morse. But neither he nor I have had any thing like your experience in old pictures. An engraver here wished to under take that picture but learning that it was for sale desisted, fearing it might leave the country before he had finished his plate. I shall not fail to remember daily your wishes both as respects old masters and the Cellinis and Fia-mingos,[2] though from what experience I have, I am not sanguine in my hopes of finding either of the latter. Small bronzes have severall times been brought to me as Cellini's; But whether his or not they were not worthy of him and I have always made it a rule to pay for excel-lence addressed to the eye rather than the ear. For a work of true beauty must have been done by some good artist or other — I have now in my eye a copy of Peter the Martyr of Titian[3] by Tintoretto; a grand original rendered with a tact, feeling and impetuosity of execution rarely met with. I shall go as high as $50. or $60 and I confess to you with shame that it was offered to me before the learned saw it and while its smoke & dirt obscured it for $30. I had not the eagle vision to see through the cloud which obscured it. Morse hankered for it and Cole thinks it a masterpiece in its way —

What you do me the honour to say of my groupe[4] consoles me, my dear sir, I thank you with all my heart. I find in your satisfaction with that work a guaranty that you will not be disappointed with your own statue. You are right in supposing I had recourse to Nature for my forms. I not only modelled but chisselled every part of them from the life. Of the heads of Raphael I had finished drawings but only a hasty sketch of the remainder. In fact the bodies & limbs in the original picture are far below Raphael's usual perfection of design. If you have seen the notices of my groupe in the newspapers you will conceive that it must have been gratifying to me to read one comment on it dictated by true feeling & real taste[5] & that too by one who is so soon to judge whether I have done that taste justice in a work for himself. To have made another copy of any work whatever would have been, just now, morally impossible. Had I let my imagination sleep and become the mere mouth piece of another inventor in the work, you would have been the sufferer; besides — those amiable ones who amuse themselves with the fair fame of their neighbours would not have allowed to slip an opportunity of attacking me as a man who soared on the wings of Italian masters, because Nature had only given him his own sorry legs to move withal.

Santarelli[6] who made a model for you in Florence is long since dead, nor is there any one to replace him. It is not the artist alone which is lost; the art is neglected; that branch is no longer taught at the academy and since the academy here becomes the depository of art, any thing overlooked by it dies, at once. I can have the cameo cut in Rome, but I cannot answer for the resemblance. They do every thing better than portrait, the experiment however will cost but little.

The Medora has been hasting since I went to Paris. The points are taken and I can speak most favourably of the marble; still you are aware that blemishes sometimes come out under the chisel which are not betrayed by the gradine.[7] I beg you will imagine me most busily employed on that figure from this time untill it is finished. To say how long it will be would be to measure what I have found to have no rule, I work with much greater facility than formerly, but as this figure is my first own poetical work and as I may not ever have such another opportunity, you will permit me I know to do my utmost. If I am not mistaken, the head alone will be worth the cherubs.

If my accounts err not, I have drawn on you for the sum of $471 $\frac{1}{19}$ for the statue. My wish was to get the statue done for $500. [I fea]r [*page torn*], however, that I shall be obliged to call on you for 500 francs more and should any thing occur to require still farther expence I may go to the amount I formerly mentioned to you, $700. — always with the understanding, however, that its cost to you is to be $500. I do not fear for the exhibition. — My groupe if as successfull elsewhere as in Boston will net me 6 or 700 dollars[8] — I have at present an idea of returning to America with your Statue. I am anxious to see the country and extend my connections. I hope particularly to interest some of the gentlemen connected with Government, with the Fine Arts. Should I have made any mistake in summing the amount I have received, I beg you will inform me of it at once. I am willing to be corrected by your acc'ts for though I keep my own with care, my occasional press of business requires that my brother sometimes sh[ou]ld attend to them & as mistakes may arise I mention this.

I am Dear Sir —
Yrs truly, Horatio Greenough —

P.S.   Owing to an attack of ague which I am at present suffering from this letter is copied by my brother from my rough-draught book — This circumstance must be my apology for occasional errors in it.

Addressed: Robert Gilmor Esqre / Baltimore.

N O T E S

All of this letter except the signature, postscript, and the word "execution" in the first paragraph is in Henry Greenough's hand.

Manuscript: Mellen Chamberlain Autograph Collection, BPL. Previous publication: Nathalia Wright, ed., "Letters by Horatio Greenough in the Library," *Boston Public Library Quarterly* 11 (1959): 80–82.

1. *A Repose in Egypt* by Francesco Albani (see Letter 30).
2. A common name among Italians for Flemish artists.
3. Titian's painting of the death of St. Peter Martyr was done for the church of SS. Giovanni e Paolo in Venice; it was destroyed by fire in 1867.
4. *The Chanting Cherubs.* In the margin of the manuscript page on which this paragraph appears Gilmor wrote: "This relates to the two 'Chanting Cherubs' at the bottom of one of Raphael's finest paintings, which Greenough copied in marble for Fenimore Cooper and which are very beautifully executed."
5. Presumably Greenough was alluding to the objections to the nudity of the cherubs.
6. Giovanni Antonio Santarelli (1758–1826), Italian gem cutter, modeler, medallion maker, and sculptor, taught cameo and gem work in Florence and several other European cities.
7. A toothed instrument, coarser than a chisel, for cutting marble.
8. *The Chanting Cherubs* was exhibited only in Boston and New York. Greenough realized about $400, most of it in Boston (see Letter 59).

41. To James Fenimore Cooper
14 January 1832

Florence Jan'y 14th — 1832.

My Dear Sir

Your letter of the 24th Ult'o[1] would have been delightful at any time but was a little world for me under the circumstances in which it found me. I had been so imprudent as to remain in my study in the evening after being warmed by exercise and the consequence was an attack of ague which robbed me of my rest for many nights — Your letter amused me in some parts and comforted me in others not a little[2] — So our Numa Pompilius[3] is little pleased with my exhibition room? I had expected this — I was in fact grieved myself that the group should have been so disposed of — but Morse I'm sure will do me the justice to believe that I had not intended it. His bust of which you speak was made from the *1st* block out of which I had tried to *extract* yours — The bust sits within a few feet of me looking grim as Goliath — I hope to make some thing of it yet.

I congratulate you on the acquisition of a fine picture for twenty five francs.[4] Such adventures occur rarely to a man — with a President of an Academy D.B.A.[5] at his elbow too — That you may do much to advantage here in purchasing pictures is certain but that you will clear your expences and put money in your pocket by no means sure — They are the sharpest nosed rascals! these thorough-bred picture mongers! I must tell you a story about one of them who brought an exquisite little picture to Cole the other day and who really wanted the money for it. My brother knocked at Cole's door — he came, and opening cautiously — whispered — "Mr Henry here is a man with a picture — don't burst out into raptures now — for I wish to buy it." My brother entered and after looking a moment at Cole's large work, the following dialogue ensued. Cole "Here it is Mr Henry" — Harry. "Faith! it's a beautiful picture — by whom is it?" Cole "I won't say now because he'll hear us — What a fine sombre tone!" Harry. "And exquisitely pencilled too — The heads are noble" — Cole. "Take care! He knows that last word I fear — he's the cunningest fellow!" Pict. Dealer — "Un bel quadro — eh Signore?" Harry — "Uh! non c'e male di chi è?" — P.

Dealer — "Del Cigoli — e lo guarentisco originale" — Cole — "Che! Che!" Harry. "I shouldn't be surprised to find it even so" — Cole — slyly but with enthusiasm of emphasis — "It's a little *gem*." P. Dealer quick and loudly — "Sicuro! è una *gemma!!*" Cole — "Come?" Picture Dealer — "La dice che è una gemma; costi' la dice bene" — Cole — "Avete Sbagliato!" P. Dealer — "Audiamo Sir Tommaso — Ho Girato il mondo e qualche cosa la so racappezzare auch'io — Se la vuol dar'mi quel che io diceva — d'innanzi va bene — se no — so — so io quel farò"[6] — Poor Cole. After all his management that unfortunate *gem* forced him to pay much more than he otherwise would have done — He had a rare bargain of it however — This is *sub rosa* for Cole is a little sensitive —

Your prophecy of war quite startled us[7] for all is dead here to an unusual degree — The illness of the G Duchess[8] alone occupies the public — The varied phrase with which the Gazette[9] informs us from day to day that she is about the same forms no mean proof of the richness of the Lingua Toscana[10] —

I am grieved to learn that Mrs Cooper has been so ill as to have need of a physician. Will you excuse me for saying that I fear your new grate and coal makes an atmosphere — (although very pleasant surely) rather too warm to leave suddenly for the outer air?

I have rec'd a letter from Mr Gilmor in which he speaks in raptures of the group — declares that he envies you the *idea* as well as the possession and assures me that he shall be most happy if his statue approaches it.

I fear my letter to Mr Chatelain found him in a state of joyous and saucy repletion, for he says in his answer that he has lately refused 150 Louis[11] for his copy — That he will sell it for 200 and cannot think of parting with it for less — I shall not write him again unless you request it.

It seems that John Bull is aroused to a degree not anticipated — As for what the clergy say about their claim to the tithes being a *vested* right, I presume it will only be necessary to shew the people that their money is taken and no equivalent given them for it, to convince them that the sooner — their priests are *divested* of such rights the better — A holder of half a dozen livings is a mere priest-broker.[12] Now if folk can't afford to pay that exorbitant brokerage they have only to recollect that it takes 2 to make a bargain — I believe those rascals would go all lengths — whatever — until they met with resistance — Look at all such animals as can't defend themselves! Abstract right is very little re-

garded — What men *can* do — they *will* do — in their collective capacity — It's a sickening fact — but I'm each day more convinced of it.
Not that I believe infants are born charged and primed with sin as
friend Morse does — It seems to be a sort of physical necessity — gravitation — that forces one man's elbow against his neighbour's stomach.

We have rec'd here several American books — amongst others a
furious attack on the American poets[13] — it's about as much like true
satire as a punch in the eye is like a repartee. This pretty work is from
Boston and is attributed to a meek but very queer friend of mine — I
can't believe it. We have 2 new Yankee painters here — Mr Alexander
and a young man of the name of Ritchie a nephew of Andrew Ritchie
of Boston.[14] Alston is hard at work and is selling pictures at good prices
as fast as he can paint them. Cole begs me to assure you that his not
seeing you in Paris was his misfortune not his fault — You will remember that he was a sourd-muet pro tempore[15] and he suffers more under
that calamity than any man I have seen — I beg you will present my
respects to Mrs Cooper who I trust is by this time recovered as also to
your family and friend Alphabet Morse. Yours truly

Horatio Greenough

Addressed: J. Fenemore Cooper Esqre / Care of Mess Welles & co /
Paris

NOTES

Manuscript: Cooper Collection, Beinecke.
1. Cooper, 2:162–67.
2. In his letter, a reply to Greenough's letter of 17 December 1831, Cooper told
   Greenough to draw on him for whatever sum of money he needed. For
   Greenough's debts to Cooper, see Letter 64.
3. Numa Pompilius, the legendary second king of Rome, was credited with
   organizing the city's religious institutions. Greenough refers to Morse, who
   tended not only to moralize but to pontificate. Cooper had written that he did
   not think Morse spoke so well of *The Chanting Cherubs* since learning it was
   being exhibited at the American Academy of the Fine Arts. See also Letter 39.
4. Cooper had written that he had bought, at a street stall, a female head of the
   Flemish school, reputed to be a portrait by Teniers of his wife, which was
   offered for 50 francs but for which Cooper bid 25 and which he got for 26.
   Morse saw it first but did not try to buy it.
5. *Di Belle Arti,* "of the fine arts."
6. "Pict. Dealer — 'A beautiful picture — eh Signore?' Harry — 'Uh– not so bad

by whom is it?' — P. Dealer — 'By Cigoli — and I guarantee it original' —
Cole — 'What! What!' . . . P. Dealer . . . 'Certainly! it is a gem!!' Cole —
'What?' Picture Dealer — 'He says that it is a gem; there he says well' —
Cole — 'You are mistaken!' P. Dealer — 'We hear you Signore Thomas — I
have gone around the world and I know how to find something out — If you
wish to give me what I was saying — before very well — if not — come —
come — I shall have that [painting.]' "

    Lodovico Cardi da Cigoli (1559–1613) was a Tuscan painter, architect,
and poet.

7. Cooper had written: "The great political Armagedden must come — I think
Germany will be likely to begin the fray" (Cooper, 2:165).
8. Marianna Carolina (1790–1832), princess of Saxony, grandduchess of Tuscany,
died March 24.
9. The *Gazetta di Firenze* was the leading newspaper in the city at this time.
10. "The Tuscan tongue."
11. A louis was worth about $3.35 at this time.
12. Greenough refers first to the Third Reform Bill, introduced in Parliament in
December 1831 and passed in June 1832; Cooper had asked what he thought
of it. Cooper had also asked Greenough what he thought the consequences
would be of Irish Catholics refusing to pay tithes to the English Church.
13. *Truth: A New Year's Gift for Scribblers* (Boston, 1831), a satirical poem by
William Joseph Snelling (1804–48).
14. Francis Alexander (1800–1880), portrait, genre, and still life painter, was
in Florence for five or six weeks in the winter of 1831–32. He painted
Greenough's portrait in Boston in 1836; its present location is unknown
(Catherine W. Pierce, "Francis Alexander," *Old-Time New England* 44
[1953]: 29–46).

    Andrew Ritchie, Jr. (1782–1862), was a painter of landscapes and battle
pieces. His nephew may have been John M. Ritchie, a portrait painter, who
lived in New York about 1844.

15. "Deaf mute temporarily." Cole was in Paris during the early part of May
1831 (Thomas Cole, *The Course of Empire, Voyage of Life, and Other
Pictures of Thomas Cole* . . . , ed. Louis L. Noble [New York, 1853], pp.
125–26).

42. To James Fenimore Cooper
Between 14 January and 8 March 1832

Saturday — Evening —

My Dear Sir

    Mr Kinloch mentioned to me this evening that he had written to you
on the subject of a petition to Congress etc etc.[1] I stated to him on the
spot the conditions upon which I was willing to undertake a statue —

He thought I had better write them to you in a form to be laid readily before such as might be inclined to favour the enterprise.

I am willing to undertake a statue in marble 7 feet in height provided one thousand dollars are advanced in three instalments at different stages of the work (say at intervals of 4 months) provided I am allowed to find subscribers for one thousand dollars among my friends in America. The statue to be delivered to the subscribers to be disposed of as they think fit — after having been exhibited for my benefit.

My reasons for being eager to attempt such a work are — That I would fain do something in the large before *habit* shall have cramped my hand to the little — That I wish to emulate others who have made statues for my country, while I'm young — That I believe that such a work would form the best possible petition, not only to Congress; of whose spirit in matters of this nature I have no very favourable opinion, but to the nation at large which if enlisted on our side will soon make itself felt in Congress, and without whose good opinion all the patronage of congress could never make us happy.

It remains for the gentlemen in question to decide whether my ambition can subserve their national spirit, and whether one chance in a hundred of owning any thing I can make, is worth the 20$ more or less which each pays to cover the expences — I confess the project has little to recommend it for the subscribers —

One thing I beg you will believe and remember — that is that I *wish* the support of your voice alone in this matter. You've done your part by me Sir and I've only to aspire to the preservation of that place in your esteem which forms no small portion of my present happiness.

> I am My Dear Sir
> Your Friend and Serv't
> Horatio Greenough

J Fenimore Cooper Esqre / Rue St Domenique / 59

Addressed: J Fenimore Cooper Esqre / Rue St Domenique S. Germ. / No 59.

NOTES

The last known letter from Greenough to Cooper before this one is dated 14 January 1832. On 8 March Cooper wrote President Andrew Jackson recommending Greenough for employment by the national government (Cooper, 2:233–35).

This letter does not seem to have passed through the mail and was probably carried to Cooper by a friend of Greenough's.
Manuscript: Cooper Collection, Beinecke.

1. Francis Kinloch (1798–1840), of South Carolina, lived in Florence (at first, studying art) from 1832 until about the time of his death, which occurred in Rome. Greenough, who knew him in America, met him in Paris in the fall of 1831 (Nathalia Wright, "Francis Kinloch: A South Carolina Artist," *South Carolina Historical Magazine* 41 [1960]: 99–100). No such petition to Congress as Greenough describes was made.

43. To Samuel F. B. Morse
Between 25 March and 23 April 1832

Accept my warmest thanks for your sympathy — the interest you express in my welfare fills no small portion of the void which my troubles may have made in my heart. As for my kind friends in the Rue St. Dominique, may the Disposer of events send them thousands of such sensations as I experienced when I read what you say of their regret at my difficulties! But I will hope that by exertion I may reach a point where to feel interest in me shall not be to suffer. You mention a certain plan, but you roll it under your tongue again in the most tantalizing way. Why won't you, in your next, sketch with your pen the plan of your picture,[1] for I'm not sure I understand it; that is, if indeed you meant I should? I don't wish to beg a secret.

You were right, I had heard of the resolution submitted to Congress, etc.; Mr. Cooper wrote me about it.[2] I have not much faith in Congress, however. I will confess that, when the spectre Debt has leaned over my pillow of late, and, smiling ghastily, has asked me if she and I were not intended as companions through life, I snap my fingers at her and tell her that Brother Jonathan talks of adopting me, and that he won't have her of his household. "Go to London, you hag," says I, "where they say you're handsome and wholesome; don't grind your long teeth at me, or I'll read the Declaration of Independence to ye!" So you see I make uncertain hopes fight certain fear, and borrow from the generous, goodnatured Future the motives for content which are denied me by the stinted Present. I still continue to think that another year will find me somewhere in Germany. I must cut through the snarl into

which four years have wound my relations, and come smack on my
feet. I'm afraid of a habit, and the habit of being assisted is one of the
most ruinous.

In the mean while I'm trying to mix a little with the world, and to
learn how to behave myself. I have hitherto read my Dante, etc., and
when thrown into contact with folk have gotten through as quick as
possible, with the idea that every word spared was so much clear gain;
but I now find that a man needs a circle of acquaintance, and have
already made several pleasant acquisitions in this way.

What shall I say in answer to your remarks on my opinions? Shall I
go all over the ground again? It were useless. That my heart is wrong
in a thousand ways I daily feel, but 'tis my stubborn head which
refuses to comprehend the creation as you comprehend it. That we
should be grateful for all we have, I feel — for all we have is given us;
nor do I think we have little; for my part I would be blessed in mere
existence were I not goaded by a wish to make my one talent two; and
we have Scripture for the rectitude of such a wish. I don't think the
stubborn resistance of the tide of ill-fortune can be called rebellion
against Providence. "Help yourself, and Heaven will help you," says
the proverb. When Leonidas stood with his three hundred in the gap
against the tide of Persian tyranny,[3] was his a rebellion against the
decree that doomed his country to defeat? No, he stood there to see it
done, and to decimate his conquerors according to the decree of the
Disposer of all. I suppose you have Brisbane with you by this time
with several new German syllogisms. If the truth were known, that
fellow went to Berlin to refit after the battering his metaphysics had
received at your hands. Hateful word that same metaphysics. Let's
have reasoning till all's blue, but let's have *hold* of something. Let's
have Poetry, too; for she raises our motives instead of poisoning them;
she makes another world, instead of topsy-turvying this.

There hangs before me a print of the Bunker-Hill Monument. Pray,
be judge between me and the building committee of that monument.[4]

There you observe that my model was founded solidly, and on each
of its square plinths were trophies, or groups, or cannon, as might be
thought fit. (No. 1.) Well, they have taken away the foundation, made
the shaft start sheer from the dirt like a spear of asparagus, and, instead
of an acute angle, by which I hoped to show the work was done, and
lead off the eye, they have made an obtuse one, producing the broken-
chimney-like effects, which your eye will not fail to condemn in No. 2.

Then they have inclosed theirs with a light, elegant fence, *à la Parigin*[a],[5] as though the austere forms of Egypt were compatible with the decorative flummery of the Boulevards. Let 'em go for dunderheads, as they are!

I'm remodeling Washington; the old model was made too long since to repeat any more. Harry is painting, and is quite a favorite with his master. The boy grows fast; I have great hopes of him. Gore is painting his mud portrait very well; he may be found at any time of the day with one of the mud-heavers of the Arno for a model: a red-headed, long-bearded, fiery-faced, green-eyed fellow, that has killed his man and cuts all his bread with a pointed knife two inches longer than the law directs. Gore has imagination; he feels character. I have the promise of certain drawings for the Academy; your bust and Cole's have both gone, directed to Mr. Morton. Cole is probably in Naples. My "Lafayette" is [boasted][6] without a strain. I congratulate you on your sound conscience with regard to the affair that you wot of.[7] As for your remaining free, that's all very well to think during the interregnum; but a man without a true love is a ship without ballast, a one-tined fork, half a pair of scissors, an utter flash in the pan. Will you give my love to the Coopers, and say to Mr. C. That I have received his note, and am awaiting his letter, of which he speaks![8]

Horatio Greenough

NOTES

The letter from Cooper to which Greenough refers in this letter was dated 15 March (Cooper, 2:235) and presumably reached him about ten days later. The date of Greenough's next known letter to Morse is 23 April.

Source: Samuel Irenaeus Prime, *The Life of Samuel F. B. Morse, LL.D.* (New York, 1875), pp. 212–14.

1. Greenough is probably referring to Morse's painting *Exhibition Gallery of the Louvre*, depicting the Salon Carré with most of the works in it and several spectators and copyists. Morse painted it in Paris at this time and completed it in America in 1833 (Prime, *Life of Morse*, pp. 227, 249). It is now in the College of Fine Arts, Syracuse University.

2. The original resolution appointing Greenough to execute a statue of Washington for the Capitol rotunda was dated 13 February 1832, and was introduced in the House of Representatives the next day. In his letter of 15 March to Greenough, Cooper said he had seen a reference to it in a recent letter from America.

3. Leonidas, king of Sparta, who opposed the invasion of Greece by the Persian Xerxes with three hundred men.
4. For Greenough's drawing, included with his letter, see Plate V.
5. "Like a Parisian." Prime has *Parigino,* which is probably a misreading of the manuscript.
6. Prime has "boxed," which is probably a misreading of "bosted," Greenough's spelling for "boasted."
7. Morse may have been temporarily interested in Susan Cooper (Cooper, 2: 375). His first wife, Lucretia P. Walker, died in 1825; in 1846 he married his young second cousin, Sarah E. Griswold (Prime, *Life of Morse,* pp. 142, 590).
8. In his short letter to Greenough of 15 March, Cooper promised to write at length in a few days.

44. To John Ludlow Morton
27 March 1832

Florence — March 27th 1832 —

My Dear Sir

This will accompany 2 marble busts which I have made within the past year — The one of our good president — the other of Mr Cole the landskape painter.[1] Cole desired me to ship to you and having no instructions from Morse and being unacquainted with his brothers[2] I have taken the liberty of doing the same with his. Should these busts arrive in season for your exhibition[3] may I beg you will find a good light for them? A glance at them will shew you what light they require and the best views of them. Perhaps it had been more discreet to avoid exhibiting them altogether made as they have been at odd moments of leisure when fatigued and dispirited — But I have no right to claim exemption from criticism — so let them take their chance.

I am most happy to learn the improvement of the institution[4] which owes so much to your exertions and perseverence. I wish I had the prospect of being one among you in body as I have long been in name and in good wishes — but I am chained.

I have read with the feelings it is calculated to rouse, Mr Dunlap's manly address to the Academy[5] — Dr Franklin said "it is hard *for empty sacks* to stand up straight"[6]; but I think we may answer that they must be *held up* before they can be filled — and I for one will confess that the independent tone taken by Mr Dunlap has raised much of my slack canvass from the ground — whether any thing is to be put into it remains uncertain.

I am in hopes of procuring several drawings by eminent artists for our academy, some indeed are already promised me —

Begging you will accept my assurances [of] friendly regard I remain Dear Sir Yours truly

[No signature][7]

J. L. Morton Esqre / Sec'y of the N Academy of Design. / New York.

Addressed: For / J. L. Morton Esqre / Secretary of the National Academy / of Design / New-York.

Endorsed: Greenough's letter / & Bill of Lading for / 2 *marble Busts* / March 27. 1832

NOTES

John Ludlow Morton (1798–1871) was a portrait, historical, and landscape painter. He served for many years as the first secretary of the National Academy of Design.

 Manuscript: National Academy of Design, New York City.

1. The *Morse* is now in the National Collection of Fine Arts, Washington, D.C.; a plaster copy, made for the Council Room of the National Academy sometime after December 1843, is in the Metropolitan Museum of Art, New York. The *Cole* is in the Wadsworth Atheneum, Hartford.
2. Sidney Edwards Morse (1794–1871), journalist, inventor, and geographer, and Richard Cary Morse (1795–1868), journalist, were co-founders in 1823 of the *New-York Observer*, a religious journal.
3. They were shown at the National Academy of Design during its annual spring exhibition in 1833.
4. The National Academy of Design.
5. William Dunlap, *Address to the Students of the National Academy of Design, at the Delivery of the Premiums, Monday, the 18th of April, 1831* (New York, 1831).
6. This is an inaccurate quotation of the proverb in any of its three versions — in *Poor Richard's Almanack* for 1740, 1750, and 1758. The final version, in "The Way to Wealth" (the preface to the 1758 almanac), was " 'Tis hard for an empty Bag to Stand upright."
7. Greenough's signature has been cut out. To the left of the cut, "signed — *Greenough*" is written in another hand.

45. To Samuel F. B. Morse
23 April 1832

Florence April 23d — 1832 —

My Dear Morse

I have been extremely anxious about you all since I learned the serious character assumed by the Cholera at Paris — I have been in hopes that you would by the time the disease was at its height have informed me of your safety — but when I consider that besides your usual occupations your leisure may have been employed in tranquilizing your friends across the water, I cannot complain of your silence. In the mean while I trust I shall have heard of you before this reaches you. A party of Americans has just gone to Leghorn to embark for the States, instead of returning through France, such is the panic produced by the details given by the French papers.

I had the P. office searched the other day but found no letters of yours — There are however 2 for Mr Willis[1] which I should have despatched immediately had I any *surety* that he were still in Paris — They are addressed simply to him — Will you do me the favour to mention this to him should he be still in Paris and if not will you inform me whither he has flown?

The "violent pains in my pocket" have been relieved by the very liberal advancement (voluntarily) on the part of Com' Biddle of the full price of a bust of W[ashingto]n which I am making for him — I have remodelled the bust so as to make it a companion for that of Gen Lafayette — This latter has not only pleased the artists but has drawn many curious and some intelligent people to my study — From these I have chosen one or two whom I visit occasionally with a sincere wish to scour away a certain ferocity which 3 years of independence and solitude has added to my natural depravity of heart —

My maternal grandfather[2] died lately at near a hundred years of age — he had been incapable of enjoyment for many months yet it seems yesterday that I saw him get into his gig with a clear eye and a firm leg — He began life with high hopes as we all do but was thrown out of his business by the war — married — and made the best of it — I am indebted to him for a good mother[3] — what I ever did to repay him for this gift I can't say — If life is such a span what matters it how it's passed so one lives and does his part for posterity — what does a ragged coat or a poor dinner matter when one thinks of a few years hence? If I'm so philosophic now friend M—— what shall I be when I have added experience to reason — Why I shall get into jail directly[4] — A letter from an uncle at Albany[5] advises me to take some lessons in fire eating and rope dancing in case I should return as he fears that an ourang outang or a calf with seven legs will at any time through[6] all the chisel can do into the shade — This is encouraging! In the mean while I have 4 marble busts in progress[7] and the Medora under full sail — I have nearly finished a pen-drawing for your sketch book and am preparing for another — Subject David singing to Saul in his phrenzy[8] — The crazy king his noble son — The young poet and war-riour will I think afford a fine variety of character and expression while the tender daughter will come in as a relief and fill that void which the absence of petticoat interest makes us feel in all works that address the heart — I have dined today with an English gentleman whose house I have frequented of late and who took the trouble of making my acquaintance — The hour was much later than I am accustomed to and I entered the room dressed with due attention and smelling sweet but with a certain wolfishness of disposition which 2 hours' protraction of emptiness is sure to produce with me — There were ladies and gentle-men and prints and picture books disposed on the tables before us — to while away the time withal — sad substitutes for beef and pudding Morse eh! but what was most conspicuous of all and called for all my gratitude was a folio of sky blue binding and superscribed in a large type as follows, "Four select views of the Action between his majesties ship Shannon and the American Frigate Chesapeake[9] drawn from Accurate sketches etc etc." I passed the greater part of the time be-tween the moment my eye had run over this title page and the an-nouncement of dinner in considering what combinations of tact and kindness could have prepared this treat for me — nor was it until I had swallowed my soup that I concluded that the gentleman in question had paid me in my own coin for the *impressions* I had un-wittingly made in telling him *whom* the various busts in my study *represented.* I made up my mind on the spot that he had a heart of the size of a humming bird's and pardoned him — Am I not a chris-tian?

My Dear Morse I know very well that this world is all a fleeting

shew — yet should I like amazingly to be with you there again in
Paris for a few short days — I would risk the Cholera and all to be
seated in your snug little chamber with Cooper too — now talking
seriously and now letting ding any how — Well! I presume the friend
of Lafayette's whom he mentions as having been arrested at Berlin
was no other than friend[10]; I suspected his sympathies with the
proletaires would get him into hot water in his favoured land of
philosophy — Germany is the place to study! said he — retirement
Sir! ha! ha! He's out so one may laugh at the joke now —

   I have been reading a remarkable book — Doblado's letters from
Spain[11] — pray get it. It contains interest for you — for me it's rather
too faultfinding — He throws in descriptions for relief but his object
was to asperse and expose — and though it may be all right I had
rather seen the truth naked and laconically told instead of that —
agro dolce[12] mixture of abuse of his countrymen description of scenery
and flattery of John Bull — He has Argus's eyes for Spanish Errors
but sees England through a prism — The book was lent me by some
friends of the author who inform me that he is to become a priest
of the English Establishment — and that he's a sincere protestant
Christian — Seeing is believing. — Count Cicognara[13] has just returned
to Venice in very bad health. We all go on as usual — Pray remember
me to the Coopers — Harry sends his love to you. He is painting —
Let me know your intentions for the summer and believe me

                                                   Ever Yours
                                                   H. Greenough —

S. F. B. Morse. Esqre P.N.A. / Paris.

P.S. I had a little note from Cooper[14] in which he promised to
write soon at length. I suppose he [is] waiting to give me some
pleasant news — pray beg him not to wait for that lest I never should
hear from him again — besides any letter from him is good news as
it informs me of the health of him and his —

Addressed: For / S. F. B. Morse Esqre *PNA.* / Poste Restante / *Paris.*

NOTES

   Manuscript: Morse Papers, LC.
   1. Nathaniel Parker Willis (1806–67), author, editor, and foreign correspondent

for the *New-York Mirror,* was in Paris from November 1831 to May 1832. His letters from abroad during this period were collected in *Pencillings by the Way* (New York, 1844).

2. Peter Bender (1745–1832) died 6 January. Born in Boston, he settled in Marlborough, Massachusetts, in 1764. After serving in the Continental Army, he became a carpenter. He married Abigail Brigham, by whom he had six children (*Vital Records of Marlborough, Massachusetts, To the End of the Year 1849* [Worcester, 1908], p. 343; Charles Hudson, *History of the Town of Marlborough* [Boston, 1862], p. 325; *Massachusetts Soldiers of the Revolutionary War* [Boston, 1896–1908], 1:934).

3. Elizabeth Bender Greenough (see note to Letter 182).

4. See n. 10.

5. Possibly Jacob Bender (b. 1781), who was said to have read law, taken the name of Hastings, and died in New York state (Hudson, *History of Marlborough,* p. 325). It is perhaps more likely that Greenough was in correspondence with his father's brother William (1772–1861), a printer, who was closely associated with the David Greenoughs during Horatio's boyhood, but there is no record of William's having lived in Albany (Greenough, p. 53).

6. Greenough means "throw."

7. Presumably those of Hayne, Lafayette, Washington, and either Cooper or Brisbane.

8. This sketch, representing episodes described in 1 Sam. 16:23, 18:10, and 19:9, seems not to have been preserved. A study for it is in the editor's collection. On the back of this study is one of Phaeton being restrained by Helios from mounting the sun chariot, possibly the subject of the second sketch.

9. The U.S. frigate *Chesapeake* engaged the British ship *Shannon* outside Boston and was captured on 1 June 1813.

10. Here, Greenough drew a profile of a man with a protruding chin, presumably Albert Brisbane (identifiable from the frontispiece of Redelia Brisbane, *Albert Brisbane* [1893]; see also the profile of Brisbane in Plate IV and Greenough's comments to Morse on Brisbane in Letter 44, which closely resemble his comments here). The man in question was not Brisbane, however, but Samuel Gridley Howe, the Massachusetts reformer and philanthropist, who, as chairman of the American Polish Committee, had gone to Prussia to distribute aid to the victims of the Polish Revolution. He was arrested in Berlin by the Prussian government in February 1832. See Samuel G. Howe, *Letters and Journals of Samuel Gridley Howe,* ed. Laura E. Richards [Boston, 1909], 1:401–19; Cooper, 2:259–64.

11. Joseph Blanco White, *Letters from Spain by Don Leucadio Doblado* (London, 1822). Born and brought up in Spain, White lived after 1810 in England and Ireland. He was ordained a Roman Catholic priest, but became a vigorous critic of the Roman Church and at last gave up belief in any but rational religion.

12. "Sour-Sweet."

13. Count Leopoldo Cicognara(1767–1834), archaeologist and writer, spent many years in Venice, but left the city about 1820 because of political differences with its Austrian rulers.

14. That of 15 March.

46.   To Thomas Cole
       19 May 1832

Florence May 19. 1832 —

My dear Cole
   I have but a moment — but will say the little I can — Your letter[1]
gave me unfeigned pleasure — I trust you will remain in Italy longer
than you had intended — I have rec'd orders to the amount of about
$600 lately[2] and am in hopes of a commission from government — My
Medora is far advanced — I have nearly chiselled Lafayette — Col
Hayne's[3] bust is quite done in the important parts. I've modelled
another Washington [and] [*page torn*] have just boasted it *without
a stain.* I've had [*page torn*] from English folk of late and have some
agreeable acqu[aintances] [*page torn*] among them. Harry is painting away[4] and Crank[5] has rea[lly] [*page torn*] done himself credit
of late — Will you give my best regards to Mr Hammett[6] the consul
as also to Persico if you see him — The redoubtable Miss Douglas
was here the other day and *impressed* me for a drawing.[7] I saw a
sketch of yours in the book — Congratulate Mr Alexander from me on
his success at Rome[8] — My love to Mr Lane[9] — Cooper has escaped
with all his family — the cholera — Morse was nervous but is clear —
Yours in all love

Hor Greenough

Addressed: For / Thomas Cole Esqre / Poste Restante / Naples.

NOTES

Thomas Cole (1801–48), the English-born American landscape painter and
founder of the Hudson River school of painting, was in Italy from May 1831 to
October 1832. In one of his sketchbooks he drew, probably in 1832, a portrait of
Greenough (Detroit Institute of Arts).
   Manuscript: Thomas Cole Papers, New York State Library.
   1. Presumably that of 16 February 1832, written soon after Cole arrived in
Rome from Florence. In it Cole gave a brief account of his trip, commented

at length on St. Peter's, and expressed admiration for the Pantheon and Michelangelo's *Moses*.

2. These orders were for two statues and a bust (see Letter 47).
3. Arthur Perroneau Hayne (1790–1867), South Carolina soldier and statesman, was at this time agent for American naval affairs in the Mediterranean. Greenough's bust of him seems not to have been preserved.
4. One of the paintings Henry was working on about this time was apparently a copy of a Giorgione (*Letters*, p. 91).
5. John Cranch.
6. Alexander Hammett was U.S. consul in Naples, 1809–46 and 1849–61, and chargé for the Two Sicilies, 1847–48. He had looked after Greenough when he was ill in Naples in 1828.
7. Harriet Douglas (1790–1872), celebrated New York heiress and lion-hunter, was at this time nearing the end of a six-year sojourn in Europe (see Angus Davidson, *Miss Douglas of New York* [London, (1952)]). On 16 May Greenough drew heads of Washington and Lafayette in her sketchbook, according to her diary (in the possession of a descendant). In 1829 John Greenough had met her in Paris, proposed, and been rejected (information furnished by Mr. Davidson).
8. Francis Alexander, who traveled in Rome and Naples with Cole, painted a portrait of Miss Douglas in Rome in April. During that time Sir Walter Scott accompanied her to Alexander's studio and complimented Alexander's painting of Mary Magdalen (William Dunlap, *A History of the Rise and Progress of the Arts of Design in the United States* [New York, 1834], 2:432–33).
9. A Mr. Lane of Boston traveled with Alexander and Cole from Florence to Naples and back as far at least as Rome. Possibly he was one of the four Lanes — Charles, David, John S., and George — listed as merchants in the *Boston Directory* for 1831–32.

47. To James Fenimore Cooper
28 May 1832

Florence — May 28th — 1832

My Dear Sir

I have not heard from you for a long time[1] — nor from friend Morse though I begged him on my knees to let me know of his escape after the cholera should have subsided — I think it possible however that his letters may have been intercepted —

Unless I mistake I have mentioned to you in my conversations with you — the cold reception I met with from Mr Everett when last in America and my surprise at it, since he had distinguished me

when a boy, by kindness to which I had no claim — I rec'd yesterday
a letter from him full of paternal congratulation and expressing an
esteem of my past and a hope of my future works, which I had
never supposed he would feel[2] — He tells me he did his utmost to
further the plan in congress — that he interceded with Mr Livingston[3]
for *liberal terms* and speaks of his conversations with those who voted
against the thing (and who he says were merely opposed to the way
in which it was brought forward) in a way to shew that he was my
active friend throughout the affair — Now this was magnanimous of
him, because if My eye can talk English I have told him that I did
not care a rush for him either one way or the other — He has heaped
coals of fire on my head — But when a man cuts one at a President's
Soire what can one do — I hope we shall understand one another
better hereafter — He speaks of the thing as decided and hopes that
you will do them (the house) the justice to find that your example
has not been lost — He concludes by offering his services in the most
obliging way — I would copy his letter if it were not a long one
for I think you would agree with me that it's a beautiful specimen
in its way — I rec'd at the same time a letter from Mr Gilmor[4] containing much very excellent advice — He does not even mention his
statue though he must think it high time it were finished — This is
delicate is it not? — I shall do him the better justice therefore —
  And now Sir I'm going to strain every nerve lest this commission
should prove the greatest misfortune that ever happened to me —
I have always made it a rule whenever a puff of good fortune came,
to look to the timbers in the hole before setting new sail — On this
occasion I've gone to the Hospital[5] and, for the first time in my
life, have dissected the dead subject — You know we generally learn
anatomy by drawing the dissections of the surgeons — This dissection
will hereafter be my constant study in the winter — In a couple of
hours one sees more of the *why* of organization and form than in
days of lecture reading or examining the living model. Its effect on
one is most stirring — It seems as one follows the knife as if God
himself were made visible and audible in the beauty strength and
fitness of our frames. Should I be disappointed in the commission,
I shall not have lost all the strength given by bearing up under its
weight even in imagination for these few weeks — Mr Hoyt[6] of New
York has ordered 2 statues of me — they are to be of 2½ feet in
height — only — In the one I shall represent Italy — in the other the
genius of our country — I would describe the compositions if this

letter were not going by the mail — I'm to have 500$ for the 2 — though I don't care to have it generally known — Mr Miles[7] has ordered his bust — I have just compleated the head in 3 sittings — How I long to see you and to talk with you on the subject of the statue! — and Morse too. What a treasure he would be to me if his veteran judgement were here to help me in this extremity! — If Morse doesn't get orders for something worthy of him it's a shame — I shall ask Mr Everett in answering his letter why they cannot employ him on the Return of Columbus to the court of Spain[8] — a subject which is worthy of government & of the art, and for which Morse is not only prepared but in which I would venture to say he would astonish every body. Morse has been dribbled away in little things and his very virtues have been made use of to keep him down — He has suffered long enough and by Jupiter Ammon he deserves better things — The picture on which he is at present employed may be of the greatest service to him in a pecuniary point of view but does not cover all his mind — and at his age it should be so — should it not? I say these things between ourselves — for generally folk have little sympathy with talents which are not in full operation —

Miss Douglass passed through here like a whir wind the other day — Willis has popped upon us after a week's quarantine at Villa Franca[9] — poetical fare and simple boards to sleep on — He is however fat and handsome and quite redolent of the french capital.

We have here two "*old gulls*" who command all our chivalry — What a pity one can't whisper on paper! The Misses Bridgen[10] — They are travelling alone in quest of health and when I see that one of them has nearly recovered from a most dangerous illness I can't but defend their spirit in so doing — They are of that form and feature which secures virtue from all outward danger — While they have conversation — manner and tact to secure them beaux wherever beaux are to be found — One of them is quite clever and If I mistake not knows you — Shall I have sittings for your upper lip or not? If I should not the old bust will serve me for the mouth was religiously modelled — But I hope you will find it for your pleasure to come this way once more — I beg you will present my respects to Mrs Cooper and the family and believe me

> Dear Sir — Yours truly —
> Horatio Greenough

J. Fenimore Cooper Esqre / Paris.

Addressed: For / J Fenimore Cooper Esqre / care of / Mess Welles &
Co Bankers / *Paris.*

NOTES

Manuscript: Cooper Collection, Beinecke.
1. The last known letter before this one from Cooper to Greenough was that
   of 22 April 1832, informing Greenough that the resolution employing him to
   execute a statue of Washington for the Capitol had passed the Committee of
   the Whole in the House of Representatives (Cooper, 2:244–45).
2. Edward Everett apparently slighted Greenough at the Presidential reception in
   Washington on 20 February 1828 (*Letters,* p. 26). In his letter to Greenough of 12 April 1832 (collection of David Richardson, Washington, D.C.),
   however, he congratulated Greenough on receiving the commission for the
   statue of Washington; reported advising that not less than $10,000 be of-
   fered for the figure and the same amount for the pedestal with $5000 to be
   paid in advance; explained that the votes against the resolution in the House
   of Representatives were cast by those doubting that a single legislative body
   had the right to appropriate money; and concluded with several flattering remarks about Greenough's works, particularly *The Chanting Cherubs.*
3. Edward Livingston was then secretary of state (see note to Letter 53).
4. That of 29 February 1832 (see Greenough's Letter 50 to Gilmor).
5. Presumably the Arcispedale di Santa Maria Nuova, where the city's Collegio
   Medico was housed. A sketch of thigh muscles by Greenough bears the
   notation, "Copied from a study at the Hospital of S. M. Nuova By Giuseppe
   Bezzuoli — 1832 —." Other surviving anatomical and hospital sketches by
   Greenough were probably made about this time. (Sketches in the editor's
   collection.)
6. Henry Shaeff Hoyt (1816?–91), a lawyer, was at this time traveling in Europe
   (Hoyt to Thomas Cole, 24 August 1832, Thomas Cole Collection, New York
   State Library, Albany, N.Y.; David W. Hoyt, *A Genealogical History of the
   Hoyt, Haight, and Hight Families* [Providence, 1871], p. 506). The statues
   which he ordered were finished about 1833 but seem not to have been preserved.
7. Henry Miles, an American merchant living in Florence.
8. Presumably Greenough refers to Morse's proposal early in 1832 to Gulian
   Verplanck, chairman of the Committee on Public Buildings, that he be employed to depict this subject and that of the departure of Columbus on two of
   the four unpainted panels in the rotunda of the Capitol (Oliver W. Larkin,
   Samuel F. B. Morse and American Democratic Art [Boston, 1954], p. 106).
   He was never awarded a commission by the government, however.
9. Willis was in Florence for a few weeks at this time, living, like Greenough, in
   Casa dei Frati. He had been detained at Villa Franca, the quarantine area
   near Nice, because he had been in Paris during the cholera epidemic
   (Nathaniel Parker Willis, *Pencillings by the Way* [New York, 1844], pp.
   44–47).
10. Anna M. Bridgen, who died in 1857 at the age of 69, and a sister were

residents of Albany (Joel Munsell, *The Annals of Albany* [Albany, 1850–59], 9:339).

48. To Samuel F. B. Morse
31 May 1832

Florence May 31st 1832

My Dear Morse

If I seem a little drowsy in this letter pray attribute it to the circumstances under which I write — Tis a luxurious morning — The sun is just peering over Capponi house and makes an emerald of every leaf of the trim garden under my window[1] — The tall poplars seem to sleep in the light — A donkey is drawing water for the garden — all is quiescent save the birds who twitter whistle and chirup as if the Devil had them — Your letter contained much to delight and something to sadden — Was it not a Mr Jackson who took charge of your presents?[2] If so I no longer doubt where the mischief lies for I have lately heard no very good account of the gentleman — If you see Mr Persifer Frazer[3] of Philadelphia on his return to Paris pray compare notes with him — he also has met with trouble from that quarter — You grieve me when you speak of going to America so soon[4] — However you know better than myself what your interests require — My Medora will bind me here untill late in the summer — and then I have 2 3 ft statues to touch up in the marble — before the [beg]inning [*page torn*] of November — If I could in any honest way get to Paris before you [lea]ve [*page torn*] I would do so were it but to see you before you go away — Cooper he's [go]ing [*page torn*] home too[5] — This world is all a fleeting shew![6] I can find one consolation in your leaving Paris however — I shall cease to yearn after the city as I have done to an extent amounting to boyishness — All the folks who have arrived from Paris since myself — have seemed to me to smell sweeter than ordinary artists — My longings will now take a more natural channel — I don't like the thought of the Atlantic between us however not at all — I don't think the sum you mention is going to hamstring the Academy by any means — If your suspicions are confirmed I hope the newspapers will put Americans on their guard — The small number of foreigners who spend their money now in Italy fall into the hands of greedy and it must be added famished people — They are quite ferocious. A cool fellow may now buy to some advantage — I for example bought a portrait of Mich. Angelo yesterday — painted in his time — here in Florence — and fine for likeness and expression. As for the painting I can only say it is *soignee*.[7] You might find a good tone and a passable colouring — Willis is above me and sound asleep I presume — I fear he finds himself a little out of his element here. He's a corinthian capital amid rough hewn stone posts — He has most estimable qualities and wants nothing but a little solitude or a little insight into the real value of the vanities of society. He's clever certainly — But has allowed himself to be too much cut up — He has chopped his mind up too fine — Do you know the Bridgens — So Do I — and regular ones they are hey? The elder has recovered in great measure her health — If I was a woman and was unmarried I would make it a *point* never to find fault with any thing or any body after the age of 20 or 21 say — It would be confounded hard I suspect from what I have seen but if it could be done I should be fully repaid for my trouble — for I should stand alone — almost — as for the commission from Gov't, I don't speak of it yet — After about a fortnight I shall be calm I think — Morse I have made up my mind on one score — Viz. that this order shall not be fruitless to the greater men who are in our rear — They are sucking now and rocking in cradles but I can hear the Pung! Pung! Puffety! of their hammers and I am prophetic too! We'll see if Yankee land can't muster some ten or dozen of 'em in the course of as many years! — If you go home you will be married. If you are married you will stay there — Pray advertize for me when you get there. Wanted a young woman of knowledge without being aware of it — very humble at finding herself found — A blonde and inclining to the petite — not slothful in business fervent in spirit serving the Lord — My love to Mr Cooper and my respectful regards to the family — Ever thine   Horatio G

Addressed: To / S F B Morse Esq *PNA.* / &c &c &c / Poste Restante / *Paris*

NOTES

Manuscript: Morse Papers, LC. Previous publication (in part): Samuel Irenaeus Prime, *The Life of Samuel F. B. Morse, LL.D.* (New York, 1875), pp. **211–13.**

1. The Palazzo Capponi, in Via San Sebastiano (now Via Gino Capponi), was the residence of Marquis Gino Capponi. The Giardino Botanico, or dei Semplici, was one of the largest in the city.
2. W. Jackson, an agent at Rome, was engaged by Morse to pack and transmit certain casts and donations he had assembled for the National Academy of Design, but apparently had not done so (Morse to Jackson, 28 April 1831, Samuel F. B. Morse Papers, LC). Greenough's later reference in this letter to the sum lost by the Academy and to unreliable Italian agents is probably also in connection with this matter. Jackson continued to act as a commercial agent in Rome for many years (John Murray, *A Handbook of Rome and its Environs* [London, 1858], p. xxiv).
3. Persifor Frazer (1808–80), of Philadelphia, was educated for the law but spent much of his time in leisure abroad (Persifor Frazer, *Notes and Papers of or Connected with Persifor Frazer in Glarslough, Ireland, and his Son John Frazer of Philadelphia, 1705 to 1765* [Philadelphia, 1906–7], 1:85–86).
4. Morse sailed for America from Le Havre on 1 October 1832 (Prime, *Life of Morse*, pp. 234, 240, 250).
5. Cooper considered returning to America with Morse but did not go until September 1833 (Cooper, 2:268, 353).
6. This sentence is the title of a poem in Thomas Moore, *Sacred Songs* (London, 1816).
7. *Soignée*, "carefully done."

49.   To Samuel F. B. Morse
3 June 1832

Florence June 3rd 1832.

My Dear Morse

As I write this almost immediately after reading yours of the 24th Ult'o you will not be surprised at incoherence or any other symptoms of a topsy turvy state of mind — I have as strong a *gizzard* as most folk but a coldness came over me as I read your good news[1] — excuse my *material* and undignified way of saying how much I was pleased. I presume Mr Cleveland[2] was mistaken in what he said of the equestrian statue. However, be it as it may, here's work and care and all the material of life for several years with the hope being enrolled among the American *Old Masters* if I do not sink under the burthen — Prosperity is indeed hard to bear. I do not think she attacks me however in a very ruinous shape — The thousand adders that have so long crawled about me have turned to a big serpent merely —

Will I come to Paris? Cruel invitation — My Medora ties me — You know Gilmor's generous treatment of me — Until he's served here am I — Lead us not into temptation. Besides I wouldn't suffer again what I did before in leaving Paris for the world[3] — I'll explain all this to you one day or night when we shall have forgathered somewhere in America our heads white and our hands dry but can say no more just now.

The Cholera is past and all's well and if the Courier Francais is to be trusted 20,000 is a cheap price for a change in the cabinet[4] — The *particular* view of these pests; famines and battles is grievous but the general one if we *could embrace* it is full of kindness as any of the more pleasing phenomena — This is pretty philosophy — especially as you all escaped the scythe — I'm afraid that "escaped" will shock your nerves. However you know my meaning is good and will overlook inadvertancies.

I have just finished the model of a bust of Mr Miles[5] — I have done your pen drawing likewise and only wait an opportunity to send it you — It was done mainly in the winter evenings without models and is a failure in so many respects that I would burn it were there not in it a proof that I have not neglected your request. Shew it I pray to none but Cooper and to him by candle for that's the light it was born in —

Willis is here and is very comfortably lodged over me — He's hard at work getting (as Cooper would say) in at the cabin windows of the Art. Verily it is harder for a camel to go through the eye of a needle than for a very accomplished young gentleman to write about what he knows little of and make it worth reading. Willis is pleasant and clever surely, but he's too much dressings and stuffing — *altogether* too much red pepper by the by for our moral latitude — The *Quomodo* is his idol rather than the quid[6] — and on that rock he may split unless his good sense and penetration are favourably developed — He's delighted here but I don't think he'll continue so —

Gore has been very sick and is still feeble — his studies want of exercise etc have affected his liver — he's in the best hands and has begun to mend.

Crank is wide awake and has done 2 very good heads from the life. A Mr Ritchie[7] of Boston is industrious at the Academy and promises fair. I'm proud of my Henry though he's not bilious enough — Cole and Alexander are expected;[8] your message to C shall be conscientiously *stated* — though I shall reserve the priviledge of holding on to him if possible for you're rich as Rothschild in company while I am poor. The plan of going home together is constructed on the nicest principles of the beau ideal —

Heidenmauer is in the press I see[9] — I look for it with eagerness — I have a proposition to make — that you and Cooper travel to Switzerland this summer say in July and I'll do the same. I hear Cooper is half inclined to do so. As for yourself I only want the plains of Italy stretched right fair before your feet to secure you for two years — I need your company I want your support I must have your advice. You have gotten me into this scrape among you and you're bound to help me out of it

> If ever I love an only son
> And he to that love shall be true,
> Of love, his duty shall be done,
> When he loves me as I love you—

That's quaint an't it? I'm always verse mad in the Spring — but get over it as soon as the strawberries cherries and other *opening* fruits ripen. I always hide these concoctions, however and pray you'll burn this without delay. I asked you in my letter the other morning to advertize for me — now if I'm impertinent sometimes you've spoilt me by your indulgence. I'll behave better next time — Where is that windmill Brisbang! I've always had some how or other a presentiment that he would *develope* trouble for himself — Pray forward the letter addressed to me — what did the man mean by an order? Does he rely on my signature rather than your word —? — You mention Col Aspinwall. Does he come lately from London? and if so will you do me the kindness (if you know him well) to ascertain from him the circumstances of my brother?[10] I have written and rewritten but all in vain and God knows I would have given my own blood if I could have thereby saved him from want — Mention this to *nobody* as you love me and ask the Col as for your own satisfaction if you feel at liberty to do so — Give my love to Cooper and present my respectful though heartfelt thanks to the family for their kind sympathy — My instances in behalf of our Academy will be worth more than formerly — there are one or two things which I propose to present myself as soon as I shall have *earned* the right to give — Adieu. Yours with all affection

Horatio Greenough

Items for the Gentleman at the office if he can understand it. I don't know the title of the clerks at the office.

Monsieur Je vous prie de vouloir bien remettre à Mons Morse une lettre à mon addresse qui doit se trouver actuellement au bureau.[11]

Horatio Greenough

Addressed: To / S F B Morse Esqre P.N.A. / &c &c &c / Poste Restante / Paris.

NOTES

Manuscript: Morse Papers, LC.

1. Apparently Morse had written that the letter from Secretary of State Livingston officially notifying Greenough of the Congressional resolution to have him execute a statue for the Capitol had been received by the U.S. minister in Paris.
2. Henry Russell Cleveland (1808–43), educator and classical scholar, was at this time attached to the U.S. legation in Paris (E. J. and H. G. Cleveland, comps., *The Genealogy of the Cleveland and Cleaveland Families* . . . [Hartford, 1899], 2:1072–73).
3. This is probably a reference to Greenough's reluctance to leave Cooper and Morse in December 1831. See Letter 37, paragraph 5.
4. Casimir Périer, the French prime minister and leader of the Liberal party, died of cholera on 16 May. The *Courier Français* had opposed his policies.
5. Nothing further seems to be known of this work.
6. *Quomodo,* "How"; *quid,* "why."
7. Possibly John M. Ritchie (see Letter 41, n. 14).
8. From Rome.
9. Cooper's novel *The Heidenmauer* was published in Philadelphia on 25 September; in London on 19 July 1832 (Robert E. Spiller and Philip C. Blackburn, *A Descriptive Bibliography of the Writings of James Fenimore Cooper* [New York, 1934], p. 73).
10. John Greenough.
11. "Sir, I pray you to be so good as to give Mr. Morse a letter addressed to me which should be found now at the office."

50. To Robert Gilmor, Jr.
   10 June 1832

Florence. June 10th 1832 —

Dear Sir

Your kind letter of Feb 29. has lain unanswered several days owing to the press of my affairs. The letter of which you speak as having been enclosed to Mr Harper[1] and as having been probably lost, was duly rec'd, though it would seem that my answer to it has not been equally fortunate.

I feel the highest gratification in learning that your confidence in my ability has not abated and I thank you for the useful proof you give me of your esteem by advising me for the future — I think with you that he who abandons the principles of study which have raised him to the execution of important works deserts himself — Surely it would seem impossible that a successful experiment should be abandoned merely on account of its success — yet my observation tells me that it is but too often the case and justifies your caution — Besides convinced as I have always been of this truth I shall confess to you that what you have said by recalling my attention to the subject and adding the seal of your authority to the conclusions of my own reason, has strengthened me not a little.

I have lately purchased several articles for you which I think will please you and am only waiting until a small case is filled to send them — The profile of Mrs Gilmor in shell, was at last finished by the kind assistance of Mr Cole, and though not so fine as I could wish, is the best that could be procured.[2]

I am giving the finishing touches to the Medora — This statue pleases here and has attracted many English to my studio — You will soon judge of it yourself — I shall ship it to New York or Boston as occasion may offer — for opportunities at Leghorn for the Southern cities are rare — I should be highly gratified if you would allow the statue to be exhibited first in Boston — I think I am sure of its reception there — I of course am still more desirous that you should be *perfectly* satisfied so that should you prefer its being transported immediately to Baltimore you will I am sure do me the favour to advise my brother Alfred

Greenough to that effect — I have directed him to order a pedestal made for the statue should you be willing to have it shewn at Boston — With regard to the receipts of the exhibition, though I am not sanguine, still I think I am sure of being able by means of it to repay you *agreeably to my promise all I have drawn on you for, over and above the sum of $500* — I do not of course include the price of pictures or other works purchased for you though God knows my Dear Sir I would fain fill your collection with chef' d'oeuvres — nor should I feel that I had done more than my duty toward you — You took me by the hand when I was inexperienced and poor and in ill health. I am not a man to forget these kindnesses — I have hithertoo been silent because I have been so poor ever since I have been abroad that I looked with a suspicious eye on my own gratitude lest it might seem to have somewhat of hope for the future as well as of love for the past — but now that I find myself commencing a career of profitable employment for Government with enough of honour if I succeed to satisfy any ambition, I may speak to you more freely. I may beg you to believe me yours not in the language of compliment but in that of truth and believe me dear Sir the power of saying this is not among the least pleasing consequencies of the improvement of my fortune — I have been baulked lately of 2 fine pictures for you owing to the news of my commission's having taken wind here among the dealers — I am sure they think I am buying for myself — I shall be obliged hereafter to make use of another in making my bargains — Desiring you will present my respectful compliment to Mrs Gilmor as also to Mr Harper and his amiable family[3] I remain Dear Sir

> Yours Truly
> Horatio Greenough —[4]

Addressed: To / Robert Gilmor Esqre / *Baltimore*
Endorsed: Horatio Greenough / ans'd 27 Sept'r

NOTES

Manuscript: Mellen Chamberlain Autograph Collection, BPL. Previous publication: Nathalia Wright, ed., "Letters by Horatio Greenough in the Library," *Boston Public Library Quarterly* 11 (1959): 82, 85–86.
    1. Charles Carroll Harper (see Letter 30, n. 6).
    2. Apparently it has not been preserved.

3. Mrs. Harper was Charlotte Chiffelle, a niece of Mrs. Gilmor's (see Letter 20, n. 8).

4. On the remaining half of the manuscript page, below the signature, appears Gilmor's notation: "It [*Medora*] was exhibited in Boston and profitably for Greenough. I tried the [American] academy in New York with Trumbull and failed in getting someone to undertake its exhibition; I then applied to Rubens Peale who had the Museum in Broadway opposite the Park, but I couldn't induce him to undertake it. In returning [?] home, I applied [in Philadelphia] to [James] Earle to have it exhibited in his and [Thomas] Sully's rooms and failing them also, tried [James] McMurtrie to get it exhibited in the large gallery where [Benjamin R.] Hayd[o]n's picture was but no one would risk the exhibition though I offered them one half the receipts. When I was obliged to bring it to Baltimore I got a person in Market Street to exhibit it for a share of the receipts. I gave Greenough the rest when he expressed himself well satisfied. RG."

Rubens Peale (1784–1864) was a museum manager and still life painter, the son of Charles Wilson Peale. James Earle was a carver and gilder. Benjamin R. Haydon (1786–1846) was an English painter and writer, whose work *Christ's Triumphal Entry into Jerusalem* was exhibited at the American Gallery from 1831 to 1846.

51. To Nathaniel Niles
    12 June 1832

                                                   Florence — June 12. 1832 —

Dear Sir.

I received your letter of May 11th yesterday and was a little surprised at learning that it was not accompanied by any parcel or package whatever — I have since been told that in consequence of the Documents[1] you mention being enclosed in a tin case they have undoubtedly been forwarded as merchandise and will arrive here in the course of Five or Six days — I shall keep this letter open for a few days that I may acknowledge the rec't of these papers.

I beg you will accept my sincere thanks for the interest you have taken in my advancement as an artist and for the plan you had formed for bringing my improved abilities before the nation.[2] I am highly gratified at the manner in which you express yourself on the subject of the order of the Government but I should do myself injustice were I not to confess to you that I look on this commission rather as the fruit of the esteem and hope of a few intelligent lovers of art than as the harvest of my own labours as an opportunity rather granted than won —

I am grateful for the offer of your kind offices and will avail myself of it with the same frankness with which you have made it. If I can serve you or any friend of yours here I beg you will command me. Begging you will present my respectful regards to Mrs Niles

I am Dear Sir Your Obliged Friend
H Greenough

NOTES

Nathaniel Niles (1791–1869), physician and diplomat, was secretary of the U.S. legation in Paris from 1830 to 1833.
    Manuscript: E. Maurice Bloch, Los Angeles, California.
1. For these documents, see Letter 53, n. 1.
2. Presumably Niles' proposal to have Greenough execute a colossal head of Washington, to be paid for by several patrons (see Letter 39).

52.   To James Fenimore Cooper
   28 June 1832

Florence. June 28. 1832 —

My Dear Sir

I have a long and not very pretty story to tell about Maria[1] but will make it as short as possible — Several weeks after I took her into my service I was robbed of a large mannikin cloth of kerseymere and the muslin shroud of Medora — This exploit lay between her and the woodman who with his boy were the only persons who had entered the room where these effects were — I attributed it to the boy — he being a *guercio*[2] and otherwise illfavoured — I employed these people no longer and continued my reliance on the good faith of Maria — It is true that I detected her from time to time in fibs — such as accounting for her absence by the sickness of her lord when I had met the gentleman in the street. But this I looked on as a thing so general here that it would have seemed — a miracle had it been otherwise — Six weeks since 2 pairs of pantaloons were stolen from the window where they were drying and I then began to look about me — I took into my service an old fellow who had been my drudge before and who having been sick offered to serve me for his food and clothing — The presence of this man in the kitchen was irksome to Maria — She became ill humoured — impatient — impertinent — Seeing that she could not dislodge the man she changed her politics and caressed him — about a week since after I had put every article of value in my house under lock and key, her husband came to me told me he had something of importance to communicate and ended by informing me that Maria had introduced into my house, during my absence, a female friend of hers to assist her — that this female friend had appropriated several articles belonging to me and that he had overheard the whole account she gave to her better half of the transaction — On my questioning Mr Fleetwood he described to me the cloth and the pantaloons — I now saw something wrong — it seemed strange that he should have overheard this thing so long after it took place — it seemed impossible that Maria could have introduced anybody during my absence into the house, for I have never been gone long — But I was confirmed in my disbelief of his testimony when he urged me to take him instead [of] the man who is with me — and when he assured me that he would remain here all night even with pleasure — I looked upon him as fearful that his wife would lose her place and willing to fib to save it for her — I still persisted in thinking that I might keep along with her untill this morning when I was informed by my landlady that a friend of hers who had seen her enter the house supposing that she came to her — cautioned her against quella Napoletana[3] as a suspicious person — I feel it my duty under these circumstances to get rid of Maria as a servant — if I can do anything for her without endangering myself or my friends I shall be happy — I have thought it my duty to lay this before you partly because I promised Mrs Cooper that Maria should want nothing which it was in my power to procure her — partly because she told me with a menacing air that she meant to write you and I would fain put you on your guard as to her representations.[4]

I am well and very busy — I find that the statue for the Rotunda will require a height of at least 12 feet — I am anxious to see what turn mat[ters] [page torn] take [page torn] a war might interfere with the execution [of] [page torn] the work — I have expected letters from

Morse with some anxiety of late — he fell into bad hands in sending
home his casts — that is made clear by the accounts of some people
lately arrived here at least as far as the character of the man is concerned — I would give some thing that [you] could see my Medora. I
think it would please you — I am now modelling a Genius of America
for Mr Hoyt — Your bust is cutting from a block which seems a lump
of virgin wax. I shall make the mouth from the old one if you conclude
not to return here. With desire that you will present my respectful
compliments to Mrs Cooper and the family I remain Dear Sir

Yours truly
H. Greenough

Addressed: To / James Fenemore Cooper Esqre / Care of Mess Welles
& Co Bankers / Paris.

NOTES

Manuscript: Cooper Collection, Beinecke.
1. Maria Fleetwood was a former servant of the Coopers, whom Greenough
   had employed in December (see Letter 38).
2. "Squint-eyed one."
3. "That Neapolitan."
4. For Cooper's reply to this letter, see Cooper, 2:267–68.

53. To Edward Livingston
8 July 1832

Florence July 8th 1832

Hon Edward Livingston / Secretary of State
Sir

Your letter of Feb'y 28th together with the accompanying documents[1] were duly received and have occupied my attention until now.

The hope of being found worthy to execute a statue of Washington
for one of the great cities of my country, has been my support through
years of solitary study in a foreign land. I have looked forward to such

an honour as the reward of a life of toil and sacrifice — I will not dissemble the confidence I have felt of the support of my countrymen at some future period, though I feared that there existed among them a diffidence of the national capacity in art; which could only be removed by persevering and successful demonstration — I accept this great opportunity with surprise at finding myself so early known and with joy that I am thought worthy of the task.

I propose to give the Statue together with its pedestal an elevation of about Twenty-five feet from the floor of the hall — I say *about,* for though I have fixed on Fifteen feet as the height of the statue itself, experiment alone will enable me to decide on that of the pedestal.[2] This size, without encumbering the hall, will fill the eye at every part of the same and the features will be recognizable even from the door of the great entrance — To make the figure less, would be to risk the effect of the whole by producing a diminutive appearance. I agree with you that the square form will be the best for the pedestal and I am confident that the effect of this quadrangular body will be happier from its being enclosed by a circular wall — Had the cylindric form any advantages (and I know of none), I should think it worth while to sacrifice them rather than to repeat the form of the hall in its embellishments — Nature constantly sets us the example of varying shapes which are to be embraced together by the eye — I am much pleased that Houdon's bust was mentioned in the Resolution as my authority for the features of Washington[3] — I have always used it from choice — I thank you for the liberty with which you permit me to understand the directions on this point and I believe I shall have occasion to profit by it.

The model of this statue will occupy at least a year — probably eighteen months. The bas reliefs will require at least three months in the clay — We will allow three months for drying the casts and transporting them to the quarries — The rough hewing and taking of the points will require ten months, the finishing will consume the residue of Four Years.[4]

I have been able to avail myself of the experience of an artist who has executed a statue of dimensions similar to those I have mentioned[5] and am willing to undertake this work for the sum of 20,000$ to be paid in annual instalments of 5000$ each — This is little, if at all more than Canova received for a statue of little more than the size of life[6] — The transport of such masses of marble and plaister and the number of assistants necessary to maintain the proper degree of moisture in the clay & to waste the useless stone — render the increase of expence more than proportioned to the increase of size.

If you will permit me I would wish to transmit you from time to time drawings of my compositions for this work — It seems to me that a statue of Washington in that situation should not be a mere image of the man to gratify curiosity, nor a vain display of Academic art, but an embodying of his spirit — The accessories should be stamped with the character of our institutions — They cannot instruct perhaps, but they may impress and confirm. The Historic facts to be recorded on the pedestal are of a different character from the statue as regards the art and I think they should be so[7] — Truth will be my first object in these. I mean by truth in this connection, not all that was, but nothing that was not. I shall adopt the dress of the time and secure as many portraits as are preserved —

Accept kind Sir my warmest thanks for your interest in my success — Believe that in exertion I will be true to my country — and that I fully feel that if I prove worthy of this task I shall not have lived in vain — I have the honour to be with respect Your most obedient Servant

Horatio Greenough

Endorsed: Greenough Horatio / Florence, 8th July 1832 rec'd 8th September / will execute the statue of Washington / for Dollars 20,000. / To be published with my / letter to him

NOTES

Edward Livingston (1764–1836), New York statesman, was U.S. secretary of state from 1831 to 1833.

Manuscript: RG 59, General Records of the Department of State, Accession 161, Item 135, NA. Previous publication: *Boston Daily Evening Transcript,* 25 September 1832; *New York Evening Post,* 1 October 1832; *New-York Mirror,* 20 October 1832; *Niles' Weekly Register,* 27 October 1832; and in other periodicals.

1. Livingston's letter (copy in RG 59, General Records of the Department of State, Domestic Letters, NA) officially informed Greenough of the resolution passed in the House of Representatives on 16 February authorizing the President to employ him to execute a statue of Washington for the rotunda of the Capitol. With it came a copy of the resolution and a plan of the rotunda. The letter was published in several periodicals in 1832, including the *New-York Mirror,* 21 July; the *Boston Daily Evening Transcript,* 27 September; *New-England Magazine* 3 (September 1832): 260–61; the *New*

York Evening Post, 1 October; and *Niles' Weekly Register,* 27 October.
See also U.S. Congress, House, *Statue of Washington,* 27th Cong., 1st sess.,
1841, H. Doc. no. 45, pp. 2–3.

2. He finally made the statue eleven feet, four inches. The original height of
the pedestal was apparently about eight and a half feet.

3. Jean Antoine Houdon (1741–1828), French portrait sculptor whose works
are noted for their realism, made the only life mask of Washington and
executed in marble a bust and full-length statue of him. The resolution
stipulated that the head of Greenough's work be a "copy" of Houdon's
(U.S. Congress, House, *Journal,* 22d Cong., 1st sess., 1832, p. 342), but
Livingston wrote that this requirement "was for the purpose of securing a
good representation of the features" and "it is presumed will not restrict
you to a servile copy, should the action of the figure, which you are at
liberty to choose, require a more animated expression of countenance."

4. For the amount of time these operations actually consumed, see Letter 143.

5. Greenough probably refers to Bartolini and his colossal statue of Napoleon,
executed between 1811 and 1813 and erected at Bastia on Corsica in 1853
(Mario Tinti, *Lorenzo Bartolini* [Rome, 1936], 1:181; Ashton Rollins Willard,
History of Modern Italian Art [London, 1900], pp. 71–72).

6. Canova received $10,000 for the statue of Washington which he executed
for the North Carolina State House in Raleigh between 1815 and 1821
(R. D. W. Conner, *Canova's Statue of Washington,* Publications of the North
Carolina Historical Commission, Bulletin no. 8 [Raleigh, 1910], p. 7).

7. Livingston had suggested that the faces of a quadrangular base might be
ornamented with bas reliefs representing the surrender of Yorktown, Washington's resignation of command of the army, his inauguration as President, and
"an inscription."

54.   To Samuel F. B. Morse
19 July 1832

Florence, July 19, 1832.

Yours of the 9th reached me yesterday and stopped my grumbling.
I could find but one excuse for your silence, and that was too painful
to be admitted, even as a conjecture, viz., that you had been drawn by
the crowd into some tremendous row, and made a revolutionary
figure at the expense of all your friends. I don't doubt you will profit
by your exhibition,[1] and I have every hope of your receiving some
handsome commission. I have written to the Government my terms; if
they are accepted I shall have a proposition to make. We will have a
knot of us here, which shall form an epoch, by the beard of Jupiter

[e flaminis]!² I see by the papers that some fellow has attacked me, says I'm an educated man, allied with *literati*, and possess every means of doing myself honor;³ it's a heavy charge, is it not? I suppose he hints I have not made use of these advantages; but he's too quick, let him wait a little. All this is as it should be; let 'em spare my character, and they may call me dunce to doomsday, and I'll be half ready to say, amen! As to going home in October, I'd give my little finger to do so, but I don't think it possible.

If I can muster the cash I'll come to say good-by to ye as far as Paris; but I'll say beforehand that I shall be a blockhead, for I know I shall come moping back with a face as long as an ox-bow. So Cooper is gone to take another pull at Johannisberg;⁴ much good may it do him; God bless him! I begin to doubt if ever I shall leave Italy; they write me that artists stand as ignorantly with the public as ever. If I return it will be to marry and become citizen, and I won't do that unless I can stand on fair ground. I've just modeled a statue half the size of life. Here he is: "The Genius of America" holding out the bud of promise and pointing to posterity. I made such a mess with the head in small that I have done it larger, to give you a little notion of the expression.⁵ I must close this. Crank is in Venice, with W. and Alexander;⁶ W. is not a man after my heart; he is corrupt, depend on it; I have been obliged to haul off, for he assumed intimacy of the closest kind. Cole⁷ is painting away up-stairs; Gore is recovered. My love to Cooper, and my respectful saluta-tion to the lilies of his household. Thine till the Dr.⁸ has had his wicked will of me.

Horatio Greenough

NOTES

Source: Samuel Irenaeus Prime, *The Life of Samuel F. B. Morse, LL.D.* (New York, 1875), pp. 214–15, 216.
1. Presumably Greenough refers to a proposed public showing of Morse's *Exhibition Gallery of the Louvre* in America. The work was unsuccessfully exhibited in New York for several weeks in the fall of 1833 (Carleton Mabee, *The American Leonardo* [New York, 1943], pp. 157–58).
2. "Jupiter of the wind." Prime has "Flaminius," which is probably a mis-reading of the manuscript.
3. An article in the *Boston Daily Evening Transcript* for 4 May 1832 urged the self-taught Connecticut sculptor Hezikiah Augur to put himself in competi-tion with Greenough, declaring that Greenough's reputation was much ex-

aggerated and explaining the matter thus: "His residence in Italy, his intimate acquaintance with the most popular American writers who have
chosen to expatriate themselves, and whose personal friendship he has acquired in Europe, have been the means by which he has acquired a notoriety,
that is daily increasing both abroad and at home."

4. This village near Mainz on the Rhine, celebrated for its wine, was on the
route which Cooper took with his family on a vacation to Belgium and Switzerland (Cooper, 2:273–348).

5. See Plate VI.

6. John Cranch, N. P. Willis, and Francis Alexander went to Venice together
about this time.

7. Cole had returned from Rome in June and remained in Florence until his
departure for America in October 1832 (Thomas Cole, *The Course of
Empire, Voyage of Life, and Other Pictures of Thomas Cole . . . ,* ed.
Louis L. Noble [New York, 1853], pp. 166–75).

8. The person to whom Greenough refers has not been identified.

55. To Samuel F. B. Morse
20 August 1832

Florence, August 20, 1832.

My eyes have been opened painfully, within a year, to the perception
of the light in which artists are held, *all the world over.* In Italy they
deserve it. You can speak of France and England better than myself;
but, in America, they do not deserve it. They are quite equal in knowledge, and light, and character, to the mass of the most refined classes,
and are totally above the rabble. You have had a proof, in your own
experience, how completely the title of artist throws into the shade the
qualities and the virtues which ought to have secured your pride from
any wound. Your experience, then, will make you (as you are a man)
safe in future. I know Congress too well to think much better of the
prospects of art now than I did formerly. 'Tis not the money we want,
'tis the consideration and weight. The money comes then, of course,
as it does to men of other respectable callings. Now, I choose to reside
in old Europe, and live secluded, and try to respect myself, rather than
be waiting at the doors of the rich, at home, for the vain, or patronizing,
or pitying proofs of their superabundance. If I am disappointed of my
statue, off I go to Germany. If I do not get the order, good-by to the

drudgery of the trade. I will make one statue, and go about my business, i.e., provided the country remains as ignorant on this point as now. Let me beg of you to hang on to the conception of the *departure* and *return* of Columbus. You are perfectly qualified to do honor to the country in such works, and should never give up the plan. Hang on like Columbus himself. You could make the first a grand picture in character and effect of composition; you would embody in the second all your scheme of color and *chiaro-oscuro*. These subjects are yours, you are theirs; have faith, and fear not. Cole is driving through, to get ready to go home, next month, *via* Leghorn. He intended to have remained here another year, had commissions in abundance, and was under full sail, when he got news of sad domestic affliction, sickness, and (you know the other word),[1] so, like the glorious fellow he is, he sent home his spare cash, and is getting ready to follow it, to struggle with all your difficulties, and mine, with a family on his shoulders. He has painted several things of high merit, and a *"Campagna di Roma,"*[2] which is a master-piece in the middle and back grounds. Cole knows as well the value and power of art as any man, and only wants the *puo sto*[3] to be a great man in art. Will he ever get it? I hope so; but, if he does, Fortune will give it him, without raising her bandage from her eyes.

So you are going home, my dear Morse, and God knows if ever I shall see you again. Pardon, I pray you, any thing of levity which you may have been offended at in me. Believe me, it arose from my so rarely finding one to whom I could be natural, and give loose, without fear of good faith or good-nature ever failing. Wherever I am, your approbation will be dearer to me than the hurrah of a world.

I shall write to glorious Fenimore in a few days. My love to Allston and Dana. God bless you!

H. Greenough.

NOTES

Source: Samuel Irenaeus Prime, *The Life of Samuel F. B. Morse, LL.D.* (New York, 1875), pp. 215, 217, 218.
1. Cole left Italy sooner than he had planned because of the news he received of an epidemic of cholera in New York and of the illness of his parents (Thomas Cole, *The Course of Empire, Voyage of Life, and Other Pictures of Thomas Cole . . .* , ed. Louis L. Noble [New York, 1853], p. 170). By

"the other word" Greenough presumably meant "death," an allusion to the
recent death of Morse's first wife.

2. Probably Cole's *Roman Aqueduct,* painted in Florence in 1832. It is now in
the Metropolitan Museum of Art.

3. *Puosto,* "post," "position."

56.   To James Fenimore Cooper
22 August 1832

Florence — August 22nd 1832 —

My Dear Sir —

You have of course rec'd my former answer to your proposal[1] — I
have only to add that it was not until this morning that I rec'd through
friend Samuel's kindness, the news of the bills having passed the
Senate[2] — without which I could not have thought of leaving Florence
and which comes now too late, as you will be sailing, probably, before
I could have time to finish my *jobs* and be with you — Had I *known*
of this commission 6 months since, I would have prepared myself to
return — It would have been the greatest of gratifications to me — but
I am now engaged until winter probably — for 2 months to come certainly — I am mortified that you should go away my creditor for so
heavy a sum as 1100 francs.[3] I shall send my brother[4] an order to pay it
you or to whom you please in Boston, as I trust I shall by the time you
arrive, have credit through my commission, if not money from my
Medora — To have seen you before you sailed would have been a great
comfort — I shall soon become a Vox clamantis in deserto,[5] for Cole is
going home too and Gore is about to leave Florence — I fear I shall not
see you again for a long time — I see your situation in America with
different eye from yours — I'm but a boy I know but my colpo d'occhio[6]
is not bad and I think you must have been bilious when you wrote —
not that I don't know — there is working at home the stuff which lies
atop here — but I think it's more imbecile and unripe than you seemed
to feel — Two months will dissipate all those clouds[7] — I hope and
trust — I have leaned very hard on you my dear Sir — but if you consider what I have attempted and with what means you will believe
that I have borne myself too as much as my knees would stagger

under — Well! I hope all is now clear — Let us see if we can show Jonathan that art is a noble vehicle of national gratitude and glory and that a man may be an *artist* without being ergo a blackguard and a mischievous member of society. Alston and Morse they say are exceptions of a high order — I can tell 'em that Alston and Morse have made the rule. I have 2 things to beg of you — that you will make me and mine useful to yourself & your friends or acquaintances — and that you will write me as often as you can find it for your pleasure — I do not wish to bore you but believe me it will give me more pain than I would inflict on any body not to hear sometimes from you — of — how you do — and how your family does —. I have many things to say but may not — What is 5 or 6 years after all? The next will not seem like the last I fear — God bless you — will you Present my respects to Mrs Cooper and the family — Horatio Greenough —

Addressed: To / J. Fenemore Cooper Esqre / Care of / Mess Welles & Co / Bankers — / *Paris.*

NOTES

Manuscript: Cooper Collection, Beinecke. Previous publication (in part): James Fenimore Cooper, *Correspondence of James Fenimore-Cooper,* ed. James F. Cooper (New Haven, 1922), 1:284–85.
  1. In his letter to Greenough of [14?] July 1832 Cooper suggested that Greenough go home with him and asked for a reply to this suggestion by the first week in September (Cooper, 2:268). Greenough's "former answer" has not been located.
  2. The resolution authorizing the president to employ Greenough to execute a statue of Washington was accidentally passed as a House bill instead of a joint congressional bill. When it came to the Senate in April, the Senate objected that the House could not act independently in the matter and struck out the appropriation clause. A joint resolution was then introduced on 25 April; it passed the Senate on 26 June and the House on 14 July.
  3. That is, the $500 borrowed in February and March 1831 and the $600 borrowed about January 1832. In his letter of 21 September 1832, Cooper told Greenough: "You are unnecessarily punctilious about our little money transactions. Return me what you have borrowed at your entire convenience" (Cooper, 2:335).
  4. Alfred Greenough.
  5. "Voice crying in the wilderness."
  6. "Point of view."
  7. In his letter of [14?] July 1832 Cooper had proposed, sarcastically, to ingratiate himself with his fellow countrymen by eulogizing aristocratic principles, referring to the criticism of him in America precipitated by his

Letter to Gen. Lafayette (1831), in which he presented evidence that the government of republican America was more economical than that of monarchical France. He concluded: "I am heart-sick and will say no more on the ungrateful subject" (Cooper, 2:268).

57. To James Fenimore Cooper
18 September 1832

Florence Sept 18. 1832 —

My Dear Sir —

I drew on you yesterday for the sum of 500 Francs — to keep along above water — I have rec'd a letter[1] from Mr Everett in which he informs me of the whole proceeding relative to the statue — and that all is now ready on that side the water — I have therefore the prospect of soon seeing you and paying you with out which I hope you will believe that *nothing* should have forced me to call on you as I have done —

My present intention is to go to Paris for a few weeks that I may secure certain books prints and casts which I have long wanted — but I cannot do this for 2 months to come at least —

I have too much to say about the statue for this bit of paper — I am full of plans and attitudes and conceptions but have as yet firmed nothing — nor shall I till I have had a grand talk or 2 with you and one with an artist or so —

I beg you will be easy about the size of my figure[2] — The Baptistery here is just about as large as the Rotunda and from the length and volume of the grand altar I'm confident that 15 feet will not be too much to fill the eye — like a great summer cloud — He'll be all alone remember — to drop into the little would spoil all — The jupiter of Phidias[3] was so large that could he have risen from his throne he would have stove the roof of the temple — I shan't go quite so far you see as authority could be had for — I beg you will present my respects to Mrs Cooper and the family and am Dear Sir

Yours
H Grin.ho!

Addressed: To / J Fenemore Cooper Esqre / À Vevay en Suisse.

NOTES

Manuscript: Cooper Collection, Beinecke.
1. Dated July 29, 1832 (collection of David Richardson, Washington, D.C.).
2. In his letter of [14?] July 1832, Cooper had written that he and Morse thought that Greenough's proposed height of twelve feet for his statue was too large, suggested that nine or nine and a half feet would be better, and wondered if Greenough should not go to America to examine the proposed site (Cooper, 2:268).
3. The statue of Zeus made by Phidias for the temple at Elis in Olympia, counted one of the Seven Wonders of the World, did not survive to modern times. According to ancient accounts it was seven or eight times the size of life (Quatremère-de-Quincy, *Le Jupiter Olympien, ou l'Art de la Sculpture Antique* [Paris, 1815], pp. 268 ff.).

58.   To James Fenimore Cooper
      Between October and 18 December 1832

My Dear Sir
   Allow me to present to you my friend Col A. P. Hayne of Carolina[1] a gentleman whose intercourse has been a great pleasure to me during his stay here in Florence — Like yourself he is a staunch American and like yourself he has done me the honour to give me his confidence as an artist —
   I feel myself flattered in being the medium of an acquaintance which I feel must be mutually satisfactory and am Dear Sir

                                   with respectful affection
                                            Yours
                                   Horatio Greenough
J. Fenimore Cooper Esqre / Rue S Domenique — S. Germain / Paris —

Addressed: J Fenimore Cooper Esqre / Rue S. Domenique S. Germ / Col A. P. Hayne — No 59 —

NOTES

Cooper returned to Paris, to which this letter is addressed, on 11 October, after a three-month vacation with his family. In his next letter to Cooper, dated 18 December 1832, Greenough inquired if Hayne had reached Paris.

Manuscript: Cooper Collection, Beinecke.

1. See Letter 46, n. 3.

59. To Samuel Cabot
   12 November 1832

Dear Sir

It was my intention to have seen you this evening but I have been prevented by the weather — I have thought it best therefore to write you the terms on which I am willing to undertake your groupe,[1] that you may have time to decide upon it at leisure — My price for the groupe will be 700 Tuscan crowns[2] — the half as is customary to be paid in advance — The remainder when the case is shipped —

For Mr Cooper's groupe I rec'd (exhibition included) about $600. — For Mr Gilmor's statue I have rec'd $700, of which I am to repay $200 on its being exhibited — You will observe that the production of my statues has more than consumed the prices paid for them — though my domestic establishment has been always of the most economical — I have only to add that the price of the bust[3] will be 100 Tuscan crowns — I ought perhaps to desire you not to mention the above particulars relative to Mr Cooper's and Mr Gilmor's statues — I have mentioned them merely to shew you that though I have increased my price I have done it but just enough to save me from what I endeavour constantly not to deserve — Debt. I am Dear Sir

Yours with respect
Horatio Greenough

Nov'r 12th 1832 —

Addressed: A Mons / Monsieur Cabot / *Casino Schneiderff*[4]

NOTES

Samuel Cabot (1784–1863), Boston merchant, took his wife and two children abroad in 1832 after the death, at the age of two, of their third child (L. Vernon Briggs, *History and Genealogy of the Cabot Family, 1475–1927* [Boston, 1927], 1:283–310). They were in Florence from 21 October to 20 November 1832, and again from 9 March to 15 March 1833 (Diary of Samuel Cabot, 1832–33, Samuel Cabot Papers, MHS; Diary of Thomas Handasyd Cabot, 1832–33, MHS). Manuscript: Samuel Cabot Papers, MHS.

1. A few days after his arrival in Florence, Cabot ordered from Greenough a small marble group of an angel leading the soul of a child to heaven, which was variously called *Ascension of an Infant Spirit, Ascension of a Child Conducted by an Infant Angel,* and (by Greenough) *Journey to Heaven.* Executed in 1832–33, it is now in the Museum of Fine Arts, Boston.
2. A Tuscan crown had the same value as a francescone.
3. Cabot also ordered a marble bust of his nine-year-old daughter Elizabeth. It is now in the possession of Dr. George Shattuck, Brookline, Massachusetts.
4. The house next to the Schneiderff Hotel.

60.   To Samuel Cabot
17 December 1832

Florence. Dec 17th 1832 —

My Dear Sir

Your letter of the 11th inst. reached me three days since — some little delay has been unavoidable in procuring information respecting pictures. I shall transmit your order for the chimney pieces by tomorrow's post. I shall bargain to have them delivered in Leghorn to your agent as considerable expence in duty and transportation will thus be saved — by way of caution however I shall tell the workman that they will be seen by you at Carrara previous to their being sent.

I have been much struck with the simplicity and elegance of your rooms in form and arrangement — I like much the project of a niche — It is almost necessary indeed, for the protection of the work from accidents — Nothing will be lost — for as you remark the statues should be placed on a turning plinth — I should prefer the situation marked by dotted lines were the groupe to be seen by day. But the other is

preferable at night on account of narrowness of the wall on that side —
by day it would sacrifice the work as it is between the windows. I
should say 5 or 6 feet for the height of the niche — 3 feet in breadth will
be necessary and if you can command 18 inches of depth I think it will
be so much the better though a foot would answer if you cannot.

I should be most happy to do any thing to shew my sense of Col
Perkins' kindness to me but the present commission rather adds to my
obligations.[1] You could not do me a greater pleasure at any time than
to ask me to buy pictures. It is a great satisfaction to me to find employment for deserving young men. I have opportunities for knowing
the cleverest among them and have seen hard times enough in my day
to sympathize with their eagerness to unite improvement to profit. The
proprietor of that fine copy of the Madonna D. S.[2] has already been
offered 70 Louis for it. He has a noble piece of dead game which he
will sell for 200 crowns and I think might be induced to take 130 or
140 for it. Do you remember the Dante consigning his Poem to a friar?[3]
That picture Bezzuoli has formerly offered to sell for 200 crowns. I
think I can give you your choice of 2 copies of the Rubens[4] at the Pitti
on your return without your being *expected* to take either — In a few
days you may hear from me again on this subject of pictures —

I have rec'd for you Mr Pisani's[5] handwork — it is very pretty — He
took the 45 crowns at which I must say I was surprised —

My brother has already removed to other lodgings and is gaining
strength daily. He joins me in presenting his respect to you as also to
Mrs and Miss Cabot and your son

Yours truly
Horatio Greenough

Sam'l Cabot Esqre / Rome.

Addressed: Samuel Cabot Esqre / Care of F. C. Cicognani — U.S.
Consul / *Rome.*

NOTES

Manuscript: Samuel Cabot Papers, MHS.

1. The "present commission" was probably Cabot's group *Journey to Heaven.*
Presumably Cabot, Perkins' son-in-law, brought a message from him to
Greenough, but about what is not known.
2. The *Madonna della Sedia* by Raphael is in the Galleria Palatina in the
Palazzo Pitti.

3. This work has not been identified.
4. Rubens is represented by several paintings in the Galleria Palatina, the most celebrated being *The Four Philosophers* and *The Consequences of War*.
5. Possibly Leopoldo Pisani, sculptor and worker in alabaster (*Guida per la Città di Firenze e suoi Contorni* [Florence, 1852], p. 258).

61.   To James Fenimore Cooper
18 December 1832

Florence — Dec 18th 1832 —

My Dear Sir —

I learned from a letter of Brisbane's received this morn'g that you expect me in Paris this winter — It was my intention to have gone though a little later — I should have gone with Brisbane but I waited the definitive answer of Mr Livingston — which by the by has not yet arrived — I learn also with the highest pleasure that you and yours are perfectly well — I have had a painful occupation for the last 3 months but all is well that ends well — B—— I dare say has mentioned to you how ill my brother has been — I had him moved to my new quarters[1] a few days since and he is I may say recovered — I have received an order for a groupe similar to yours in which I propose to represent a young angelic figure conducting a babe to the other world — The points of expression will be the contrast between the ideal forms and face of the cherub and the milky fatness and shew-baby, half doubting, half pleased look of the child — I shall be paid 700 Francesconi for this work. I mean if my circumstances will permit it to exhibit it gratuitously — I have received also several orders from your friend Col Thorn[2] who is however so occupied in *living* that I fear it will be some time before he can find leisure to come to arrangements — I'm at work on your bust at present. It is the prettiest stone in my rooms and is far advanced. I have been sadly disappointed in not being able to finish Com Biddl's Washington as soon by 3 months as I had hoped to do — But I hope he will excuse it when he learns the reason. What do you hear of Morse? Is his academy above water still? Will he return to Italy — The American Consul made a blow a few days since which I think worth relating for the *character* it displays — There was a family of Bells[3] here from Philadelphia to whom it would seem he was factotum. Among other things they requested him to conduct them to see my studio — Whew! a Year since he used to answer such requests by stating that Mr Greenough was a strange sort of a man! — rather odd! — and that he had rather be excused — on this occasion however he sent a servant into the study to ask if certain Americans could see the rooms — I said certainly — Open went the doors — Good morning to you Mr Greenough — This is Mr Bell — and his daughter — etc etc — It was upward of 2 years since I *had seen* the man and I was taken by surprise — Had it not been for a pretty little American face under the bonnet at his elbow he should not have passed it so sugarly *I reckon.* They say he has inherited property lately — I hope it is true — he is a man who ought never to be without ample means. I wish to come to Paris much — But shall probably be detained here now for several months — I wish to secure a cast of the model of Washington which is in Gen Lafayette's possession[4] — He was kind enough to offer it — I think a squeezing (or calque as the French say I believe) might be made without the slightest danger to the model — Peale set my portrait up at auction the other day.[5] That was pretty was it not? I'll be bound now he hadn't the slightest idea that he was doing any thing at all indelicate. — You may remain in Paris all the next summer Brisbane says. Will you let me know if this is correct for I must go there before the summer is past and would fain arrange it so as to see you — How do you progress in the little room — where we sat with Morse one night and had such a grand discussion of the means of renovating art? have you made another book?

The Jarvis'[6] are here and are very useful — They give us prayers on a Sunday and waltzing — tea and cakes on Wednesday. The Dr is the same fat oily man of God — sleek as oil itself — but reminds me too strongly of what Rev. Dr Gardner[7] said of him ever to gibe — and that was that he was too d——d slobbering in his manner — I heard a sermon there the other morning very well read indeed — Have you seen one Col Hayne of Carolina? I gave him a letter to you — he asked it — I wrote you apprising you of it but have rec'd no news (directly) of you since.

The number of Americans here is quite unprecedented — They are from all parts of the country — We have had a rumour here of the loss of the Constellation[8] frigate among the Greek islands. Will you mention in your next if it be true for we shall never know from the papers at this distance of time —

I am quite curious to see the progress Master Paul has made since he and I foregathered. Present I pray you my respectful compliments to Mrs Cooper and the family and believe me Dear Sir Yours truly

Horatio Greenough

F. C. Cooper Esqre

Rue St Domenique — S G I shan't forget the number as long as I live —[9]

Addressed: J Fenimore Cooper Esqre / Care of Mess Welles & co / Bankers — / *Paris.*

NOTES

Manuscript: Cooper Collecton, Beinecke.

1. Casa Ximenes, 6718 Borgo Pinti.
2. Herman Thorn (1781–1859) of New York was purser of the *Wasp 18* in 1809 and 1810 when Cooper was attached to it. He lived much of his life abroad. In later years, after coming into money from his wife's family, he was an ostentatious social figure; his lavish entertainments, richly dressed attendants, and frequent quarrels over small charges were often reported in newspapers (see, for example, the *Boston Daily Evening Transcript,* 1 September 1836, 9 October 1845). (Joseph O. Brown, *The Jaunceys of New York* [New York, 1876], p. 22; *New York Evening Post,* 1 August 1859.)
3. Possibly members of the family of Henry Bell, a miller, whose son Samuel became a prominent merchant in Philadelphia. Presumably the party included a Mary Bell and her daughter, who were in Rome during the latter half of 1833 (Leo Francis Stock, ed., *Consular Relations between the United States and the Papal States* [Washington, 1945], 1:38–39).
4. A copy of Houdon's bust.
5. It was eventually acquired by the Greenough family.
6. Samuel Farrar Jarvis (1786–1851) was rector of St. Paul's Episcopal Church, Boston, from 1820 to 1825. He went abroad in 1826 and remained in Europe until 1835. See Franklin Bowditch Dexter, *Biographical Sketches of the Graduates of Yale College,* 5th ser. (New York, 1911), pp. 770–79.
7. John Sylvester John Gardiner (1765–1830) was from 1805 to his death rector of Trinity Episcopal Church, Boston.
8. The *Constellation* was one of the vessels in the Mediterranean Squadron, maintained from 1815 until the Civil War, which regularly patrolled Levantine waters. During the 1820's and early 1830's those waters were the center of extensive piracy. The ship was not lost, however. It saw service in the Civil War, and in 1894, was made a stationary ship at Newport, Rhode Island.
9. "S G": "St. Germaine." Most of Greenough's letters written to Cooper while

he was living at this address, including this one, have the name of Welles &
Co. cancelled and the street address added, presumably in another hand.
Evidently Greenough frequently did forget Cooper's street number.

62. To James Fenimore Cooper
29 January 1833

Florence — Jan'y 29th 1833.

Dear Mr Cooper

I have not heard from you since you left Switzerland except indirectly — I learned however from Brisbane that you were well some
weeks since — Excuse my calling your attention again to the Statue —
Mr Livingston rec'd my letter — he published it — Six months and upward have elapsed yet I get no answer[1] — Could you do me the favour
to learn through some friend what they mean to do about it — I can't
begin without money — Delay will be of no service to them and very
distressing to me — I would fain have avoided importuning any body —
but my friends here tell me that those official gentlemen sometimes
require the spur[2] —

I am somewhat in a quandry whether I ought to fix myself here
during the execution of this work — I fear I may become anchored for
life — Still I see many obstacles to the study and exercise of my art in
the States — The choice of country in this case amounts to a choice of
life — Like the ass between 2 bundles of hay I cast my eye from
continent to continent and sigh that I can't plant one foot in the
states and the other on the boot — chisel here with one hand and hold
up to the christening font there with the other. Hithertoo I have
trodden on every sprouting inclination which threatened to shade or
encumber my profession — shall I change tactics? Pray give me your
advice — I seek it seriously because I think I have reached one of those
cross roads of life where the choice of path has a great influence on
subsequent happiness — I hear Friend Brisbang has a new eye[3] — I
think we must call this his metaphysical eye — He told me gravely
that he meant to make "that *social tact* for which the French are so
remarkable" the subject *of careful study* this winter. Dei immortales!

The Yankees are at this moment all at court. Oh tempora! Willis they say makes quite a figure. He goes to Rome shortly — whether it be with a thorn in his side I know not though I fear he has sighed for a *thorn*[4] — The talent dates report friend Samuel with a hard belly ache but nothing serious — What say you of Carolina? I think I see *symptoms*, but don't apprehend any thing fatal yet.[5]

I had written thus far when yours of the 19th inst reached me[6] — I'm in hopes there will be no bloodshed — what a responsibility those men in Carolina are taking upon themselves! I can't tell you what the Italian Gazettes say. I never look at them — Republic or no Republic John Bull never need look for any thing very consolatory to his vanity on our side the water — *I reckon* — I find my colossus sits heavy on your stomach still — The hall is 76 feet high and 96 feet wide — There's my ground Sir — go into the Louvre, find a room of that dimension and imagine the statue. It won't be heavy — depend on't. You would be amused to see the effect produced here among the artists by the rumour of commission. I find myself provided with a set of friends and foes in a jiffey — I know not which incommode me most — It is not pleasant to eat with hungry fellows looking through the window at you. I could tell you some droll things — Basta[7] — My journey to Heaven groupe is far advanced — I feel confident it will take quite as well at least as the former one — Angels never wear clothes you remark[8] — This comes strangely from *you* — I never saw one that was not dressed and very tastefully too — I make 'em both stark naked — The conversation that passed between me and the gentleman who ordered the groupe was a scene — I fought hard and carried the day — the little fellows are to be provided with alabaster fig leaves which shall fall at a tap! of the hammer when the discerning public shall have *digested* the fruit of the knowledge of good and evil.

Kinloch is living here under the same roof with me. He is the oddest and at the same time the best fellow in the world — There's no nullify about him — I assure you he tr[em]bles [*page torn*] for his *niggers* — I think with reason —

It makes me melancholy to hear you talk of writing your last Romance[9] — You mean to give way —? I didn't know there was any body to take it — Still if you would turn your attention to one or two thorough legitimate national comedies I think you would put the topmost stone on the pyramid. Posterity! There's the quid for you to chew while the curs are barking. On the whole I think you have better reason to be contented with your lot than any American who never entered public I mean official life — Will General Lafayette allow me a calque of his bust of Washington — Jaquet[10] can do it without risk and I find it difficult to procure a good one in America — If I get money I come to Paris in May — If not I go to the ———— in June at farthest — With respects to Mrs Cooper and the family I remain dear sir

Yours truly.

H Greenough

Addressed: To / J Fenimore Cooper Esqre / Care of Mess Welles & co / Bankers / *Paris.*

NOTES

Manuscript: Cooper Collection, Beinecke. Previous publication (in part): James Fenimore Cooper, *Correspondence of James Fenimore-Cooper,* ed. James F. Cooper (New Haven, 1922), 1:307–10.

1. See Letter 53 and n. 1 to that letter. The delay was caused by the fact that President Jackson had understood $5000, the amount of the first installment, to be the total cost of the work and had referred the approval of the sum to Congress to be considered at its next session.
2. For Cooper's reply to this part of Greenough's letter, see Cooper, 2:370–73.
3. Brisbane had apparently acquired a monocle (Cooper, 2:371).
4. Willis was apparently flirting with one of the five daughters of Col. Herman Thorn, famous for their beauty and wealth (Joseph O. Jauncey, *The Jaunceys of New York* [New York, 1876], p. 22).
5. A state convention called by the South Carolina legislature in November 1832 had declared the tariff act null, and when President Jackson proclaimed the state had no power to do so, a volunteer military force was raised. Conflict was averted by the passage of a compromise tariff.
6. In this letter Cooper asked what Greenough thought of the situation in South Carolina, what the Italian gazettes said of it, and speculated that England might side with the southern states against the national government. He also commented again about the proposed height of Greenough's statue: "Thirteen feet seems to me to be a devil of a pile of stone to put into the rotunda" (Cooper, 2:368).
7. "Enough."
8. Cooper had written of Greenough's group, *Journey to Heaven,* for Samuel Cabot: "I do not know that angels wear clothes and I know nothing superior to fine displays of the human figure, but I distrust the effect of your contrast" (Cooper, 2:368).
9. Cooper had written: "I am nearly half through my last romance [*The Headsman*], for the pen and I have quarrelled. The country is getting to be too big for men of my calibre. I must give way to my betters, of which it would seem to be full, by their *talk*" (Cooper, 2:368).

10. Presumably Georges Jacquot (1794–1874), French sculptor, who studied in
    Rome and Florence from 1820 to 1826.

63.   To James Fenimore Cooper
10 April 1833

Florence April 10th 1833.

My Dear Sir

Allow me to present to you my friend Lieut't Auchmuty[1] of the U.S.
Navy who has been passing the winter in Florence and is on his way
to America.

My friend will give you an account of the Americano-Italian colony
here — which is still flourishing — Lest you should not have received
my last I will repeat that Chatelain's copy[2] is sold — Desiring my best
respects to Mrs Cooper and the family I remain

Dear Sir
Yours truly
Horatio Greenough

J Fenimore Cooper Esqre / Paris —

Addressed: J Fenimore Cooper Esqre / Rue S. Domenique — S. G. /
No 59. / Lieut Auchmuty — / Paris.

NOTES

Manuscript: Cooper Collection, Beinecke.
1. Henry J. Auchmuty (d. 1835) became a midshipman on 10 May 1820 and a
   lieutenant on 17 May 1828. Apparently he retired to a farm in Westchester
   County, New York, in 1834 (*Letters,* pp. 93–97).
2. His copy of Raphael's *Transfiguration.* Greenough's "last" letter to Cooper
   has not been located.

64. To James Fenimore Cooper
15 May 1833

Florence — May 15, 1833.

My Dear Sir

I received the day before yest'y a letter from Mr Livingston[1] inform-ing me that the President accepts the conditions on which I offered to make the Statue and enclosing a warm letter of introduction to Mess Baring Brs & co — My earliest care is to refund to you the sums of money you have from time to time advanced me — These sums I find debited as follows.

Decemb'r	1831	F 500
Feb'y	1832	300
July	1832	300
Sept	1832	500
		F 1600[2]

I shall take the opportunity of the departure for Paris of my friend Mr Wall of New Bedford to send you this sum — As for the seven Francesconi with which I had credited myself at your order, I send that also to stand to my account for bankers' commissions and I beg you will retain a note of how much you paid Mess Welles for the above 1600 as I of course mean to defray all expences —

When and Where shall I see you? I have questions to ask. I have plans to shew. I want your aid — My Medora is gone[3] but to divert my melancholy I have set up an Achilles[4] of 7 feet which will I fear nail me for the summer — I am in hopes to get Lord Normanby's theatre[5] for a work room — Do You come to Switzerland this season? If so I'll see you, come what will of it — I have been very hard at work of late — 5 months more will see me free of all small jobs — Will you remain in Europe yet until autumn? If so I have a favour to ask of you a favour which Morse promised me but which I suppose he was too much occupied to remember — What is he about? — Mrs Cooper I learn is improved in health — will she not *persuade you* to defer y'r return home for the present. I had slily made all preparations for decamping myself but was prevented by finding Mr Cabot expected his groupe would be finished as early as possible in which he was perfectly right — I should like that you should see my Achilles — he's a whacker — I must conclude. I have a hundred letters to write and a model waiting my order to undress — Is Mr Harris[6] minister? Where is Mr Niles?[7] I beg you will remember me to Mrs Cooper and the family and believe me Dear Sir

Yours
Horatio Greenough —

PS   In case you should be absent from Paris I shall direct my friend to pay Mess Welles for your account. —

Addressed: To J Fenemore Cooper Esqre / Care of Mess Welles & co / Bankers. / *Paris.*

NOTES

Manuscript: Cooper Collection, Beinecke.
1. Livingston's letter to Greenough of 30 March 1833 was published in U.S. Congress, House, *Statue of Washington,* 27th Cong., 1st sess., 1841, H. Doc. no. 45, pp. 3–4; a copy is in RG 59, General Records of the Department of State, Domestic Letters, NA.
2. The five hundred francesconi which Greenough borrowed from Cooper in February and March 1831 were not included in this total, presumably because that sum covered the transportation of *The Chanting Cherubs* to America, for which Cooper said he would pay. In his reply of 13 June to this letter of Greenough's, Cooper said that any charges for the loan were out of the question (Cooper, 2:384).
3. It was shipped about this time (see Letter 68).
4. This work was evidently not completed. For Cooper's comments on it, see Cooper, 2:384.
5. In his residence, Palazzo San Clemente in Via San Sebastiano (now Via Gino Capponi).
6. Levett, or Leavitt, Harris, who had served as U.S. consul and as chargé d'affaires in St. Petersburg, was at this time chargé d'affaires in Paris.
7. Here Greenough drew a profile, presumably of Niles.

65. To James Fenimore Cooper
28 May 1833

Florence. May 28th 1833.

My Dear Mr Cooper —

I wrote you on the 9th inst.[1] to say that I should forward to you the sum of 1600 fr by my friend Mr Wall of New Bedford — finding however that my friend was going to Venice and would perhaps spend some weeks on the road I have obtained from Mr Kinlock an order on Welles for the amount above mentioned and have only to beg that you will make a note of what you paid for these monies that I may make it up to you. (Of course I suppose there were commissions etc). I have written you several time[s] [*page torn*] but hear nothing of you — I am about to take a run to Leghorn to see 2 [*page torn*] of [*page torn*] there — I'm so lean that I'm afraid my bones will com[e] th[rough in go]od [*page torn*] earnest and all from pure comfort and happiness — [I] [*page torn*] have been so long working away without knowing what was to become of me in 3 months from any given time that I lose my identity when I set about a job with every means and appliance — If you'll come down our way I shall be happy — however I suppose your family rather draws you in the other direction — I meant to have been with you ere this but the fact is that I had despaired of doing any thing this year about the statue and so put an Achilles 7 feet high which it would be wrong to leave — I feel a great void under my waistcoat — I suppose I always shall — Did you ever feel really satisfied? Where is Morse? I must conclude for I have all my travelling arrangements to make — Pray present my respects to Mrs Cooper and the family.

Yours
Horatio Greenough —

F Fenimore Cooper Esqre Paris.

Addressed: To / J Fenimore Cooper Esqre / Care of Mess Welles & Co / Bankers. / *Paris.*

NOTES

Manuscript: Cooper Collection, Beinecke.
1. A mistake for the 15th.

66.   To William Allen Wall
[May?] 1833

My Dear Sir
  Having a disagreeable cold I beg you'll excuse me today. — if you'll come to my house and smoke a cigar I should be happy to have y'r comp'y.

Yours truly
Horatio Greenough

Addressed: W. A. Wall — Esqre — / *Present.*[1]

NOTES

William Allen Wall (1801–85), a landscape painter from New Bedford, Massachusetts, was in Europe from 1831 to 1833. He was in Florence in May 1833 (see the first paragraph of Letter 64).
  Manuscript: Charles Roberts Autograph Letter Collection, Haverford College Library.
  1. *Presente,* "in this city."

67. To Edward Livingston
24 July 1833

Florence July 24th, 1833.

Hon Edward Livingston / Secretary of State
Sir

In the month of May I rec'd from the Department of State a letter informing me that the President accepted the conditions on which I offered to make the Statue of Washington for the Rotunda of the Capitol and enclosing a credit on Mess Baring Bros London for Five Thousand Dollars, being the first annual instalment. In the month of June I received a Duplicate of the same. I accept the conditions stated in the above document relative to the refunding any sums rec'd by me from the Government, in case of my death or inability before the work shall be commenced; as also that in case of my death or inability to proceed after the statue shall have been commenced, the same shall be delivered to the Government in the state in which it shall have been left by such demise or inability.

I shall be happy in furnishing the Department from time to time with drawings of the several plans and compositions for the work.

I remain Sir
With respect
Your Most Ob't Serv't.
Horatio Greenough

Addressed: Hon. Edward Livingston / Secretary of State — Dept of State. / Washington.
Endorsed: Rec'd *Sept 26*

NOTE

Manuscript: RG 59, General Records of the Department of State, Accession 161, Item 135, NA.

68.   To Robert Gilmor, Jr.
   25 July 1833

Florence July 25th 1833.

Dear Sir

Your statue[1] is probably now arrived in America, as it was shipped more than six weeks since. It has been executed amid many distractions — its progress has been interrupted by many accidents. I have never allowed myself to bestow on it my jaded or ineffective moments. It has been a great object with me to perfect it. I now leave it to yourself and to the Public to judge it. In placing it I beg you will let it receive the light at an angle of from 25 to 30° — I trust you will agree with me that the light should be one, and even that veiled.

I am preparing to ship 3 pictures which I have purchased for you — A portrait of M Angelo, which though probably a copy, is I think by one of the Alloris[2] — I consider it a highly valuable picture as do all the connoisseurs and artists who have seen it. Two Landskapes on copper by Zuccherelli the master of Wilson.[3] The English continue to appropriate by force of money the best of every thing that turns up in the way of pictures. I shall continue to be on the alert, but cannot say I have high hopes of any thing choice at present. I have been this summer much employed on a statue of Achilles 7 feet high, but have been interrupted by an attack of small-pox, from which I am at present convalescent. I shall soon send you my plans for the Statue of Washington and beg you will favour me with your opinions of them.

I annex an account which I believe to be exact, of the several sums which I have from time to time rec'd from you and of what I have expended for your account. I make my account in Francesconi or Tuscan crowns which are $\frac{1}{20}$ more than the Spanish dollar. You will observe that the 100$ for which you sent me an order on Mess Grant & Co on the acc't of Mrs Gilmor's bust was incorporated with the 500$ which I drew for the statue — I wish no further recompence for that bust as the model was so munificently paid.

Francesconi		Francesconi	
1830. 17 March – drew	95	⌠Statue of Medora	475
——— 23 July.	251	⟨Copy of Salvator Rosa . .	10
——— 20 Dec.	65	⌡Battle pieces on slate. . .	2½
1831. 8th April	116	Case for do	1
——— 23 July.	50	Picture by Albano	112
1832. 4 Feb'y	100.	case and expenses . . .	4
——— 17 Aug't	50.	Carvings on ivory wood &c	4
Drawn.	727.	⌠Portrait of M Angelo . . .	7
Rec'd less commissions	7.²⁄₁₀	⟨2 pictures by Zuccherelli .	60
Your credit	719.⁸⁄₁₀	Case and custom house exp	2
		Your Debit	677½

$$719\tfrac{8}{10}$$
$$677\tfrac{5}{10}$$

Balance due to you $42\tfrac{3}{10}$

You [will] [*page torn*] inform me if my account stands true to your
payments to Mess Grant & Co – if not I consider myself bound to make
up every deficiency, as I am more likely to [have] made an error or
omission than they.

I have never seen any thing like Mr Derby's Venus.[4] Should I find
time I will try to make one myself. I have rec'd a letter from Mr Miller[5]
at Paris. I am impatient for his arrival here. I have several times heard
of your being ill – With request that you will present my compliments
to Mrs Gilmor I remain Dear Sir – Your Obliged Friend & Serv't.

                                                    Hor. Greenough

Addressed: Robert Gilmor Esqre / Baltimore.
Endorsed, in Gilmor's hand: H Greenough / ansd. 8. Oct 34

NOTES

Manuscript: Charles Roberts Autograph Letter Collection, Haverford College
Library.
1. The *Medora.*
2. There were three Italian painters named Allori: Alessandro (1535–1605) and
   his son Cristofano (1577–1621) of Florence, and Angiolo (1502–72), a
   painter and poet born near Florence. Cristofano and Angiolo were more
   noted for portraiture than was Alessandro.
3. Francesco Zuccherelli (1702–88), Tuscan landscape painter, spent many
   years in England. Richard Wilson (1714–82), English painter, turned to

landscapes after Zuccherelli admired one of his early attempts in this genre during his sojourn in Italy.

4. See Letter 30 to Gilmor and n. 8 to that letter.

5. Alfred Jacob Miller (1810–74), portrait and Indian painter, spent several months in Italy at this time. His diary contains an account of his visit (diary in possession of L. Vernon Miller, Baltimore).

69. To Samuel F. B. Morse
18 November 1833

Florence, November 18, 183[3]

. . . . I have finished my design for the statue in clay, half [the] size of life, and the drawing will in a few days be ready to send to Washington. I have had the greatest difficulty in finding a place big enough to do the work in. At one time I feared I should be obliged to go to Rome; however, I am at length suited, and shall have my man-mountain up by the close of February, if not sooner. I will give you a [sketch][1] to convey a general notion of the composition.[2] I can't say I have fixed any thing, still it will require strong reasons to change the general action it has seemed to me characteristic of the man. I had and still have the notion of making him hold the sword, as in the sketch on the other leaf, but I fear it will not be so distinct as I made it in the first sketch; the arm would almost entirely hide it, you observe, as seen in front. We shall see how it pleases at headquarters. I suppose Mr. Cooper is with you before this:[3] God bless him! Pray, ask him to write me, if it were only a few words; I should be so happy to see his hand once more. . . .

H. G.

NOTES

Although Prime dates this letter 1832, it must have been written in 1833, since it refers to Greenough's clay model of his *Washington*, completed in the fall of 1833, and to the drawing of the model, sent to Secretary of State Livingston on 28 January 1834 (see Letter 73).

Source: Samuel Irenaeus Prime, *The Life of Samuel F. B. Morse, LL.D.* (New York, 1875), pp. 218–19.

1. Prime has "scratch," probably a misreading of the manuscript. For the sketch, see Plate VII.

2. The letter to this point was printed in the *New York Journal of Commerce*, 11 March 1834, with slight variations from Prime.
3. The Coopers arrived in New York on 5 November 1833 (Cooper, 3:3).

70. To William Dunlap
1 December 1833

Florence, Dec. 1st, 1833.

Dear Sir —

Your letter, introducing Mr. Fay,[1] was presented to me by that gentleman, in person, the day before yesterday. You will be happy to learn that he has entirely recovered his health. He has taken a comfortable and pleasant apartment for the month. I look forward to the winter with less dread, in hopes of enjoying his society. I beg you will rest assured, that my best services, in behalf of any friend of yours, are at your command. The nature of my occupations prevents me from personally assisting strangers here so far as I could wish; but I can always command a few moments, to attend to the necessary, the indispensable.

I thank you for the opinion you express of what little I have done in the art of sculpture: I have not yet had the time to do much. I fear that the circumstances under which I began my career will ever prevent me realizing my idea of what sculpture should be. Still the effort may be useful to future artists, and yield some works of a relative and special value. I cannot pretend to occupy any space in a work consecrated to American art. Sculpture, when I left home, was practised no where, to my knowledge, in the United States. I learned the first rudiments of modelling from a Frenchman, named Binon,[2] who resided long in Boston. My friends opposed my studying the art; but gently, resonably, and kindly. It would require more time than you would find it profitable to spend, to listen to the thousand accidents that shaped my inclination to the study of this art. I might perhaps interest you more by mentioning the many instances in which I have been comforted, assisted, advised, induced, in short, to persevere in it by acquaintance and friends. I could tell you of the most generous efforts to assist me, on the part of men who scarcely knew me — of the most flattering and encouraging notice by elegant and accomplished women — but I might hurt or offend those who have so kindly helped me; and (what I shrink from also for myself), I fear there would be a fearful disproportion between the seed and the fruit.

Mr. Cogswell,[3] who now keeps an academy at Northampton, contributed perhaps more than any one to fix my purpose, and supplied me with casts, &c. to nurse my fondness of statuary. Allston, in the sequel, was to me a father, in what concerned my progress of every kind. He taught me first how to discriminate — how to think — how to feel. Before I knew him I felt strongly but blindly, as it were; and if I should never pass mediocrity, I should attribute it to my absence from him. So adapted did he seem to kindle and enlighten me, making me no longer myself, but, as it were, an emanation of his own soul.

Dr. [G.] Parkman,[4] during my sophomore year, proposed to assist me in obtaining some knowledge of anatomy. He supplied me with bones, preparations, &c. every week; as also with such books as I could not get from the college library. He not only continued this kindness during the three years of my remaining college life, but lent me generous assistance in forwarding my studies by travel. I began to *study* art in Rome, in 1826. Until then I had rather amused myself with clay and marble than studied. When I say, that those materials were familiar to my touch, I say all that I profited by my boyish efforts. They were rude. I lived with poets and poetry, and could not than see that my art was to be studied from folk who eat their three meals every day. I *gazed* at the Apollo and the Venus,[5] and *learned* very little by it. It was not till I ran through all the galleries and studios of Rome, and had had under my eye the genial forms of Italy that I began to feel nature's value. I had before adored her, but as a Persian does the sun, with my face to the earth. I then began to examine her — and entered on that course of study in which I am still toiling.

Fenimore Cooper saved me from despair, after my second return to Italy. He employed me as I wished to be employed; and has, up to this moment, been a father to me in kindness. That I ever shall answer all the expectations of my friends is impossible; but no duty, thank God! extends beyond his means.

I sigh for a little intercourse with you, gentlemen, at home: I long to be among you; but I am anchored here for the next four years. I will not risk a voyage before my statue is done. I think it my duty not to run away at the first sight of the enemy.

When I went, the other morning, into the huge room in which I propose to execute my statue,[6] I felt like a spoilt boy, who, after insisting upon riding on horseback, bawls aloud with fright at finding himself in the saddle, so far from the ground! I hope, however, that this will wear off. Begging you will remember me kindly to our common friends, and particularly to wicked Morse,

I am, dear sir,
Yours, truly,
Horatio Greenough.

NOTES

William Dunlap (1766–1839), playwright, theater manager, painter, and historian, spent most of his life in New York, where Greenough met him in 1828. In 1833 he was assembling material for his *History . . . of the Arts of Design in the United States* and had requested that Greenough give him an autobiographical sketch.

Source: William Dunlap, *A History of the Rise and Progress of the Arts of Design in the United States* (New York, 1834), 2:420–22.

1. Theodore Sedgwick Fay (1807–98), author and diplomat, went to Europe with his bride in 1833 and spent most of the rest of his life there. He was in Florence from the fall of 1833 to the summer of 1834, and described his activities during this period in a series of travel letters called "The Minute-Book" which were printed in the *New-York Mirror* in 1834 and 1835.
2. John B. Binon executed a bust of John Quincy Adams and at least a model of a bust of Washington (Binon to Adams, 21 January, 3 February, 2 May 1819, MHS; Adams to Binon, 7 February 1819, 11 October 1821, Adams Papers, MHS; *New-England Palladium & Commercial Advertiser*, 30 March 1819; the *Boston Directory*, 1820).
3. Joseph Green Cogswell was at this time director of the Round Tree School, Northampton, Massachusetts. See note to Letter 152.
4. Dunlap has "J. Parkman."
5. The *Apollo di Belvedere*, and presumably, the *Capitoline Venus*.
6. Greenough executed his *Washington* in the villa in Via Piazzola, opposite the Collegio della Querce, now known as the Villa San Paolo.

71. To Washington Allston
8 December 1833

Florence. Dec 8th 1833.

Dear Mr Alston

I had hoped to have been nearer you by this but have concluded that it would be wrong to risk a long journey before my model is

compleated. I have heard of you often — but not so often or quite so
directly as I could have wished. Has not your picture from the
Italian been engraved?[1] I should like much to see the composition —
I learned with pleasure that you had declined a picture for South
Carolina on account of your engagements[2] — My poor brother Harry
after struggling against the influence of this climate has at length returned home — I know it will not be necessary to ask of you before
hand the favour of your counsel and assistance for him in prosecuting
the study of painting — but I think I can tell you in a few words what
you might not see at once — that he wants encouragement — not excitement for his fibre won't bear it, but gentle and soothing encouragement. To expect much of him seems to palsy him, to be pleased with
what he has effected frightens him less — He is good and pure of
heart to an uncommon degree. I can't squeeze out of my correspondents any satisfactory news of Mr Dana[3] — I trust Harry will give
me [a] treat in that way — The number of artists has much increased
in America within a few years — I begin to hope that we shall be
numerous enough soon to keep each other warm — I firmly believe
that — our claims to respect and encouragement are more fairly
viewed in the U States than elsewhere and I do not say this rashly —
In France they come nearest us but it savours of nationality perhaps
more than of the love of poetry. In Italy the mass with the finest
susceptibilities are too ignorant too corrupted to comprehend or feel
as they should — The English tone of Art seems to me a sickly exotic
— I can't speak of their real connoisseurs because I never have fallen
in with them except they were artists — but I have known a greater
number of educated refined English who did not care a pin for Art
than of every other nation put together. I have just seen the first
number of a National Portrait Gallery — in which is one of Harding's portraits — right well engraved — It has comforted me much —
The portrait is of Carroll and is excellent.[4] I shewed it at the coffee
house last evening and it surprised the Italians. This book reminds
me that Mr Dunlap wrote me he was also concerned in a work relating to art and Artists in America and he said he meant to speak of
me — asked the time and place of my birth and accounts of what
turned my attention to Sculpture. Now I have just begun to work
and to make my attempts a matter of public print further than the
news of the day seems to me to risk blowing up of a bladder for those
who are to follow to jump on — He says he has obtained much valu-

able information respecting art in [the] U S from you — I am delighted that a pen is at work in putting down what you have seen
and known of this — It will be invaluable — But I hope I do not ask
too much when I request you when you write him to say in a few
words the substance of what I feel on this point. If as a beginner in
the regular practice of Sculpture I have a local and temporary importance (which may be) he may easily say in a note of 30 lines all I
ever did. My pride more than any modesty is concerned in this. I
have made a model of 2½ feet of the Statue of Washington. I have
made him seated — looking straight forward — with a sheathed sword
in his left hand and with his right pointing to heaven. He is dressed
in a large mantle whose hem is embroidered with stars. He sits on a
massive chair ornamented with fruits flowers and Naval and Military
trophies — the large spaces on the back of which are filled by bas
reliefs representing virtues personified. The hind posts of the chair
are surmounted on each side by an Eagle — I shall try to have the
sketch pass through Boston on its way to Washington that you may
give me your opinion. I beg you will pity me as a sojourner in the
land of strangers — I am a poor land-bird at sea — I am tired — but
there is as yet no lighting place — I can't turn waterfowl — My notions
of men and things are just what they were when I sail'd. A few years
and I shall I trust sit by you and smoke and look out a window at the
trees and sky of Cambridge — It will seem but a moment then —
these months and years of absence — I hear nothing of John[5] — His
heart must be made of stern stuff. I only hope he will be true to himself since he seems to forget us — Naturally his impulses were generous and kind — but he was unfortunate — Begging you will present
my respectfull remembrance to Mrs Alston — to the Misses Dana and
to our Poet[6] who is become every bodies' Poet at last that you will
tell the Master than I pine to laugh and cry with him. I remain —
Yours truly — Horatio Greenough

Addressed: Washington Alston Esqre / Boston. Mass.

NOTES

Manuscript: Dana Papers, MHS.
1. No record of any such engraving seems to exist.
2. In April 1833 a committee representing the city of Charleston, South

Carolina, requested Allston to paint Joel R. Poinsett, first U.S. minister to Mexico, unfurling the American flag from the window of his house as he was about to be attacked by a mob, the purpose of the committee being to counteract sectional animosities by emphasizing the value of union. Allston declined the request, alleging a press of engagements (Flagg, pp. 263–67).

3. Probably R. H. Dana.
4. Chester Harding (1792–1866), portrait painter, had a studio at this time in Boston. Greenough met him in Washington in 1828. An engraving of his portrait of Charles Carroll (1737–1832), of Carrollton, Maryland, signer of the Declaration of Independence, member of the Continental Congress, and U.S. senator, appeared in *The National Portrait Gallery of Distinguished Americans. Conducted by James Herring, New York, and James B. Longacre, Philadelphia, under the superintendence of the American Academy of the Fine Arts* (New York, 1834), vol. 1, no. 3. Greenough visited Carroll with Robert Gilmor, Jr., in 1828.
5. John Greenough.
6. Elizabeth Ellery (1789–1874) and Sarah Ann (1791–1866) Dana were sisters of Edmund T. and R. H. Dana (Clarence Winthrop Bowen, *The History of Woodstock Connecticut* [Norwood, Mass., 1932], 4:235). By "our Poet" Greenough presumably refers to R. H. Dana, whose *Poems and Prose Writings* (Boston, 1833, 2 vols.) had recently appeared.

72. To Winslow Lewis
16 December 1833

Florence Dec 16. 1833.

My Dear Sir

I send you herewith a letter of introduction to our Consul at Rome[1] which may be useful to you in case of need — I return you also the map of the U.S. with many thanks for your politeness and desire that you will not pass through Florence on your return without coming to see me — Wishing you a pleasant journey I remain —

Yours truly
Horatio Greenough

Mr Lewis — / at Mad. Homberts.[2]

P.S. present my respects to your companion[3] and say I shall be happy to see him on his return.

Addressed: Mr Lewis — / at Mad Hombert's / No 19. —

NOTES

Winslow Lewis (1770–1850), a native of Cape Cod, inventor, and lighthouse builder, married Elizabeth Greenough, Horatio's aunt (John H. Sheppard, "Brief Memoir of Dr. Winslow Lewis," *NEHGR* 17 [1863]: 8–9).
   Manuscript: Mrs. Nina Howell Starr, Gainesville, Florida.
   1. F. C. Cicognani.
   2. Mrs. Fanny Hombert operated the Hotel Europa in the Palazzo Ferroni on the Piazza Santa Trinità (Federigo Fantozzi, *Pianta Geometrica della Città di Firenze* [Florence, 1843], p. 53).
   3. Unidentified.

73.   To Edward Livingston
28 January 1834

Florence. Jan'y 28. 1834.

Sir
   Agreeably to instructions received from the Department of State, I transmit you a drawing from the small sketch in clay of the Statue of Washington on which I am employed.[1] I trust it will be needless to explain at large that this drawing is not intended to shew what the statue will be in its several parts, but only to convey a general idea of the position, action and sentiment of the figure, its dress and the nature of its accessories.
   I have not represented any one action of the man, but have given him a movement which seems to me characteristic of his whole life. I wish while I impress the beholder with the idea of Washington, to remind him that Washington was an agent. I have chosen the seated posture as giving a repose not incompatible with expression. To have represented any one action would have been difficult from the nature of our art, its limits and the unity of person prescribed by the subject. For historic sculpture, bas reliefs and medals have great advantages over single figures, nor indeed can these be forced into that walk, without a sacrifice of their proper value and beauty.
   In the dress I have endeavoured to make the figure decent, dignified and simple. If on the one hand it be not the dress of Washington's time or nation, neither is it peculiarly the dress of any age or

people. It has not been without much reflection that I have set aside
the dress of Washington's time. I am aware of the value of truth in
the representation of the person of a great man — I feel that as an
honour to his memory it ought to perpetuate all that was really his
in his appearance; but it seems to me that the fashion of his dress
cannot be considered as such and where that fashion would interfere
with the main object of the work, by calling the attention to trifles, I
think it should give way to considerations of what is natural and
permanent. In looking at the portraits of some of the kings of France,
we forget the man in wonder at the size and structure of the wig.
And when we remark the volume and weight of the robes, the in-
convenient and uncouth forms given to every portion of the attire,
it is not our taste only that is shocked, our sense also suffers.[2] Such
in kind if not in degree must be the sensations of posterity in looking
at a literal representation of the dress of Washington's time. To yield
to scruples about misrepresentation and to follow out the principle,
would be to confine ourselves to the size of life instead of a colossal
dimension — to place the statue on a low platform instead of elevating
it on a pedestal, nor would the work be compleat until it were
coloured to the life. Wax figures dressed in real clothes but satisfy
these cravings after reality and how far they fully represent a person
dead or absent, may be left to the warmest advocate for matter of
fact to decide. We have lately seen that the popular feeling in France
required a literal representation of Napoleon in the statue placed
upon the column of the Place Vendome[3] — The case however was
different. Napoleon affected a practical simplicity of costume. The
dress became then a feature of character — The imperial robes had
been quite as literal in point of fact. Still I believe that when years
shall have passed away and the idea of the man shall have been con-
densed to the conciseness of a maxim (like that of Alexander or
Caesar) in the minds of the many, this costume will stand between
the beholder and the object of his interest and become disguise.

A middle course has also been recommended between the literal
and the ideal. It is said that the garments of the time may be sculptured, but so masked in the detail as not to be recognized at a certain
distance and thus it is affirmed, that we have the advantage of breadth
and simplicity at a distance, with all that is so dear to the antiquarian
on a close examination. This however plausible seems to me a mistaken view of the matter. No skill of the sculptor can make such a

statue at any distance, comparable in effect to one in which the drapery is arranged for the relief and harmony of the composition, while antiquarian curiosity is as much interested in the prominence of a buckle or a button as in its mere outline.

I consider my work therefore as addressing itself to a people who are familiar with the facts of Washington's life, with his character and its consequences, who have learned from books and tradition all that is to be known about him and I would fain sculpture an image that shall realize in form that complex of qualities which is our idea of the man, apart from what was common to him with other gentlemen of his day.

The square columns which support the chair behind, as also the continuation of the same above the cushion, are ornamented severally with garlands of fruit and flowers — military and naval trophies — implements of agriculture — commerce and manufactures. Since this drawing was made I have thought proper to change the footstool for a step — which will occupy the same space in breadth but will extend in length from one to the other side of the chair in front. I think also of changing the position of the left arm for a more extended one. In the head you will not look for a portrait as the drawing is made from a rapid sketch. In the statue itself I propose to give the hair its natural direction, as in the drawing it discords with the figure and in that form constitutes a portion of the costume of Washington's time.

I have to request that the drawing which accompanies this letter, may not fall into the hands of any engraver or lithographic draftsman, as it might if multiplied, give general false impressions of what the work will be. With a request that I may be favoured with such observations as may occur to the several gentlemen to whom you may shew this sketch

I remain Sir
With respect
Your most ob't Serv't
Horatio Greenough

Addressed: Secretary of State / Department of State — / Washington.
Endorsed: Rec'd May 14.

NOTES

Manuscript: RG 59, General Records of the Department of State, Accession 161, Item 135, NA.

1. In his letter to Greenough of 30 March 1833 (copy in RG 59, General Records of the Department of State, Domestic Letters, NA), Livingston had written that it would be "agreeable to the President" for Greenough to furnish the Department of State with drawings of his design for the statue from time to time. See Plate VIII.

2. Probably Greenough refers chiefly to portraits of Louis XIV. Hyacinthe Rigaud's painting in the Louvre and Bernini's bust at Versailles show him with an elaborate wig and voluminous garments.

3. The first statue of Napoleon I placed on top of the column, designed by Pierre-Nolasque Bergeret and erected between 1806 and 1810, represents the subject in imperial robes, resembling Caesar. It was taken down by the Royalists in 1814 and replaced by a large fleur-de-lis surmounted by a white flag. In 1831 Louis Philippe had a new statue put up, by Charles Émile Marie Seurre, representing Napoleon in a greatcoat and three-cornered hat. In 1863 this statue was replaced by a copy of the original one.

74.   To Samuel F. B. Morse
       24 May 1834

Florence, May 24, 1834.

My Dear Morse:

I am not displeased that my statue calls forth remarks;[1] now is the time to hear and profit by them. I trust I shall be found open to conviction and desirous to learn; but I fear the making a statue of this kind, requires more attentive and instructed thought than most of our able men can spare from their occupations. I am pleased that the *artists* find my design significant. Your hint, or rather Mr. King's hint, about the constitution, is surely valuable; and if the object of the statue were to *instruct* people about Washington, it might have been anticipated by me. To put into his hand a scroll or a book would be easy; but as books are very like each other on the outside the meaning would be uncertain; and doubt in a statue is feebleness. We raise this monument because Washington's face and form are identified with the salvation of our continent. That sword, to which objections are made, cleared the ground where our political fabric was raised. I would remind our posterity that nothing but that, and that wielded for years with wisdom and strength, rescued our rights, and property, and lives from the most powerful as well as most *enlightened* nation of Europe. I look on the military career of Washington as being, though not perhaps *his* highest glory — *our* greatest obligation to him. I can conceive of his having died at the close of that struggle without any very bad consequences to our institutions. But a sword in the hand is an access[o]ry which adds little to the *contents* in any way; in art it is important. If people would consider the abstract nature of sculpture — its elements — its limits — they would cease to look to it for information on points which are better explained by other arts in other ways. They would as soon expect to hear Washington's dress described in a 4th of July oration as to see it sculptured in an *epic* statue. It is to the *man* and not to the gentleman that he would do honor. To embody in the work the abstract of a political creed, or the principles of a political party, might ensure protection for my work just now. But just now I can do without it. — I am pleased that you and your friends think my composition, in the main, significant.[2] Those who imagine that I would dress Washington in a Roman costume misunderstand me. The time is past when civilized nations are distinguished by their dress. — If the United States ever had a national garb, I can conceive patriotic zeal interested in its preservation. But what distinguished the dress of Washington from that of Peter, Leopold, or Voltaire, or Burke? In many statues the dress of the time is most useful. In a statue of Howard,[3] or Fulton, or Watt, or any other simple improver of the arts or institutions of society, I should think it very proper then to mark the date of his career, by exhibiting him in that circle of usages where he merely served. But the man who overthrew a tyranny, and founded a Republic, was a hero. When he sits down in marble immortality in the Hall of the Capitol, his dress should have reference to the future rather than the past; there should be about him nothing mean and trifling, or above all, ridiculous; which latter adjective, I hold to apply in its full extent, to the modern dress generally, and to that of Washington's time particularly. Three statues have been made of Washington: one by Houdon, representing the General, made with every advantage, and with an accuracy of detail that will ensure it, in its way, the first place among the representatives of the man: one by Canova representing a Roman in the act of thinking what he shall write: one by

Chantry, representing him holding a scroll in one hand and a piece
of his cloak in the other. I have heard these statues, in their time,
examined and criticized by the country. I find nothing in the interest they excite to tempt me to follow either. I choose to make another experiment. If it fails, the next sculptor who attempts the subject
will have another beacon in this difficult navigation: the rocks will
not increase: the sooner light-houses are on them the safer. Only
don't send us landsmen for pilots. I am, my dear Morse, yours,

H. Greenough.

NOTES

Source: *New York American*, 4 August 1834. A few minor spelling errors
have been corrected.
1. The excerpt from Greenough's Letter 69 which appeared in the *New York
   Journal of Commerce* on 11 March 1834 brought forth a letter, published
   on 2 April, to the editor of the *New York American*. The author, Senator
   John Pendleton King of Georgia, objected to the sword and the costume of
   Greenough's figure, declaring that Washington's hand should be laid "upon
   the book of the Constitution" and suggesting that a suit of Washington's
   clothes be sent Greenough for use as a model. Morse had sent a copy of
   King's letter to Greenough, seconding the suggestion of substituting the
   Constitution for the sword, though he disagreed in general with King (*New
   York American*, 4 August 1834).
2. According to William Dunlap, Morse called the sketch Greenough sent him
   "sublime" (*Diary of William Dunlap*, ed. Dorothy C. Barck [New York,
   1931], 3:777).
3. John Howard (1726–90) was an English prison reformer.

75.   To Samuel F. B. Morse
      24 August 1834

Paris.[1] August 24. 1834.

My Dear Morse
   Your letter introducing Mr Bryant[2] was delivered to me here by
that gentleman — I regretted much not being with him in Fl. on his
arrival there, but I have requested Mr Kinloch and Mr Miles to see

him comfortably settled — I am grieved to hear that you have decided on confining yourself to portrait[3] — I would almost rather you would suffer a little and give us at least one picture which should embody all your acquirements — Of course I cannot pretend to advise you — I believe that situated as you are I should do the same — I flatter my-self so — As for your growing old I must think that a little nervous-ness of yours for I am sure you can more safely count on 20 active years than most young men —

I am here for a few days only and am very busy procuring books, casts and other objects connected with my studies — I am not yet sure that I shall not be obliged to go to London, but shall not If I can help it — I am anxious to learn the situation of my brother[4] & to see if I can do anything for him — I have written him again & again but not having his address my letters I fear have never reached him — I have great comfort here in the company of Mr Mason[5] who was so lately with you all and who gives me such delightful anecdotes and such copious news about you — You can't think how flat Paris is — no Cooper no Morse — all changed — I've lost my confidence in my impressions for I find the society in which I lived when here be-fore threw a charm over every thing. The very Louvre seems mediocre and Luxemboerg[6] makes me laugh — that ever I should have thought so highly of it — But I am I dare say as far on one side the truth now as I was before on the other — I am convinced now that the French are not a people of *genius* in art — (There's no other word — but that of genius though it's a vague one.) The same frippery taste which gives all the frequented streets of Paris that Vanity fair aspect creeps into their serious efforts — obtrudes itself along with the really beauti-ful of their nature and even usurps the society of the grand in their monuments — and the effect is to me melancholy — In all merely practical works I think them great — Their wars disciplined them — they were obliged to look to the end and the matter — The stern exigences of military despatch and hostile operation — obliged them to drop the graces as they call them and to lay aside the monkey — They are in Art — but the slaves of fashion — They are now converts to the German doctrines and nothing but Ghirlandaio — and Giotto and Signorelli and so on will serve their turn.[7] Do you remember some caricatures in sculpture which we thought very clever by Danton?[8] — They came to be the vogue — and he has been *producing* at a fearful rate — Instead of continuing however merely to *change*

character he dropped to caricature of feature and form and has exhausted monstrosity deformity — pathology — Strange! that a man who
had so finely sketched the voluptuous self complacency of Rossini[9]
should aim at making the rabble laugh with a huge nose and a
whopper-jaw — The Magdalen is finished on the outside and is surely
a rich and magnificent monument. The tympanum is filled with an
alto relievo of Christ appearing to judge the world, the angels of
love and of wrath on either side and the good and evil — blessed and
punish'd[10] — The Saviour is a diluted reminiscence of Thorwaldsen's
— Flaxman left the artist nothing new to say about blessing and
damning — the execution though somewhat round and heavy is beyond other works of its class here — We must give the credit of making sacrifices for art to the French — they sweep away whole arron-
dissements for a coup d'oeil — a grand perspective compensates with
them for a thousand inconveniences — You might think yourself gaz-
ing at the dress scene of a Theatre — The architects have evidently
had carte blanche — but the salt of art is wanting. There is more
beauty and more art in Florence than in Paris in spite of all this show
— I shall return to Florence with an unwillingness to leave it again
but for my own home — I prefer the Italians with all their faults to
any other people — I thank God I've seen people that can beat them
all hollow at cheating — I dare say that when one has learned to live
here it's quite like any other town but I want to get back to my own
nest — and my own clay — and my own hammer. Mason has taken a
carriage to go on in and I have agreed to join him; several others[11] are
going about the same time and we hope to form a sort of caravan —

I beg you will present my kindest remembrances to Weir — I hope
his situation at West Point will not be too engrossing for him[12] —
Leslie[13] missed it in going to America and I fear almost as much in
returning to London — He had several (2) instances of his prices
being disputed before he left London as I learned from a source In
which I put the greatest confidence and the person told me he attributed L's leaving England to disgust on that account. You will be
happy to hear that Mr Wyatt[14] the English Sculptor is daily rising in
reputation. In his walk he has no superiour. He has lately had a commission from the King of the Sicilies (a nymph of Diana).[15] I trust
that I can give you my notions without any danger of your shewing
my letters to any body but Cooper. It is that belief only that induces
me to talk away so flippantly.

When you write me again will you tell me all about Cooper and his family — Is not Mrs Cooper very happy now? At home with all her children safe about her and her husband's company and her social position — but is she well — And he what does he say what does he think of the world — Does he like some of us sigh and fear that Solomon was right when he said there's nothing new under the Sun — I am not one of 'em mind — Steam and printing are new — Hurrah! for our side! We had a very serious attempt made here the other day to *fly* —Twas at the Champ de Mars — They shewed the apparatus at 20 sous the head — twas not a bad investment — I went with a party to look at it — twas a contemptible sham affair — a dandy who was of our party twitched his gills and quoted Hudibras — "Doubtless the pleasure is as great" "Of being cheated as to cheat —"[16] I am Dear Morse

> Yours as ever
> H Greenough

Addressed: Samuel. F. B. Morse P.N.A. / New-York.

NOTES

Manuscript: Samuel F. B. Morse Papers, LC.

1. Greenough was in Paris—where he went to secure certain authorities for modeling his *Washington,* chiefly a copy of Houdon's bust—from late in August until 6 September 1834.
2. William Cullen Bryant was in Paris in July and August 1834 and traveled to Florence in September. For a description of some of his experiences during this European trip, see his *Letters of a Traveller* (New York, 1850).
3. Apparently Morse made this decision partly because of his disappointment that Cooper did not purchase his *Exhibition Gallery of the Louvre,* as was expected, for some $2500; he sold it in July to George Clark of Cooperstown for $1200 (*Samuel F. B. Morse: His Letters and Journals,* ed. Edward L. Morse [Boston, 1914], 2:27–28).
4. John Greenough.
5. Jonathan Mason, Jr.
6. The Musée du Luxembourg.
7. Domenico Ghirlandaio (1449–94), Giotto di Bondone (*ca.* 1266–*ca.* 1337), and Luca Signorelli (*ca.* 1441–1523) typified the pre-Raphaelite painters who at this time were enjoying a vogue, especially with German romantics.
8. Jean Pierre Dantan (1800–1869), French sculptor, is chiefly noted for his portrait caricatures.
9. Dantan's bust of Gioacchino Antonio Rossini is in the Musée de Versailles.
10. The church of La Madeleine, on the Place de la Madeleine, in the style of a

Roman temple, was begun in 1764, altered by order of Napoleon, who intended to make it a "Temple of Glory" for the French army, restored to use for divine worship in 1816, and finished in 1842. The pediment has a relief of the Last Judgment by P. H. Lemaire.

11. Among the others were Col. Joseph M. White (1781–1839), territorial delegate to Congress from Florida, and his wife. The party went by way of Venice.

12. Robert Weir taught drawing at the U.S. Military Academy at West Point from 1834 to 1876.

13. Charles Robert Leslie (1794–1859), historical, portrait, and genre painter born in London of American parents, was brought up in Philadelphia. In 1811 he went to England, where he studied at first under Benjamin West and Allston. He taught drawing at West Point for a short time in 1833, but returned to England and there spent the rest of his life.

14. James Richard Wyatt.

15. The present location of this statue is unknown.

16. Samuel Butler, *Hudibras,* pt. 2, canto 3, l. 1.

76. To John Forsyth
8 October 1834

Florence. Oct'r 8th 1834.

Hon John Forsythe / Secretary of State / Department of State —
Sir

Agreeably to the contract I have entered into with the U.S. Government, I was to have received early in the present year an instalment of Five Thousand Doll's. I presumed until now that a press of public business had occasioned the postponement of this remittance. I can defer no longer begging that the payment may be made as the operations I am engaged in require a great expence and I am in danger of being interrupted for want of funds.

I am Sir with respect
Your Most Ob't Serv't
Horatio Greenough.

Addressed: Hon John Forsythe / Secretary of State / Dept of State / Washington D.C.
Endorsed: Rec'd Decr. 7.

NOTE

John Forsyth (1780–1841) was secretary of state from 1834 to 1837.
    Manuscript: RG 59, General Records of the Department of State, Accession 161, Item 135, NA.

77. To Emanuele Fenzi
[1834?]

My Dear Sir
    I was aware of your holding a credit in my favour for 300 Francesconi — for account of Mr Greene[1] — The credit for which I enquired was one of 22 or 23 napoleons on account of Martin Brimmer Esqre[2] — I shall write to Mess Grant by today's post — It is possible he may have lodged the amount in their hands I am

> Dear Sir
> With respect
> Your most ob't serv't
> Horatio Greenough

Cav. Emanuelle Fenzi

Addressed: Al Ill's'mo[3] / Sig Cav. Emanuelle Fenzi / S.R.M.[4]

NOTES

Emanuele Fenzi was a prominent Jewish banker in Florence, with whom Greenough had his account during most of his residence in the city (T. A. Trollope, *What I Remember* [New York, 1890], 2:12, 141, 289; Giovanni Duprè, *Thoughts on Art and Autobiographical Memoirs,* trans. E. M. Peruzzi [Boston, 1886], pp. 69, 157, 354). He was a Cavaliere in the Ordine Insigne Sacro e Militare di S. Stefano Papa e Martire (*Almannaco Toscana* [Florence, 1834]).
    This letter is dated on internal evidence; see n. 2, below.
    Manuscript: Carteggi Fenzi, Biblioteca e Archivio del Risorgimento, Florence.
    1. George Washington Greene was then living in Florence (see note to Letter 84).
    2. Martin Brimmer (1793–1847), Boston merchant and public servant, was in

Florence in the spring of 1834 (Martha Babcock Amory, *The Wedding Journey of Charles and Martha Babcock Amory* [Boston, 1922], 1:172, 177, 179).

3. *Al Illustrissimo,* "To the Most Illustrious."

4. *Suo Riverite Mano,* "His Esteemed Hand."

78. To John Forsyth
27 February 1835

Hon. John Forsyth / Secretary of State. Department of State.
Sir

Your letter of Dec 8th 1834.[1] with the accompanying letter of credit reached me duly through the U.S. Consul at Leghorn. I was not before aware of the necessity of an annual appliance for the payment of each instalment.

I have made considerable progress in the work on which I am employed for the Government. The first year was almost entirely consumed in finding and preparing a room of the proper dimensions — After waiting in vain a copy of Houdon's Washington, I was obliged to go [to] Paris myself to procure one.

I take advantage Sir of this opportunity to propose a measure, which I think cannot fail to be advantageous in many respects. I propose that when the model of the Statue of Washington is finished, a cast of it be forwarded to the capital and erected on its pedestal in the situation which is intended for the work in marble — That it remain there six months or a year, as may be thought advisable, before a blow is struck in marble. I would take advantage of that interim to model there, the bas-reliefs which are to occupy the sides of the pedestal, as they will contain many portraits which I find it impossible to procure at this distance —. There is also a great disadvantage in not being able to consult any one acquainted with the persons and events represented in that portion of the work. I have been induced to this proposal, by the various and contradictory opinions of my design, which have reached me from sources entitled to the highest respect.

As this operation will be attended by an expense of about 1500$,

I trust it will be thought just that [the] Gov't should pay it if my model is approved, as it will save the sum of 10000$ in case it should be condemned.[2]

                                             I am Sir —
                                    Your Obedient Servant
                                       Horatio Greenough.
Florence Feb'y 27. 1835.

Addressed: Hon John Forsyth / Secretary of State. / Department of State / Washington D.C.
Endorsed: Rec'd. April 13

NOTES

Manuscript: RG 59, General Records of the Department of State, Accession 161, Item 135, NA.
1. Copy in RG 59, General Records of the Department of State, Domestic Letters, NA.
2. In his reply to Greenough of 17 April 1835 (copy in RG 59, General Records of the Department of State, Bureau of Accounts, Letters Sent, NA), Forsyth wrote that he was not authorized to promise payment of any sum other than that named in the contract.

79.   To Washington Allston
      7 March 1835

                                    Florence, March 7th 1835.
My Dear Mr Alston
    I remember that when with you once at Cambridge, I asked your opinion on some doubtful point relating to Art and that you said, an answer to my question would cost you at least 3 cigars — Sure I am that it would require that number to fit me to describe to you my gratification in reading the verses you wrote on my groupe, which lately reached me in a letter from my brother Harry.[1] I believe my Dear Sir that gratified vanity was not the foremost or strongest of my pleasures — for your verses were as far from being addressed to

minds of the many as my composition was from being adapted to their tastes.

They say there's no love without hope — This I don't believe, but I do believe that a correspondence requires 2 people to make it — I say it from experience and by way of apology to you for my long silence which has not been occasioned by any change in my tastes or character — but simply from the discouragement of your silence[2] — I called a spirit from the vasty deep — He would not come when I did call to him — But though like the clownish wooer I have said nothing, like him I've thought the more. I am happy in an excuse for addressing you again. I throw aside all fear of being irksome to you and I proceed to give you my news. And first of all let me tell you that John G—— with whom I have established a regular correspondence is comfortable and likely to be still more so — He is at Islington in a very decent house has one or two respectable persons lodging with him and seems to drive quite a promising business in portrait though in a small way — I am so happy that he has had the character to go through with it! It wrings tears out of me that I can't put him in a way to gratify a little his ambition which you know is strong in him. After 3 years of married life he speaks with much affection of his wife and I think therefore that it's a good match.[3] At the same time that he writes cheerfully and even jocularly he shows clearly that he has grown thoughtful and cautious — I always felt that John had a vast deal of good in his nature though circumstances and his temperament combined against him — We shall see — I hope he will yet be a happy man —

I can as regards myself only talk to you of my statue which is my life — I have hopes of casting it next autumn — I propose exhibiting the cast in the Rotunda and giving Government the choice of taking or refusing the work as they may think fit. I have as authorized by the Vote in Congress made the work after my own heart — Had they ordered this or that costume or action I might have been blamed for disregard of orders — They can now only question my taste and skill and as I give them their entire freedom as regards the marble I think they cannot complain. As a bargain I am not eager for it — though the price is a fair one, as far as I can judge from my expences hitherto — and as for the honour of filling that spot I want to be sure or at least have hopes that it is to be an honour and not a disgrace before I strike a blow in stone.

I received a letter from Mr Everett a few weeks since in which he tells me he fears my plan will never do in our country — He takes a view of the matter directly contradictory to that he has hithertoo taken and at this moment when the work may be said to be done[4] — I question neither his sincerity nor the friendliness of his motives but I draw from his various and inconsistent advice the strongest arguments in favour of an artist's thinking for himself and acting resolutely from his own convictions — I beg you will show this letter to no one. I would not harm Mr E even in his reputation as a connoisseur for the world — I have made up my mind to look for the approbation of a few — I rest my hopes of comfort during my life upon ground which has little relation with the success of my work with the world — Was it not always so? Yes and it will always be so — Do not imagine that I think I have join[ed] [*page torn*] the glorious company of men in advance of their age — I do not — [But of?] [*page torn*] this I am convinced that he who looks to what is abstractly right [in?] [*page torn*] any employment or occupation whatever must give up what Alfieri calls glorietta[5] — and the attempt is as fatal to him as the greatest success — Mr Mason has been here the greater part of this winter. He is as you have no doubt heard married — to [a] young and sprightly widow with all the qualities to make a good wife as the world goes[6] — He is in person and appearance as young as I left him 10 years ago — I have made about 15 busts this winter[7] — I have had a statue rough hewn which I wish to finish but have not time — Love prisoner — to wisdom[8] — his feet are chained and the bird of Minerva sits by on the stone where his chain is fastened. I have tried to represent that twisting impatience which a boy manifests at restraint in his form and an expression of treachery and mischief in his face. I have been grieved to hear of Mr Dana's[9] illness — I hope he is recovered entirely — I heard a strange story of the recovery from many years' melancholy of the brother of Dr Foster[10] — is this true? — I hear nothing of poor Newton[11] — I propose to model at Washington the bas reliefs of my pedestal while my model is exhibiting — I find it quite out of the question to attempt it here. I can't get the portraits — and the events represented I know too superficially to trust myself — I hope then My Dear Sir to see you in less than a year from this date — Among the thousand tender and happy anticipations which are linked to that hope — the thought of looking once more on your face and on the master's is among the strongest — I beg to be remembered to the master and his brother — to the ladies of the family — and am Dear Sir —

Yours

H Greenough

P.S. Your nephew is here[12] — just arrived — he looks enough like you to give me great pleasure in seeing him. He will remain until spring and then to England — He is studying or to study rather at the gallery —

Addressed: Washington Alston Esqr. / Boston Mass —

NOTES

Manuscript: Dana Papers, MHS. Previous publication (in part): Flagg, p. 224.

1. Allston's poem, "On Greenough's Group of the Angel and Child," appeared in the *Boston Daily Advertiser*, 30 December 1834. It was reprinted, with minor alterations, in his *Lectures on Art and Poems* (New York, 1850), pp. 363–65.
2. The only letter from Allston to Greenough which seems to have been preserved is that of 25 July 1836 (collection of David Richardson, Washington, D.C.).
3. John Greenough was living at this time in Islington, a district in London. He married Maria Underwood of London on 20 February 1832 (Greenough, p. 41).
4. In his letter to Greenough of 15 December 1834 (collection of David Richardson, Washington, D.C.), Everett reported that the drawing of the statue which Greenough had sent Livingston had been objected to because of the action of the right hand and the nudity. He also expressed the opinion that it was "too dangerous to address a work of art to a degree of refinement, which does not exist, among those who are to behold it," and concluded by saying that he wanted Greenough to make a popular as well as a good statue. This advice was inconsistent, as Greenough says in this letter, with that of Everett's letter to him of 29 July 1832 (collection of David Richardson, Washington, D.C.), in which he said he was "much pleased" with Greenough's idea for the design of the statue and urged him to read accounts of Phidias' statue of Zeus at Olympia, which in fact, was the general design after which Greenough patterned his own.
5. "Small glory." The source of the quotation has not been identified.
6. In 1834 Jonathan Mason, Jr., married Isabella Cowpland, daughter of an English merchant living in Florence (Harvard University Archives).
7. Among them were those of Bryant, Capt. Alexander Claxton, Mr. and Mrs. David Sears, Col. and Mrs. Joseph M. White, and presumably William Griffin and a "Mme. Para." That of Sears is now in the Somerset Club, Boston; of White, in the New-York Historical Society; and of Mrs. White,

in the Mary Buie Museum, Oxford, Mississippi. The others have not been located.

8. It is now in the Museum of Fine Arts, Boston.
9. Presumably R. H. Dana.
10. John Foster (1782–1836) was a graduate of Harvard in 1802. His brother Thomas (1805–31) was a physician. (Lucius R. Page, *History of Cambridge, Massachusetts, 1630–1877* [Boston, 1877], p. 547.) Since boyhood John had had a nervous disease for which he did not receive proper treatment, and at last, he became a recluse. After going into seclusion, he was well until his brother's death deranged him again (Sophia Peabody to Elizabeth Palmer Peabody, 23 June 1831, Berg Collection, NYPL).
11. Gilbert Stuart Newton (1794–1835), London history and portrait painter who had been brought up in Cambridge and Boston, was long troubled with mental disorder and died insane.
12. George Whiting Flagg (1816–97), son of Allston's half-brother H. C. Flagg, Jr., was a genre and portrait painter.

80. To Josiah Quincy
14 July 1835

Florence — July 14. 1835.

Dear Sir

This will accompany a catalogue of the celebrated library of Count Boutourlin[1] — which is now offered for sale by his heirs — The collection was made under the most favourable circumstances and is in the first order — The person who has the care of this library and to whom is entrusted the sale of it, has requested me to forward a catalogue to the U States — The family are unwilling to divide it — They consider it a monument to the old count — Three hundred thousand Francs is the least (they say) they can take for it — I have taken the liberty of forwarding the catalogue to you, hoping that as Professor Ticknor[2] is about to revisit Europe you may think it worth the pains of examining this collection, which even here is considered unique — With the request that you will remember my respectful compliments to Mrs Quincy

I remain Dear Sir
Your obliged friend & servant
Horatio Greenough

Hon Josiah Quincy / President of Harvard University/ Cambridge

Addressed: Hon Josiah Quincy / President of Harvard University / Cambridge. Mass.

NOTES

Manuscript: Miscellaneous Manuscripts, G, NYHS.

1. Count Dimitrii Petrovich Buturlin (1763–1829), Russian general, military writer, and director of the Imperial Library in St. Petersburg, was a noted book collector. The catalogue which Greenough sent Quincy was apparently *Catalogue de la Bibliothèque de Son Exc. M. le comte D. Boutourlin* (Florence, 1831). The collection was sold in Paris between 1839 and 1841.

2. George Ticknor (1791–1871), scholar and teacher, was professor of French and Spanish at Harvard when Greenough was a student there. He had just resigned his post and was about to go to Europe to collect material for his *History of Spanish Literature* (1849).

81.   To Robert Gilmor, Jr.
        28 November 1835

Florence, Nov 28, 1835 —

My Dear Sir

I received this morning your very kind letter of Sept'r 24th and am not a little relieved at learning that you have at length seen Medora and that on the whole you are not disappointed — Your generous effort in my behalf is as your conduct toward me always has been worthy all gratitude. I am sensible of the sacrifice you must have made in so long denying yourself a sight of a statue so long expected & of which rumour had already spoken favorably. Accept dear Sir my thanks for all this kindness.

I am mortified and grieved that there should be any difficulty in placing the figure.[1] I think that if I were with you I could contrive a place for it, but perhaps you have more experience in arranging these objects than I have. I beg you will remember what I formerly said I was willing to do in case the figure was not in all respects what you wished — I am still perfectly willing either to take the statue off your hands or to replace it by one to which you shall not have the same objections. I am now finishing in my moments of leisure a figure of Love captive in which I am embodying a conception of Petrarch in the "Trionfo della Castità."[2] His godship stands chained to a rock on which the bird of wisdom stands centinel. His arrows lie broken at his feet, his hands are crossed behind him in the attitude of helplessness — in his face I have attempted to mingle lurking mischief with shame — I think it my best figure thus far and should you after seeing it wish to exchange Medora for it it shall be yours — I think it possible that Mrs White[3] of Florida who wishes something of mine would take the Medora in case you should be willing to part with her —

I have at length brought the model of Washington to a close — I shall continue to caress it until New year's when it will be cast — I ought perhaps to say to you what I think of my success but I will leave it to yourself to judge me when you see it & will content myself with assuring you that I have done my utmost — You are evidently not aware that Government did not accede to my proposition of sending the model to Washington — The responsibility falls entirely on me and I am ready to take it — I have acted conscientiously — At all events it will probably sooner or later give way to a more successful effort of some more [favo]red [?] [*page torn*] artist — I trust that a few may be found [to?] [a]pprove [*page torn*] the course I have taken — I loo[k] forward with confidence to your support at least for my intentions — Be assured that the many proofs I have had of your esteem are a balance for all the mortifications I have met with in my arduous profession — Begging to be respectfully remembered to Mrs Gilmor I remain Dear Sir

Respectfully Yours
Horatio Greenough

Addressed: Rob't Gilmor Esqr / Baltimore. / Pr Sully
Endorsed, in Gilmor's hand: Horatio Greenough / Sculptor / ans'd 10 March 36

N O T E S

Manuscript: Mellen Chamberlain Autograph Collection, BPL. Previous publication: Nathalia Wright, ed., "Letters by Horatio Greenough in the Library," *Boston Public Library Quarterly* 11 (1959): 86–87.

1. Edward Everett recorded in his diary for 11 March 1835 that Gilmor had opened the case containing the *Medora* but could not decide where to place the statue (Diary of Edward Everett, Everett Papers, MHS).
2. In this poem Amor assails Laura but is defeated, Laura being armed by several virtues including "Senno" ("wisdom"). Amor is bound to a column, his arrows are broken, and ultimately he is taken to the temple of "Pudicinzia" ("chastity") in Rome.
3. Ellen Adair White (1801–84), celebrated belle, was the wife of Col. Joseph M. White. After White's death she married Dr. Theophilus Beatty.

82. To Richard Henry Wilde
November 1835

My Dear Sir

I must call on the Channings[1] tonight but will join you in the course of the evening — Not being willing that your opinion of my continence should depend on any such devilish bad reasons as you adduce I hasten to inform you that I left the theatre only long enough to smoke half a cigar and that I was when you left it standing immediately behind the prompter — Mr Thomson's[2] servant told me as I came out that your man had been looking for me — Au reste a theatre in Florence is an antidote to unholy passions — I have sometimes found great relief in this way from the ballet — but find that each successive year it is necessary to go a little *nearer* — I'm now as I said right behind the prompter — the next year will take me behind the scenes and what will be requisite after that God knows.

Till 9 adieu

yours

H Greenough

Addressed: R H Wilde Esqr / Chez Schneiderff.

NOTES

Richard Henry Wilde (1789–1847), Irish-born American lawyer, congressman, and poet, was in Italy from the autumn of 1835 to the autumn of 1840.

This letter is dated on internal evidence; see n. 1, below.

Manuscript: Editor's collection.

1. William Henry Channing (1810–84), Unitarian clergyman and author, was in Europe in 1835–36, together with his mother; Miss Sarah Gibbs of Newport, Rhode Island; and Miss Gibbs' nephew George Gibbs. They were in Florence in November 1835 (Octavius Brooks Frothingham, *Memoir of William Henry Channing* [Boston, 1886], pp. 28, 39, 107, 121; see Channing to Greenough, 11, 23 September, 23 December 1835, collection of David Richardson, Washington, D.C.).
2. Col. James Thomson, a New Yorker, was resident in Florence for many years.

83. To James Fenimore Cooper
15 December 1835

Florence Dec 15 – 1835 –

My Dear Mr Cooper

I have heard of you at last thank God![1] though indirectly – Chapman[2] says that you & yours are well and most happy am I to hear it – I doubt not that you have the best reasons for so long a silence – indeed I find you continue your literary labours in spite of your rash vow –

I have read the Monnikins[3] & was much amused and instructed too by parts of it – others I could not comprehend – not being au courant of measures and men at home – your description is fresh as ever and your yankee is glorious – I had once imagined giving my notions on Italy France England – America as respects those topics that lie within the range of my judgment, in the form of Travels in the East by a Boston Boy – Italy I meant to designate as the Empire of Già fù[4] England as the island of Sellemall (Bulwer has I since see a borough Buyemall)[5] France as the Kingdom of Ornsiorano[6] – America as the Republic of Peroravabbene[7] – you have not only forestalled the main idea but have of course hit many things which I never saw – Still I think that in what relates to art & one or two other such matters they would bear shaving all over again.

Well! as you used to say every now & then & a very kind hearted habit it was in a world like this – I have done my statue – The die is cast – I have sailed right in the wind's eye or so near it as to set all a shaking – I think I shall amuse you one day with the anecdotes connected with this work — I have done my utmost and am as thin as Don Quixote and almost as wild — I have had a hard job of it my friend but I begin now to look on the whole as vanity & vexation etc — it's always the way you know when we have had our wicked wills — My block is quarried & weighs 5 tons — I don't expect to make any money by this work but I still cherish a hope that it may find favor & give me a place in the esteem of the country of all classes and every party — If it does not I shall have the satisfaction of feeling that I have not sacrificed my art to any hopes of gain or favour or tem- porary reputation — The work is conscientious Sir & is a thousand miles ahead of any thing I have yet done. So say the knowing & so I think — I speak to you col cuore sul labbro.[8] I believe the old Hero is there and he looks like Old Hundred[9] *you may depend* —

I shall probably visit America the following summer for 6 or 8 months — I shall look forward to meeting you & yours with a joy and an affection not different from that [which] waits me in my own home — What man ever found a juster or more indulgent friend than you have been to me — I feel grateful to you but I take & always have taken some credit to myself for your opinion of me — Present my respects to Madame & the ladies as also to Mr Paul who is probably a tall stripling ere this. What is that wicked Morse about now? sousin' up niggers & writin' anticatholic pamphlets — love to all — addio

Yours

Hor — Greenough

Addressed: James Fennimore Copper Esqre / New — York — / Pr Francis Depau

NOTES

Manuscript: David Richardson, Washington, D.C.
1. The last known letter from Cooper to Greenough before this letter was that of 13 June 1833.
2. John Gadsby Chapman.
3. *The Monikins* was published in London on 4 July; in Philadelphia on 7 July 1835 (Robert E. Spiller and Philip C. Blackburn, *A Descriptive Bibliography of the Writings of James Fenimore Cooper* [New York, 1934], p. 81).
4. "Already was."
5. Edward George Earle Lytton Bulwer-Lytton (1803–83), first Baron Lytton, used this name in his satirical novel *Pelham* (1828) for a borough in possession of the lords of Glenmorris.

6. "They decorate themselves."
7. "For the present it goes very well."
8. "With the heart on the lips."
9. Presumably an expression derived from the name "Old Hundred," designating the seventeenth-century tune composed for Psalm 100, to which the Doxology is also sung. It was used in the nineteenth century to mean to go about something with great enthusiasm and gusto; that is, in the way in which the Doxology was traditionally sung.

84. To George Washington Greene
[February?] 1836

My Dear Greene
    I enclose the Culprit Fay[1] which has at length been returned to me and beg you will accept my thanks for the loan — I like it much — I think it shows more imagination than any of our Am. poetry that I have read — parts are exquisite —
    I enclose also your verses[2] and have read them again & again with a fault finding spirit but can only object to one image and beg you will give no other weight to my opinion than the habit of composing in a different art may entitle it to.

> While from the rapid wing of time,
> Hope drew new charms & Love new power —

My fancy in spite of me draws the picture as I read — The wing of time is a distinct object. Hope & love present themselves readily at your call but the action & its objects are not so clear — intelligible certainly — but not homogeneous with the other parts of the image — Censure me in your wisdom & awake your senses that you may the better judge — A thousand thanks for the pie which was and is excellent — respects to Madame.

Yours.
H Greenough

Addressed: G. W. Greene, Esqr

NOTES

George Washington Greene (1811–83), critic, historical writer, and teacher, spent much of his early life in Europe. He was in Florence early in 1829, when presumably he and Greenough first met. From 1837 to 1845 he was U.S. consul in Rome.

This letter must have been written about 27 February, on which date Greene wrote Longfellow that he had shown Greenough the poem to which Greenough alludes in this letter (Longfellow Correspondence, Houghton).

Manuscript: Editor's collection.

1. *The Culprit Fay and Other Poems* (1835), by Joseph Rodman Drake.
2. Twenty-two untitled lines composed about the death of Mary Storer Potter Longfellow, wife of H. W. Longfellow (Greene to Longfellow, 27 February 1836).

85. To John Gibson
Before April 1836

My Dear Mr Gibson

Allow me to present to your acquaintance my friend the Hon. R. H. Wilde of Georgia U.S.A.

I trust to the kindness you have always shown me to excuse a liberty to which I am prompted by the desire that a gentleman for whom I have the highest regard may be enabled to appreciate yourself as all the world does your works.

I need not beg you to make him known to Mr Wyatt but must request that you will remember my best compliments to him.

> I am Dear Sir
> Respectfully yours
> Horatio Greenough

Mr Gibson

Addressed: Mr Gibson — / Sculptor — / Rome — / Hon R H Wilde / of Georgia —

NOTE

John Gibson (1790–1866), English neoclassical sculptor, went to Rome in 1817 to study. He worked in the studios of Canova and Thorvaldsen and finally established his own studio.

Wilde was in Rome by 20 April 1836; see his letter to J. K. Paulding of that date, published in the *Knickerbocker Magazine* 8 (1836): 447–54, under the title "Secret History of Tasso."

Manuscript: Bryant-Godwin Collection, NYPL.

86. To James Fenimore Cooper
30 July 1836

Boston.[1] July 30th 1836.

My Dear Mr Cooper

When I arrived here from Washington I found my father in a feeble state of health[2] — he had long been sinking gradually and he kept his place among the family three days only after I met him — He suffered no pain but lay on his bed from weakness — He conversed cheerfully and made his toilette until within 24 hours of his death — He breathed his last the 27th inst with out a groan and his last words were of joy to see his children around him. "My trust is in an unknown God!" These were the words that conveyed the creed and the hopes beyond the grave, of an honest and benevolent man, who had heard the Gospel preached during a long life in silence. I know not what your faith may be, but I offer you an example of a happy death, without any other security for the future than natural religion gives to an upright & benevolent mind.

When I compare the simplicity and kindness of his last words to us with the mannered jargon of the priest whose duty it was made to console this family — his helter skelter quotations from the Old & New testament[s] to prove that we should rejoice in the event, and his clap trap & stage effect to rip open the soothed wounds of bereavement, I cannot but think that Christianity is in the heart & in the heart only — any admixture of head-work spoils all — and in those of the trade all is spoiled. I write this in confidence — I would not will-ingly throw my father's character or my own to the blood-hounds of charity & brotherly love —

I may be kept here longer than I had feared by the arrangements that it now becomes my duty to assist in making for the family. I hope I shall see you before I sail. I trust I shall at least hear from you. I was ill at Washington but am recovered — I read your letter to your countrymen[3] with pleasure — I fear you were mistaken in the origin of the obnoxious article of the American and I believe that the *country* is as warm an admirer of your works as ever it was — More of this if we meet. Pray present my respectful regards to Mrs Cooper and the family and Believe me

Yours
Hor. Greenough

Addressed: J. Fennimore Cooper Esqr / Cooperstown Ostego C'y / New York.

NOTES

Manuscript: Cooper Collection, Beinecke. Previous publication: James Feni-more Cooper, *Correspondence of James Fenimore-Cooper,* ed. James F. Cooper (New Haven, 1922), 1:366–68.

1. Greenough left Florence early in April, sailed from Le Havre on 16 May, and reached New York on 10 June. He proceeded to Washington and from there went to Boston about the middle of July.
2. David Greenough became ill about February 1836 (*Letters,* p. 110).
3. Cooper's *A Letter to His Countrymen* (1834) was a warning to Americans that they were undermining their political principles by imitating European practices. It was precipitated by a hostile review of *The Bravo* by "Cassio" in the *New York American,* 7 June 1832. The author was an American, Edward Sherman Gould, but Cooper thought him a Frenchman antagonized by Cooper's antigovernmental role in the French finance controversy. He further felt that the general objection in America to his "European" novels was partly due to that controversy (Robert E. Spiller, *Fenimore Cooper: Critic of his Times* [New York, 1931], pp. 222–30).

87. To Richard Henry Wilde
18, 19 August 1836

Nahant. August 18th, 1836.

My Dear Mr Wilde

I thank you most heartily for your letters which have reached me duly & to which I have not replied only because I have not had a moment, I will not say of leisure, but of time. I have been so constantly engrossed that some of my intimate friends who are near me, I have not yet seen. You may have heard indirectly that I went immediately to Washington on my arrival in the country, & that I fell ill there — I returned to Boston about 5 weeks since, in time to see my father's face and hear his voice once more. He took to his bed 3 days after I arrived and sank gradually asleep. I have lost the man on earth whom I esteemed and loved the most & who was rather a companion, than a governor of my youth. I am fled hither for a day or two, to escape the hurry and fatigue of my city employments. There is a southeast storm and I see little of the *beauty* of Nahant while the wind is too gentle as yet for the sublime. One who has been at sea in a gale however has little interest in these terra firma glimpses of the sea storms — Notwithstanding (what a long word!) the many changes that have taken place here, I felt soon quite at home & I could find it in my heart to settle down here and dream no more of foreign lands, or of any advantages not enjoyed here. Every thing is more to my mind than I had feared; It is true I have not mix'd much in society or come in contact with any party, political or religious; but I love a country where one can do this, or rather where *I* can do it. Mr Greene will have told you that I think I have remedied the defect of light in the Rotunda.[1] I am confident that I can get *any* light *I want* there, if they will give me leave. I find (entre nous) very little doing in the way of art. Portraits are the only pictures — and bank notes the best engraving I have seen. The Architecture flounders on in obstinate Greekism and at enormous expence. No one dreams of making other than wooden floors and the most costly dwelling houses are lathed & wainscotted into utter tinder-boxes. Rail Roads alone seem to be *understood.* Go ahead! is the order of the day — The whole continent presents a scene of *scrabbling* and roars with greedy hurry — They are chipping out a colossus and one must stand clear of the *flinders*. Of politics I shall say nothing as my ideas are getting more & [more] [*page torn*] Tory [*page torn*] me — & I feel about them much as the old gentleman did about his infirmities, who always rejoiced when he suffered from the stone, that he was free from Gout and when twinged by the Gout thanked God that he was free from the stone. I find the well-informed gentlemen of this country entertaining the most liberal opinions on the subject of Art, and I believe that their views of it are in advance of the powers of the Artists. Truly Sir! we complain of the public and I'll be hanged if they are not ahead of us. I would rather have the advice (and be backed by them in short) of a knot that I could form in Washington of 8 or 10 gentlemen than by that number of men to be selected in any part of Europe whe[re] [*page torn*] I have been.

Boston 19th. I pray you will say to Mr Sloane[2] that I have the *promise* of some seeds for him and that in case I am detained here this winter which is possible I will send them to him. Remember me kindly to the Thomsons. — Col. Wh[ite][3] [*page torn*] and Madame are here. She has been quite ill, but our east wind and fresh hallibut & mackerel have quite restored her. I shall say nothing of your plans till I learn how you have decided and will merely recommend that you go not to the east, lest the fatigues and climates of [that?] [*page torn*] quarter deprive me of another friend — Poor Lowell[4] has died in the flower of his age a victim to the determination to go over land to India — [*page torn*] [re]member the lovely Mrs Otis?[5] I never thought her beautiful till the night before last when her father in law led me to her bedside and shewed me a corpse — I never saw more symmetry of feature! Ah Sir it was a bitter lesson that sight! I cast her face and must attempt a bust — I have not seen Mrs Baker[6] but hear that she is well. They are gone on a journey. My love to Liverati and to Marchio[7] — as for Greene and Arno[8] I shall write them in a few days.

Yours truly
Hor Greenough —

Addressed: Hon. R H Wilde / Care of Mess Fenzi & Co / Florence / Tuscany / Mess Wells & Greene[9] Havre

NOTES

Manuscript: Editor's Collection.

1. When he examined the rotunda, Greenough found that if his statue were placed in the center, where the congressional resolution decreed it should be, it could not be properly seen, since it would be directly under the light from the dome. He decided the best place for it would be between the center of the rotunda and the door leading into the library.

2. Francis Sloan (*ca.* 1795–1871), English geologist and philanthropist, lived in Florence from about 1824 until his death (Clara L. Dentler, *Famous Foreigners in Florence, 1400–1900* [Florence, 1964], pp. 200–221).

3. Joseph M. White (1781–1839) was a delegate to Congress from the territory of Florida from 1825 to 1837.

4. John Lowell (1799–1836), Boston merchant, traveled extensively after the deaths of his wife and two daughters in 1830 and 1831; he died in Bombay.

5. Emily Marshall Otis (1807–36), famous Boston belle and wife of William Foster Otis, died on 17 August. Greenough's bust of her is now in the Boston Athenaeum.

6. Possibly Deborah Smith Mott Baker (d. 1838), wife of Walter Baker (1792–1852). Trained for the law, he went into the chocolate manufacturing business in Dorchester.

7. Carlo Ernesto Liverati (1805–44) was a history and genre painter living in Florence. Presumably Marchio was a workman in Greenough's studio.

8. Arno was Greenough's greyhound, which he bought in January 1835. G. W. Greene was occupying his quarters in his absence.

9. Possibly this was a branch of Samuel Welles' banking firm (see Letter 27, n. 5).

88. To Charles Pelham Curtis
1 September 1836

Dear Sir

I have received with great pleasure your letter informing me of the honor done me by the Phi Beta Kappa Society in electing me a member of that Society and I regret extremely that my engagements prevent me having the pleasure of dining with them today.

With respect
Yours
Horatio Greenough

C. P. Curtis Esq

NOTE

Charles Pelham Curtis (1792–1864) was a Boston lawyer.
    Greenough was elected a member of the Harvard chapter of Phi Beta Kappa
on 1 September 1836. A dinner was held that night (Harvard University
Archives).
    Manuscript: Lemuel Shaw Papers, MHS.

89. To Romeo Elton
23 September 1836

Boston. Sept 23d. 1836.

My Dear Sir
    I had hoped to have seen you at least for a few moments on my
way from N. York – but I was at that time slightly indisposed, and
you are aware that the steam communications of modern days have
but little sympathy with friendships whose objects lie *between* the
great points of locomotion. I have been very busily employed in
modelling portraits[1] since I arrived here and am now preparing to
leave this country for England – It would be a satisfaction to me to
see you on my way to New York, though I fear the yankee hurry is
communicated to all my movements, & that I shall pass your city
without stopping –
    I beg that you will at all times command my services for yourself
or any friend of yours who shall come to Italy and that you will
recommend me to the remembrance of Mrs Elton – With respect

Yours
Horatio Greenough

Addressed: Rev R. Elton – / Professor at Brown University / Providence. R.I.

NOTES

Romeo Elton (1790–1870), clergyman and professor, taught Greek and Latin at
Brown University from 1825 to 1841. In 1827, during his European sojourn to

prepare himself for this position, he and Greenough traveled together from Rome to Naples.

Manuscript: Brown University Library.

1. Those of Emily M. Otis and Samuel Appleton, and possibly of Henry Clay, John C. Calhoun, and Jonathan Mason, Jr. That of Appleton is now at Harvard University; the last three have not been located.

90. To Romeo Elton
23 September 1836

Boston, Sept 23d, 1836

My Dear Sir

Your favor of the 22d inst has just reached me. I am most happy to hear that there is a prospect of obtaining for Mr Greene an office like the consulate in Italy[1] — Mr Greene's acquaintance among the Italians — his familiarity with their language — the respect in which he is held by gentlemen of rank & consideration in that country — will make him most useful to his country men in such a situation — The circumstance that he is a man of sterling merit & of talents ought surely to give him a preference over foreigners of whom several in that country, are to my knowledge, rather a hindrance than an assistance to our people.

It is a positive fact that several American consuls have had an understanding with the local polices, not to sign any passport until the American consulate seal should be affixed — thus forcing the traveller to expend in Italy, at least 25 or 30 Dollars for a signature which is of no other use than to furnish a pretext for charging 2 dollars for each signature — I beg my Dear Sir that if what I have said should be any way useful to Mr Greene you will make such use of it as you think proper.

I am Dear Sir Yours
Respectfully
H. Greenough

Prof Elton

Addressed: Professor R. Elton / Brown University / Providence — R.I.

NOTES

> Manuscript: RG 59, General Records of the Department of State, Applications and Recommendations for Office, 1837–45, NA.
> 1. Elton, who had been a professor of G. W. Greene's at Bowdoin, saw him in Florence in 1836 and became interested in obtaining a diplomatic post for him. Greene took office as U.S. consul in Rome on 9 January 1837. He was removed on 25 July 1845 for misappropriation of funds.

91. To James Fenimore Cooper
23 September 1836

Boston Sept'r 23d. 1836.

My Dear Mr Cooper

I am uncertain whether this will find you at Cooperstown — but hope it [will] reach you readily through Mr Morse. I am about to embark again for Europe. I find that my business calls me and as my brothers are quite competent to manage the settlement of our family affairs, I shall return to Italy in company with my eldest sister[1] whose health is delicate to a degree that makes us dread a winter's exposure here.

I shall go to N. York on the 27th or 28th inst. Shall you return to town in season for me to see you between that and the 10th Oct. when I sail? Pray let me know as I shall make an effort to come to you if you do not.

I am sure I shall give you pleasure by informing you that my father's estate proves a very valuable one and that with proper management our numerous family will be all provided for[2] — which I think important for the female part of it especially. My affairs are in a very prosperous state, and I return to my mud and my hammer more convinced than ever that there's no place for an artist like his own studio — Why can't you go to Florence now?

I end with this question.

Yours affectionately
Horatio Greenough

Jas Fennimore Cooper Esqr. / New York

Addressed: James Fennimore Cooper Esqr

NOTES

Manuscript: David Richardson, Washington, D.C.
1. Louisa Greenough was an amateur painter. She remained in Florence until the summer of 1839. Early in the 1870's she returned and spent the remainder of her life there. See Letter 15, n. 7.
2. David Greenough's estate was heavily mortgaged at the time of his death, but under the administration of Henry it eventually enriched his heirs.

92. To John Gorham Palfrey
3 October 1836

New-York — Oct 3d '36

My Dear Sir

I regret extremely that the press of my affairs prevented my waiting on you in person before I left Boston. I had hoped to have offered for your approval some hints on Architecture and Building and a few remarks on the probable *avenir* of Art in our country. But I have not been able to finish what I had begun — If in the few days that remain to me on this side the water, I can put my loose sketches[1] into any form I will send them to you through my brother;[2] only requesting that you will judge them severely, *and that you will not mention to any one that I am the writer,* as I may have done a rash thing to speak of an art which I do not profess — I feared to take up the subject of Washington's portraits as it would make me an advocate of my own choice which I wish to do only in my work itself. I have had much pleasure here in observing the progress of the Artists and the interest taken by the Public in their labours. At the house of the late Mr Reed[3] I found a gallery of American works of which New York may well be proud — Mr Durand[4] has furnished several fine portraits and a picture of an Itinerant Merchant in the Wilkie[5] style which do great credit to the versatility of his genius. Mr Flagg[6] a very young artist has several fine productions and Mr Mount[7] of this neighbourhood has shewn an originality of invention a tact of hitting off yankee character truly surprising, added too to a fine execution — clear, bright, American atmosphere and harmony of colour — his pictures are a most valuable lesson to all young artists.

Begging that you will command me if I can ever be of use to you as resident in Florence I remain Dear Sir

Yours with respect
Horatio Greenough

Rev. J. G. Palfrey — / Cambridge

Addressed: Pr Steamboat / Rev J. G. Palfrey / Editor of the North American Review / Cambridge. Mass.

NOTES

John Gorham Palfrey (1796–1881), Unitarian clergyman, editor, and writer, was from 1818 to 1831 pastor of the Brattle Street Church in Boston. From 1835 to 1843 he owned and edited the *North American Review.*

Manuscript: Editor's collection.

1. These sketches, which Greenough apparently hoped might be printed in the *North American Review,* have not been preserved. The substance of them is probably contained in his essays "Remarks on American Art" and "American Architecture," which appeared in the *United States Magazine and Democratic Review* for July and August 1843, respectively.

2. Probably Henry.

3. Luman Reed (1787–1836), New York merchant and art patron, gave a floor of his house on Greenwich Street to his collection, which was open to the public one day a week. After his death the collection was given to the New-York Historical Society.

4. Asher Brown Durand (1796–1886), engraver and painter, was first commissioned by Reed to paint a portrait of President Jackson and subsequently to paint portraits of all of Jackson's predecessors in office, of Martha Washington, and of Reed himself. Durand's other picture to which Greenough refers was *A Peddlar and his Wares.*

5. Sir David Wilkie (1785–1841) was a Scottish genre painter.

6. At least thirteen paintings by George Whiting Flagg were in Reed's collection.

7. William Sidney Mount (1807–68), genre painter, was represented in Reed's collection by *The Fortune Teller, The Truant Gamblers, Bargaining for a Horse,* and *Haying Scene.*

93.   To Washington Allston
   22 November 1836

. . . [*page cut off*] He[1] lives at Islington comfortably, and has in Newman Street one of the best studios I have seen — He has a numerous acquaintance. . . . [*page cut off*] What shall I say of the world of English Art: The sight of much in so short a time has bewildered me and you must excuse any incoherence in what I may say. As a school I think the English below the French — single men have pieced the thrall that holds the mass, but these are inferior to the 2nd rate men of Paris. When I look at the works of Hogarth of Wilson and Gainsborough I marvel at the supremacy of Reynolds, unless the pen he considered his sceptre instead of the pencil — I cannot allow the frowsy and beplastered portraits I see here with his name, though at a distance they look like works of the old masters, to be comparable as works of art to Stuart's or Copley's portraits. Hogarth seems to me to be their greatest man — Wilkie's best are stinted are eked out in comparison with him — He is the Fielding[2] of the English school — English in his subjects — in his style he is the natural rich product of the soil and worth all the hot house luxuries of the imitators. You will perhaps be surprised when I tell you that moden (late) buildings of [*page torn*] city are reflections of Paris — Instead of the Palladian magnificence of W[hite]hall [*page torn*] and other old palaces, they content themselves with the eternal portico, the new fangled Pompeian ornaments, and paint stucco & plate glass complete the 9 days' wonder[3] — I like Chantry's portraits both the busts and the full lengths better than any other modern ones I have seen — I cannot think him an inventor — his imitators of whom are 4 5ths of the English sculptors are poor enough — I would say someth[ing] [*page torn*] of the beautiful water colour pictures but have not space — I beg you to be remembered to Mr Dana and his brother and to Mrs Alston and am Dear Sir with affectionate respect

Yours
Horatio Greenough

London Nov 22 1836
to Washington Allston[4]

Addressed: Washington Alston Esqr / Care of Mr Alfred Greenough / Boston. Mass. / 24th Nov.

Endorsed: Forwarded by Your ob't Servant / Alfred Greenough / 40 India Whf / Boston 4 Jan 1837

NOTES

Most of the first page of the manuscript for this letter has been cut off, leaving at the bottom of the recto only two lines and, directly above them, the words "you in person"; the verso of this manuscript page contains only the last three lines ("What . . . . I think the").

Manuscript: Dana Papers, MHS.

1. John Greenough.
2. The English novelist and dramatist Henry Fielding (1707–54) crowded his works with details of life in his day, which he often satirized.
3. The Palace of Whitehall was destroyed by fire in 1691, and only its Banqueting Hall, designed by Inigo Jones and built in 1622, was restored. It is this building, a superb example of Palladian architecture, to which Greenough refers. Ornamental designs similar to those on buildings in Pompeii enjoyed a great vogue for many years after the discovery of that city in 1748.
4. Greenough was in London for about two weeks after leaving New York. These two lines are in another hand.

94.   To Guillaume Tell Poussin
        30 March 1837

Florence 30th March '37.

Major Poussin

My Dear Sir

I have much pleasure in introducing to your acquaintance and in recommending to your kindness the Bearer of this Emilio Santarelli[1] Sculptor a gentleman more known from the excellence of his own works, than from the circumstance of his inheriting the name of the most celebrated of modern Engravers in precious stones. May I ask of you the favor of procuring for him an acquaintance with such of your Parisian artists as you may think it useful for him to know? I beg you will afford me an opportunity of serving you here in like manner. I have not seen Mess. Gray[2] and Cogswell since Feby. but expect them daily. Accept my assurances of the highest consideration and believe me Dear Sir

Yours very truly
Horatio Greenough

Addressed: Major Poussin / Rue Cadet — No 24. / Paris. / Emilio Santarelli / of Florence

NOTES

Guillaume Tell Poussin (1794–1876), French soldier, engineer, and author, was particularly interested in America. In 1848–49 he served as French minister to the United States. Presumably Greenough met him in Paris in 1831.
    Manuscript: Gratz Collection, American Painters, Sculptors, Engravers, HSP.
  1. Emilio Santarelli (1801–86), Italian sculptor, became professor of sculpture at the Academy of Fine Arts in Florence in 1832.
  2. Francis Calley Gray (1790–1856), Boston lawyer, politician, and one-time president of the Boston Athenaeum, devoted himself chiefly to public affairs. He and J. G. Cogswell passed through Florence early in the year, en route from Paris (where Greenough had seen them) to Rome, and shortly afterward they returned to Florence.

95.   To Samuel F. B. Morse
      11 May 1837

Florence May 11th '37 —

S F B Morse Esqr
My dear Sir.
    I have requested my brother to forward to you, provided you should be willing to do me the service, a picture belonging to a friend of mine, which I am desirous to exhibit and if possible to sell. I wish to exhibit with a view to profit and I thought that you might give the charge of exhibiting it to some indigent person, who might derive a benefit in serving me. I wish it to be so located as not to be exposed to fire, though I shall have it insured. The room where it is shown

should have the sun, but kept out by a tracing paper screen. I need
not tell you that the light should be concentrated on the work by
means of pieces of baise, shutting out the rest of the room. If you
would take the trouble to give it one hand of light varnish to refresh
it, I shall be obliged. It is the work of M. Alexander Le Blanc[1] a
painter of much eminence here, and a particular friend of mine.
Should you think him worthy a seat among your honorary members I
am sure he would be gratified. In case you find a person willing to
give it his attention, I shall be willing to make such a compensation
for his services as you may see fit to allow. We want $1500. for the
picture if we sell it, but if no hopes are entertained of getting that
sum, we will let it go for 1000. I have procured you newspapers —
they shall be sent you directly — They were to have been delivered
yest'y — Love to Cooper and his — shall write again soon, am full of
occupations but well.

Yours sincerely
Horatio Greenough

Addressed: S. F. B. Morse Esqr P.N.A. / at the N. York University[2] /
New. York —

NOTES

Manuscript: Charles Roberts Autograph Letter Collection, Haverford College
Library.
   1. Alexandre Leblanc (1793–1866) was a French landscape and history painter.
      At his death Greenough owned a painting by a Leblanc, probably Alexandre,
      of the interior of the Siena Cathedral. From 1838 to 1841 Greenough and
      his wife lived in Casa Lablanc, on Via di Bardi in Florence, possibly the
      property of Alexandre Leblanc. Apparently nothing came of Greenough's
      proposals to Morse.
   2. Morse was appointed Professor of the Literature of the Arts of Design in
      New York City University in 1835 (Samuel Irenaeus Prime, *The Life of
      Samuel F. B. Morse, LL.D.* [New York, 1875], p. 292).

PLATE I. Drawing of mounted warriors. From a draft of a letter addressed "My Lord," written after 31 July 1829 and consisting only of the words "During Mr Cooper's residence in Florence he did." Editor's collection.

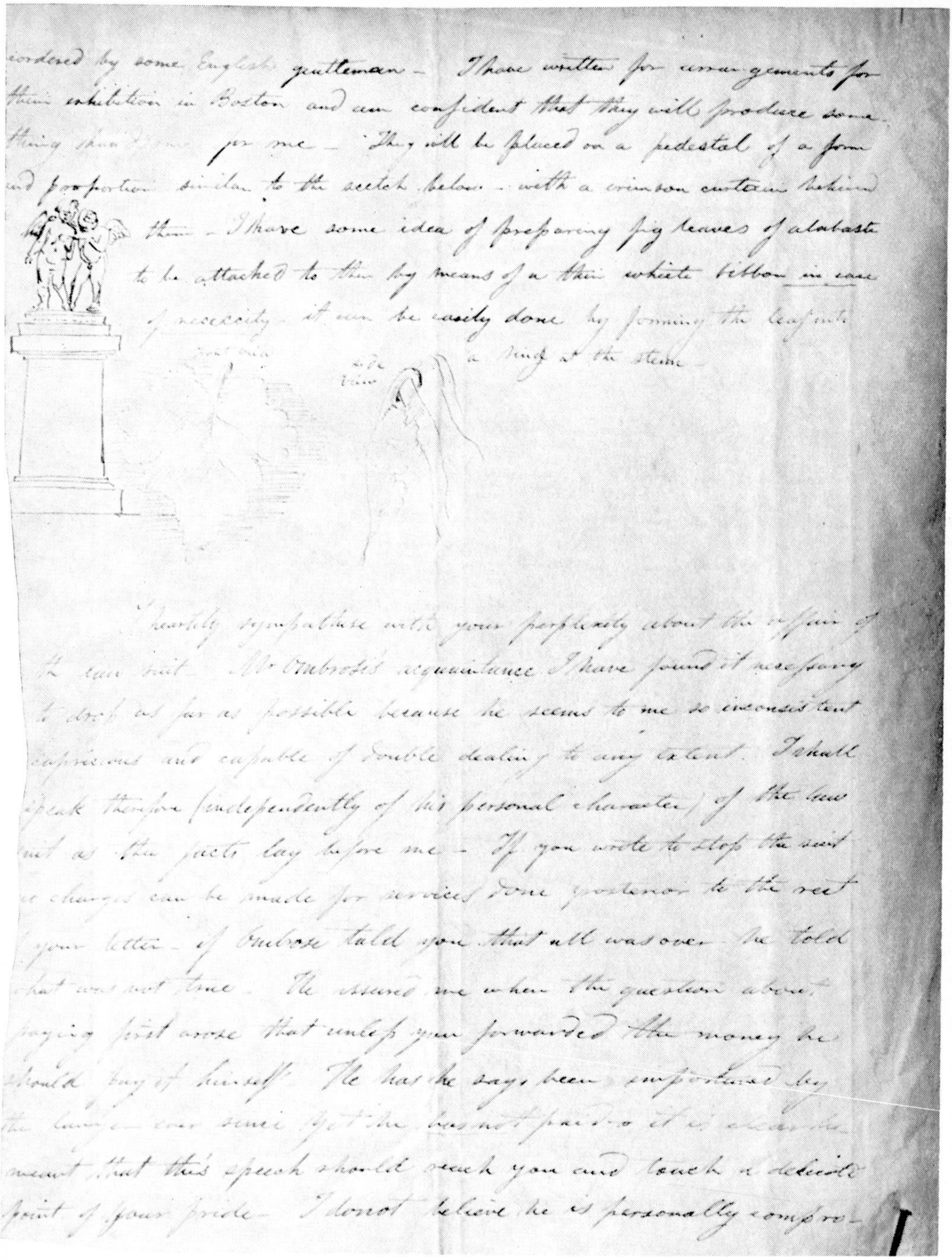

ordered by some English gentleman — I have written for arrangements for their exhibition in Boston and am confident that they will produce something handsome for me — They will be placed on a pedestal of a form and proportion similar to the sketch below — with a crimson curtain behind them — I have some idea of preparing fig leaves of alabaster to be attached to them by means of a thin white ribbon in case of necessity it can be easily done by forming the leaf into a ring at the stem

I heartily sympathize with your perplexity about the affair of the law suit. Mr Ambrose's acquaintance I have found it necessary to drop as far as possible because he seems to me so inconsistent ... and capable of double dealing to any extent. I shall speak therefore (independently of his personal character) of the law suit as the facts lay before me — If you write to stop the suit ... charges can be made for services done ... to the rest ... your letter — if Ambrose told you that all was over he told ... that was not true. He assured me when the question about paying first arose that unless you forwarded the money he should pay it himself. He has he says been importuned by the lawyer ever since yet he has not paid ... it is ... meant that this speech should reach you and touch a delicate point of your pride — I do not believe he is personally compro-

PLATE II. Drawing of *The Chanting Cherubs* and alabaster leaves to be used in exhibition of the group. From a letter book copy of Greenough to James Fenimore Cooper, 20 December 1830 (Letter 25). Editor's collection.

be resolved into one of these two - want of knowledge - want of mind
of the faculty to see consequences - I ask pardon for this garrulity
and will close this before it gets worse by a sketch and explanation
of my plan for a National Monument - The ground plan is thus
The white spaces at the corners are the foundations of the Dies a, b. which
are 4 - on the Eastern one I design Columbus seated pondering on the
globe - on the north a   Mother from clasping her infants while
the Indian   steals behind them - on the west Piety
Philip seated amid the   bones of their fallen brethren - on the
south Civilization as a   [Female] seated with the implements of
industry in her hands   while the [Boy] is represented at her
side as reading   on the side c and on the other
corresponding   sides - I should [des]
four points   of the history of the [Rev.]
of oppression   Remonstrance - Resistance -
Independence   these I should represent
in the form of historic bas reliefs. The whole I would surmount with a statue
of Washington in the act of resigning his authority as General in chief -

I have designed this monument not so much from any hope
I have of ever being so respectably employed as from a thirst
to get vent in something large - I like to think about great
works though my stars have forbidden their execution

I pray you will remember my respectful regards to Mrs Cooper
and the family -   I remain Dear Sir
                                        Yours sincerely
                                        Horatio Greenough

PS on the [rect] of your letter authorising
my drawing for the balance I took up to
[ ] of 50 Francescone at Florence and shall
avail myself of your last for the drawing for the remainder

PLATE III. Design for a national monument. From Greenough to Cooper,
7 March 1831 (Letter 28). Cooper Collection, Beinecke Rare Book and
Manuscripts Library, Yale University.

PLATE IV. Miscellaneous drawings. The profile labeled "expects to be lathered" is of Samuel F. B. Morse; that next to it may be of James Ombrosi, who had a large nose; that bearing the notation "a promising lad" is probably of Paul Cooper; and the small profile with protruding chin is of Albert Brisbane. From a draft of Greenough to Washington Allston, October 1831 (Letter 34). Editor's collection.

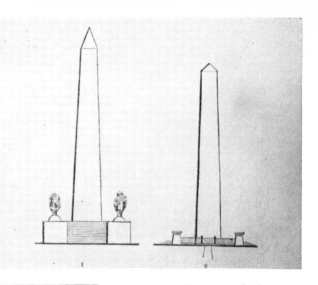

PLATE V. Design of the Bunker Hill Monument proposed by Greenough (left) and design of that to be built (right). From Greenough to Morse, between 25 March and 23 April 1832 (Letter 43). Printed in Samuel Irenaeus Prime, *The Life of Samuel F. B. Morse, LL.D.* (New York, 1875), p. 214.

PLATE VI. Drawing of *The Genius of America*. From Greenough to Morse, 19 July 1832 (Letter 54). Printed in Prime, *Life of Morse*, p. 216.

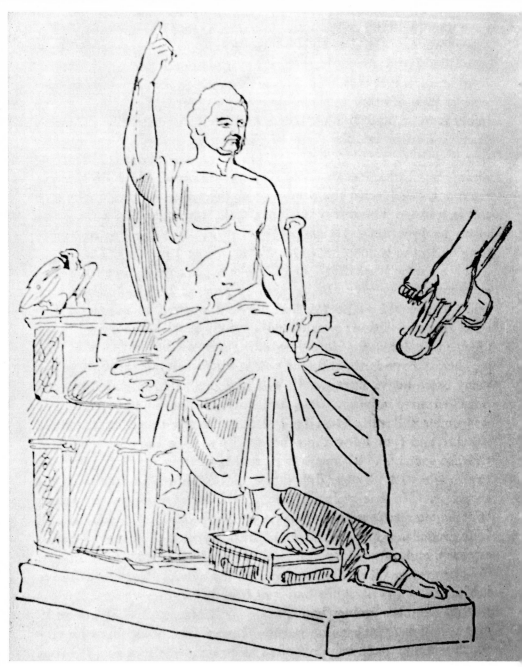

PLATE VII. Drawing of the model of *Washington*. From Greenough to Morse, 18 November 1833 (Letter 69). Printed in Prime, *Life of Morse*, p. 218.

PLATE VIII. Drawing of the model of *Washington*. From Greenough to Edward Livingston, 28 January 1834 (Letter 73). RG 59, General Records of the Department of State, Accession 161, Item 135, National Archives.

Florence. July 12. 1840.

My Dear Sir

The constant press of my affairs has hitherto prevented my having the pleasure of writing to you. I am preparing Washington's Statue for shipment in October. I have varied the back of the chair since you saw it by making it of ornamental open work — by this means I enable the Spectator to enjoy the outline of the entire figure from behind. as well as from the other sides — The work is much enriched and though the additional expense is great I cannot repent the step.

SIMULACRUM ISTUD
ad magnum libertatis
exemplum — nec aine
ipsa duraturum · HG
Cives americanus —
faciebat.

In the midst of these certainly industrious and praiseworthy efforts to do my art well, I have received a letter from Mr Vail acting Sec'y of State, in which he takes me to task with very little ceremony on account of the time I have been occupied in this work and which he closes by assuring me that I need hope for no more moneys until the Gov't get official report upon the progress of my group. How this is to be done I know not as the Consul at Leghorn is dead and Mr Greene has had no orders from Gov't to leave his post for this object.

[left margin, written vertically:] In making known what I have here written they you will be governed by discretion. I prefer of course if an attempt is making to prison the public mind against my work. These you will make these facts known if the subject is at all dwelt upon it —

PLATE IX. Drawing of the chair for *Washington*. From Greenough to Charles Sumner, 12 July 1840 (Letter 145). Sumner Correspondence, Houghton Library, Harvard University.

96. To Richard Henry Wilde
   [May?] 1837

My Dear Sir

Being obliged to go to the Studio at an early hour I write instead of coming to you in person — I have occasion to ask your good offices with the Austrian Minister,[1] through such friends as you can move in my behalf — My case is this — The Duke of Modena[2] in the plenitude of his financial wisdom has laid a duty of 2 franks per metrical pound, on plaister models entering the "felicissimi stati."[3] This law takes about 60 Napoleons out of my pocket, smart money for enjoying the priviledge of spending 3 or 4 hundred more in Carrara. Now I am told that by applying through the Austrian minister I can get permission to enter my cast *"in transito"* for one year say — Will you have the goodness to enquire of the English or French minister,[4] whether they are willing to ask such a favor of the Austrian Ambassador or if they will give me line of introduction to him, that I may plead my own case.

I had intended to ship my marble to Leghorn as a last resort, rather than pay this (as it seems to me) extortionate duty, but I find that the rogues have calculated it to a nicety & that my marble will stand me in the same amount in transportation before I can get it to Leghorn — With regret that I am forced to annoy you with such a matter I am

Respectfully Yours
Horatio Greenough

R. H. Wilde Esqr
Thursday M'g

Addressed: R H Wilde Esqr / Casa Vernaccia

NOTES

This letter was apparently written not long before that of 6 June 1837 (Letter 97), in which Greenough refers to his difficulty in deciding whether to send the

cast of his *Washington* to Carrara or have the marble sent to him in Florence.
Manuscript: Department of Rare Books and Manuscripts, BPL.

1. Count Adam Reviczky von Reviczky (1786–1862), a native of Hungary, was Lord High Chancellor there until 1836, when he became Austrian minister to Tuscany; later he retired to a monastery, where he died (*Pallas Nagy Lexikon* [Budapest, 1897], vol. 14). He succeeded in getting permission for the cast of the *Washington* to be sent to Carrara duty-free (see Letter 152).
2. Francis IV (1779–1849) of the d'Este family.
3. "Most happy states."
4. Ralph Abercrombie and a M. Bellocq, respectively (*Almanacco Toscano* [1837]).

97. To John Forsyth
6 June 1837

Florence June 6th 1837.

Hon John Forsyth Secretary of State / Depart't of State.

Sir. When I received from the Secretary of State, the commission to execute a Statue of Washington, I was unprovided either with a Studio fitted for the work of such magnitude, or with the authorities upon which I could rely to form a likeness. I went to Paris to obtain a cast of Houdon's head, after having in vain tried to procure it through the assistance of others. I also ordered a copy to be made from the original portrait by Mr Stewart.[1] The delay occasioned by these preparations and in making necessary alterations in the building which I had selected as a work-room (and which had been a church) prevented my setting up the skeleton of the statue until Sept'r. 1834. The model was finished and cast in Feb'y 1836.

I was cautioned by the more experienced against commencing upon my marble, while the plaister was still moist, as in such large masses its weight often proves too great for its consistency and it settles however well armed and secured. I took advantage of the interim of its drying to visit the room where it is proposed to place it; and I found on my return here, that in fact the great weight of the right arm and drapery attached to it, had bent the trunk several lines out of its relation to the plumb. The correction of this defect has cost some time.

I thought after examining the Rotunda with reference to my statue that the latter would require somewhat more of ornament in the accessories than I had at first intended. I am now executing six figures in low relief, to fill the empty spaces on each side [of] the chair. These are allegorical — On the one side I represent Agriculture with Trade and Facture on each side of her, on the other Legislation, the Land and Marine forces. This addition to my original plan will occupy several months.

It is hardly necessary to state to you that as a stranger and alone, I have difficulty in making fair contracts, and in having them faithfully executed. My block of Marble at this moment waits my decision, whether it shall be transported hither at an enormous expence or remain till the model be sent to it, in which case it cannot be rough hewn under my constant and immediate inspection. I shall probably attempt the first mentioned course.[2]

My object in addressing you at this time, is not only to give account of the present state of the work, but to beg respectfully that I may have official assurance, that while I sacrifice my eagerness to complete this monument, to the best interest of my employers, I am not incurring blame for a delay unforseen and inevitable & I am sure that if my health is spared, this statue will have been executed in as short a time as is ever allotted to works of its size and importance.

I am sir with the highest respect
Your most obedient Servant
Horatio Greenough

Addressed: Hon John Forsyth / Secretary of State / Dept of State / Washington D.C.
Endorsed: Rec'd July 26th 1837 — / Mr Hill

NOTES

Manuscript: RG 59, General Records of the Department of State, Accession 161, Item 135, NA. A duplicate of this letter, also in the National Archives (RG 59, General Records of the Department of State, Miscellaneous Letters Received), differs from this one in a few minor details.

1. Presumably that in the Boston Athenaeum, painted in Philadelphia in 1795 or 1796. It was not Stuart's first study of Washington, which he destroyed, but one of several copies he made of it. See William T. Whitley, *Gilbert Stuart* (Cambridge, 1932), pp. 94–95, 219.
2. The model was sent to Carrara.

98. To John Forsyth
1 July 1837

Hon John Forsyth / Secretary of State. Department of State.
Sir

I have this day received your letter of April 4th '37 informing me that the President wishes me to communicate a design of a group for one of the platforms that flank the steps in front of the Capitol; together with proposals for the execution of the same. Your letter was not accompanied by a contract entered into with Mr Persico, to whose composition of "Columbus Discovering the New World,"[1] it is proposed that I should produce a *pendant,* so that I am left in doubt both as regards the size of the work, and the amount proposed to be devoted to its execution.

I know of no single fact in profane history that can balance the one so wisely chosen by Mr Persico as the subject of his group. I shall be obliged therefore to submit to the adoption of one of less import, and to rely upon the resources of the Art, for filling the space allotted to me. I propose to make a group, which shall commemorate the dangers and difficulty of peopling our continent, and which shall also serve as a memorial of the Indian race, and an embodying of the Indian character; a matter of great interest to no distant posterity — a subject which with due respect, has not been exhausted by the gentlemen whose bas reliefs adorn the Rotunda.[2] It will be my immediate care to forward to you my design, which I hope to do, by the month of August.

I have consulted some of the abler artists here on this choice of subject. It has been objected to me in one instance that it is not a distinct individual historical fact, & it has been recommended to me to represent instead of it, Washington raising from the ground the figure of America.[3] I am assured I should thus be clear and balance figure for figure. But it seems to me that these objections to my first invention are not well grounded — first; though its intention may not be quite clear to those who are imperfectly acquainted with our early history, it is distinct and unequivocal to every American eye. If not an individual historical fact, it will embody a whole class of facts, and perpetuate the ideas and sentiments connected with them. I object to the Allegory which I have mentioned, that it borders on common-place, and may be considered superfluous, since Washington's agency in achieving our liberties, is more distinctly told elsewhere in the same edifice. I mention these two subjects as they seem to me at this time, the best adapted to the situation, but I shall be most happy in being advised in choosing between them or listen with great pleasure to another, should the more experienced be willing to suggest it.

The advanced state of the work on which I am at present employed, and the length of time during which it will be wrought upon mainly by my assistants, will enable me to devote a large share of my attention to this group. I regret very much that I am not informed of the time accorded to us for completing these works. To conceive, is the task of a moment — to digest arrange and model is not so speedily effected — to render a group in marble finished ad unguem[4] is a herculean undertaking, and I have long since come to the determination, that no motive shall tempt me to promise that which I cannot be sure of performing Viz. my utmost at a given day. I shall look to you therefore to weigh my claims to the character of a thorough workman and an upright artist, & I shall beg of you to urge with the President the expedience of allowing me my own time, retaining the right of withdrawing the commission if I prove inactive or dilatory. Should the conditions made by Congress a part of this note exclude the terms on which alone I can serve them, I shall be most happy to be the medium of your communications with any other artist whom you may [choose] [page torn] to [fill] [page torn] my place. As regards the price fixed for the [work] [page torn] I shall be satisfied with the same sum paid to m[y] [page torn][5] collaborator, be that what it may.

I am Sir
Your Most Ob't Servant
Horatio Greenough

Florence
July 1st '37 —

P.S. Since writing the above, I have been informed by my brother that you have stated to him, that it necessary that I should apply for the remaining instalment of the price of the Statue of Washington. I beg therefore that you will make as early an arrangement as may be convenient for the payment of it — as owing to the present difficulties,

I am in danger of being delayed in my operations for want of funds.[6]
My address is — "Florence Poste Restante."

Addressed: Hon John Forsyth / Secretary of State / Dept of State /
p. Havre / Washington, D.C.
Endorsed: Rec'd Sept 2d 1837 / Mr Dickins to be ret'd [?]

NOTES

Manuscript: RG 59, General Records of the Department of State, Miscellaneous Letters Received, NA. A duplicate of this letter, also in the National
Archives (RG 59, General Records of the Department of State, Accession 161,
Item 135), differs from this one in a few minor details.
1. Persico had modeled a group of this subject, which he proposed for one of
   the blockings of the steps on the east front of the Capitol, by the spring of
   1836.
2. The bas reliefs are the *Conflict between Daniel Boone and the Indians* by
   Enrico Causici, the *Treaty of William Penn and the Indians* by Nicholas
   Gevelot, and the *Preservation of Captain John Smith by Pocahantas* by
   Antonio Capellano.
3. Greenough's sketch of this subject is in the editor's collection.
4. "Perfectly."
5. The missing words in the last two sentences have been supplied from the
   duplicate of the letter.
6. Alfred Greenough wrote Secretary of the Treasury Levi Woodbury on 15 May
   1837 asking if he could receive for Horatio the last installment due on the
   Washington (RG 56, General Records of the Treasury Department, Miscellaneous Letters Received, NA). Woodbury referred the letter to Forsyth,
   who replied that Horatio had not received the money because he had not
   asked for authority to draw it, because the statue was not finished, and because payment could be made to Horatio only (Forsyth to Woodbury, 22
   May 1837, RG 56, Letters from Executive Officers, NA). Woodbury communicated these facts to Alfred in a letter dated 25 May 1837 (Alfred to
   Woodbury, 30 March 1838, RG 56, Miscellaneous Letters Received, NA).

99. To Laura Elizabeth (Carson) Brevoort
   3 October 1837

My Dear Madam
    I hasten to enclose you the Bill of lading of the Chimney Pieces I
have had made for Mr Brevoort[1] — The present stagnation of the
American trade has prevented their being shipped until now — they
have lain long in the magazines at Leghorn. I need not tell you how

much I have fretted at this delay, being aware that they should long since have been in New York — I beg you will represent to Mr Brevoort that owing to the present state of American credit here I have been called on to pay charges on these cases as follows — in francesconi & pauls & crazie[2]

		pauls	
Storage — reception — expedition	Fi 5. — 5	cr	
Shipping or boat expence . . .	Fi 7. — 4.	2.	
Postage and papers		3.	4.
Francesconi	13.	2.	6

I shall debit Mr Brevoort with this sum — I remain Madam

With respect
Yours truly
Horatio Greenough

Florence. Oct'r 3d. 37.

NOTES

Laura Elizabeth Carson (b. 1798) was a native of Charleston, South Carolina. She married Henry Brevoort of New York in 1816 (records in the South Carolina Historical Society, Charleston).
    Manuscript: Hart Collection, Archives of American Art, Smithsonian Institution.
  1. Henry Brevoort (see note to Letter 114) had ordered four pieces of white Carrara marble and a fifth of yellow (Brevoort to Greenough, 28 January 1838, collection of David Richardson, Washington, D.C.).
  2. A paul was worth about 10¢ at this time; a crazia was worth 1¼¢.

100. To Andrew Stevenson
10 October 1837

Florence Oct'r 10th 1837.

To / His Excellency Andrew Stevenson
My Dear Sir
    I can hardly expect that your memory should retain the details of the Contract entered into with me by the American Government, for

the execution of a statue of Washington — One of the articles however, stipulated that I was to be furnished with the sum of $5000 per annum, for four years, which has accordingly been done without any application or demand on my part, until the present year. My Brother, Alfred Greenough of Boston, has received in answer to his enquiry on this subject, a letter from the Secretary of State,[1] informing him that funds have been placed in London for the above object; but that no advice has been given me of the same, 1stly, "Because the Statue is not finished" 2ndly "Because I have not made application for funds." Now the contract stipulates that the 4th instalment shall be paid, *not on the completion of the work,* but at the expiration of the 3d year — No mention is made of any application from me as necessary — & in fact the preceding instalments have been regularly forwarded without such a step on my part.

As my work is in danger of interruption for want of funds — (the present state of Exchange having rendered what I have, literally unavailable), I have written to Mess Rothschilds[2] requesting them to inform me if they hold funds for my disposal, and I have taken the liberty of addressing you at this time, in the hope that your influence may induce them to authorize my drafts for at least 2000 Dolls. I have made application to the Sec'y of State, but as the answer cannot reach me these two months, I grieve to be obliged to suspend for want of money, particularly now that the cholera and other unforeseen calamities, have already thrown so many obstacles in my path. Begging that you will excuse this call upon your kindness & that you will present my compliments to Madame Stevenson

I am Dear Sir
Respectfully Yours
Horatio Greenough

Addressed: His Excellency / Andrew Stevenson / Envoy & Minister Plenipotentiary / of the U.S. of America / London.
Endorsed: Rec'd. Oct 21

NOTES

Andrew Stevenson (1784–1857), of Virginia, was U.S. minister to Great Britain from 1836 to 1841. Presumably Greenough met him and his wife in London late in 1836.

Manuscript: Andrew and John White Stevenson Papers, LC.
1. See Alfred to Levi Woodbury, Secretary of the Treasury, 15 May 1837 (RG 56, General Records of the Treasury Department, Series K, Miscellaneous Letters Received, NA) and John Forsyth to Woodbury, 22 May 1837 (RG 56, Series A.B., Letters from Executive Officers, NA).
2. Nathan Mayer Rothschild and Sons was the banking house of the American government in England. For Greenough's letter to them, see "Unrecovered Letters."

101. To Richard Henry Wilde
Before 14 October 1837

Mr Dear Sir

I have seen the lawyer — the presence of the American consul is not necessary — his cognizance of the act[1] is not necessary — but it is usual to fortify similar papers in such manner — which can be done by *sending* the instrument *to him* for signature — I have consulted Miss Gore[2] on the choice of place & she prefers being married by an English clergyman — and of course will be married at the minister's if he will give his consent, or at our house, if *the ceremony can be performed* here by an *English* clergyman.

The contract in Italian can express in general terms the conditions stipulated in the settlement prepared by you[3] — I fear I shall be obliged to ask you to represent to Mr Abercrombie[4] the present state of this matter — his answer must now be our guide. I write instead of coming to you because I am fatigued.

Yours truly
Horatio Greenough.

Addressed: R. H. Wilde Esqr.

NOTES

Manuscript: Gratz Collection, American Painters, Sculptors, Engravers, HSP.
1. Greenough's marriage, which took place on 14 October 1837.
2. Louisa Ingersoll Gore (1813–91), called Eliza in her youth, was the daughter of Boston merchant John Gore. Her brother John C. Gore had been a

fellow art student of Greenough's in Florence a few years earlier (see Letter 14, n. 33). She and Greenough met in Paris in 1836. Early the next year she and her stepfather traveled to Italy, stopping briefly in Florence on their way to Rome; and in the spring they settled in Florence.

3. The most notable condition of the contract was that both parties should maintain separate estates. It is registered in the Stato Civile nel Comune di Firenze, vol. 90, fol. 161, c. 2. A copy, made 17 October 1837, is in the editor's collection. The ceremony is also recorded in the marriage register of the Church of the Holy Trinity, Florence.

4. Ralph Abercrombie, the British minister to Tuscany from 1836 to 1839. The marriage ceremony was performed at his residence, the Palazzo Panciatichi Ximenes, by the Reverend Henry Hartopp Knapp, chaplain of the Anglican community.

102.   To Gino Capponi
7 November 1837

To the Marquis Capponi

Mr Gibson[1] an English Sculptor of celebrity who is at present in Florence, having expressed a wish to see the beautiful drawings by Sabatelli[2] in your possession, I am induced to trespass on your kindness for a permission to that effect, as it is the only pleasure I can do a gentleman for whose character & talents I have the highest esteem. I would have waited your return to town, but that I fear the news of the cholera having ceased at Rome may induce my friend to return thither.

I am much obliged by the sight of a fine bust of Lorenzo dei Medici which was left here with your name several days since. It agrees well with my own[3] — perhaps is less noble — but may be more true — Mr Greene desires to be remembered to you, he is well.

Your Obliged friend & Serv't
Horatio Greenough

Florence. Nov. 7th '37.

Addressed: To The Marquis Capponi —

NOTES

Marquis Gino Capponi (1792–1876), Italian historian, statesman, and member of an illustrious Florentine family, had a wide acquaintance among foreign as well as Italian politicians, philosophers, writers, and artists. Greenough met him soon after settling in Florence.

Manuscript: Carteggi Capponi, Biblioteca Nazionale.

1. Benjamin Gibson (1811–51), brother of the sculptor John Gibson and his assistant in Rome, was in Florence at this time (information furnished by Clara L. Dentler, Florence).
2. Presumably Luigi Sabatelli (see Letter 20, n. 2). Capponi's large collection of art objects included portraits of himself and of Pier Capponi, one of his ancestors, by Sabatelli (Pietro Thouar, *Notizie e Guida di Firenze e de' suoi Contorni* [Florence, 1841], p. 416).
3. Presumably a bust which Greenough owned, not one which he executed.

103.   To John Forsyth
         15 November 1837

Florence Nov'r 15 – 1837.

Hon John Forsyth / Secretary of State / Dep't of State.
Sir –

I herewith enclose the design of a second group[1] which I have composed for the platform in front of the Capitol – in which I have endeavoured to convey the idea of the triumph of the whites over the savage tribes, at the same time that it illustrates the dangers of peopling the country. I have thought it best not to waste time in making laboured drawings until I shall have been made acquainted – 1st on which side of the stair-case it is intended my group shall stand – 2d what is the general form of the composition made by Mr Persico, as it is necessary for Architectural congruity that the two masses should harmonize to a certain extent. – 3d The exact area on which the group will stand – 4th The height of that surface from the esplanade in front of the building –

I have written to Messrs Rothschild to request a payment of a portion of the instalment which I learned from my brother had been lodged with them, and received for answer that they could not advance without instructions to that effect from the Department of State.[2] Allow me to call your attention to the letters that passed between Mr Livingston & myself when this work was ordered of me, and I trust that on examination of them, you will find that I have asked nothing inconsistent with the stipulations of that contract. If the execution of the work consumes more time than I had anticipated — this must be attributed to the distances that have stood between me and my resources, & my materials. Should I not make it clear that I have used all the dispatch consistent with the obstacles I have encountered, I am ready to abide by any decision which the severest justice can form against me. In the mean time, I beg that if the order for payment has not been forwarded, that it may be done as early as convenient, since my continuation in this task has obliged me to resort to unpleasant, and disadvantageous means of procuring funds — I am Sir with the highest respect

Your Ob't Serv't
Horatio Greenough

Addressed: Hon John Forsyth / Secretary of State. / Dept of State. / Washington D. C.
Endorsed: Paris, 29 November, 1837 — forwarded by Mr Forsyth's / obedient servant, / Daniel Brent / Rec'd Jan. 10' 1838 —

NOTES

The body of this letter is in Louisa Greenough's hand.
     Manuscript: RG 59, General Records of the Department of State, Accession 161, Item 135, NA.
  1. This sketch has not been preserved, but it probably depicted a pioneer woman with an infant being saved by a pioneer man from an Indian wielding a tomahawk, the essential design of Greenough's group *The Rescue.*
  2. See "Unrecovered Letters." The letter from Messrs. Rothschild is in the collection of David Richardson, Washington, D.C., and a copy of it is in the Rothschild Archives, London.

104. To Thomas Handasyd Perkins
[Fall 1837?]

. . . I became possessed, a few months since, of casts from the celebrated statues by Michael Angelo, representing Night and Day.[1]

They are *proof casts,* made to try the moulds ordered here by the King of the French,[2] and were by the terms of contract, a perquisite to the moulder. They are for all purposes of study and criticism identical with their originals and are in the best state and quite new. . . .

NOTES

Thomas Handasyd Perkins (1764–1854) was a prosperous Boston shipping merchant and a noted philanthropist. Perkins visited Greenough in Florence in May 1835 in the course of a European tour; his manuscript diary for the period, including an account of the visit, is in the Samuel Cabot Papers, MHS.

This letter is dated on the supposition that it was written at the time Greenough shipped the casts of the Michelangelo statues to Perkins, probably three or four months before Perkins evidently received them (see n. 1).

Source: *Catalogue of the First Exhibition of Sculpture in the Athenaeum Gallery* (Boston, 1839), p. 7.

1. The *Giorno* and *Notte* are figures beneath the statue on the sarcophagus of Giuliano dei Medici in the New Sacristy in the church of San Lorenzo, Florence. At the same time Greenough acquired the casts of Michelangelo's *Aurora* and *Crepuscolo,* beneath the statue on the sarcophagus of Lorenzo dei Medici, and the statue of Giuliano, in the same room, all of which he kept for himself. Perkins presented the casts of *Giorno* and *Notte* to the Boston Athenaeum in 1838, where they were exhibited the following year. A print of them appeared in *Ballou's Pictorial Drawing Room Companion* 8 (1853): 201. They have apparently been destroyed.
2. Louis Philippe (1773–1850).

105.   To Edward Elbridge Salisbury
         2 December 1837

Florence Dec'b'r 2d — 1837 —

Dear Sir,

I learn from a letter of J McLean Halsey Esqr[1] that you have become the proprietor of two small statues which I have undertaken for that gentleman. Allow me to answer as briefly as I can the questions proposed to me by my former employer. These statues are about two feet high — That of Aristides[2] is quite advanced in marble, that of Washington is yet uncommenced. I propose to make the latter of the same size as the other; in a modern dress, but wrapped in a cloak — & leaning on his sword. I prefer as pedestals green marble, only, because I think it relieves the statues better, besides, that in our climate a large mass of white chills the eye I think, but, I of course don't wish to make my own caprice on this point a law for others' tastes. I shall wait your answer to this, in case you may have any thing to suggest on the subject of the statue of Washington and am —

Dear Sir
Yours truly
Horatio Greenough

NOTES

Edward Elbridge Salisbury (1814–1901), Oriental scholar, studied in Europe from 1837 to 1841 and in 1842–43. In April 1837 he visited Greenough's studio in Florence, at which time Greenough was in America. Salisbury's manuscript journal of his travels is in the Salisbury Family Papers, Yale University Library.

The letter, except for the complimentary close and signature, is in Louisa Greenough's hand.

Manuscript: Salisbury Family Papers, Yale University Library.

1. John McLean Halsey (1817–42), of New York, assumed responsibility for two orders his father had placed with Greenough after his father's death at sea on 6 June 1837 (Jacob Lafayette Halsey and Edmund Drake Halsey, *Thomas Halsey of Hertfordshire, England, and Southampton, Long Island, 1591–1679, with his American Descendants to the Eighth and Ninth Generations* [Morristown, N.J., 1895], pp. 210, 243). Salisbury apparently met the Halseys in the summer of 1837.

2. Greenough's statue of the Athenian general is a copy of one formerly so-called in the Museo Nazionale, Naples, now thought to be of Aeschines, an Athenian orator of the same period; it is now in the Yale University Art Gallery.

106. To Edward Elbridge Salisbury
3 January 1838

Edw'd E. Salisbury Esqr
My Dear Sir

I have been highly gratified by your proposal to commute the order of a statue of Washington for one of a more poetical character. I enclose you a rough sketch of a *bas relief* of the subject from the Revelations.[1] I think the action better suited to that branch of sculpture than to the full relief — I wish you to look at this sketch merely as an expression of the general features of the composition & not as a sample of form or character — I think the bas relief particularly well adapted to our walls and style of lighting and furnishing a house — The subject of Joshua[2] I dare not attempt — I doubt if our art has compass enough to convey the full majesty of the miracle. Raphael has come off but so so in his attempt to embody it.[3] Poetry may soar beside those great scriptural symbols but sculpture I fear at least my sculpture must be content to attempt humbler themes.

Allow me to mention to you 2 subjects of a different character — In the 5th Book of the Paradise Lost at the close you will find a description of Abdiel walking through the rebel host — worthy of a marble representation — Another which indeed it were almost vain to attempt yet it were worth the disgrace of defeat to have expressed it partially would be the figure of the Saviour in the act of driving from the temple the money changers — not the expression of brute or of human anger but the radiant indignation of a god whose love itself becomes bitterness at the sight of such profanation in whose hands the scourge is but a type of condemnation. If I were to make the bas relief above mentioned it would cost you about 300 crowns — as for the statues it were hardly worth while to make them less than life and they would cost a great deal. I need not go into any detail as I

know our houses are not prepared to receive works of size. I beg if
you have other subjects to suggest that you will do so and also that
in your answer to this you will give me some account of the prospects
of the Halsey family[4] for whom I have felt much pain. Begging to
present my respectful regards to Mrs Salisbury I remain Dear Sir

Yours very truly
Horatio Greenough

Florence 3d Jan'y. '38

Addressed: Edwd. E. Salisbury Esqr / care of Mess Welles & Co /
Bankers Paris.

NOTES

> Manuscript: Editor's collection.
> 1. Revelation 22:8, 9 describes Saint John's falling on his knees to worship the Angel and the Angel admonishing him not to do so at the end of his vision. Apparently Salisbury suggested the subject.
> 2. That is, of Joshua's commanding the sun to stand still. Salisbury probably also suggested this subject.
> 3. In one of the Loggie in the Vatican.
> 4. "Halsey family" is canceled, in another ink, presumably by another hand. See Letter 105, n. 1.

107. To Edward Elbridge Salisbury
30 January 1838

Florence Jan'y 30 — 1838 —

E. E. Salisbury Esq'r

I was much pleased by the suggestions of your letter of the ———
and shall adopt them entirely in the plan of the bas-relief.[1] I propose
to give the figures 18 inches height — the form of the bas-relief will
probably be a square. To convey the full force of the expression you
describe is not easy, and I will own to you that I fear I shall disappoint you — still, I will do my utmost.

The statue of Abdiel I have long contemplated modelling for myself, and will give you the marble at as low a price as the work can be done for.[2] — If we make it less than life it cannot be larger than three feet without having a dwarfish appearance — of that dimension I should ask 600 Francesconi — If I were to copy the model of the full size that I mean to make it, it could not be furnished for less than 4000 — Nor should I be the gainer of a dollar by the bargain — such a task is the finishing of a statue. I have come to a point in the exercise of my art when it is necessary that I should rather seek to perfect a few works, than to despatch many. I often work on simple busts for a length of time that gives about two dollars a day for my labor. I do not mean that such is my constant employment, if it were, of course I should be working at a very great expense instead of profit — I beg you will not speak of the above circumstance, as I do not wish to be understood as dissatisfied with the reward of my labors — I am far from it. — It is impossible for me to promise at what time this work would be completed, unless I should learn whether the Government has chosen me to make one of the great groups for the staircase of the Capitol — If such be the case, I should require at least three years, as I could give only a portion of my time to the model.

With respectful regards to Mrs Salisbury

Believe me Dear Sir

Yours truly

Horatio Greenough

NOTES

Except for the complimentary close and signature, this letter is in Louisa Greenough's hand.

    Manuscript: Salisbury Family Papers, Yale University Library. Previous publication (in part): E. E. Salisbury, "Two Letters of Horatio Greenough," *Magazine of American History* 18 (1873): 331.

1. Salisbury ordered a bas relief of Saint John and the Angel (see Letter 106, n. 1). It was completed about 1841 and is now in the Yale University Art Gallery.

2. The statue is now in the Yale University Art Gallery.

108.   To Washington Allston
        18 February 1838

Florence, Feby. 18th 1838.

My Dear Mr Alston —

Since I left you now more than a year since I have scarce had
time to collect my thoughts sufficiently to write — I addressed you a
few lines from London because I thought you would be happy to
hear a rather pleasanter account of my brother[1] than others which I
presumed had reached you. I am sorry to say that the poor fellow has
since been again in trouble owing to the simple fact that his expences
are considerable & his means very small — I fear that he will never
get sufficiently free from embarrassment in that country to be able to
begin properly — and at his age — what can I expect? I often shudder
at what may be his fate, for his impulses are as strong as ever and
his experience seems only to prick skin deep —

I heard of your health lately from Mr Brimmer[2] who remained here
a few days on his way to Rome and who amused me not a little by
crumbs that had fallen from Stewart's table and remarks of his own
— I heard of you also from Mr Powers[3] who is now fairly settled here
and is doing himself great honour in his busts. Since my return here
I have besides the work upon my colossus finished a group for Mr
Sears[4] and a full length portrait for Col Thomson which represents
one of his boys playing at battledoor — My intention was to have
made the companion figure representing the brother standing ready
to receive the shuttlecock[5] — I have also made the model of a Venus
for Mr Lowell[6] and have had of course a dreadful battle with the
figure — this being the first female figure entirely naked which I have
attempted except in sketches and drawings — or in bas relief — I have
attempted to combine symmetry with expression and beauty with
innocence taking the more poetic sense of the character and considering the mother of Beauty and the patroness of the graces as
simply such — In making this study I have had occasion to examine
Nature pretty widely & to scrutinize the received models of antiquity
very closely — I submit a few remarks on the Venus dei Medici to your
judgement beginning by confessing that if but one statue of a female

could be saved — I should say let it be this — The head is scarce
worth speaking about, though very beautiful as I presume it has been
forcibly married to this trunk, and belonged originally to a smaller
figure — I find the length from the *nates* to the heel very great — too
great by far — long limbs not being characteristic of the sex but
rather the reverse — I find the pubis superficial — bas relief like, and
as a consequence the muscles of the inside of the thigh going to a
false insertion considerably *outside* the real one — I find the thighs
and legs though exquisite less I will not say marked but emphasized
than even younger figures in real life — I cannot believe this round-
ness and smoothness to be other than architectural or mechanical
when so far carried & must believe that the science laid out in commencing so rare an ensemble was forgotten or laid aside and the
ultimate touches addressed to the eye sensually — I use the word
sensually as denoting that finish which appeals to our love of what
is smooth even and graduated — The ancles (inner) have an emphasis which cannot be found in a female whose bones are otherwise
delicately formed — the feet beautiful as they are seem a little geo-
metric in some of their outlines — want the compound [?] waves
and the play of half tint given by the actual bone and muscle — I
have finished my model and am about to cast it — I am so interested
in the study of this class of figure that I think of remodelling it while
my ideas are awake on the subject to try a few experiments —

I am in treaty for a statue of Abdiel a figure which you may remember suggesting to me many years since — I almost dread it I confess
— for I fear that the accessories which will be necessary to indicate
his nature as an angel may have a fantastic look — but the angel
character embodied in a form worthy the words of Milton and alive
with kindling and just indignation were a flight above the Apollo[7] —
Alas! I feel, believe me Sir, how far I am from being worthy to speak
of these great works but I have always thought it best aim at what
we dream of in our warmest aspirations rather than to measure our
strength and mark out our course by the rules of logic — I am come
now to the determination that I will hereafter make fewer works and
spend more time in preparing them — The run which has been made
upon me and which I have been not always at liberty to check owing
to my situation has not been favorable to the creation of ideal forms
— I find the imagination, at least mine — will not bear fruit by plow-
ing manuring & sowing — I can work in that way but the work seems

to me to want color flavor odour — I must let the sun shine and the rain fall only on the ground whence I would see a real flower of the heart & of the soul spring — I must now express my wonder how you who are in the midst of a people who are the most exacting in the world in their expectations of performance how you have been able to build a wall between your vine and their thirst and give them only old wine when they would have hurraed at new cider![8]

   . . . [*page cut off*] Mr Powers has finished Mr Webster's bust in marble, and really I think it one of the very finest portraits I have ever seen — He is now about a head of Judge Marshall — Col Baldwin's bust is nearly compleated.[9]

   . . . [*page cut off*] by command myself — I have recently finished the preparatory studies for my large groupe — Washington goes forward bravely & I am in hopes of putting him up in July 1840 —

Ho Greenough[10]

NOTES

Manuscript: Dana Papers, MHS.
1. John Greenough.
2. George Watson Brimmer.
3. Hiram Powers, sculptor, arrived in Florence in the fall of 1837 (see note to Letter 109).
4. David Sears (1787–1871), Boston merchant, was traveling in Europe with his family at this time (Robert C. Winthrop, "Memoir of the Hon. David Sears, A. M.," *ProcMHS*, 2d ser., 2 [1886]: 405–29). The group on which Greenough was engaged, called *Forest Children,* was of the two Sears children, Grace and Knyvet Winthrop. It is now in the Massachusetts Historical Society.
5. The first of these statues evidently appears in William J. Hubard's 1839 portrait of Greenough in his studio, now in the Valentine Museum, Richmond, Virginia. Their present location is unknown.
6. John Lowell (1769–1840) was a Boston lawyer and political pamphleteer. Greenough's statue for him, *Venus Victrix,* is now in the Boston Athenaeum.
7. Presumably the *Apollo di Belvedere.*
8. The next manuscript page has been cut off, leaving only the last three lines on the recto ("Mr. Powers . . . compleated") and on the verso ("by command . . . July 1840").
9. Busts by Powers of Daniel Webster are in the Chicago Art Institute and the Boston Athenaeum. His bust of John Marshall is in the Library of Congress. His bust of Laommi Baldwin (1780–1838), Massachusetts civil engineer, is in the Boston Athenaeum.
10. The signature is in another hand.

109.   To Hiram Powers
       Between 20 February and 4 March 1838

My Dear Powers

   Dr Andreini[1] was not at home. I have sent for him — I have thought as coolly as possible on my way here of your situation.

   I have great confidence in Dr Andreini and am moreover a believer in the Italian system. My belief arises from my experience[2] — an experience limited it is true but which thus far rules my conviction — If your child[3] dies under Dr Andreini's treatment he will have died easily, of disease, and you cannot reproach yourself with a decision formed in ignorance of what course to pursue — If you blister and give him mercury you may feel that he has been tormented to no purpose — Judge and decide — I feel it my duty to give you my opinion and I say *I* should not take the course mentioned by the gentlemen whom I left with you.

Yours.

Hor Greenough

NOTES

Hiram Powers (1805–73), Vermont-born sculptor, who grew up in Cincinnati, began his career in 1835 and, in 1837, went to Florence, where he spent the rest of his life.
   This letter is dated on internal evidence; see n. 3, below.
   Manuscript: Editor's collection.
1. Vincenzo Andrieni, Italian physician, was on the staff of the Arcispedale de Santa Maria Nuova in Florence (*Almanacco Toscano* [Florence, 1836]).
2. Presumably Greenough refers to the treatment of his illness of 1827–28 by an Italian physician who did not apply strong measures (see Letter 28).
3. James Powers, five years old, became ill about 20 February suffering from what had been diagnosed as brain fever. Andrieni was called in, but the child died on 4 March (information furnished by Clara L. Dentler, Florence).

110.   To Edward Elbridge Salisbury
23 February 1838

E E Salisbury Esq'r
My dear Sir

Yours of the 7th inst reached me yesterday. I think we may produce a very good effect with the figure of Abdiel of 3 feet, provided it can be seen by itself, and properly lighted. I will now give you the items of Mr Halsey's commissions, as they stand on my hands.

Statue of Aristides —	150 F
" " Washington	150 "
2 truncated columns to serve as pedestals	50 "
	350 "

I find no record of any other payment having been made, and beg you to inform me if the gross amount only was mentioned. Mr Halsey may have included in the expense, the price of the money which was very high at that time. The price of the medallion[1] made for Mr Halsey since his father's death is 80 Fi after deducting which from the above amount, leaves 270. Fi. deducting 150. the price of the Aristides we have 120 paid on the bas relief — and the pedestals unpaid — I shall be perfectly satisfied by the payment in May as you propose — You will suit your own convenience entirely in paying me the whole or the half.

It may be that 20 Fi were paid me afterwards by Mr Halsey, but I do not remember, nor can I understand any reason for it. I find no trace of it in my letters or accounts but I am so much occupied that I may have neglected to note it. Is it possible I may have the pleasure of seeing you during the execution of these works?

I remain dear sir
Yours truly —
Horatio Greenough

Edw'd E. Salisbury Esqr
Florence, Feb'y 23d 1838.

NOTES

Manuscript: Salisbury Family Papers, Yale University Library.
1. Nothing further seems to be known of this medallion.

111. To Hiram Powers
28 March 1838

My Dear Powers
    I send you the translation of your note to Andrieni — I have taken the liberty to omit the clause in which you mention the complex nature of the disease as likely to embarrass etc because I feared it was liable to misinterpretation —
    I send also the print rec'd from Mr Brimmer[1] —

I remain Dear P
Yours
Horatio Greenough

28th March. '38

Addressed: H. Powers Esqr — / Present.

NOTES

Manuscript: Editor's collection.
1. George Watson Brimmer.

112. To Richard Henry Wilde
ca. April 1838

My Dear Wilde
    In looking over my memoranda this evening I find that Dr Warren[1] requested me to say to you that he found the preparations of Segato[2]

at Bologna *"very pretty"* but that he did not purchase them. "For one he asked 50 — Louis — for another 200 Louis" etc — Not remembering to have communicated the above I hasten to do so and ask your pardon for the delay.

Yours truly
Horatio Greenough

Addressed: R. H. Wilde Esqr / S.R.M.

NOTES

This letter is dated on internal evidence; see n. 1, below.
   Manuscript: Editor's collection.
1. John Collins Warren, Boston surgeon, was in Florence from 4 March to 14 March 1838 (see note to Letter 122).
2. Girolamo Segato (1792–1836), Italian traveller and scientist, discovered a system of preserving the bodies of animals and human beings without changing their form, mass, or color, but he did not leave an explanation of the process.

113. To James Fenimore Cooper
6 May 1838

May 6, 1838

. . . The statue of Washington, after cruel delays, from cholera, quarantines and the state of the roads, is now in full progress. The marble promises well, and we are near the surface. The block weighed 130,000 lbs, when we commenced on it. It is fast losing its chips. . . .

I have just finished a Venus Victrix,[1] and am now preparing a statue from the Paradise Lost — Abdiel as described at the close of the Fifth Book.[2] . . .

NOTES

Source: *Boston Daily Evening Transcript,* 7 July 1838.
1. See Letter 108, n. 6.
2. See Letters 106 and 107.

114. To Henry Brevoort
9 May 1838

Florence May 9th [1838]

Dear Sir

The object of the present is to inform you that your chimney Pieces have been finished now several days and only wait an opportunity for shipment. I have as yet been unable to go to Carrara and can therefore say nothing of the prices on which you insist.[1] I trust I shall be at Carrara however in a few days.

Your Ob't Serv't
Horatio Greenough

H. Brevoort Esq.

[Addressed to Brevoort in Paris.]

NOTES

Henry Brevoort (1782–1848), member of a prominent New York family, was a New York merchant ("Famous New York Families, XXXVII: The Brevoorts," *New York Evening Post,* 2 November 1901).

Source: Typed copy of letter manuscript, supplied by Isaac Mendoza Book Store, New York City.

1. The five mantle pieces which Brevoort had ordered through Greenough reached New York late in 1837, after long delay. On 28 January 1838, Brevoort wrote Greenough (collection of David Richardson, Washington D.C.) from Paris complaining about the delay, the price, the fact that a black and yellow one had been substituted for the yellow (which had been broken in shipment), and the fact that all four white ones were of the same pattern. He enclosed sketches of three designs, together with the price of each asked by dealers at Carrara, and demanded a reduction in the prices on the white pieces and the replacement of the broken one by a yellow piece. Apparently Greenough had obtained new pieces as Brevoort had ordered.

115.   To Hiram Powers
        4 July 1838

Carrara July 4th '38

My Dear Powers
    I consider myself as very fortunate in having found a copy of the
Hebe[1] of the required size — without a stain* worth mentioning —
It is not entirely done but may be finished shortly. The only defect if
such it can be called is that the clustering locks behind the head are
made separate & joined —[2] but of course in such a way that no one
would ever be aware of it unless you told him — I think you could
not *contract* for such marble for less than 600 Francesconi — The man
asks 400 as his last price — The one that went to New Orleans cost a
great deal more & was spotted — badly. I can do nothing about the
pedestal till you give me its dimensions & style. They are looking out
for your sculptor but I have no great hopes, we will see —
    Sister[3] is at Massa 5 miles hence & very comfortable — I have
walked about 15 miles today & nearly as much yesterday & begin to
get my spirits again. These mountains are glorious — and the shepherds and bush whackers that I passed this morning at work on their
dark sides, singing like larks right under God's own sky seemed to me
as happy people as I ever saw — Address me Alla Locanda delle
Quattro Nazioni[4] — Massa di Carrara — Love to all —

Yours in haste
Horatio Greenough

* I did not see one of any sort whatever.

Addressed: Hiram Powers Esqr / Poste Restante / At Florence

NOTES

Manuscript: Editor's collection.
1. Conventionalized busts of Hebe, Greek goddess of youth, were popular during the neoclassical period. A few months earlier Greenough had secured
   one for Powers, but it had a blemish (information furnished by Clara L.
   Dentler, Florence).

2. Here Greenough drew a profile of such a head.
3. Louisa Greenough.
4. "At the Inn of the Four Nations."

116.   To Hiram Powers
   25 [August 1838?]

My Dear Powers
   It has occurred to me this evening that perhaps you had occasion for the money today. If so pray tell me of it. I have but about 20 Fi in the house but will let you have that immediately and the balance on Monday.

Yours truly
Horatio Greenough

Saturday even'g 25th

Addressed: Hiram Powers Esqr

NOTE

The first Saturday which fell on the twenty-fifth of a month after Powers arrived in Florence was 25 November 1837. The next was 25 August 1838. It seems more probable that Powers and Greenough were having some financial transaction at the latter date, which was about the time Greenough was securing a bust of Hebe for Powers and Louisa Greenough was staying with the Powerses, presumably paying her share of the household expenses.
   Manuscript: Editor's collection.

117.   To Hiram Powers
   [August?] 1838

My Dear Powers
   I wished to have thanked Mrs P——[1] for her extreme kindness to sister L before I left Flor[2] — pray do so for me — I cannot help fear-

ing that she may prove a hindrance to you in case of Madame's confinement. Still I hope and trust that she will compensate for this by attentions and a sympathy which servants know not of — I pray that you will allow her to furnish her quota of the expenses of your ménage while she is with you not from a wish to confine my obliga[tion] [*page torn*] as much as possible, but because I think we can have a better face in asking such a favor another time if need be and because I know not how far you may find it convenient to take increased family under your care at this time — I pray you to preserve yourself and yours and to wish me well. Yours affectionately

Horatio Greenough

Addressed: Miss Louisa Greenough / Poste Restante / Florence.

NOTES

Half the folded sheet, presumably containing the letter to Louisa Greenough, has been torn off.
   This letter is dated on internal evidence; see n. 2, below.
   Manuscript: Editor's collection.
   1. Elizabeth Gibson Powers (information furnished by Clara L. Dentler, Florence).
   2. Louisa Greenough stayed with the Powerses shortly before and at the time of the birth of Louisa Greenough Powers, 10 September 1838. Greenough and his wife customarily left Florence late each summer to escape the heat. They may have done so at this time.

118.   To David Hoffman
21 September 1838

Florence Sept 21st '38

David Hoffman Esqr / Baltimore
Dear Sir
   After delays and interruptions such as never before interfered with the execution of any work of mine, I have at length finished your head or rather I may say *half length* for such in fact it is —

I have made a Heloise to embody the expression conveyed by Pope
in the lines

> "Rest dearest name for ever unrevealed!
> Nor pass these lips in holy silence sealed!
> Hide it my heart! within that deep disguise
> Where mixed with God's his loved idea lies!"[1]

Tis a *veiled* Magdalen in short — but a Magdalen who has to reproach herself with no grosser sin — I have aimed at beauty of feature
allied to devotion and a heaven directed aspiration — Have I succeeded? I know not but I send you my dear Sir the fruit of much
toil and I hope it may please you — Begging to be remembered respectfully to Mrs Hoffman I remain

Dear Sir
Yours very truly
Horatio Greenough

P.S. This bust will be shipped by the first opportunity from Leghorn[2] —

Addressed: David Hoffman Esqr / Baltimore —

NOTES

David Hoffman (1784–1854), Baltimore lawyer, teacher, and writer, traveled
in Europe in 1833–34. At that time he ordered a work from Greenough, leaving
the subject to the sculptor (Diary of David Hoffman, 14 May 1834, Manuscript
Division, NYPL).
   Manuscript: Editor's collection.
1. An inaccurate quotation of Alexander Pope's "Eloisa to Abelard," ll. 9–12.
   Greenough's bust evidently appears in William J. Hubard's portrait of him
   (see Letter 108, n. 5). Its present location is unknown.
2. The postscript is in Louisa G. Greenough's hand.

119. To George Washington Greene
1 November 1838

Florence Nov 1st '38.

My Dear Greene

I doubt not that you have that trust in my friendship toward you to have attributed my silence for several months past to the right cause. I should have written many times but for the state of hurry anxiety & bustle in which I have lived, a state which with me entirely kills the conversible faculty a[nd] leaves me as soon [as] I retire from toil and battle only fit to mope and smoke or read merely to stop thought —

If I were to tell you the tithe of what I have gone through in 8 months of excitement and botheration of one kind and another you would give me credit for a tough gizzard — however I am now firmly entrenched in my new house[1] and feel easy once more — I beg that when you see the Misses Brimmer[2] you will explain to them that my wife has been prevented from answering Miss Eliza's most welcome letter by a serious illness (entre nous the poor girl has miscarried 2ce this year and this last was a gravidanza[3] of 2 months so that it was not without danger) — She is still confined to her room but I am happy to say that she is mending very rapidly.

Sister Louisa will probably leave us in the spring and I dread her going — I shall beseech my mother to send me another younger sister in her stead — Capponi was at my house about a fortnight since and spoke much of you. He is looking very well better than you ever saw him.

We artists are about to make an effort [to] have something like a club — some 5 of us are determined nasca quel che su' nascere[4] to see each other once a week in rotation at our respective houses. Do You ever see Gibson or Wyatt or Dessalavy or Hogan?[5] If so pray remember me to them. Col Thomson has taken the big Casa Ximenes and is I suppose about to astonish the natives with a second edition of Milor as they used to call Burghersh[6] — Have you seen Grunde's book![7] I think he shews much talent but he is evidently writing at a mark and crams us and the English both in the grossest manner — He is an adventurer and has the stamp of that character on every page as in every feature but he's not an ordinary one.

Prescott's book[8] seems to have taken right well in England as in America of course — I have the first volume but can't say I feel hungry about it — I think he has made a mistake (in the long run) for his reputation with posterity in turning to Europe for a subject when so many of our local histories cry for a hand to record them and when the traditions that would render them so interesting hereafter are dying daily. I would rather take my chance as an American author with a volume of annals of Salem than with a history of the Decline & downfall of the Turkish Empire (ceteris paribus[9] of course). I beg you will present my kind regards to that naughty little woman[10] there on the other side of the fire place and my respects to her parents.

Yours affectionately

Hor Greenough

Addressed: Geo W Greene Esqr / U.S. Consul / Rome.

NOTES

Manuscript: Editor's collection.
1. Casa Leblanc in Via di Bardi.
2. Eliza Oliver and Sarah Brimmer, then traveling abroad, were sisters of Martin Brimmer.
3. "Pregnancy."
4. "Come what may."
5. T. Dessoulavy, English landscape painter, lived for a long time in Rome. John Hogan (1800–1858), Irish sculptor, lived in Rome from 1824 to 1848; Greenough drew Hogan's statue *Eve Startled at the Sight of a Dead Bird* in the sketchbook he began in Rome in 1828.
6. John Fane, eleventh earl of Westmorland (1784–1859), known as Lord Burghersh until he succeeded his father in the earldom in 1841, was from 1814 to 1830 the official English resident in Florence, living in the Palazzo Panciatichi Ximines. The entertainments and musicals which he and his wife gave there were lavish. Upper-class English were frequently called "Milord" or "Milor'."
7. Francis Joseph Grund (1805–63), German author, was highly critical of England and America in his work *The Americans, in their Moral, Social, and Political Relations*, 2 vols. (London, 1837). He had been in Florence in 1837 (John Farrar to Willard Phillips, 29 December 1837, MHS).
8. William Hickling Prescott (1796–1859), historian, published his first important work, *The History of Ferdinand and Isabella,* in 1837.

9. "Other things being equal."
10. The Greenes' daughter.

120.   To George Washington Greene
         6 [January?] 1839

Florence. Dec [January?] 6th. '39.

My Dear Giorgio

This will be handed to you by my friend B. D. Greene Esqr of Boston who is about to visit your city in company with his lady and his mother. His sisters and brother in law are of the same party.[1] Allow me to present them to your acquaintance and warmly recommend them to your kind offices.

I shall answer your kind letter accompanying the papers from Washington[2] by the first opportunity — The ladies & Mr Russell[3] join me in kind regards to your wife and family.

I saw Capponi this morning who gave me very good accounts of you all.

I remain Dear Giorgio

Yours affectionately
Horatio Greenough

Addressed: Geo. W. Greene Esqr / U.S. Consul / Rome. / B. D. Greene Esqr / of Boston

NOTES

This letter is dated January on the basis of internal evidence; see nn. 1 and 2, below.

Manuscript: Joseph Downs Collection, Henry Francis du Pont Winterthur Museum.

1. Benjamin Daniel Greene (1793–1863) of Boston devoted himself to scientific pursuits. His wife was the daughter of Josiah Quincy and a childhood friend of Louisa G. Greenough. His mother was Elizabeth Clarke Copley Greene; his sisters were Mary Greene Hubbard Sturgis and Mary Copley Greene

Amory; his brother-in-law was James Sullivan Amory. The group was in
Florence from 11 December 1838 to 7 January 1839, and from 24 to 28
March 1839. Mrs. Greene's diary for the period is in the Massachusetts
Historical Society. See also M. A. De Wolfe Howe, ed., *The Articulate Sisters*
(Cambridge, Mass., 1946), p. 5; "Marriages and Deaths," *NEHGR* 17
(1863): 77; ibid., 20 (1866): 169; "Necrology of the New-England Historic
Genealogical Society," *NEHGR* 39 (1885): 89; ibid., 42 (1888): 324.

2. Late in December 1838 Greenough received, through Greene, a letter from
acting secretary of state Aaron Vail (22 October 1838, copy in RG 217, Records of the General Accounting Office, Fiscal Section, NA) stating that his
second design for a group for the Capitol had been accepted. It also contained articles of agreement between Greenough and President Van Buren,
the dimensions of the blocking, and a copy of Persico's proposals to the Committee on Public Buildings, made the preceding year.

3. The ladies were Greenough's wife and sister Louisa. Joseph Russell, a Boston
merchant, married Louisa G. Greenough's widowed mother (Boston city directories; will of John Gore, Suffolk County Registry of Probate).

121. **To Emanuele Fenzi**
   23 January 1839

Cav. Princ. Em Fenzi —
My Dear Sir
   The period which you fixed as that when you hoped to procure an
audience from the G. Duke for my friend Mr Delavan[1] having arrived, I waited upon you 4 days since to explain to you that that
gentleman had been obliged to leave town. He requested me however to present his thanks for the prompt & kind manner in which
you had come forward in his behalf, and hoped that on his return
here, he should have it in his power to thank you in person — Accept
also my best acknowledgements of your indulgence toward myself
and excuse a delay in this communication which was occasioned by
its being *post day* when I called, and by an indisposition of my own
since that time.

                                        Yours respectfully
                                        Horatio Greenough

23d Jan'y '39.

NOTES

Manuscript: Carteggi Fenzi, Biblioteca e Archivio del Risorgimento, Florence.
1. Possibly Edward Cornelius Delavan (1793–1871), who operated the Delavan House, Albany.

122. To John Collins Warren
1 March 1839

Florence. March 1st '39.

My Dear Sir —

Your favor of Dec'r 30th reached me a few days since — I learn with much pleasure the arrival of your bust,[1] and your favorable opinion of it. The bust of your father[2] is also ready, but I have detained it with a view of sending at the same time the medallion which I am making for Mrs Warren[3] — I have already purchased a small copy in alabaster of the Cathedral of Pisa (price $16) and shall forward it by the first opportunity. I note your instructions with regard to the marble columns, 4 in number, and shall forward them with your other bust. As you do not mention the kind of marble you wish, I shall consult my own taste, and hope at no great cost to furnish such as will please you.

I presented your respects as desired to the several gentlemen mentioned in your letter through Dr Burci[4] — I mentioned to the latter your fears respecting the preparations — he is sanguine in his hope that *nothing* will be injured, as he assures me he packed them himself in a way to prepare them even for rough handling. I communicated to him your kind wishes, and the hopes you held out in case he be disposed to try his fortune in the states — He received the message with a grateful acknowledgement of your kindness, and professed himself highly flattered by the notice you had taken of his abilities, and the confidence you had shewn in his character — With a truly *Italian* caution however (as regards long voyages, & other similar undertakings) he represented to me that his prospects here, though moderate, nay narrow, were sure, and that not having means to undertake a long voyage, and to wait in a distant land for an oppor-

tunity to become known, & employed, he feared to go unless some
definite plan of employment were proposed — some post in an anatomical School offered, or other similar means devised of making
him at once respectable, and ensuring him against the chance of
appearing as an adventurer instead of *waiting his turn* in this School.
I represented to him that I understood your letter to imply a wish to
serve him, which from my knowledge of your influence, and my
opinion of your means fully ensured him against the situation he
seemed so much to dread — he was, I thought, about to accept, but
concluded the conversation with a request that I would make known
his views, & feelings to you — That I would lay before you his hopes
here, & his fears in America, and assured me that in case you could
devise some means of placing him in the position he wished, he
should think seriously of going at once to you.

I have again & again seen the gentleman who holds Segato's preparations, & the skulls[5] — He is doggedly determined not to part with
any *portion* of the collection — He is in easy circumstances — holds
them for a small debt, & I suppose takes a pride in shewing them to
strangers — I have attacked him directly, & indirectly, face to face, &
through his foreman, but with no success. Continuing therefore, to
keep in mind your wishes with respect to these skulls, should any
opportunity offer, or any change be effected, I must assure you that
[I see?] [*page torn*] no present chance of obtaining them.

I regret much to inform you of the death of Dr Nespoli,[6] who died
a month since very suddenly, and who is mourned by every one — he
was truly a great physician and a good man — I knew him well, &
was under obligation to him. The G Duke has very handsomely continued to his family the salary he received as court physician — Dr
Andreini has lately married a very young woman — I observe that Dr
Combe[7] is come to blow up the embers of Phrenology among the
Boston people — The want of modesty in the ground these philosophers have taken has given me feeling towards the whole theory,
which is very well expressed by 2 words in the Ars Poetica "In-
credulus odi"[8] — The ladies and Mr Russell join me in respectful
compliments to Mrs Warren and the family. We heard of my brother's
engagement to Miss Parker[9] with the highest gratification — I confess
that I feel every day more & more as living in exile, when I see the
connexions of my family embracing so large circle of valuable friends
— but I have chosen my path, & I must travel it — I beg you to com-

mand me at all times for yourself & friends, and that your health and happiness may be long continued to your family, and the public is the fervent wish of

Your friend & servant
Horatio Greenough

Addressed: Dr John C. Warren / Boston. Mass. / Emerald

NOTES

John Collins Warren (1778–1856) was a Boston surgeon, author, and member of the faculty of the Harvard Medical School from 1809 to 1847. He was in Florence from 4 March to 14 March 1838, during which time he visited Greenough, and presumably had his bust modeled (Edward Warren, *The Life of John Collins Warren, M.D., Compiled Chiefly from His Autobiography and Journals* [Boston, 1860], 1:315–17).

Manuscript: J. C. Warren Papers, MHS.

1. It is now at the Harvard Medical School.
2. John Warren (1753–1815), surgeon, was attached to Washington's forces during the Revolution; afterwards, he practiced in Boston. Greenough's bust of him is at the Harvard Medical School.
3. Nothing further seems to be known about the medallion.
4. Carlo Burci (1815–75), Italian surgeon, was at this time professor of pathological anatomy at the Arcispedale di Santa Maria Nuova, Florence.
5. See Letter 112.
6. Angiolo Nespoli was court physician and provost of the Royal Medical College in Florence (*Almanacco Toscano* [Florence, 1836]).
7. George Combe (1788–1858), Scottish phrenologist, made a lecture tour of Canada and the United States from the fall of 1838 to the early summer of 1840.
8. "Incredulous, I abhor" (Horace, *Ars Poetica,* l. 225).
9. Susan D. Parker and Alfred Greenough were married 25 April 1839 (Greenough, p. 41).

123. To Richard Henry Wilde
6 March 1839

My Dear Mr Wilde

I have never received a testimony of the effect produced by my poor labours more gratifying to me than that contained in the verses[1] which my wife has just laid before me — Whether I consider the beauty and pregnant meaning of the verses or the feeling which dictated them on your part I am equally gratified. I am sure I shall not be accused of overweening vanity if I own that I am proud of such a mark of your high opinion — I love to receive such praise & I love to give it — May I be enabled to render the Statue worthy of your verses! May you enjoy a thousand fold the unmixed pleasure they have given me — Overwhelmed as I am with the burthens of responsibilities I feel unequal to, situated in many respects in a trying and perplexing position, I should be indifferent to the welfare & happiness of all connected with me were I not often weighed down to the earth by my load — I feel then truly grateful for a voice that stirs my blood like the sound of [a] trumpet and that by assuring me I have not labored all in vain, bids me hope for a fair result to my future toils. With truly grateful feelings toward you for this new proof of your interest and your friendship Believe me

Sincerely yours
Horatio Greenough

6th March '39.

NOTES

Manuscript: Autograph File, Houghton.
1. Wilde's "On Greenough's Washington." The only known manuscript version is contained in a poetry album of Mrs. Greenough's (collection of David Richardson, Washington, D.C.). It has been printed in Nathalia Wright, "Richard Henry Wilde on Greenough's Washington," *American Literature* 27 (1956): 556–57.

124.   To George Washington Greene
29 March 1839

Florence 29th March 39

My Dear Greene

I have written immediately on the receipt of your last to Mr Everett & have urged on him by every motive that I thought ought to weigh with him your claims to a portion of the honor & profit to be reaped in this field about to open[1] — I had equal regard in my letter to your claims as a man your wants as an aspirant and your dignity as a gentleman — I hope I have done the thing right — nous verrons! Between ourselves I think the opportunity far below your merits since I read the article on Italian Romance[2] — I truly grieve that you should look as an advantage to such a job — I will urge the journey in my next letter to Washington — Pray give my love to Mrs Greene & to Mr Crawford[3] who must be a good man since you all love him.

addio & much love from all
here Yours
H Greenough

Have you seen Stevens of N York's travels in Africa the Holyland & Russia etc.?[4] Very interesting I do assure you and very very very clever to my notion.

Addressed: Geo W Greene Esqur / U.S. Consul — / Rome —

NOTES

Manuscript: Joseph Downs Collection, Henry Francis du Pont Winterthur Museum.
1. Edward Everett was at this time a member of the Massachusetts Board of Education, which was sponsoring the publication of a series of books on a variety of subjects for use in schools. Evidently Greene proposed to write one on literature, and Greenough wrote Everett on 29 March 1839 recommending him. In his reply (Letter Book, Everett Papers, MHS), dated 20 May 1839, Everett said the books had to be approved unanimously by the board mem-

bers and he could not promise that Greene's would be accepted. He also suggested a volume on the history of the arts, presumably to be written by Greenough.

2. Greene's "Historical Romance in Italy," a review of *Raccolta di Romanzi Storici originali Italani* (Florence, 1830), which appeared in the *North American Review* 46 (1838): 325–40.

3. In 1835 the American sculptor Thomas Crawford (1813–57) went to Rome, where he spent most of the rest of his life.

4. John Lloyd Stephens (1805–52), writer and traveler, published *Incidents of Travel in Egypt, Arabia, Petraea, and the Holy Land* in 1837 and *Incidents of Travel in Greece, Turkey, Russia, and Poland* in 1838.

125.   To Robert Gilmor, Jr.
1 April 1839

Florence, April 1st '39.

My Dear Sir

I hasten to answer your very obliging letter of Feb'y 27 and perhaps I ought to apologize for not having before addressed you on the subject of the Monument.[1] I agree with you that Trophies will be the most appropriate and effective ornaments for the Base of your Column, but I should be afraid to decide on their proportions or shape without putting up a model of painted canvass to represent one corner at least of the Base — by means of such a model and the draft of the height and ground plan I think I should venture to design & superintend these ornaments. It would be impossible for me to say what price they would cost as that would depend on their size and workmanship — Should your committee be inclined to trust them to me, I will engage to see them well made after my designs at as reasonable a rate as can be done — I do not pretend to offer any great Bargains because I employ the best workmen & pay them at a high rate — Should your great object be to have the thing finished cheaply, do not think of me — I cannot say either that I can finish them at a given day — as I have suffered too much mortification and loss from the failure of my agents to fulfill their contracts ever to think of binding myself when I cannot bind them — I will attend to them and do not wish any thing more than a reasonable compensation for the time to be devoted. I cannot *risk* losing any thing & therefore cannot undertake to ship them or do more than deliver them in Leghorn — after which they are at the risk of the committee. I fully believe that the trophies could be made in marble and transported and set up for 10,000$ but I really think *Bronze infinitely preferable* — In marble these objects would soon become discoloured and the joints and seams at least blackened and they would have a paltry appearance — Should your committee think of Bronze I should recommend Milan as a city where they might be probably cast cheaper than at Paris — Have you thought of Berlin castings in Iron?[2] I believe they would have a very good effect — I should prefer them to marble — Bronze would be much more expensive than marble — of the cost of Berlin castings I can give no estimate.

I regret very much not having it in my power to offer at once to make these trophies at a given price — You will excuse me however when I tell you that I have met with pretty severe losses from want of caution in this matter — Should your committee think of employing me I beg you will induce them to open a credit in my favor for the execution of *one* Trophy say at 1500$. From the workmanship & price of that one I shall be enabled to decide on the cost of the whole while you will have a sample of execution should you think proper to have the rest made at home — I believe that Mr Willard[3] of Boston is fully adequate to the ma[king of?] [*page torn*] these works. I fully understand and justify your unwillingness to buy Mr. Hoffman's bust until you [have?] [*page torn*] seen it — I made it for 300$ as I had been obliged [to put?] [*page torn*] him off several years. I could not make the same again for less than 500 D. My wife whose father[4] you knew was highly pleased by your interest in her, and your kind recollections of her parents — She is my only comfort in this exile apart from my profession — I hope and trust that I shall have the pleasure of presenting her to you in June 1840 — when I expect to accompany my Statue of Washington to America — Mrs Greenough joins me in kind regards — Yours truly

                                        Horatio Greenough

PS Since the above was written we have seen your nephew[5] who remained here a few days on his return from Rome — he left several days since for Vienna — though delicate & thin he seemed well & in good spirits.

Addressed: Robert Gilmor Esqr / Via Havre pr Packet / Baltimore —

NOTES

Manuscript: Editor's collection.
1. The monument to George Washington in Baltimore. It consists of a shaft, erected between 1816 and 1824, and a figure of Washington on top, executed by Causici and placed there in 1829. Nothing came of Gilmor's idea of ornamenting the base with trophies.
2. A Berlin iron is a fusible variety of cast iron, from which figures and other delicate articles may be manufactured.
3. Solomon Willard (1783–1861) was a Boston architect and stone worker.
4. John Gore (1789–*ca.* 1817) was a Boston merchant. His wife was Mary Green Babcock.
5. Robert Gilmor (1808–75) was the son of Gilmor's brother William.

126. To Edward Elbridge Salisbury
28 April 1839

Florence April 28. '39 —

My Dear Sir

In answer to your inquiries respecting the actual state of the works I have on hand for you, — I have the satisfaction to inform you that the Abdiel is entirely out in the marble and that it is free from stain or vein or any blemish whatever, and as there is not in any part of it a thickness of more than $\frac{1}{20}$ of an inch over the ultimate surface I feel safe in assuring you that you will have every reason to be satisfied on that score — The bas relief waits only for the blocker to be free from the Abdiel to commence that also — I hope to finish both in the course of the summer — Had I been able to procure another rough-blocker I should have been far advanced in the bas relief. You will perhaps be surprised when I tell you that the bas relief has cost me more time and a greater expense of models in short a greater outlay than the Abdiel — yet such is the fact, and I truly believe that I could have made 2 busts which would have yielded me 800 Francesconi in the time that I have spent on that composition — Yet I have done it willingly, and cheerfully and have twice modelled it entirely with a view of perfecting it as far as lay in my power — As you are the first American gentleman who has ever ordered a bas relief, it is but right that you should enjoy the benefit of taking the sharp edge off my curiosity and eagerness to sculpture one — The statue of Aristides is much admired. It is also free from stain — I note your instructions respecting the packing and shipping and shall attend carefully to the same — You are perhaps aware that I deliver my work cased and baled, & that subsequent charges on it are at the expense of the purchaser — Accept my thanks for your delicacy in not hurrying me in the completion of these works. Believe that I shall be unremitting in my attention to them, and that they will be a sample of what I can do — Called on as we daily are to choose between speed and safety — an honest name hereafter, and the approval of our own conscience, or gain, and the temporary approval of our employers — it is a great comfort to be *encouraged* to *obey* rather the dictates of the art — than the suggestions of a mere mercantile punctuality — I wish it were once well known that no man can state how long he will be employed in embodying poetry in marble — we should be saved much mortification, and our friends some disappointment.

I am about commencing a colossal group by order of the U.S. Gov't to be placed on one of the blocks which flank the great stair-case on the east Front of the Capitol — Th[e] [*page torn*] group is intended to commemorate the danger[s] [*page torn*] of our first contact with the Aborigines, & I think is susceptible of great dramatic interest as of great variety of form & character & expression.

I remain Dear Sir
Your Obliged Friend & Serv't
Horatio Greenough

E. E. Salisbury Esqr / London

Addressed: Edward E Salisbury Esqr / Care of Mess Baring Brothers & Co / Bankers / London

NOTE

Manuscript: Salisbury Family Papers, Yale University Library. Previous publication (in part): E. E. Salisbury, "Two Letters of Horatio Greenough," *Magazine of American History* 18 (1873): 331.

127. To James Fenimore Cooper
[Spring 1839?]

. . . I think you lose hold on the American public by rubbing down their shins with brickbats as you do. . . .

NOTE

Source: Thomas R. Lounsbury, *James Fenimore Cooper* (Boston, 1884), p. 156. According to Lounsbury, this excerpt from Greenough's letter refers to Cooper's *Home as Found,* which was published in November 1838 (Robert E. Spiller and Philip C. Blackburn, *A Descriptive Bibliography of the Writings of James Fenimore Cooper* [New York, 1934], p. 100).

The date is conjectured on the basis of the publication date of *Home as Found* and the time required for a letter to cross the Atlantic (two to three months).

128. To Charles Greely Loring
5 July 1839

Florence, July 5th 1839.

Charles. G. Loring Esqr / Boston
Dear Sir

Your favor of the 21st May reached me today — I beg you will accept my thanks for having delayed remittance in hopes of an improved rate of exchange. I note your minute of our account and thank you for the clear and satisfactory details of the same — I perceive from the extract you give me of Mr Clay's[1] letter to you, that my letter of advice never reached him — I shall lose no time in giving him the explanation he requires.

I accept my dear Sir with pleasure the task you so flatteringly entrust to me —. I will do my portion of it at once, and with every precaution to ensure what you wish — From Florence, whence hundreds of copies are yearly sent to America, you can scarce expect any very startling *novelty* — I hope to be able to send you in addition to the Madonna some other small work — Your directions respecting packing and shipment shall be attended to — I beg you will say to Mr Sprague[2] that tho' I feel some anxiety in purchasing for a person with whose tastes I am not familiar, yet I shall not hesitate to do it, begging him to excuse me if I happen to send him exactly what he does not wish, as I can only promise to use my judgment in the matter and to act as for myself.

Accept my acknowledgements of your delicacy in requiring that I regard this commission as one of business — Allow me rather to regret that I can only be of service to yourself & friends in such a trifle —

It was my wish & intention to have made your acquaintance more fully when in Boston, but a calamity which befell me there, under circumstances that rendered me peculiarly vulnerable, took from me what I have of energy and of philosophy[3] — I look forward to the hope of meeting you under more happy auspices — I shall probably accompany the colossal Statue of Washington to America in 1840.

I have brought this work so far forward that the uninitiated would suppose it finished & when I tell you that I have chiselled and modelled over the surface of a figure 8 times in bulk that of Chantry, you will allow that I have been diligent. The chiselling this figure has been of great service to my health. It is hard bodily labor — and I would recommend it to your dyspeptic gentlemen of Boston that they should keep a lump of granite in their wood houses and pass their leisure in making Washingtons — I beg that you will excuse my orthography, which has suffered by dabbling in foreign tongues and my grammar too, as I passed my youth in studying Greek — I never should have suspected either but for my wife, who not having received a *liberal education* is pretty well versed in her mother tongue — She begs to be remembered to you. . . . [*page cut off*][4]

Horatio Greenough

Addressed: Charles G Loring / Boston Mass. / Via Havre — / pr New York *Packet*

NOTES

Charles Greely Loring (1794–1867), Boston lawyer, was engaged by Greenough in 1838 to handle his accounts (*Letters,* p. 125).
   Manuscript: Charles Greely Loring Papers, Houghton.
1. Presumably Henry Clay (1777–1852), Kentucky statesman. Greenough executed a bust of him about this time. Its present location is unknown.
2. Probably Charles Sprague (1791–1875), Boston banker and poet.
3. Greenough probably refers to the death of his father, coupled with the experience of taking a death mask of Emily M. Otis.
4. The last lines of the manuscript have been cut out; the signature is not in Greenough's hand.

129. To George Washington Greene
   10 July 1839

Florence July 10th 1839

My Dear Greene.
   Your letter reached me yesterday — You do not say whether the *"publishing committee"* asked of you a work on the subjects mentioned by Mr Everett — I presume from your silence that such was the case — It seems to me a strange conduct on their part to have said nothing on the subject of remuneration — I should rather think said remuneration was not considerable or they would have *talked* about it. I am very happy to learn that your income is so nearly all you require, and think you ought not to sacrifice yourself to any hope of immediately freeing yourself from debt, but rather to go on developing your literary plans in your own way — such I believe would be the better in the end for all —
   I shall be very happy to give the young sculptor[1] you mention such assistance as is in my power — work he can have at once on Mr Crawford's and your recommendation of his qualities as an artist and as a man — I can not pay more than 10 pauls per diem however, because I find it necessary to pay workmen of that class all alike —
   The group is advancing, and I wish with all my heart that you would come and report on it.[2] I shall cast it by Christmas probably —

at least a portion of it, for the composition enables me to finish one portion first — We are expecting soon Mr Clevenger of Ohio[3] Sculptor — of whom my brother[4] writes me in the highest terms — We shall soon be provided with many able chisels —

Did you ever read Paulding's Letters from the South?[5] I have been reading them lately, and truly admire them —

Le io potessi arrivare quella bricconcella della Sig'a Carlotta per Bacco! non so cosa non farei — la mi morde, la mi stuzzica con Post-scritti — con ogni sorte di impertinenza — Finora sono stato buono, ma poi tutto finisce. Voglio che la canti subito una mia canzone favorita, ed io saro la nello spirito a sentirla — Capponi sta malinconico assai — credo che voglia viaggiare fra breve

Addio Giorgio mio Caro —[6]

Horatio Greenough —

The above letter Dear Mr Greene you will at once perceive is not in my husband's handwriting. I stand convicted of forgery. The fact is, he left the *original* letter with me this morning to seal, & send to the Post-Office — I dexterously poured the ink over it — & as it was impossible to send you so lugubrious a Document — nothing remained for me to do but to copy it myself — Please keep my secret — With love to Signora Carlotta believe me with sincere regard —

Your friend — Louisa I Greenough

NOTES

Manuscript: Horatio Greenough Papers, Duke University Library.
1. Possibly Della Lunga, mentioned in Letters 133 and 134.
2. Throughout 1839 Greenough asked Greene to come to Florence to inspect his group for the east front of the Capitol, since further payments to Greenough were contingent upon the receipt of a certificate signed by the American consul at Leghorn or Rome, to the effect that the work was progressing satisfactorily. Greene refused to do so without a government order, and though Greenough requested one, none was given.
3. Shobal Vail Clevenger (1812–43).
4. Presumably Henry.
5. First published in 1817.
6. "If I were able to reach that rogue of a Signora Carlotta, by Bacchus, I don't know what I wouldn't do. She bites me, she provokes me with post-scripts — with all sorts of impertinence — Till now I have been good, but then all has an end. I wish she would sing immediately my favorite song,

and I would be there in spirit to hear her. Capponi remains melancholy still. I think he wants to travel soon. Goodbye, my dear George."

130.   To Charles Greely Loring
15 July 1839

Florence July 15. 1839.

Charles. G. Loring Esqr / Boston —
My Dear Sir
   I have succeeded in purchasing for you 3 Pictures as follows —

Copy of the Madonna della Seggiola in a very rich frame — painted on panel	Francesconi 130 —
Copy of the Madonna del Gran Duca also by Raphael — in a handsome frame	Francesconi 105.
Original Madonna by Carlo Moratti[1] a very sweet picture — framed	Francesconi 60
Spent for cases, cordage, postage & Custom House permit —	Francesconi 12
	307

Should I be able to procure another picture before the "Noble" sails (which will be about August 10th) I shall send it by that opportunity — I cannot take it upon me to decide for whom these pictures shall be respectively, I will merely say that the copy of the Madonna del Granduca should go with the Carlo Moratti, as together they come to less than half the amount produced by your remittance; while the Madonna della Seggiola and the Carlo Moratti would come to more than half that am't. I consider myself very fortunate in being able to furnish such pictures as I have sent you at such short notice. I am of opinion that in case of sale they should bring you double what they cost you — Sweet and lovely as are these Madonnas, do not believe that they render *perfectly* their originals — They do not — they are like waxen flowers compared to the real breathing blossom — I am of opinion that such copies are merely gratifying to individual taste —

they never can teach a young mind or waken genius — they are the result of a mechanic process totally different from the synthesis of the original master — They are *translations* not *copies* —

As soon as I shall have furnished the 4th picture I shall give you an entire account — of the outlay of your remittance — I shall direct to Z Cook Jr N—— York[2] and unless something new should present itself I shall not write by the vessell that takes the pictures — Accept Dear Sir my assurance of grateful attachment.

Horatio Greenough

Addressed: Charles. G. Loring Esqr / Boston Mass. / Via Havre — / Pr New. York Packet.

NOTES

Manuscript: Charles Greely Loring Papers, Houghton.
1. Carlo Maratti (1625–1713) was an Italian painter and etcher.
2. Zebedee Cook, Jr. (1786–1858), insurance man and horticulturist, was president of the Mutual Safety Insurance Company, New York.

131. To Emanuele Fenzi
    16 July 1839

Pregiatissimo Sig Fenzi

Le rimando insieme colla presente il Rapporto del Sig Martelli,[1] insieme coi documenti che gli servono di corredo — Il rapporto mi pare fatto con una scrupolosa esatezza sia riguardo alla qualita del prodotto delle cave, come pure in rispetto alle difficolta attuali e gli ostacoli da incontrarsi in appresso —

Io avrei voluto conoscere oltre la spesa di staccare un bloccho di 100 palmi[2] e. g. il costo del trasporto di esso dalla cava al poggio, dal poggio alla marina. Io credo che si vedra che tale operazione e costosa assai nel metodo attualmente adoperato, oltre che dubito che molti blocchi di grande valore sono soggetti a rompersi ed *intronarsi* nello scendere per quei ravaneti. Infatti perche hanno finora languito queste cave con un prodotto almeno eguale a quello di Carrara? Per ragione della spesa del trasporto — Io dubiterei sempre del esito di una lotta coi Carraresi, coi mezzi stessi dei Carraresi — perche quest' ultimi hanno una riputazione oramai stabilita — Marmo di Carrara da per tutto, vuol dire marmo di squisita bellezza — Non potendo dunque vendere a miglior prezzo di loro — mi pare che saranno sempre preferiti loro nei grandi mercati.

Io credo che uma strada di ferro di semplice costruzione darebbe allo Stabilimento i mezzi di comandare a Carrara per un pezzo, e di farle fronte per sempre — tale strada non avrebbe bisogno di alcuna forza motrice, eccetto la gravita medesima del prodotto — essa renderebbe lucrosi infino i frammenti che ora sono d'ingombro — essa farebbe si che l'introito seguirebbe le spese senza quei lunghi intervalli che ora devono essere framessi.

Concludo con dire che il Sig Martelli benche abbia accennato l'aumento ognora crescente del consumo di marmo non si e fermato sopra come mi pare che avrebbe potuto — prego V. S. di operare queste cifre e di rammentarsi che le cave di Carrara scarseggiano del marmo di prima qualita —

Il Sig Powers sta preparando per il Sig Borrini[3] un rapporto di quanto gli pare necessario, per rendere *l'exploitation* di queste cave facile e lucrosa — Egli, avendo assai piu conoscenza di simili lavori che non ho io, potra dare maggior valore alla sua opinione, la quale e conforme alla mia, cioe che conviene dare una grande attivita a queste cave e di communicare colla marina per mezzo di una strada di ferro — Qualora non fosse creduto opportuno il fare tale strada dal poggio alla marina — il farla dalle cave al poggio e di tutta necessita per impedire la rovina dei miglior blocchi, cioe dei *piu grandi.*

Pregandola di compatire questi pochi cenni di quanto mi e occorso di dire sul rapporto.

mi professo di V. S.
Umilissimo Serv't
Horatio Greenough

Adi 16 Luglio 1839

TRANSLATION

Most worthy Signor Fenzi

I am sending back to you along with this letter the report of Sig. Martelli,[1] together with the documents which complete it — The report strikes me as made with scrupulous care both with respect to the condition of the product of the quarries as with respect to the actual difficulties and the obstacles to be encountered shortly afterwards.

I wished to know more than the cost of removing a block of 100 palmi[2] — that is, the cost of transport from the quarry to the hill, from the hill to the seacoast. I think it evident that such an operation is costly enough because of the method actually employed, besides which I suspect that many blocks of great value are liable to be broken and cracked in the lowering in those quarries. In fact, why has this quarry hitherto languished with a product at least equal to that of Carrara? Because of the cost of transport — I am always dubious about the outcome of a struggle with the people of Carrara, even with the same means as the Carrarians — because the latter now have an established reputation — Carrara marble is considered marble of exquisite beauty everywhere — Not being able to sell, then, at a better price than they, theirs will always be valued more in the great markets.

I think a railroad of simple construction would provide the Firm with the means to be in authority over Carrara for a long time and to stand up to it forever — such a road would not require any motor power, except for the weight of the product itself — it should even make profitable the broken pieces that are now in the way — it would cause profits to follow expenses without those long delays which must now be interposed.

I conclude by remarking that Sig. Martelli, although he has pointed out the ever-rising increase of marble consumption, has not dwelt on it, as it seems to me he could have — I beg you to work these figures and to remember that the quarries of Carrara are wanting in marble of the highest quality —

Mr. Powers is preparing a report for Sig. Borrini[3] of what seems necessary to him, to make the *exploitation* of these quarries easy and lucrative — Having much more knowledge of similar operations than I have, he will be able to give greater weight to his opinion, which is similar to mine — that is, that it is fitting to apply great activity to these quarries and to communicate with the seacoast by means of a railroad — In case it should not be considered convenient to make such a road from the hill to the seacoast — the construction from the quarries to the hill is absolutely necessary to prevent the destruction of the better blocks, that is those of *great weight.*

Begging you to excuse these few indications of what has occurred
to me to say on the report,

I am your
most humble servant,
Horatio Greenough

16 July 1839

NOTES

Manuscript: Carteggi Fenzi, Biblioteca e Archivio del Risorgimento, Florence.
1. Giuseppe Martelli (1792–1876) was a Florentine architect and engineer.
2. A *palmo* (pl. *palmi*) is a linear measure equal to 3.94 inches.
3. A secretary of the Grand Duke.

132.   To Hiram Powers
[16? July 1839]

My Dear Powers
I saw Mr Borrini last night. He mentioned to me that he would
probably see you this evening — he was in hopes to obtain from you a
letter setting forth your opinion touching the means to be used in
order to render the Quarries productive as well your notion of
the nature of the road as of the mechanical contrivances for letting
down the marble from the hill[1] — Mr Frenzi told me on Friday last
that both the G Duke & G Dutchess[2] are very eager to have something done. If therefore you could draw up in a few words your
notions on the above points you would much oblige.

yours faithfully
Horatio Greenough

Studio — Tuesday morn'g

NOTES

This letter is dated on internal evidence. It seems to have been written about the same time, if not on the same day, as Letter 131. In addition, 16 July 1839 was a Tuesday.

Manuscript: Editor's collection.

1. At this time Greenough and Powers were trying to work out plans whereby the marble quarries at Carrara could be made more productive and the marble more quickly obtainable; they also hoped to open a new quarry near Carrara, and to improve the methods of transporting the stone. See Letter 131. Nothing was done at this time, however.

2. Maria Antonia, Princess of the Two Sicilies, Granduchess of Tuscany (b. 1814).

133. To John Greenough
[August 1839?]

My Dear Brother

I send you herewith the following sums to be disposed of in this manner —

To della Lunga the Roman[1]	Fi — 5
To Tomberli	Fi — 4
To Bistarino	Fi 4
To Poldo	Fi 4
To Franzoni	Fi 3
To Pietro	Fi 2
To Antonio	Fi 2.

I beg you to send for della Lunga at once and stop his work as I do not wish any thing more done until my return — you will hand him the enclosed. You will find 5 Fi for yourself in the envelope. I should be obliged if you could shew yourself occasionally in the studio to keep the fellows in order.

Yours

H———o

Addressed: John Greenough Esqr / Alla Querce[2] — / S.R.M. / with 29 / Francesconi —

NOTES

John Greenough (1801–52), eldest child of David and Elizabeth B. Greenough to reach maturity, a painter by profession, was in Florence from the spring of 1839 to 1841 (Nathalia Wright, "John Greenough, an American Artist," *Old-Time New England* 50 [1959]: 43–52).

This letter is dated on the conjecture that it was written soon after Greenough's employment of the Roman Della Lunga (who, if he was the "young sculptor" mentioned in Letter 129, was hired after 10 July), certainly while Greenough was absent from Florence, and probably during his visit to Carrara in August 1839 (*Letters*, p. 131).

Manuscript: Waterston Papers, MHS.

1. See Letter 129, n. 1.
2. A neighborhood on the outskirts of Florence, on the slope of the hill of Fiesole, where Greenough's studio was located.

134. To George Washington Greene
15 September 1839

Florence, 15th Sept'r '39.

My Dear Greene

I duly received the rasps which are excellent — accept my best thanks for them — pray say to Mr Crawford that I am much obliged by his attention to this want of mine and that I shall be happy if it is in my power to serve him — The portion of your letter in which you mention the price is quite illegible — so that you must write again and I will send you the monies by the first clever fellow that goes Rome-ward — Sumner took leave of us last evening and is probably sleeping now at Scarica l'Asino[1] on the Bologna road — I like and admire him though we had some pretty sharp discussions — he being somewhat bitten with Anglicism — Antislavery etc — but I felt truly proud to see a young business like lawyer casting behind him the greed of gold & the ambition of little greatness and compleating his education by travel & study — I feel a great regard for him and am most proud of the expressions of sympathy & approbation which he has honored me withall — Della Lunga goes on well — he is now modelling & I find that his *forte* — he seems better adapted to invent & execute his own ideas than to follow another as a mere assistant —

I am looking for Cooper's Naval History[2] but have not yet seen it. Marryatt's book[3] has not reached me.

If it were not for the fear of boring you I would order another dozen rasps of the same sort and a dozen fine ones — I cut them very fast just now —

I wish indeed that Government would commission you to inspect my work — I mentioned it to Paulding[4] in my last — We shall see —

I am told that the crop of Yankees this year promises well for you — I pass my evenings pretty regularly now in a room-full & must plead that excuse and a very hard day's work for the shortness of my letter — I am pretty regularly done up every day now — this running up and down ladders to see one's effect is severe exertion — Pray give our love to your dear lady and Believe me

Yours
Horatio Greenough

NOTES

Manuscript: Editor's collection.
1. Scaricalisino, a former post stop near the town of Monghidoro, on the route from Florence to Bologna. Charles Sumner had just visited Florence for several days (see note to Letter 137).
2. The *History of the Navy of the United States of America* was published in May 1839 (Robert E. Spiller and Philip C. Blackburn, *A Descriptive Bibliography of the Writings of James Fenimore Cooper* [New York, 1934], p. 103).
3. Presumably Greenough refers to *A Diary in America, with Remarks on Its Institutions,* published in June 1839, by Frederick Marryat (1792–1848), English novelist, who spent from April 1837 to late 1838 in the United States.
4. James Kirke Paulding was then secretary of the navy (see note to Letter 138).

135. To James Fenimore Cooper
28 September 1839

. . . The figure of Washington is finished in the main, and none but an adept would suppose it had not received the last finish. The accessories and *bas reliefs,* will occupy me during the winter, together with certain parts of the [naked?], which are not yet to my mind.

My marble has turned out well, for, though the stone weighed 40,000 lbs, there is not a mark in it, that will catch the eye, from a distance of a half radius of the Rotunda, and its color is a sober even gray, one tint lower in tone, than the usual statuary marble, and much better adapted to the work. I have studied every portion of the work over again from the life, in marble. I hope and trust to land it in America, by July 1840. . . . I have sculptured on one side of the chair (the figure is seated in a curule chair) the rising sun, in which Apollo is lashing his steeds up the eastern sky, in the other the infant Hercules rocked in a shield (for a cradle) is strangling the snakes sent to destroy him &c &c. . . .

Mr. Powers has exhibited here four busts; Mr. Webster, Mr. Adams, Mr. Baldwin, the engineer, and the Rev. Dr. Lowell of Boston.[1] They have placed him, at once, at the head of this department of sculpture, and, are pronounced, with generous frankness, by all artists, to be "equal, if not superior to any ancient heads of the class of portraits." This noble rank, thus immediately taken by Mr. Powers at the head of this branch of his profession, is highly honorable to the country, as he came to Europe a finished artist, without other instruction than such as the western towns offered. . . .

NOTES

Source: Quoted in James Fenimore Cooper to an unidentified editor, between 19 October and 11? November 1839, Cooper Collection, Beinecke. The date is given by Cooper in his letter. Previous publication: Cooper, 3:438–39.
1. Powers' bust of John Quincy Adams is now in the Pennsylvania Academy of the Fine Arts, Philadelphia. The present location of his bust of Charles Lowell (1782–1864), minister of the West Unitarian Church in Boston, is unknown. For the location of the other two busts, see Letter 108, n. 9.

136. To James Fenimore Cooper
ca. September 1839

. . . [*page torn*] pain a very scurrilous attack on Mr Paulding in a paper edited by Mr Willis[1] — in which the writer after asserting that Mr P. is dead as an author proceeds to kick his carcase most manfully

— he triumphs over his 60 years and his grey hairs!! From a certain saucy & flippant command of English conjoined with an absence of all decency and dignity I suspect that Willis himself wrote that article — this is not very important any way but it is disgraceful that money seeking authors should thus impudently outrage all decency the instant they come into the market — I think that such fellows could be kept in order if they who *can would* do it. What makes this ludicrous is that Willis ought to be abler than any man of his age to say if the shoe he feels a posteriori "be Spanish or neat leather."[2]

. . . [*page torn*] I was pleased to see that Commodore Elliott who has so long enjoyed the confidence and support of his country is mentioned honorably by you & and that he won his medal and promotion by courage and conduct & not by going on his knees to Perry as the would be aristocrats around me have endeavoured to convince me[3] — there's great *injustice* in a certain class of pretending people at home — they have all the impudence of an aristocracy without its manners or its conscious force. . . .

Addressed: James [*page torn*] / Coop[er] [*page torn*] / via Harve / p'r New York
Endorsed, in Susan Cooper's hand: 1839 / H. Greenough

NOTES

All that remains of the manuscript of this letter is the bottom half of the recto and verso of one page; the upper half has been torn off.

The date has been conjectured on the basis of the postmark, which reads "New-York, Nov. 25."

Manuscript: Cooper Collection, Beinecke.

1. "Paulding the Author Disinterred," *Corsair* 1 (1839): 104–5, was a review of Paulding's *Works,* 14 vols. (New York, 1835–36). The *Corsair* was edited by N. P. Willis and Dr. T. O. Porter.
2. "Some have been beaten till they know
   What wood a cudgel's of by th' blow:
   Some kick'd until they can feel whether
   A shoe be Spanish or neat's leather."
   (Samuel Butler, *Hudibras,* pt. 2, I, l. 221)
3. In the Battle of Lake Erie in 1813, Jesse Duncan Elliott (1782–1845), master commandant, failed to bring the *Niagara* to the aid of Oliver Hazard Perry (1785–1819), commander of the American naval forces, thus precipitating a long-lived controversy. In his *History of the Navy* Cooper refrained from criticizing Elliott. As a result he was violently attacked by friends of Perry, to whom he responded by instituting a series of libel suits.

137.   To Charles Sumner
16, 18 November 1839

Florence — Nov'r 16th, [18] '39.

My Dear Sumner —

Yours of Nov'r 9th[1] has just reached me and was most welcome — I am truly obliged by your kind expressions regarding the little commission you were so good as to undertake for me at Vienna — The pumice arrived in due time & has proved excellent —

I met Mr Kenyon[2] near my Studio a few days since — he was walking with an acquaintance of mine, who introduced me to him — he spoke much of you and I need not say in terms that made me seek a farther acquaintance with him — I accordingly invited him to see my statue, which he promised to do — I have not yet seen him — If I do I shall certainly endeavour to cultivate his acquaintance; but as an invitation has been given & accepted, J think I cannot with propriety take any further steps myself.

I look upon your advice respecting the accessory ornaments of my chair as having been most well-timed and fortunate for me[3] — not that I think the figures you object to can not be rendered poetical as well as effective, but because as you convincingly observed — I ought in a *first great* work, appealing to great national sympathies, to keep clear, quite clear of debatable ground — so as to carry with me all hearts and all consciences as likewise all tastes as far as the Art (as in me) will allow —

I had intended to have no word, unless of our mother tongue, written upon my statue; but I have been seduced from my determination — Listen now, "et mihi Delphica lauro cinge volens — comam."[4] In modelling the rising Sun the verse which you may — must remember, flashed athwart my memory as I studied my horses — "Magnus ab integro saeclorum nascitur ordo!"[5] I immediately determined to carve it under my bas relief, upon the base of the chair — I now set about a *pendant* for the Infant Hercules and soon found it as you will see — "Incipe parve puer cui non risere parentes!"[6] Instead of the negro I have placed Columbus on the left hand of the chair — he leans against the pilaster and is pondering upon a globe which he holds in his hand. I am not yet decided whether to make an Indian for the other side or a figure of Virgin America raising her veil and shewing a star upon her front — What say you to Liberty with the epigraph dos. pace sta! troppa roba[7] is it not? The bas relief of Hercules and the snakes is far advanced in the marble — the Columbus is nearly modelled — Capponi embraced me when I told him that I meant to put Columbus there — He was truly delighted and his approval of my mottoes knew no bounds — he repeated the first and thereon hung a 20 minutes of most eloquent prophecy — I cannot say to you how my blood is stirred by finding that you and he and 2 or 3 more have felt and been moved by my statue — Has it not been born amid the sneers of ignorance and pretension? — nursed in solitary determination — wet with my tears — The cold eye of hatred has been on me — I have withstood but I have unter [uns?][8] [*page torn*] been *happy* only when *alone* — Nothing so withering so exhausting as the Vox clamantis in deserto — Nothing so bitter as ignorant scorn for attempted services — proffered light — Was it not always so? I am sure I have fared far better than generally falls to the lot of men, who undertake new things.

If you should have leisure pray tell me your impression of the works of Shinkel[9] the architect, as regards distribution & adaptation, *organization* in short. That's the germ of future architectures — Science to decide on forms and arrangement of parts — Taste & fancy in a hand formed by the exemplaria graeca[10] for the ornament — there is an architecture that will require all the light of this age to embody it and all the genius of antiquity to adorn it — an E pluribus Unum style sine qua, non [to] have anything worthy our country —

We are expecting Miss Sedgwick[11] — Lady Davy[12] who was with me the other day was in raptures about her. I don't hear from Giorgio[13] very often — I have begged him to get the Secretaryship of Cambreling[14] who they say goes to Turin — If you can move any wires in this matter pray do it — I think Giorgio calculated to rise in that department — do you not? Statesman perhaps no — but diplomate why not? in Italy too — Who else can do one half what he can? that is to be had — My wife and Mr Russell join me in kindest wishes for your health and happiness — pray let me hear of you if possible more than once before you embark.

Yours sincerely

H G——gh

P.S. I have received J Q Adams' jubilee oration delivered at N Y last April[15] — It is godlike — The clearest exposition of true American principles & policy — the most eloquent enforcement of them — His heart is full of hope — What a blessed old man who can look back on a life of honorable & high & successful exertion — forward to an approving posterity & to a God whose will he has done! — Longfellow has published a book of which, much praise.[16] Rufus Dawes a novel entitled Nick Mate[17] — Biddle's[18] promise to pay turns out not empty wind but mere paper for the time at least — I do not cannot believe in this system. It is the most tremendous irratamentum maloroum[19] in our country — If the Sub-Treasury issues paper without an easy means of testing its vaults I shall become a nothingarian —

18 Nov. — When I inform you that I have met Mr Kenyon several times and that I have had several long conversations with him you will not doubt the impression he has made on me — he is a most *finished* man — He begs me to say that he shall write before you leave Berlin — He dines with me the day after tomorrow & I with him the day after — I have engaged Mr Kemble Charles to meet him. Also Wilde, Bezzi[20] & Powers & shall try to get Capponi — If they are all like him in England I think we shall get along with them.

In the right-hand margin alongside the beginning of the fourth paragraph of the letter:

I have written an inscription for my own account to go on the plinth of my statue behind — As my Latin was never great & is now rusty I beg your file for it — Hoc simulacrum, quod libertati superstitem fore — Noluit — Horatius G——gh inv. 1832 — plastice pinx. 1834 — collocav. 1840[21] —

On two separate sheets enclosed with the letter:[22]

Mem —

Artificial Pumice — colour a creamy white (with a slight tinge of peach blossom tint sometimes but oftener yellowish —)

Texture firm but granulated and falling in a coarse powder when rubbed on stone — Adheres to the tongue — seems a pulverised silicous substance amalgamated in some kind of earthy paste & burnt.

I believe it is to be found at Vienna A — If Mr Sumner could ascertain where it is to be found and who should be addressed to procure it he will much oblige me —

Any person polishing metals or glass would be likely to know about it —

Addressed: A Monsieur / Monsieur Charles Sumner / Poste Restante — / Á Berlin — [23]
Endorsed: Greenough / Florence / Nov. 16th / Recd. at Berlin / Dec 4th 39

N O T E S

Charles Sumner (1811–74), lawyer and U.S. Senator from Massachusetts, traveled in Europe from 1837 to 1841. Greenough drew a sketch of him, presumably during his visit in Florence (sketch in editor's collection).
 Manuscript: Sumner Autograph Album, Houghton. Previous publication (in part): Charles Sumner, *Memoir and Letters of Charles Sumner,* ed. Edward L. Pierce (Boston, 1877–93), 2:96–97.

1. In his letter Sumner said he had obtained the pumice which Greenough had requested with the aid of the U.S. consul in Vienna (manuscript owned by H. E. Luhrs, Shippensburg, Pennsylvania).
2. John Kenyon (1784–1856), English poet and philanthropist, had many friends among the literati and intellectuals of England and America. Sumner had written that he had heard Kenyon was in Florence and that he would write Kenyon to tell him of Greenough's statue.
3. Sumner had written that he would like to have Greenough's statue entirely harmonious and classical, and for that reason, would reject Greenough's proposed accessory figures of a Negro, an Indian, and Washington passing the sirens.
4. An inaccurate version of "And, willing, crown my head, Melpomene, with Delphic laurel" (Horace, *Odes* 3.30.16).
5. "The great sequence of ages is born anew" (Virgil, *Eclogue* 4.1.5).
6. "Begin small boy on whom parents have not smiled!" (ibid., 63).
7. "Thus. May there be peace! Too much stuff."
8. "Between ourselves."
9. Karl Friedrich Schinkel (1781–1841), German functional architect.
10. "Greek models." See Horace, *Ars Poetica,* l. 268.
11. Catherine Maria Sedgwick (1789–1867), Massachusetts novelist, wrote an account of her visit abroad at this time in *Letters from Abroad to Kindred at Home* (New York, 1841).
12. Lady Jane Davy (1780–1855), whose second husband was Sir Humphrey Davy, the distinguished English chemist.
13. G. W. Greene.
14. Churchill Caldain Cambreling (1786–1862) was a member of Congress from 1821 to 1839 and U.S. Minister to Russia in 1840–41.

15. It was delivered on 30 April, the fiftieth anniversary of the first inauguration of Washington. Subsequently it was printed as *The Jubilee of the Constitution* (New York, 1839).
16. *Hyperion,* published in August 1839.
17. Rufus Dawes (1803–59), Boston author and editor, who was a fellow student of John Greenough at Harvard, published his historical romance *Nix's Mate* in 1839.
18. Nicholas Biddle (1786–1844) was president of the Bank of the United States from 1822 to 1839.
19. *Irritamentum malorum,* "incitement of evil."
20. Charles Kemble (1775–1854), English actor preeminent in comic roles, was a member of the famous family of actors of that name. Giovanni Aubrey Bezzi was a Piedmontese political refugee who settled in Florence.
21. "This statue, which he was unwilling to be about — to be outliving liberty — Horatio Greenough designed 1832 — put in plaster 1834 — set up 1840."
22. This note on pumice, written on two separate slips in Greenough's hand, was preserved with the letter. It was probably carried by Sumner upon his departure from Florence.
23. Sumner replied to this letter on 8 January 1840, that he approved the first of Greenough's proposed mottoes but felt the second was a taunt to England, thought the exchange of Columbus for the Negro a good one, and preferred the Indian to the Virgin America (manuscript owned by H. E. Luhrs, Shippensburg, Pennsylvania).

138.   To James Kirke Paulding
14 December 1839

Florence Dec. 14th '39.

J K Paulding Esqr.
My Dear Sir
I have been deterred from sending my lately finished works to the United States by the accounts which I have received from my friends of the duty levied upon statuary in general — I have been assured that every statue and bas relief must pay a duty of 30 pr cent — at which rate the work I now hold ready for shipment, would pay on its delivery in America the sum of 1230 Dolls. I trust it is useless for me to urge that this sum must ultimately be paid by me; the buyers of course will insist upon a corresponding reduction of price — The sacrifice is entirely out of the question, and I fully believe that this law will act as a prohibition, not for mean & paltry ornaments in marble,

but for works of high art. I shall hold what objects I now have therefore until spring, in the hope that this duty will be either removed or so modified as [to] enable us to make contracts more to our advantage. May I ask of your kindness the favor of setting this matter in a true light with the President[1] & such other gentlemen connected with the Government as can move effectually in producing the desired change. I should not thus importune you did I not believe that the levy of this tax on works of art produced by native citizens abroad, was an oversight.

I hear from Rome that Mr Crawford the Sculptor of New-York has lately produced a statue of Orpheus[2] which does him high honour — he is most advantageously known there not only for abilities of a high order, but for an amiable and estimable character. He is not much known at home generally, from the circumstance of his having formed himself in Italy. When I tell you that his situation at Rome is very trying, from an ambition he has of finishing some work in marble before he returns to America & from his not possessing any means except those drawn from his profession, I am sure that I shall bespeak a kind word from you in his behalf with such of his fellow citizens as you may know desirous of bringing forward a talent of a high respectability which belongs to the State of New York —

The Statue of Washington continues to advance regularly. I am now carving on the chair the rising Sun with the motto — "Magnus ab integro saeclorum nascitur ordo." I have nearly decided upon a green marble for my pedestal, having found that granite would cost me more than remains of the money devoted to this monument.

The Group goes on prosperously and Mr Chapman's casts and drawings came most opportunely. I hope he has received his armour[3] etc but hear nothing from him.

I recognized your pen at once in the gift from fairy land[4] — which was truly a treat to us all. My wife was delighted with the novelty you have given to that form of invention — This is what we want — not a starveling and puritanical abstinence from works of fancy & taste [but] [*page torn*] an *adaptation* of them to our institutions and a harmonizing of them with our morals or what we mean shall be such —

I hear less eloquence on the subject of Mr Biddle's genius in financiering than formerly. An English gent'n called on me lately and after asking me if I had seen the papers went on to remark that Jourdan[5] was losing his health — "Now I don't like this" said he — "Biddle you know, his health was bad — I don't like to see 2 gentlemen of their abilities get sick in managing so flourishing an institution. I shall sell out!" I have lately received a specimen of marble from the island of Paros.⁶ It is so like that from Stockbridge⁷ that no one can distinguish between the 2 — I remain dear Sir Yours faithfully

H Greenough

Addressed: J. K. Paulding Esqr / Secretary of the Navy / pr *Erie* / Washington D.C.
Endorsed: Referred to the / Secretary of State / for perusal [?] & returned / without comment, / *JKP*

NOTES

James Kirke Paulding (1779–1860), New York writer and statesman, was secretary of the navy from 1838 to 1841.
    Manuscript: Editor's collection. Previous publication (in part): William Irving Paulding, *The Literary Life of James K. Paulding* (New York, 1867), p. 273.
1. Martin Van Buren.
2. It is now in the Museum of Fine Arts, Boston.
3. Presumably that which J. G. Chapman bought in Florence, reported to have been worn by Giovanni dei Medici (Henry T. Tuckerman, *Book of the Artists* [New York, 1867], pp. 219–20). The casts and drawings were requested by Greenough for use in modelling part of his group *The Rescue.*
4. *A Gift from Fairy-Land,* published in 1838.
5. Samuel Jaudon (1796–1874) was second in importance to Nicholas Biddle in the administration of the Second Bank of the United States. He became cashier in 1832, and in 1836 was sent abroad as its agent to raise funds. See Edwin Jaquett Sellers, *Jaudon Family of Pennsylvania* (Philadelphia, 1924), p. 31; Bray Hammond, *Banks and Politics in America from the Revolution to the Civil War* (Princeton, 1957), pp. 472–73, 507–9, 520.
6. A Grecian island, one of the Cyclades.
7. The marble of West Stockbridge, Massachusetts, had a reputation for resistance to weather exceeded by no other in the world (Charles Powers Smith, *The Housatonic* [New York, 1946], p. 255).

139.   To Gino Capponi
    ca. 25 December [1839?]

My Dear Sir

Whenever it suits your convenience you will find me at my *studio*
from 10 A.M. until 4 P.M. I have not been able to restrain myself from
working a little at your bust,[1] so that you will find it rather more advanced than when you last saw it. I need not assure you that it will
give me the greatest pleasure to receive you here at my house, should
you have leisure in the evening — I always pass that part of the day in
my *library*[2] — (Lucus a *non* lucendo).[3] Wishing you many happy returns of the season

> I remain your friend & Serv't
> Horatio Greenough

The Marquis Capponi —

Addressed: To The Marquis G. Capponi —

NOTES

This letter is dated on the conjecture that "the season" is Christmas (see the last
sentence of the letter) and on the fact that Greenough reported his bust of
Capponi "nearly finished" in February 1840 (*Letters,* p. 132).
    Manuscript: Carteggi Capponi, Biblioteca Nazionale.
  1. Greenough's bust of Capponi, which stood for many years in the Directors'
     Room of the Academy of Fine Arts in Florence, was apparently destroyed
     during World War II by order of Benito Mussolini, along with other works by
     citizens of the nations with which Italy was at war (information furnished by
     Clara L. Dentler, Florence).
  2. Greenough had a sizable library, judging from the catalogs of his books sold
     at auction after his death. See *Auction Sale . . . Dec. 12th and 13th,
     1890 . . . Including Portion of the Library of the Late Horatio Greenough,
     Sculptor, of Boston and Florence, Italy* (Boston: C. F. Libbie & Co.), and
     *Auction Sale . . . May 7th, and 8th, 1895 . . . Together with the Remain-
     ing Portion of the Library of the Late Horatio Greenough, Sculptor of
     Boston and Florence, Italy* (Boston: C. F. Libbie & Co.).
  3. "A grove from not being light," quoted when an absurd derivation is given
     for a word, as *lucus* ("grove") from *non lucendo* ("not being light"), since
     a grove is dark. The phrase may also be used to indicate a *non sequitur.*

140.   To George Washington Greene
        6 February 1840

My Dear Greene

I write you in great haste and in much anxiety — My group[1] is modelled and ready for casting — *The moulder* of Florence is ill of a lung fever and will not soon be able to resume his work — I wish you to attempt to send me an able moulder — pray consult Mr Gibson about it — The group is a complicated one and it requires a skillful workman — If you can engage one pray send him on by the courier — you know my address. Casa Leblanc Via Dei Bardi — The moulder can find assistant workmen here — the group is of 2 figures — size of life — pray write me at once what you can do —

Yours in haste
Horatio Greenough

Dalle Studio
6th Feb'y '40

N O T E S

Manuscript: Editor's collection.
1. *The Rescue.*

141.   To John Forsyth
        8 February 1840

Florence Feb'y 8th 1840 —

Hon John Forsyth / Secretary of State
Dear Sir

The object of the present is to lay before you such facts with respect to the works I am executing for the Government as require the consideration and action of the same, and such information as in your former communication I was directed to afford the department.

The Statue of Washington is now so nearly completed, that I have hopes of being able to deliver it in the course of the next summer. Having always found it impossible to foresee the exact time when a work even of moderate size will be done, I cannot request that any arrangements may be made for transporting this statue at a given period — Should it be contemplated to transport this work in a Government's Ship and could I be informed at what time a vessell may be expected to return to the States from the Mediterranean, I should use every effort to secure it a summer passage by working at night. The more important and difficult portions of the statue are sculptured. The accessories employ me at present.

I have made enquiries of the prices of different materials for a Pedestal — My wish was to have made it of one solid block of Granite, from the Quarries of Quincy, Mass. I find however that the price of such a pedestal carefully dressed with the hammer will be somewhat more than Ten Thousand Dollars,[1] and this exclusive of the cost of transportation from the Quarries to Washington. As I am uncertain whether it is expected that I should be at the expence of the pedestal myself, I of course cannot undertake to furnish one at such a price — If it is expected that I shall provide the pedestal, I shall be obliged to have recource to a granite core in blocks covered or encrusted with a coloured marble of Italy — this pedestal besides being inferiour to one of Granite for its effect and beauty will have a character unworthy of its position as being visibly pieced and encrusted and threatening decay. It will be seen from my accounts that the elaboration of this statue has consumed such a portion of the money paid me for it, as to make it impossible for me to furnish such a pedestal as it requires, at my own expence.

The main group of the subject for the East Front of the Capitol is modelled and ready for casting. At this critical moment a combination of circumstances has deprived me of the assistance of a competent Moulder — the one I usually employ being dangerously ill and the others in the employment of the French Gov't and of one of the English nobility. I have written to Rome for one however and hope that this delay and disappointment will be only disadvantageous in point of expense.

I beg leave to press upon you the necessity of my receiving the second instalment of the price of the Group this year and earnestly request that it may be laid before Congress at a time to ensure the action of that body. The journals of my expences which will be presented to you at the time of the delivery of the Statue of Washington, will I trust be ample apology for this importunity, situated as I am where credit is unavailable and where the failure of a supply of hard money is followed by an immediate stoppage of all active service —

I cannot conclude this letter without mentioning the very distinguished rank as an artist of Mr Hiram Powers of Cincinnati and expressing my hope that such a genius as his will find employment from the government. His works are duly esteemed by the citizens of all countries and as efforts have been made to engage his services by persons connected with the Court of Sardinia[2] I feel anxious lest we may lose him — a loss which will be disgraceful to our country connected with the adoption as has been the case in some instances of foreign artists of inferiour reputation.

> I have the honor to be Dear Sir
> your ob't and humble Servant
> Horatio Greenough

Addressed: To The Hon John Forsyth / Secretary of State. / Dept of State / Washington D.C.
Endorsed: Rec'd 24 March / Mr Dickins

NOTES

Manuscript: RG 59, General Records of the Department of State, Accession 161, Item 135, NA.

1. Greenough overestimated the sum; the pedestal which was finally obtained from Quincy cost $1900.
2. No record of any such negotiations have been preserved in the Powers Papers, National Collection of Fine Arts, Smithsonian Institution (information furnished by Clara L. Dentler, Florence).

142.   To Gino Capponi
        1 May 1840

To The Marquis G. Capponi

Accept my dear Sir my grateful acknowledgments for the portraits[1] you have sent me — Precious as they must be from my sense of the virtues and talents of those whom they represent, they are doubly so as a gift from you.

The favorable opinion of my statue expressed by your daughters affords me the highest gratification — I pray that you will say to them that I am proud that they, who so venerate the heart & mind of *Washington*, should find any thing worthy of him in the monument I have carved.

I will not fail to deliver your message together with the portrait to Miss Sedgwick this evening.

I remain dear Sir
Your friend & Servant
Horatio Greenough
Friday May 1st '40 —

P.S.   Miss Sedgwick accepts with many thanks the portrait[2] which she recognized at once — though she finds that a great change has taken place in the original.

Addressed: To The Marquis G. Capponi / Via S. Sebastiano.

NOTES

Manuscript: Carteggi Capponi, Biblioteca Nazionale.

1. Presumably portraits of Capponi and one or more of his daughters. Portraits of his daughters Marianna and Ortensia were painted shortly before 1838 by Carlotta Bonaparte, daughter of Joseph Bonaparte (Andrea Corsini, *I Bonaparte a Firenze* [Florence, 1961], p. 69).
2. Presumably of Capponi.

143.   To Aaron Vail
         26 June 1840

Florence June 26th 1840.

A Vail Esqr / Acting Secretary of State
Sir

I have received a letter from your department of the date of May 22nd[1] expressing the "regret and surprise" of the President that the Statue of Washington is not completed "notwithstanding the reasons" presented by me "in explanation" — The surprise that I should question my obligation to furnish the pedestal — and the intimation that no further supply of money can be afforded me on account of the Group on which I am employed, until a consular certificate of its present state of forwardness is received by your department.

By an examination of my correspondence with your Department it will appear that the Model of the Statue of Washington could not be commenced until October 1834, that it was cast in Feb'y '36 having occupied in modelling it — 16 months. It will also appear that obstacles beyond my controul prevented the model and the Block of marble from meeting until November '37 — that the operation of rough hewing was finished in March '39, making 17 months devoted to that portion of the work, while from March '39 to October* '40, when I shall have completed the Statue, we have 19 months devoted to carving and finishing it.

The entire space occupied therefore by the execution of this work has been 52 months or 4 years and four months — ie 4 months more than I had mentioned as the time necessary for its execution. As regards the intervals of inaction between the respective dates here given, I have heretofore fully explained them — they have given me an uneasiness as much greater than that felt by any other person, as my interest in the speedy and happy completion of my task has been greater than that of any other person.

With regard to my obligation to furnish the Pedestal, I must have very imperfectly explained myself, if I left an impression on your

* If it seem fit to the President I should prefer shipping the Statue from Leghorn.

mind that I meant to question what is expressly stated in the contract and repeatedly referred to by me in my correspondence. I rather inquired if it were not proper to give the Statue a *pedestal* of *Granite,* stating it as my opinion that *such a pedestal* would be the most proper and expressing the hope that I should not be called on for the entire expense of *such a Pedestal.* Now as the expense of a granite pedestal is so very great my remarks on that subject tended only to this that I found it hard that I should be expected to give 4 years of my life and 25000$ in consideration of the sum of 2000$ to be paid me by the Government. If it be asked why I *proposed* a *Granite pedestal* instead of furnishing one of marble my answer is that though the latter costs only 300$ while the former will cost more than twice as many thousand, I conceive that the superiority of the granite for *effect* and *character* is such as to entitle it to an unhesitating preference and in so doing consider myself Sir as doing my duty — humbly submitting myself to the rebuke of the President insofar as my incapacity to judge of such matters shall be found to have interfered with a *proper* and *just* sense of my obligation and its discharge.

In obedience to that sense of my duty in acting by the *spirit* of my contract I shall take no steps with reference to a Pedestal until the statue is erected and I promise myself the approbation of those who are to come after me in this art in so doing. While I place that confidence in the justice of the government to believe that when my work is before them, I shall not be found to have spared either labor or expense in its service and that so far from endeavouring to get rid of my obligations while I exacted the full price of my work, I have done double what the contract exacts of me both in labor and expense.

The condition annexed to the farther payment for the group is one which unfortunately it is not in my power to comply with. The consulate at Leghorn is vacant by the death of the late Mr Appleton[2] while the Consul at Rome has repeatedly stated to me that he cannot leave his post for such an object without the express order of Government. I hope therefore that I may be allowed to supplicate and I do hereby supplicate that I may be allowed to give up the farther prosecution of this groupe and that a reasonable time (for instance 1 year) may be allowed me for the reimbursement of the sum already received on account of the same. Whatever may be my ambition to serve the Government in the capacity of Sculptor I cannot purchase it at the price of such a misconstruction of my motives and misunderstanding of my conduct as that contained in the letter now before me. I am Sir with the highest respect

your Obedient Servant
Horatio Greenough

Addressed: A Vail Esqr / Acting Secretary of State / Dept of State / Washington D.C.
Endorsed: Rec. 21 Aug / Mr Dickins

NOTES

Aaron Vail (1796–1878) was chief clerk of the State Department from 26 June 1838 to 15 July 1840.

    Manuscript: RG 59, General Records of the Department of State, Accession 161, Item 135, NA.

  1. A copy is in RG 59, General Records of the Department of State, Domestic Letters, NA.

  2. Thomas Appleton.

144.   To James Kirke Paulding
       28 June 1840

Florence, June 28th 1840.

J K Paulding Esqr / Secretary of the Navy
Dear Sir

    I have lately received from A. Vail Esqr Acting secretary of State, a letter expressing the "surprise and regret" of the President that the Statue of Washington is not completed, "notwithstanding the reasons presented" by me "in explanation." The same letter contains much argument to prove what certainly I never could have intended to deny, Viz that my contract obliges me to furnish a pedestal and bas reliefs. It closes by intimating that I need expect no more money on account of the Group, until a consular certificate of the state of advancement of that work shall have been received and approved by his department.

As it seems clear to me that Mr Vail's letter was written without a full knowledge of what has been before urged by me and particularly in my letters to yourself, I have contented myself with simply giving him an account of the time employed on the Statue of Washington, from which it appears that I shall have spent in October next 4 years and 4 months in its execution and as I trust at that time to have completed it, I think it must be allowed by all ingenuous and fair minded men, that considering it is the first colossal work I ever undertook, the difference of 4 months between the time anticipated as necessary for its execution and that actually consumed in it, is not sufficiently great to warrant such a cracking about my ears of the twopenny whip of his brief authority. As for the intervals of inaction that unavoidably delayed the sending my model to Carrara and the getting the marble down from the mountains, they have been thoroughly justified by me in my correspondence with the Gov't and shall be laid before the public in a form and with the proofs necessary to establish my claim to entire justification in respect to them.

I have concluded to wait until I raise the Statue in the Rotunda before fixing on the height or ornaments of the pedestal, and when the work shall be so situated it will appear whether I have sought to defraud Gov't of my exertions or whether I have acted for the best in not repeating on the Pedestal, the stories already told by pictures on the wall. I say it will appear, but alas! if I am to judge of what awaits my efforts by the utter ignorance of the exigencies and claims of Art, betrayed by these gentlemen who seem to think that to make a colossus is as purely mechanical an operation as to frame a boat or build a chimney, I have little to hope but mortification and rebuke instead of praise or reward — I mean for a time Sir, for I believe that those who fulfill their duty with the zeal and self sacrifice that I have done, cannot fail in the end of being approved.

The conditions exacted from me before paying a further instalment on the group are out of my power to comply with — The Consulate at Leghorn is vacant by the death of the late Mr Appleton — the Consul at Rome has repeatedly assured me that he cannot leave his post to inspect my group without an express order from Gov't. Under these circumstances, I trust it will seem just to the President that I should no longer be held to the completion of that work and I beg you by the friendship which you have always shewn me, to use your influence to get me clear of the obligation, granting me twelve months to repay the money already received on account of the same. If I am guilty of the neglect which alone can justify such a letter as I have received from the Secretary of State, surely I can well be spared any further calls on my incapacity. If I am innocent as I hope will be seen when my work reaches its place of destination I trust I shall not be expected to stand as a butt for the spleen of illnature or malevolence.

You my Dear Sir and you alone can sympathize with me. You can imagine what would be your feelings if called on to write a work of high poetry and deep feeling with the stings and the racket of illnature and of ignorance bursting in upon your retirement and overwhelming your aspirations.

I am well aware that in a country like ours where the processes of Art are imperfectly known we are subject of being misunderstood and misconstrued — I know that the abuse of the trusts reposed by Gov't have been such as to warrant severe scrutiny and untiring watchfulness, but I think I have had my share of such suspicion and so help me God nothing but bitter necessity shall induce me to again subject myself to it. I remain Dear Sir With respectful compliments to y'r lady

Your Friend & Serv't
Horatio Greenough

P.S. I have stated in my letter to Mr Vail that the Statue shall be ready for Shipment in October. I have mentioned also Leghorn as the port where it will be most advisable to ship it. In my opinion it were better that the Statue should not be moved from its present position, until I receive advice of the arrival of the vessel which is to receive it & for these reasons. I have engaged the same men to remove it from hence who brought it hither — They have a waggon built expressly for this Statue — by so doing I shall have it in my power to transfer the statue at once from the waggon to the lighter, without the danger of trusting it in the hands of people inexperienced in moving such large Statues and ignorant of the precautions necessary in so doing. I trust that it will not be expected that I should accompany this work to America. Having sacrificed so valuable a portion of my life to the vain hope of earning a title to the respect of my countrymen and finding myself here deprived of an opportunity to engage in any new work by my engagement in the Group and denied the means of prosecuting that by the untimely exaction of official proof of my assertions and that when such proof is not to be had, I hope that it will seem fit to the gentlemen entrusted with this business to allow me to remain here and do something toward the making up for the injury my interests have sustained — particularly as the Contract stipulates nothing respecting such a journey.

I beg you My Dear Sir to consider such portions of the present letter as express my own private feelings as purely confidential and while I assure you that I shall go on with the group with such means as I possess, until I am released from the contract, to believe that I am not the man to receive the treatment of a culprit without taking every measure in my power to place my conduct in a full and fair light.

The Statue of the reigning Grand Duke of Tuscany by Professor Demi[1] was modelled before the Washington was commenced. It went to the quarries at the same time with the Washington — It is still there & the blocking of it is but now finished. The Statue of the late Dutchess of Lucca by Professor Bartolini which still stands incomplete in his Studio was modelled *before I came to Florence to study.*[2] I have been enabled to carry this colossus through in the time I have done only by assiduity and a most liberal expenditure — securing a preference wherever I had a competitor whether for workmen or for materials for [?] the latter.

I beg leave again to express my full sense of the impossibility of gentlemen connected with Government giving sufficient time and attention to all the detail of private claims to avoid sometimes urging the letter of the law to the injury of the service — but as my tranquility is more necessary to me than any renown to be gained by its sacrifice — I hope that you will grant me your kindly assistance in releasing myself from any further engagement which brings me within the liability of such misconstructions of my conduct as are implied in Mr Vail's letter to me.

I am Dear Sir
Sincerely Your friend & Serv't
Horatio Greenough

Addressed: J. K. Paulding Esqr / Secretary of the Navy / Washington D.C. / Via Havre / p New York / packet

NOTES

Manuscript: American Academy of Arts and Letters.
1. Paolo Demi (1797–1863), a native of Leghorn, executed a statue of Leopold I for the Piazza Carlo Alberto in that city. It was destroyed in the 1849 revolution.
2. Bartolini's monument to Maria Luisa di Borbone, Queen of Etruria and Duchess of Lucca, was commissioned in 1824 and erected in the Piazza Napoleone, Lucca, in 1843 (Mario Tinti, *Lorenzo Bartolini* [Rome, 1936], 2:43–44).

145. To Charles Sumner
12 July 1840

Florence — July 12 — 1840

My Dear Sir

The constant press of my affairs has hithertoo prevented my having the pleasure of writing to you — I am pressing Washington's Statue for Shipment in October. I have varied the back of the chair since you saw it by making it of ornamental open work — by this means I enable the spectator to enjoy the outline of the entire[1] figure from behind as well as from the other sides — The work is much enriched and though the additional expense is great I cannot repent the step.

In the midst of these certainly industrious and praiseworthy efforts to do my utmost, I have received a letter from Mr Vail acting Sec'y of State, in which he takes me to task with very little ceremony on account of the *time* I have been occupied in this work and which he closes by assuring me that I need hope for no more moneys until the Gov't get official report upon the progress of my group — How this is to be done I know not as the consul at Leghorn is dead and Mr Greene has had no orders from Gov't to leave his post for this object.

I have accordingly written the Sec'y to say that the Washington will be ready in October and begging that I may be allowed to with draw from the further prosecution of the group and have 1 year given me to pay the 4000$ already received on acc't of the same — Indeed I feel that I should be doing a very unjustifiable thing to go on toiling in the service of persons who want alike the confidence to trust me and the capacity to understand — I have not earned in making the Washington the wages of a clerk in any counting House of respectability — and the group would infallibly *cost me* every farthing voted for its execution. Should my petition be granted, which I hope to effect by my presence in October, I shall endeavor to make arrangements with one of the State Governments for its execution on terms more advantageous — As it is — I am prevented by my contract from undertaking any thing of importance and denied the means of fulfilling it. Had I not had other resources the Washington might have been seized for my debts & I been put in prison.

The Washington will have consumed in Oct 4 years & four months active labor — the intervals during which it has lain inactive have been explained to a day in my correspondence with Gov't; of such explanation, though satisfactory it would seem at the time, nothing is now said but I am rated like a defaulter — I beg you if you have it in your power to make known these facts and to add the following —

The Statue of the reigning G Duke of Tuscany which was modelled before the Washington and went to the quarries before it — still lies there a mere sketch.

The Statue of the Dutchess of Lucca which still stands unfinished in the rooms of the principal Sculptor of Florence was modelled before I commenced the study of Art.

The Pegasus[2] ordered by this Gov't in '28 and modelled in '29 is still unfinished.

I have driven the Washington on with all the dispatch consistent with the difficulties to be overcome and the exegencies of Art — I have done i[t] [on]ly [*page torn*] by constant assiduity and free expenditure.

I have lately been much gratified by an order from the Countess Reviczky wife of the Austrian Minister here to make a full length portrait of her daughter.[3] It is already modelled —

Mr Crawford is here and well — He seems to me a fine spirited young man — I fear that some of his canons of Art have been received with too little examination from the current philosophy of modern Rome, but he is young and has the proper spirit for an artist.

Powers is going on nobly with his Eve[4] — pray remember me in all affection to Alston & his brothers — the hope of meeting them so soon outweighs with me all the vexations I foresee in plunging once more among the waves of business & politics. Pray tell me how you are occupied and believe me

Yours
H Greenough

In making known what I have written I beg you will be governed by the state of public opinion. If an attempt is making to poison the public mind against my work I hope you will make these facts known. If the subject is asleep don't wake it —

Addressed: Charles Sumner Esqr / Care of Henry Greenough Esqr / Boston Mass. / Via Havre / pr New York / Packet

NOTES

Manuscript: Sumner Correspondence, Houghton.
1. Here Greenough sketched the back of the chair. See Plate IX.
2. This work has not been identified.
3. The wife of Count Reviczky was the Baroness Szidonia Szumlanszky (b. 1818). They had two children: Ada (b. 1838), who became a nun, and Alexis Elek (d. 1886). (*Pallas Nagy Lexikon* [Budapest, 1897], vol. 14; Ivan Nagy, *Magyarorszag csaladai* [Hungarian families] [Budapest, 1862]; information furnished by F. Redo, General Director, Orsz. Szepmuveszti Muzeum, Budapest.)
4. This statue, showing Eve before the Fall, is now in the Cincinnati Art Museum.

146. To Richard Henry Wilde
ca. 24 July 1840

Sunday Morn'g

My Dear Sir

I received a letter from Rome yest'y informing me that our friend Kinloch is dangerously ill[1] and asking the address of his family — the letter reached me too late for me to reply by return mail. Should you know to whom I can write in such a juncture I beg you will give me the name and address. Mr Middleton[2] I believe has the care of Kinloch's property but I know neither his name or in what part of Carolina he lives — Mr Everett who is now in Paris begs me to present him to you & expresses much satisfaction at the prospect of meeting you[3] — Miss Sedgwick in a letter from Frankfort begs me to assure you that one of her chief regrets in leaving Europe is that she has been obliged to give so short a time to Florence — I am sorry to add that she says Mr Sedgwick's health does not improve.[4]

I learn that Dante's portrait[5] is found at last and congratulate you thereon — It will make an appropriate frontispiece to your work[6] if what I hear of it is true — With much esteem

Yours faithfully
Hor Greenough

Addressed: R. H. Wilde Esqr / Casa Vernaccia

NOTES

This letter is dated on internal evidence; see n. 1, below.
    Manuscript: Department of Rare Books and Manuscripts, BPL.
1. Francis Kinloch died in Rome on 23 July 1840 (RG 59, General Records of the Department of State, Dispatches from U.S. Consuls, Rome, NA). Greenough's informant was probably G. W. Greene; see Letters 148 and 149.
2. Probably Henry Middleton (1770–1846) of Middleton Place near Charleston, South Carolina, who served at various times as state legislator, congressman, and minister to Russia.
3. Edward Everett, with his wife and son, were on their way to Florence, where they spent nearly a year, from November 1840.
4. Theodore Sedgwick (1780–1839), brother of Catherine Maria Sedgwick and a lawyer and writer, died from the effects of a stroke on 7 November 1839.
5. On 21 July 1840, a contemporary portrait of Dante was recovered beneath whitewash on a wall in a room in the Bargello in Florence (originally the chapel of the palace of the Podestà). Apparently Wilde instigated the search, but credit for the discovery was claimed by the Anglo-Italian G. A. Bezzi and the Englishman Seymour Kirkup. See Edward L. Tucker, *Richard Henry Wilde: His Life and Selected Poems* (Athens, 1966), pp. 57–59.
6. Wilde's projected work "The Life and Times of Dante, with Sketches of the State of Florence and of his Friends and Enemies" was to consist of two volumes, but only one was written. The manuscript is in the Library of Congress. Between Books 1 and 2 is a sketch of Dante made by Kirkup from the painting in the Bargello (Tucker, *Richard Henry Wilde*, pp. 55–56).

147.   To Edward Elbridge Salisbury
       26 July 1840

Florence 26th July 1840

E. E. Salisbury Esqr
My Dear Sir

Though I have not yet heard of the success of my friend Mr Preston's motion to abolish the heavy duty laid upon Sculptured Marble[1] yet I am induced to send your works without further delay — not doubting that in his hands the measure will be carried & being desirous of getting the work home before winter. The Abdiel and Aristides will go in a few days — the bas relief I wish to perfect somewhat farther before sending it.

If I did not observe that the same delays and even greater occur with every artist of my acquaintance who labours conscientiously I should be quite mortified at the time absorbed by your commission — let me hope that you will not be disappointed in the possession of what I now send you. I remain Dear Sir

With respect
your friend & Serv't
Horatio Greenough

NOTES

Manuscript: Editor's collection.

1. William Campbell Preston was at this time a U.S. senator (see note to Letter 172). On 11 February 1840, he introduced in the Senate a bill to reduce duties on the importation of art. It was indefinitely postponed on June 1840, on the grounds that it was improper for the Senate to originate a revenue bill (*Congressional Globe*, 26th Cong., 1st sess., 1840, pp. 184, 480).

148.   To George Washington Greene
7 August 1840

Florence Aug't 7th '40 —

My Dear Giorgio

I have taken the only steps in my power to secure the effects of poor Kinloch — I have directed a notary to make out an application to the Guidice Civile di Prima Istanza,[1] who assures me that on its presentation he will order an inventory made out and the seals affixed. I beg you will give me some account of Kinloch's illness for as yet I have only heard that he died suddenly. My poor wife has been unfortunate again[2] but is now recovering — She begs me to present her love to Madamina.

I should think that your letter to Forsyth would amply justify your conduct in your office — indeed had he *kept the run* of your communications with him he would have treated the silly representations as they deserved.[3]

I think you were wrong to characterise Mr Waugh's[4] conduct as base — simply because it was unnecessary & because the *facts alone* would have enabled him to apply the epithet as he read y'r document which would have made it shorter & sweeter & more business like — I think too that you erred in mention'g the claims of y'r grandfather[5] to the national gratitude — because that no American will ever forget them and because our institutions do not recognise such claims as descending by inheritance —

I hope & trust truly that sooner or later you will have a situation proportioned to your own merits & Believe me that I think it will require something more than is to be expected from Mr Forsyth to assure you that — I will not fail to deliver your message to Mr Paulding p'r first opp'y.

Yours in haste
Horatio Greenough

PS   Saw the Marquis last ev'g. He was in g[ood] [*page torn*] health and not a little animate[d at s]ome [*page torn*] symptoms visible in the political horizon —

Addressed: Geo. W. Greene Esqr / U.S. Consul / Rome.

N O T E S

Manuscript: Editor's collection.
1. Municipal Director of First Applications.
2. She had a miscarriage.
3. Greene was notorious for various irregularities in his financial negotiations, both personally and as U.S. consul. Greenough is probably alluding to some such matter in this paragraph and the next. No correspondence about it between Greene and Forsyth seems to be preserved in the National Archives.
4. Samuel Bell Waugh (1814–85), portrait and landscape painter, was in Italy from about 1833 to 1841.
5. Nathaniel Greene (1742–86), Revolutionary general.

149.   To George Washington Greene
        18 August 1840

Florence, August 18th, 40.

My Dear Greene

I have taken every step in my power to secure the effects of Kinloch and am sorry to say without success. After having amused me all this time and sent me from one office to another and gotten several dollars from me, they find my credentials insufficient & tell me that nothing less than a carta di procura bene legalizzata[1] will avail me.

The best thing that can be done in this juncture is to warn the family for there is no consul here & Mr Appleton is dead and his luogotente[2] incompetent.

I have derived more credit from the bust of the Marquis Capponi than from all I have ever done before in that line. I am now finishing the Group by adding the only remaining figure.

Pray give me an account of Kinloch's illness — My wife joins me in compliments to yours — remember us to Mr Crawford.

Yours truly
Horatio Greenough

NOTES

Manuscript: Editor's collection.
1. "Fully certified power of attorney."
2. "Lieutenant."

150.   To Giovanni Battista Niccolini
        30 September 1840

Pregiatissimo Sig Segretario

Ho ricevuto la Sua in data di ieri accompagnata dal Diploma della R. Accadémia delle Belle Arti di Firenze.[1] Questo onore che in ogni tempo doveva essermi caro per il rispetto che porto agli artisti che compongono tale instituzione, mi e in questo momento di doppia consolazione, dovendomi presentare in patria con il frutto di cinque anni di fatica.

Sommo poi e il piacere col quale veggo che ella si degna di accordarmi delle parole di simpatia e di conforto — parole che sono di un valore inapprezzabile per chi non ha vissuto lunghi anni di solitario esiglio. Queste parole o Signore sono state per me l'acqua nel deserto — esse mi hanno commosso profondamente. Pregandola di accettare le mie professioni di gratitudine e di venerazione Sono

                                        Suo Servitore Devotissimo
                                            Horatio Greenough
Di casa Adi 30 Sbre '40

TRANSLATION

Most esteemed Signor Secretary

I received yours of yesterday accompanied by the Diploma of the Royal Academy of the Fine Arts of Florence.[1] This honor, which would be welcome at any time because of the respect I bear for the artists who compose such an institution, is of special comfort to me at this moment, since I am about to appear in my country with the fruit of five years of work.

I derive great pleasure, then, from seeing that you are pleased to grant me words of admiration and encouragement, words of priceless value to one who has long lived in solitary exile. These words, Sir, have been for me like water in the desert; they have moved me deeply. Begging you to accept my professions of gratitude & of respect, I am

Your most devoted servant

Horatio Greenough

From home 30 September '40

NOTES

Giovanni Battista Niccolini (1782–1861), Italian dramatic poet, was at this time secretary of the Academy of Fine Arts in Florence.
    Manuscript: Accademia di Belle Arti, Florence.
  1. The diploma, dated 13 September 1840, admitted Greenough to membership in the Academy with the rank of Professor of the First Class. It is now in the editor's collection.

151.   To Richard Henry Wilde
After 30 September 1840

My Dear Mr Wilde

Your note has just been put into my hands — I supposed that you had written to Mr Russell —

I believe the address you ask is Fitch Brother's & Co[1] — I have always addressed them thus & have never lost a letter.

I have been gratified by the nomination[2] — it was made by Pampaloni, Santarelli & Demi. I certainly was agreeably disappointed in the result — I hope to soon find time to call on you to arrange with you about your portrait.[3]

Your truly

Horatio Greenough

Friday — M'g

Addressed: R. H. Wilde Esqr / Casa Vernaccia

NOTES

This letter was apparently written shortly after Greenough's notification of his
election to membership in the Academy of Fine Arts, Florence; see the third
paragraph.
    Manuscript: Editor's collection.
  1. U.S. Navy agents in Marseilles.
  2. To membership in the Academy of Fine Arts.
  3. Presumably the bust of Wilde which Greenough modeled and cast. Wilde
    was to have had the marble for the cost of the stone but never felt that he
    could afford it.

152.   To Joseph Green Cogswell
       13 October 1840

Florence Oct'r 13 — 40

My Dear Mr Cogswell —
    This will accompany 2 Pamphlets which were presented to me by
an intimate friend of their author — who is ambitious (entre nous) of
seeing whether they will produce some effect in America. He was
desirous that Dr Channing[1] should have one and I have accordingly
written his name in it — and beg you to send it to him — He left the
other at my own disposal and I beg you will keep it — The author is a
man of *esprit* and if you remember the influence of the clergy here I
think you will say a man of courage too —
    I have ventured also to address to you a parcel for Col Trumbull
doubting if it might find the good old man still living — If such should
be the case I still hope you will say a good word in behalf of the
enterprise which it is intended to forward which is to procure subscribers for a monument to Morghen the famous engraver[2] — If a
hundred Dollars or two could be procured it would be a great service —
In case a subscription can be gotten up for an object so purely foreign
to the interests of America and so merely a homage to genius — I beg
that you will put me down for 10 Dolls.

Should Col Trumbull not occupy the post of President — I beg that the letters & medal be presented to his successor[3] — The Florentine Association corresponds on this subject with Col Trumbull because Morghen was an honorary Member of the *old* Academy —

I have recently had the honor of being chosen Professor of this Florentine Royal Academy without a contrary vote, a circumstance not less *surprising* than agreeable to me as it is the immediate consequence of the exhibition of the *Washington* here.

I am at present employed in finishing a full length of the Daughter of the Count Reviczky the Austrian Envoy to this court — a gentleman to whose kindness I owe the introduction of my Statue into the State of Modena, where the quarries are, free of duty — If this circumstance could be mentioned in some journal in the manner which so liberal an act on the *part of an Austrian minister* deserves, I should be truly much obliged, as we have no minister here and it is quite out of my power to make a return in kind for the favor I have received —

I look with much pleasure to the Spring when we trust we shall be with you my dear Sir. My [wife] who was never in better health and Mr Russell join me in kindest regards.

Yours truly
Horatio Greenough

I have 2 beautiful heads far advanced by a very able man for Mr Goddard[4] —

NOTES

Joseph Green Cogswell (1786–1881), librarian and bibliographer, was teaching mineralogy and geology and acting as librarian at Harvard when Greenough was a student there. At this time Cogswell was living in New York.
    Manuscript: Editor's collection.
1. William Ellery Channing (1780–1842) was minister of the Federal Street Unitarian Church in Boston from 1803 to his death.
2. Raffaello Sanzio Morghen (1758–1833) was professor of engraving at the Academy of Fine Arts in Florence.
3. Trumbull, who died in 1843, resigned as president of the American Academy of the Fine Arts in 1836. His successor, who was still president in 1840, was Rembrandt Peale.
4. Possibly William Giles Goddard (1794–1846), professor of belles lettres at Brown University, or Calvin Goddard (1768–1842), a judge, of New London, Connecticut.

153.   To Charles Sumner
         24 October 1840

Florence Oct'r 24th '40 —

My Dear Sumner

I hasten to acknowledge the receipt of your welcome letter of the 31st Ult'o. I have been prepared to sail since the first of this month but am well pleased that they have not sent for the statue for 2 reasons — first because I can at my leisure heighten the effect of my work this winter and second because it has become an object of considerable attention to the people of this country and to foreign travellers and it seems but fair that I should have an opportunity of becoming known. In the meanwhile the President of the Academy[1] sought an introduction to me this summer and visited my Studi[o] and I was made professor of this Academy at their annual meeting in August without a contrary vote, Bartolini having left the room on my nomination — This is the man who cries aloud that *I* trample on *him* — though I never lost an opportunity of doing justice to his works.

My model of the group is done and cast and I now breathe freely — Madame Lenzoni[2] was at my studio and invited me to her soiree's where I met a very agreable society —

Sir George Back[3] of North Western celebrity and by the by a most agreeable person tells me that Kenyon is the prototype of Pickwick and now I remember that Miss Sedgwick and I agreed that all of excellent and admirable in Pickwick was very like Kenyon — Powers has nearly finished a Statue of Eve which will give him the rank as a Statuary which is due to him. *Between ourselves* I find it somewhat cold and measured but it has great qualities — Wilde embarks in a few days for America —

I am right glad that nothing has happened to induce you to open a defense of my conduct with reference to the Statue — Whatever may be its claims as a work of Art a moment's sight of it will at once defend me from all charges reflecting on my industry — I have never seen 2 such works for size as the Washington and the Groupe modelled for the capitol produced in less time unless they were merely decorative and gotten up without ambition and without scruple. You are silent with regard to your own occupations — pray let me hear something in your next —

It is a favorite dream of mine to induce Alston to come to Florence with me on my return — how he would grow young here —! Italy is so improved since he was here. What would I not give to see his Beatrice or the Saul or the Jeremiah or one of the Jew's heads[4] in the Florence Gallery — Why can't you get up a subscription & send one here from the Athenaeum in compliment to the Duke & ask a specimen of his school — Voila de la civilization! pray think of it —

Present me I pray to Alston and Mr Frank Gray and such of our common friends as are interested in us —

Yours truly
H Greenough

Addressed: pr *"Columbia"* / Charles Sumner Esqr / Boston Mass —

NOTES

Manuscript: Sumner Correspondence, Houghton.

1. Pietro Benvenuti.
2. The last descendant of one branch of the Medici family, celebrated for the salon she held twice a week in her house at Certaldo (George Ticknor, *Life, Letters, and Journals of George Ticknor,* ed. George S. Hillard [Boston, 1876], 2:36, 48).
3. George Back (1796–1878), British admiral and Arctic explorer, was knighted in 1839.
4. Allston's *Beatrice* is now the property of Miss Ellen Bullard, Boston; his *Saul and the Witch of Endor* is in the Museum of Fine Arts, Amherst College; his *Jeremiah Dictating his Prophecy of the Destruction of Jerusalem to Baruch the Scribe* is in the Yale University Art Gallery; one of his heads of a Jew is at the Boston Athenaeum, another is in the Museum of Fine Arts, Boston, and a third is owned by Mr. Victor Spark, New York.

154. To John Wakefield Francis?
[1840?]

. . . It [the *Washington*]¹ contains two of the most improving and sublime ideas that I know of, and the most necessary to be *felt,* viz. the duty of all men toward God — the duty of great men toward the human race. However I may have failed for want of art to make these ideas clear, speaking eloquent, I shall never fail to feel a warmth at my bosom that I chose them for my theme;—my Washington is the *apotheosis of abnegation* — he is a conductor standing between God and man, the channel of blessings from heaven, and of prayer and praise from earth. I have struck a bold blow; — I have thrown to the winds the fear of ridicule, carping and one-sided criticism; and I have made all the enthusiasm, that a real American feels about his country, my guide. The stately coldness of aristocratic pride I have shunned; the hyberbole of exaggerated emblems and boastful assumption seemed not worthy of real greatness. I have left the hackneyed common-places of art alone — what will come of it I know not. . . .

NOTES

John Wakefield Francis (1789–1861), New York physician, helped organize several medical and welfare associations, and was active in many cultural and charitable enterprises.

This portion of "a recent letter" from Greenough was quoted in Francis' address at the second annual meeting of the Apollo Association in New York, 30 December 1840.

Source: *Transactions of the Apollo Association* (New York, 1840), pp. 10–11.

1. The printed text has "It (the statue)."

155. To John Forsyth
5 January 1841

To The Hon. The Secretary of State

Sir

I herewith enclose the Consular certificate of the state of the group on which I am employed, by which you will observe that the model is entirely finished. The certificate is also signed by the president of this Royal Academy who being an artist of great eminence, may be supposed capable of judging of the *manner* in which the work is done — I have the honor to inform you again that the Statue of Washington is finished and can be ready for carriage with 7 days' warning at any time — I shall be forced to draw upon the Treasury for One Thousand Dollars in the course of the present month.[1] The marble of the group was quarried a few weeks since but owing to the state of the weather has not yet been transported from the mountains.

With respect your Ob't Serv't
Horatio Greenough

Florence 5th Jan'y '41 —

Consular certificate, on a separate sheet:

The undersigned having examined the model of a group in Plaister executed by Horatio Greenough for the eastern front of the Capitol at Washington hereby certify that the said group is ready for execution in marble the entire design being compleat and finished according to the approved rules of the Art.

In token whereof they here set their names[2] & the Consular Seal.

Florence Decr. 20th. 1840
J. Binda
U.S. Consul in Tuscany

I sottofirmati avendo esaminato il modello di un gruppo in hesso seguito da Orazio Greenough per la facciata di Levante del Campidoglio a Washington dichiavoro colla presente che il detto gruppo e pronto per eseguirsi in marmo l'intero disegno essendo terminato e finito secondo le regole dell Arte.

In fede di quanto sopra —
Cave Pietro Benvenuti[3]

Addressed: P Brittanica / Hon John Forsyth / Secretary of State / Dep't of State / Washington D.C.
Endorsed, on letter: Rec. 26 Feby. / Mr. Dickins; *on address sheet:* Respectfully referred / to the Secretary of the / Treasury. / Dept. of State. / Feby. 26th. 1841. / Mr Barclay[4] / Please state / the several pay- / ments if more / than one paid / to Mr. G. / Mc C Y[5] / The amount paid Mr / Greenough is $19,744.18 / JDB; *on the consular certificate:* Recd. with H. Greenough's Jan'y 5th 1841

NOTES

Manuscript: RG 56, General Records of the Treasury Department, Series K, 1841, Miscellaneous Letters, NA.
1. See Letter 157.
2. From this point on, the first column is in the hand of J. A. Binda, the U.S. consul in Leghorn from 14 July 1840 to 23 April 1861.
3. The signature is in Benvenuti's hand.
4. John D. Barclay, clerk in the Register's Department.
5. McClintock Young; see Letter 198, n. 1.

156.   To Gino Capponi
         8 January 1841

To the Marquis Capponi
    Having exhibited the Statue of Washington last evening by torch light[1] I was so much impressed by the superior effect of the work as seen in that manner that I ask of you the favor of exhibiting it in the same manner to such of your friends as are disposed to honor it with a visit — I will venture to name half past Seven P.M. as an hour when the statue may be seen at any time if I could be warned of the visit by 3 o clock P.M.

                              I remain Your friend & Serv't
                              Horatio Greenough

Addressed: To the Marquis G. Capponi / Via S Sebastiano / SS. RR. MM[2]

NOTES

This letter is dated on internal evidence; see n. 1, below.
   Manuscript: Carteggi Capponi, Biblioteca Nazionale.
1. Greenough's exhibition of *Washington* by torchlight took place on 7 January
   1841 (Diary of Edward Everett, 7 January 1841, Everett Papers, MHS).
2. *Sue Riverite Mani*, "His Esteemed Hands."

157. To Levi Woodbury
   13 February 1841

To The Hon The Secretary of the Treasury / of the United States /
Dept of the Treasury / Washington D.C.
Sir.
   Having forwarded to the Secretary of State a certificate of the
progress of the group of Statues which I am executing for the Gov't of
the U States (the want of which document was assigned as a reason
for the dishonor of my former draft)[1] I have drawn on you this day for
the sum of One Thousand Dollars in favor of Mess Edwards & Co of
Paris[2] and hereby request you to duly honor the bill. Should some
unforeseen obstacle prevent this bill's being duly paid I beg that you
will inform Henry Greenough of Boston of it as I have instructed him
in such event to protect my draft. I beg leave to represent that my
operations are much embarassed by the delay of the second Instalment
and hereby request that the entire amount may be put at my disposal
as early as convenient

                                          Respectfully
                                          Your Ob't Serv't
                                          Horatio Greenough
Florence Feby. 13th '41.

Addressed: To The Hon / The Secretary of the Treasury / Dept of the
Treasury — / Washington D.C. / United States / Steamer Caledonia /
via Halifax 4 March

NOTES

Levi Woodbury (1789–1851), politician and jurist, was secretary of the treasury from 1834 to 1841.

Manuscript: RG 56, General Records of the Treasury Department, Series K, 1841, Miscellaneous Letters, NA.

1. For $1,000, drawn in February 1841, Alfred Greenough covered the draft for Horatio.
2. H. Edwards and Company was a banking firm, possibly American, in Paris.

158.   To Daniel Webster
12 March 1841

To The Hon The Secretary of State

Sir

In conformity with the promise made to the Dep't of State at the time that I undertook the execution of the Statue of Washington, I herewith transmit an account of the expences incurred in the performance of that duty.

I have been induced to this step Firstly on account of the great expence attending works of a colossal dimension, in which indeed the expenditure increases in a geometrical ratio with the increase of weight; that the high price I have fixed may be justified to the country. Secondly Because great as has been the expence attending this work, there is scarce an item in the account which is not 50 pr cent lower than the work or the article charged could have been had in the U. States. Viewed in this light the document may serve as a guide in future contracts of a similar nature.

In my charges for Postage I have confined myself to what has been paid for letters from or to agents of Gov't, though the correspondence with private individuals for objects connected with the work has been even more extensive and costly.

In my charges for casts etc I have limited myself to such as could serve me only in this work, making no mention of a far greater number which may be hereafter useful.

I have not charged the rent of my Studio during these years when the Statue was out of it, though I should not have retained it but to receive the monument on its return.

This work has occupied my entire attention during Four years and Five months — in its execution, the time passed in making journeys and otherwise employed with reference to it, has been nearly one Year. I have expended the Sum of Ten Thousand Four Hundred and Thirty Five Dollars — *My position* has increased my *private disbursements* to a degree that would have made it impossible for me to fulfill my contract, had I not possessed other means than those furnished by the contract itself.

The delays attending the execution of this work have been such as I could not foresee or prevent, they have embittered the fulfillment of my duty more by far than the difficulties of an untried branch of art. They have been explained at length in my former letters to the Dep't of State

I am Sir with the highest respect
Your Ob't Serv't
Horatio Greenough

Florence, March 12th 1841

*Account of expenses incurred in modeling the statue of Washington —
1834, — '5, — '6.*[1]

Portrait of Washington, copied after Stuart, by F. Alexander[2]	$200 00
Casts of the head by Houdon, in the chateau at Fontainebleau	12 00
Drawing of my sketch sent to the Secretary of State	42 00
Rent of studio, from January to May, 1834	10 00
Do. for the years 1834, — '5, — '6	176 40
Construction of a large window in the studio	50 92
Stove, pipe, and setting up	15 75
Color washing the walls of studio	7 89
Modeling clay for the statue	34 65
Large trough for do.	14 72
Tubs, sieves, and benches for do.	5 50
Modeling stool, screw fastened, bronze castors, iron rail . . .	69 30
Assistant workmen for setting up statue and painting it . . .	2 50
Plinth of chestnut plank for model	21 25
Stool for lay figure, bronze castors	21 00
Iron skeleton for lay figure	2 25

Life model for lay figure	11 30
Moulding and casting do.	16 50
Iron column for the body of the statue	10 00
Do. bars for the arms and legs, and blacksmiths' work	21 00
Moveable scaffold on castors, made to raise and lower	36 75
Two smaller platforms, with steps and on castors	12 05
Frame for cloths around the statue to preserve moisture	5 60
Cotton cloth consumed in keeping the statue damp at night	36 75
Repairs of wood and iron work	11 05
Salaries of the life models who stood for the naked	166 95
Servant of the studio during the years 1834, — '5, — '6	228 25
Salary of my foreman, who, being occasionally occupied in other work, is charged for only one year during the modeling	480 90
Kerseymere cloth, from which the drapery was copied	12 60
Syringe for moistening the model during the day	8 40
Plaster of Paris for casting, and wages of the moulders	190 05
Hire of windlass, and wages of five men to raise the mould	13 25
Fuel consumed in 1834, — '5 in the studio	31 50
Postage of letters to and from Government agents	19 25
Moulds and casting of the back of chair, bas reliefs, and other ornaments	26 25
Cases in which the models went to Carrara	35 70
Repairs of damage sustained by the studio	15 75
Anatomical preparations and casts from the antique	47 25
	$2,123 95

Account of expenses incurred in finishing in marble the Statue of Washington, including the purchase of the block and the transportation of the monument to Leghorn, 1839, — '40, — '41.

Lease of studio during the years 1839, — '40, — '41	$189 00
Opening a new and larger window in the same	37 80
Purchase of timber to strengthen the vault	57 75
Repairs of damage sustained by the building	31 50
Replacing the window on expiration of lease	18 00
Price of blocking the statue, inclusive of the purchase of model and carriage of the model, on its return to Florence	2,570 25
Case of timber in which the statue was transported to Florence	68 25
Cost of transport from Carrara to Florence — eleven yoke cat-	

tle, fifteen men 262 50
Blocking the bas reliefs after the statue arrived here 146 20
Blocking statues of Columbus, the Indian, and back of chair . 158 10
Cutting the letters of the inscription 36 75
Stonecutters' work on the plinth and square part of chair . . 63 00
Finishing the ornamental work of the chair 63 00
Wages of my foreman during the years 1839, — '40, — '41 . . 1,029 00
Do.   assistant workmen   Do.   Do.   . . 720 00
Do.   servant of studio   Do.   Do.   . . 235 20
Purchase and repair of tools 63 00
Fuel during the years 1839, — '40, — '41 . . . . 60 00
Repairs of stool on which the statue was wrought 33 60
Drawings carefully made from every part of statue, in case it
  be lost 70 00
Journey to Paris to collect authorities for the head of Wash-
  ington 230 00
Cost of the cases made in Florence for the finished work . . . 140 00
Journey to Carrara during the blocking of the statue 27 00
Postage   Do.   Do.   Do. 7 00
Postage with the United States agents 35 00
Cost of transporting the finished statue to Leghorn 330 00
Paid to Captain Delano for the right he had reserved of trad-
  ing with the statue on board[3] 1,500 00

                                                            $8,181 90
Paid for damage done to trees on the road from Florence . . 60 00
Paid for assistance extra on the road 30 00
Paid for my own journey to Leghorn 27 00
Paid for my foreman's expenses in Leghorn 13 00

                                                            $8,311 90

Addressed: Hon Daniel Webster / Secretary of State / Dept of State / Washington D.C.

NOTES

Daniel Webster was secretary of state from 1841 to 1843 and from 1850 to 1852.
    Manuscript (without expense account): RG 59, General Records of the Department of State, Accession 161, Item 135, NA. Previous publication (in-

cluding expense account): U.S. Congress, House, *Statue of Washington,* 27th
Cong., 1st sess., 1841, H. Doc. no. 45, pp. 4–6.
1. A draft of this account, given in francesconi and pauls, is in the editor's
   collection.
2. Francis Alexander copied Gilbert Stuart's portrait of Washington for Greenough.
3. John A. Delano was captain of the *Sea,* the ship which transported the statue
   to America. See Letter 162 for an account of this payment.

159. To Daniel Webster
16 March 1841

Florence March 16th 1841.

To The Hon The Sec'y of State
Sir

I received on the 9th inst a letter from the Sec'y of the Navy[1] informing me that orders had been forwarded to the Commander in
chief of the U.S. Naval force in the Mediterranean,[2] to learn from me
when the Statue of Washington would be ready for Shipment and to
send the Sloop of War Cyane to Leghorn to receive the same, should its
dimensions and weight be such as to admit of its being safely transported in that ship. In the event that such should not be the case, the
Sec'y informed me that he had given instructions to barter an American
merchant ship suited to the transportation of the Statue.

On the 10th inst I received [a letter] from Com. Isaac Hull informing
me of the above instructions and advising me that the sloop of War
Cyane having already sailed for the U States when the orders of the
Sec'y of the Navy were received, he should proceed to Leghorn for the
purpose of chartering an American ship for the transportation of the
statue. He inquired the dimensions and weight of the monument, as
also when it would be ready for shipment. In my answer which was
dispatched on the following day I informed him that the Statue had
been finished for several months past that its dimensions were as
follows

              Length—10 feet 6 inches
              Height— Do   Do

Width— 6 feet   Do
Weight somewhat under 20 Tons.

I informed him that in order to avoid the risk of storage in Leghorn
and that the statue might be taken at once on board, I should not
commence moving the same until I heard of the arrangements being
made to receive it and to this I was the more induced from the doubt
entertained by men of business that such a ship as is required for the
transportation of this monument can be found at so short a notice as
the Hon the Sec'y of the Navy has supposed.

I have lately exhibited to the public in this city the model of the
Group on which I am employed for the U.S. Government and which is
intended for one of the blockings which flank the stairs of the entrance
of the Eastern front of the Capitol. The Marble for the same is now in
process of quarrying and I shall hasten the work as far as is consistent
with the demands of the Art. I cannot however let slip this opportunity
of raising my voice once more on the subject of the material to be
employed in executing this group — Intended as it is to stand in the
open air exposed to a climate far more destructive than that of Florence
I cannot but think that bronze were far preferable to marble. The
Bronzes erected during the reign of Cosmo the First[3] are as fresh and
sharp at this day as when erected — the colour they have assumed from
exposure adds to their grandeur and makes them not less venerable as
monuments than beautiful as feats of Art — The marbles erected during
the same reign, have lost that unity of colour which is the first element
of effect in Statuary — they retain their original snowy whiteness in
those parts not subject to be granulated by the rain & frost, while they
are positively black in all the more prominent & exposed portions. So
evidently is their destruction threatened that this Gov't has recently
transferred 2 valuable marble groups from exposed situations to the
collonade of the Lanzi,[4] where they will be hence forward sheltered.
That the expence of making this group in Bronze will far exceed the
sum voted for its execution in marble is sure, yet I cannot but think it
would be as economical as preferable in point of taste to adopt the
former material.

                    I am Sir with the highest respect
                              Your Ob't Serv't
                              Horatio Greenough

Endorsed: Apr 27. Mr. Dickins

NOTES

Manuscript: RG 59, General Records of the Department of State, Accession 161, Item 135, NA. Previous publication: U.S. Congress, House, *Statue of Washington,* 27th Cong., 1st sess., 1841, H. Doc. no. 45, pp. 7–8.
1. Paulding to Greenough, 8 December 1840 (copy in RG 45, Naval Records Collection, U.S. Navy General Letter Book 28, NA).
2. Isaac Hull (1783–1843), famous for his victory in leading the *Constitution* against the *Guerrière* in 1812. Paulding's letter to him, dated 8 December 1840, was published in *Statue of Washington,* p. 10. For portions of Hull's correspondence relating to shipping the *Washington,* see Isaac Hull, *Papers of Isaac Hull,* ed. Gardner Weld Allen (Boston, 1929), pp. 320–27.
3. Cosimo dei Medici (1519–74).
4. Giambologna's group of Hercules slaying the Centaur and an antique group of Ajax supporting the body of Patroclus were moved to the Loggia di Lanzi in the Piazza Signoria in 1840.

160. To Lady Rosina Wheeler Bulwer-Lytton
Before 8 May 1841

My Dear Lady Bulwer

I cannot express to you how much I have been gratified by the indulgent opinion you have expressed of my efforts in Sculpture — Living, as I have done amid a people whose *sympathy* for Art is nearly exhausted, while their connoisseurship is in full vigor, I should have contented myself (I fear) like their own artists with the sleepy and indifferent toil of the *studio,* had not the confidence of my countrymen (who you know are unrivalled in hoping great things)[1] called me to the execution of a monument which awoke every stronger and better feeling in me —

My wife has told me that you wished an explanation of the details of the Statue of Washington and I hasten to give them as briefly as I can, begging you meanwhile to excuse any wrong I may do the Queen's English, because I have dabbled so much in foreign tongues as to lose somewhat of my vernacular —

Being intended to fill a central position in the Capitol of the U.S. I have thought fit to address my Statue of Washington to a distant posterity and to make it rather a poetical abstract of his whole career than the embodying of any one deed or any one leading feature of his life — I have made him *seated* as *first magistrate* and he extends with his left hand the emblem of his military command toward the people as the sovreign — He points heavenward with his right hand. By this double gesture my wish was to convey the idea of an entire abnegation of Self and to make my hero as it were a *conductor* between God and Man — Though the Presidential chair is very like any other chair, I have thought it my duty to make that on which Washington is seated mean something with reference to the country — It is too large to be left dumb — I have represented the superior portion richly ornamented with acanthus and garlands of flowers while the body is solid and massive — by this I meant to hint at high cultivation as the proper *finish* for sound government and to say that man when well planted and well tilled must flower as well as grow — By the figure of Columbus who leans against the back of the chair on the left side I wished to connect our history with that of Europe — By that of the Indian chief on the right to shew what state our country was in when civilization first raised her standard there — The bas relief on the right side of the chair represents the Rising Sun which was the first crest of our national arms — under this will be written "Magnus ab integro saeclorum nascitur ordo —" In that on the left side I have represented the Genii of North and South America under the forms of the infants Hercules and Iphiclus — the latter shrinking in dread while the former struggles successfully with the obstacles and dangers of an incipient political existence.*

Such is my invention — The Italians have been indulgent in their opinion of the *work,* but I am not the less anxious for its fate in my own country — Here it has been like an *opera* of which they do not understand or feel the words — there it will be the words that will be thoroughly examined for of music they have less knowledge — Let me enjoy this opportunity of assuring you that the approval of such as yourself would console me under any condemnation on either side of the water for I know not whether I could derive more inspiration from the sight of your loveliness or strength and hope

---

* Motto for left hand Bas relief "Incipe parve puer cui non risere parentes."

from the approval of your taste & judgment. Pray excuse my slovenly
writing — my orthography is my own and I punctuate by the grace
of God as the Kings say which means in a graceless manner. My
wife means to kidnap you for a drive if possible on this day — I am
vexed that I cannot join you.

I am Dear Lady Bulwer
With sincere respect
yours
Horatio Greenough

Friday morn'g[2]

NOTES

Rosina Wheeler Bulwer-Lytton, Lady Lytton (1802–82), wife of the first Baron
Bulwer-Lytton, lived much of her life on the Continent. She was in Florence in
the spring of 1841. She drew on this letter for her article "Modern Arts and
Artists in Italy," *Court Journal*, 8 May 1841, pp. 1186–87.
    Manuscript: Miscellaneous Manuscript Collection, LC.
  1. At this point in the manuscript, Lady Lytton drew two asterisks and wrote
     at the bottom of the page: "Then decidedly my dear Isaac Ironside *you* also
     are an American!" Whom Lady Lytton meant by "Isaac Ironside" is not
     known.
  2. On the last page Lady Lytton wrote: "To I. I. Read this letter of Green-
     ough's the great American Sculptor and you will see that you *must* be an
     American! It was written while he was Still engaged on his Colossal Statue
     of Washington at Florence which is now at Washington."

161.   To Gino Capponi
After 8 May 1841

Pregiatisso Sig Marchese
    Non manchero' di fare pervenire al Sig Prescott[1] l'involto che
ella mi fa l'onore di confidarmi.
    La Corvetta e arrivata alla fine[2] e tutto mi promette che la mia
Statua sara imbarcata fra 15 giorni. Sento con piacere dal capitano
di questo vascello che tutta l'affizialità della flotta fu scandalizzata
dal patto conchiusa tra il Commandante e la casa di Marsiglia.[3]
    M'incarico col piu grande piacere di vigilare sull' esecuzione della

testa di Washington — Mi prometto il piacere di vederla fra poco per sentire alcune spiegazioni riguardo alla grandezza ed al materiale di essa. Mi creda Sig Marchese con sentimenti di ammirazione e di grato animo

Suo fedelmente
Hor Greenough

TRANSLATION

Most esteemed Signor Marchese

I will not fail to make sure that the package you did me the honor to entrust to me reaches Mr Prescott.[1]

The sloop finally arrived[2] and everything promises that my statue will be embarked in fifteen days. I hear with pleasure from the captain of this ship that the entire official corps of the fleet was shocked by the agreement concluded between the Commander and the house at Marseilles.[3]

With great pleasure I pledge to be vigilant about the execution of Washington's head. I look forward to the pleasure of seeing you shortly to receive instructions regarding its size and material. Believe me, Signor Marchese, with sentiments of admiration and gratitude

Yours faithfully
Hor Greenough

Addressed: All Ill'mo Sig / Il Sig March. Gino Capponi / SS. RR. MM.

NOTES

This letter is dated on internal evidence; see n. 2, below.
    Manuscript: Carteggi Capponi, Biblioteca Nazionale.
1. William Hickling Prescott.
2. The *Sea,* on which the *Washington* was transported to America, arrived at Leghorn on 8 May.
3. See Letter 162.

162.   To Daniel Webster
12 May 1841

Hon Daniel Webster / Secretary of State.
Sir

After many delays occasioned in the first instance by rumors of war and afterward by negotiations between Com. Hull and Mess Fitch Broth's & Co of Marseilles, the Ship "Sea" Capt'n Delano is at length arrived at Leghorn to receive the Statue of Washington; as is also the U.S. Sloop of War Preble, whose commander[1] is charged with the duty of overseeing and assisting the shipment.

Com. Hull informs me that he has allowed the Captain of the "Sea" the priviledge of touching at one or more Ports in the Mediterranean to complete his cargo before sailing for America, after which he is allowed to discharge such cargo at any port in the U. States not south of Norfolk Va. before proceeding to land the Statue at Washington.[2] I learn from Capt'n Delano that the sum of Five Thousand Dollars had been demanded by him for the transportation of the Statue without any other cargo and that Com. Hull had offered Three Thousand Five Hundred dollars — Deeming the delay and risk to which the arrangement made by Com Hull will subject the monument as too great to be justified by a saving of Fifteen Hundred dollars, I have written to Mess Fitch Broths & Co to offer them that sum and I have preferred the risk of ultimately sacrificing that amount to the disgrace and danger of trading about in this Sea with a National Monument to Washington under the hatches.

I may be found to have acted without due consideration for the opinion of Com. Hull, but I beg leave to represent that though I have been paid for this Statue I have still an interest in it — The interest of a father in his child. It is the birth of my thought. I have sacrificed to it the flower of my days and the freshness of my strength. Its every lineament has been moistened with the sweat of my toil and the tears of my exile — I would not barter away its association with my name for the proudest fortune that avarice ever dreamed. In giving it up to the nation that has done me the honor to order it at my hands, I respectfully claim for it that protection which it is the boast of Civilization to afford to Art and which a generous enemy has more than once been seen to extend, even to the monuments of his own defeat.

Should it seem fitting to the gentlemen with whom rests the decision of the question, that I should myself pay the sum I have offered on my own responsibility, I request that I may have early notice of such decision. I take this opportunity of urging the payment of the Second Instalment due on the Group on which I am at present employed and for want of which I am subjected to inconvenience. I am at present waiting the return to Florence of the Engineer Misuri[3] who is at present engaged in transporting hither an enormous Vase of Granite for this Government. His return may be delayed three or four days. He is the only person here to whose skill & experience I am willing to confide the Statue.

> I have the honor to be Sir
> With the highest respect
> Your Ob't Serv't
> Horatio Greenough

Florence May 12th 1841.

Endorsed: June 15th / Mr. Dickins

NOTES

Manuscript: RG 59, General Records of the Department of State, Accession 161, Item 135, NA. Previous publication: U.S. Congress, House, *Statue of Washington,* 27th Cong., 1st sess., 1841, H. Doc. no. 45, pp. 8–9.
1. Ralph Voorhees (d. 1842) became a commander in 1837.
2. Hull's charter with Delano through Fitch Brothers, dated Toulon, 23 April 1841, is printed in *Statue of Washington,* pp. 13–14.
3. Unidentified.

163. To Daniel Webster
2 June 1841

Hon. Daniel Webster / Secretary of State
Sir

With regard to the measures to be taken to raise the Statue of Washington from the Hold of the Ship — Capt'n Delano who will witness the putting it on board, will be most capable of giving instructions if any be necessary —

When the Statue shall have reached the Hall where it is to stand — I recommend raising it *in the frame* after removing the planks which cover the same — The height at which it is to stand elevated above the floor of the hall, must be decided by experiment — The elevation which I recommend is this, that at the distance of 30 feet from the Pedestal in front the *fold of skin above the navel* may be *visible* and *not hidden by the knees* — If that fold *be hidden at that distance* my work is *sacrificed.* The greater the elevation that can be effected with that datum the more the Statue will harmonize *architecturally* with the vase which is to receive it.

The timbers which form the frame are marked alphabetically in the order in which they are to be removed — With regard to the ornamental parts of the statue, they are in separate cases and should be all unpacked after the figure is in its position — I have merely to say that the figure of Columbus is on the left side of the Statue that of the Indian chief on the right — the joints will sufficiently accuse their relative positions.[1]

Should it be decided that the pedestal is to be of marble and to be furnished by me — the core of the same may be built of common stone and temporarily covered with Stucco to represent the finished marble — I enclose a drawing of the pedestal as I have conceived it, but leave it to the better judgement of the Gov't Architect to decide whether that form and those ornaments & [mo]uldings [*page torn*] will accord with the finish of the Hall.

I cannot close this letter without once more repeat[ing] [tha]t [*page torn*] in my mind the pedestal should be of one piece of solid hammered granite of Quincy and that the statue should stand *between the centre* of the *Hall* and the door of the Library *at mid-distance.*

I am Sir With the highest respect
Your Ob't Serv't
Horatio Greenough

Leghorn 2nd June '1841.

Addressed: Hon Daniel Webster / Secretary of State / Washington — D.C.
Enclosure: Drawing of pedestal

NOTES

Manuscript: RG 59, General Records of the Department of State, Accession 161, Item 135, NA. Previous publication (without the drawing of the pedestal): U.S. Congress, House, *Statue of Washington*, 27th Cong., 1st sess., 1841, H. Doc. no. 45, pp. 9–10.
  1. Here Greenough drew an outline of the back of the chair, indicating the positions of the figures of Columbus and of the Indian.

164.   To Gino Capponi
ca. September 1841

My Dear Sir

The papers entrusted to me for Mr Prescott were packed in the case containing the bust of Franklin[1] — they were accompanied by a note addressed to the gentleman who should be charged by Gov't with the duty of opening the case, in which he was requested to deliver them to Mr Laurence of Boston[2] with request to forward them at once to their address.

I am *sure* that the papers are safe and attribute this delay to the fact that the pedestal not being prepared, the cases had not been opened when Mr Prescott wrote you.

I will not fail to address Mr Lawrence on this subject as soon as possible and hope to have a speedy answer of a more satisfactory character.

With grateful attachment
Yours respectfully
Horatio Greenough

Monday Morning

P.S. I send herewith the last volume of Andryane[3] for which accept my renewed thanks.

Addressed: To the Marquis Gino Capponi / Via S. Sebastiano.

NOTES

The dating of this letter is based on the fact that the *Sea*, with Greenough's *Washington* and the papers from Capponi to Prescott, reached Washington on 31 July 1841.

Manuscript: Carteggi Capponi, Biblioteca Nazionale.

1. Presumably that now in the Senate chamber of the Massachusetts State House, Boston.
2. Presumably Abbott Lawrence (1792–1855), Boston merchant.
3. Alexandre Phillippe Andryane, *Memoires d'un Prissonier d'État,* 2 vols. (Paris, 1837–38).

165. To Gino Capponi
[1841?]

Greenough Statuario presenta i suoi complimenti al Sig Mar'e Capponi e lo prega di avere la bontà di dirgli il titolo dell' opera chiesta dal Sig Ticknor e quanti volumi gli furono mandati l'anno scorso — avendo il Greenough (non sa come) smarrita la lettera del Sig Ticknor.

[No signature]

TRANSLATION

Greenough the sculptor presents his compliments to Signor Marchese Capponi and begs him to have the kindness to send him the title of the work requested by Ticknor and how many volumes were sent him last year — Greenough having mislaid (he doesn't know how) the letter of Mr Ticknor.

[No signature]

NOTE

This letter is written on the same stationery as are Letters 161 and 164 to Capponi.

Manuscript: Carteggi Capponi, Biblioteca Nazionale.

166.   To Hiram Powers
Between 25 August and 28 September 1842

[Paris]

My Dear Powers.

This will be carried by Mr Brown[1] a brother-sculptor, who is fortunate enough to have come abroad with few engagements, and who
from his appearance seems to promise an agreable addition to our
society. I am expecting to hear from my wife — If she is not preparing
to come out to join me and return to Florence, I shall go to America in
Oct'r.

I hear not one word from Government—perhaps when my wife
writes, she will be able to give me some news — Gen'l Cass[2] says that
he supposes they have neglected my affairs, very much for the same
reason that they have lost sight of their own.

I find nothing new of real and lasting interest in Art — the Galvano-
plastic method of casting in copper, has been carried to a point of
which I had no notion — I have seen a Christ on the cross as large as
life and *perfect* in every part — They also cover by the same means
the most delicate plants, flowers, insects with a very thin coat of copper, which retains the exact form of the object over which it is diffused,
with of course that difference in sharpness which the superposition of
the metal creates — but this in many objects is scarce perceptible to
the eye, and I was convinced that the objects were bona-fide casts,
until they broke them and shewed me the leaves, petals, etc within.

Mr Everett was here for a day or two, but though I called, I had the
disappointment of finding him out.

They all complain here of the heat, but I have never passed a
summer more agreably with regard to climate.

Mr Brown will give you all that is known of Mr Petrich's affair.[3]
There seems to be a great mystery about it.

They have a machine here for making reduced copies of busts and
statues, which seems to work well — If I return to Florence I shall
probably bring a copy of the Laocoon made by it.

I have been here now long enough to have a thorough trial of Paris
as a home and I far prefer Florence as a residence for an artist. The

hurry and rush of business — the overwhelming interest of politics — The ten thousand clever and amusing nothings in the shape of theatrical entertainments raree shows etc leave but little taste or disposition in the public — for the quiet and proper appreciation of art — Hence the crowd of pretenders — the shop window exhibitions — the seizing on every passing event that promises a momentary interest and *all* for *money* — They are ferocious in their sympathies — Their pictures all run bloo[d] [*page torn*] and their marble is in the agonies of death. Strange to say they alternate between bawdry and murder — and if you hear of a beautiful picture it's an even chance whether it represents the killing of a man or the getting of a child or something near it.

I hear from Mr Livingston that you have commenced a statue of a captive girl.[4] I am quite impatient to see it. I have been studying here but I know not with what fruit. I beg you to present me kindly to Mrs Powers and to Mr Kellogg[5] of whom I retain a very agreeable remembrance — Yours

H Greenough

Addressed: Hiram Powers Esqr / Fav'd by Mr Browne / Florence —

NOTES

The Greenoughs and Mr. Russell left Florence for Paris about the middle of June 1842, and Mrs. Greenough and Mr. Russell sailed for America from Le Havre on 16 July. Greenough planned to remain in Paris until her return in the fall.

This letter was apparently written not long after Edward Everett left Paris on 25 August 1842 (Diary of Edward Everett, 25 August 1842, Everett Papers, MHS); see the third paragraph of the letter. Greenough sailed for the United States on 28 September.

Manuscript: Editor's collection.

1. Henry Kirke Brown was on his way to Italy (see note to Letter 188).
2. Lewis Cass (1782–1866), statesman and general, was U.S. minister to France, 1836–42.
3. Ferdinand, or Frederick August Ferdinand, Pettrich (1798–1872), Dresden-born sculptor, was active in the U.S. by 1838. It was proposed to have him ornament the pedestal for Greenough's *Washington,* and he modeled four bas reliefs for it, but the project was successfully opposed by Senator W. C. Preston. The affair to which Greenough probably refers is the mysterious stabbing of Pettrich by unknown assailants late in May (*Boston Daily Evening Transcript,* 1 June 1842).
4. Powers finished his *Greek Slave* in 1843. A copy is in the Corcoran Gallery, Washington, D.C. "Mr Livingston" is possibly Robert L. Livingston (1775–

1843) (Edwin Brockholst Livingston, *The Livingstons of Livingston Manor* (n.p., 1910), p. 557).
5. Miner Kilbourne Kellogg (1814–89), New York-born painter, lived in Italy from 1841 to 1845.

167. To John Ward?
1 November 1842

Boston.[1] U.S.A. 1st Nov'r '42

My Dear Sir

I embarked on the 28th S'ber at Havre — in a gale of wind and came with the gale almost the entire voyage — We had a passage of 21 days — which is remarkable at this season — I have had the pleasure of finding my family and friends well.

I write this in much haste and I beg you to inform me by the first steamer how you are — whether you have sold the picture at Paris — how Mr Ruddock[2] is etc. My address here is care of Thos. B. Curtis Esqr.[3]

I enclose a line to a Mr Thorburn[4] a celebrated miniature painter which I beg you to send to him as it relates to a money transaction which has annoyed me not a little.

Yours very truly
Horatio Greenough

Addressed: Mr J. Ward / No 51 Gibson Square / Islington.

NOTES

John Ward, English landscape painter, exhibited at the Royal Academy from 1808 to 1861. In 1828 he lived in Newman Street, in 1855 at 4 Compton Street, both in Islington.
Manuscript: E. Maurice Bloch, Los Angeles, California.
1. Greenough sailed from Le Havre on 28 September, arrived in New York on 22 October, and went immediately to Boston.
2. Presumably Samuel Ruddock, English sculptor, who exhibited at the Royal Academy for many years beginning in 1856.

3. Thomas Buckminster Curtis (b. 1795), naval officer, merchant, and banker, of Boston, married Greenough's sister Laura on 14 June 1838 (Greenough, p. 41).
4. Presumably Robert Thorburn (1818–85), a native of Scotland.

168.   To Francis John Higginson
13 November 1842

Boston, Nov'r 13th '42.

My Dear Friend

I have been absolutely forced to take a room in an inn where I can be alone in order to prepare myself for my journey to Washington — I find so many brothers and sisters in law and out of it — so many nephews and nieces, so many old friends and so much that is pleasant to do and see and hear that I have scarce had time to shave myself since my arrival — Here I am in a snug little parlour of the Bromfield house, where thank God! there is no fire and I can talk to you a moment without fear of apoplexy or suffocation.

I am disappointed that I could not come to you as I had intended, but I am forced to run at once to Washington by my pecuniary affairs. I wish it to be strictly *entre nous* — but the Gov't have never paid me the instalment due on the group which I am making for them, nor have they given me a word of explanation of the matter though the money was voted more than a year ago.

They placed the Statue of Washington just where I repeatedly begged that they would not place it,[1] and they never even acknowledged its arrival or took any steps in reference to myself after it came home — This was neither courteous nor proper. I am now about to see how it is placed and what can be done with it. Perhaps my dear Francis you think that I must be unhappy at so much indifference if not dislike for my work. I am not unhappy. I have done my utmost and I believe that there is more *Art* in my statue of Washington than in all else that I have done [by] a *thousand fold.*

I find people here becoming thank God! more moderate in their *party* feelings. I have no doubt we shall learn soon to be independent in our views of the national interests and above all that we shall shake off the dependance upon English opinion — which still continues to rail at us about Slavery as though it were a *recent invention* of *our own,* while the lords refuse to yield one jot of their priviledge to *starving freemen* and while the concentrated thunders of the Empire are forcing Opium upon the poor Chinese[2] — England owes her greatness and her prosperity not a little to her characteristic contempt for abstract truths and her tact in taking practical advantage of every abuse. She now proclaims maxims and advances theories of utter, pure, Christian philanthropy, while she acts upon calculations as ferociously selfish as those of the Romans or their barbarian conquerors — I am very curious to see Congress once more — I do not doubt that the choosing "whole hog" men has filled those halls with unprincipled & bungling fellows — But I trust that a change is at hand. I cannot say how happy I am in finding Stephen[3] a man after my own heart — He understands this country better (I think) than any body with whom I have talked about it. I hope that you will write me at Washington where I shall be in ten days — Present me kindly to your lady and believe me

Ever Yours
Horatio Greenough

Addressed: Francis J Higginson / Brattleboro —

NOTES

Francis John Higginson (1806–72), a classmate of Greenough's at Harvard, practiced medicine most of his life in Brattleboro, Vermont (Harvard University Archives; Edmund Janes Cleveland and Horace Gillette Cleveland, comps., *The Genealogy of the Cleveland and Cleaveland Families* (Hartford, Conn., 1899), 2:1064).
     Manuscript: Miscellaneous Papers, MHS.
1. In the center of the Rotunda.
2. A reference to the Opium War (1839–42).
3. Stephen Higginson Perkins (1804–77) was a Boston merchant (Cleveland and Cleveland, *Genealogy of the Cleveland Families,* 2:1064).

169.   To Robert Maskell Patterson
        27 November 1842

Washington, D.C. Nov. 27th '42.

Dear Sir

Your favor of the 25th inst reached me this morning and gave me
the highest pleasure, both as a mark of your esteem for me as an artist,
and as relating to contemplated modifications of the coinage.[1] I have
thought much on this subject and should deem myself most happy if
by any aid of mine your views could be furthered.

However easy it may be to find fault with the coin as it now stands,
I believe you will agree with me that any great change in it is a matter
exceedingly perplexing and difficult.

I am particularly anxious to learn your opinion on the following
points — Should the several coins be similar in design, though varying
in size? I have remarked that such a similarity has its advantages, as
in the Spanish Dollar Half, Quarter, eighth & sixteenth of a dollar.
Should every coin of whatever sort bear upon one of its faces and in
a most conspicuous position, its denomination and value in full Roman
letters?

I have at various times prepared designs for coins of the United
States — I shall be happy to lay them before you when I have had a
fuller explanation of your own views; at present I will merely say that
the objects to which I have mainly directed my attention are, Nationality and Simplicity — to secure these, it would be necessary that
each part should have a distinct and palpable meaning and that all
such images as from their vagueness are forced to have their name
written on them, should be omitted.

The machine for reducing the medallion intaglio to the size of the
coin insures us I think a union of design and execution such as has not
hithertoo been seen, I am sure that I need not enlarge on the advantages of such a coinage — the combination of beautiful form and
graceful arrangement with the most effective practical organization in

every department of the Mint shews me that you are prepared to instruct me on this head.

I am Dear Sir

Very respectfully

Your Obliged friend & Serv't

Horatio Greenough

R. M. Patterson Esqr

Addressed: R. M. Patterson Esqr / U.S. Mint / Philadelphia —
Endorsed: From Horatio Greenough, / Washington. / Nov. 27. 1842 /
Rec'd. [November] 29. [1842]

NOTES

Robert Maskell Patterson (1787–1854) was director of the U.S. Mint at Philadelphia from 1835 to 1851.
    Manuscript: RG 104, Records of the Bureau of the Mint, U.S. Mint at Philadelphia, General Correspondence, NA.
    1. Patterson's letter (RG 104, Records of the Bureau of the Mint, U.S. Mint at Philadelphia, General Correspondence, NA) asked Greenough to submit designs for American coins.

170.   To Robert Maskell Patterson
10 December 1842

Washington, D.C. Dec 10th '42

Dear Sir

    Agreeably to the suggestions of your second letter, I herewith transmit several sketches of coins, made without reference to the existing law.[1] I regret that not having with me my portfolios, I am forced to send rude outlines made from memory instead of accurately elaborated designs.

    In No 1 you will remark that I make one more desperate struggle to drive the heraldric eagle off the field. I need not say how much more of symmetry is attainable in *lettering* the face of this coin, even in retaining its general features.

To the group of corn in No 2 I am very partial, not only because it is one of the few fruits which form a staple from Maine to Georgia, but because it strikes me as capable of much variety and richness of effect, added to a simplicity always desirable.

I send these sketches that I may learn your objections to them and that I may be guided in my future efforts — Requesting that you will retain them for me as they are but sketches I remain

Dear Sir very respectfully
Your friend & Serv't
Horatio Greenough

R. M. Patterson Esqr / U.S. Mint.

Addressed: R. M. Patterson Esqr / U.S. Mint / Philadelphia.
Endorsed: From Horatio Greenough, Esq / Washington. / Dec. 10. 1842. / Recd. [December] 12. [1842]

NOTES

Manuscript: RG 104, Records of the Bureau of the Mint, U.S. Mint at Philadelphia, General Correspondence, NA.
1. In this letter of 2 December 1842 (copy in RG 104, Records of the Bureau of the Mint, U.S. Mint at Philadelphia, General Correspondence, NA) Patterson explained the law regarding the design of coins, agreed that each coin should have its value marked on one side, and emphasized that he wished Greenough to be absolutely free in making his designs.
Greenough evidently submitted three designs, none of which seems to have been preserved. In the first he did not have the figure or bust of Liberty (which appeared on the half cent, cent, half dime, and dime) and substituted for the heraldic or spread eagle (which appeared on the quarter, half dollar, and dollar) an imperial one. In the second he had a sheaf of Indian corn on one side, on the other the figure of Liberty on her knees before the eagle. In the third, omitting both Liberty and the eagle, he represented Industry and Plenty on one side, Agriculture (in the form of a classical figure sowing grain) and Mechanics on the other (Patterson to Greenough, 28 December 1843, RG 104, Records of the Bureau of the Mint, U.S. Mint at Philadelphia, General Correspondence, NA).

171. To John Quincy Adams
12 December 1842

Dear Sir

I am induced by the opinion I have always entertained of your appreciation of Art, and by the experience I have had of your kindness, to ask your advice and assistance in the position in which I find myself.

The Statue of Washington though it occupies the best position in the Rotunda, is almost entirely in the shade. My wish is that it should be placed in the grounds to the East of [the] Capitol and that it should be sheltered by a wooden building which may ensure its being seen in a proper light. If it should then prove worthy of preservation it might be covered by a more durable building — I am the more desirous that such temporary shelter may be afforded it as I am confident that the experiments which might be made in wood will ensure a better proportion and more effective form than any which theory could decide upon. And here I will venture to assert that if such experiments had preceded the ultimate organization of the more important members of the Capitol itself, much inconvenience would have been avoided and much of expense saved, while the expression of make-shift and afterthought which is every where impressed upon the internal arrangement, would have been changed for a clear relation of harmonious parts uniting in a grand whole.

It was my intention to have accompanied the Statue of Washington to this country had I been invited to do so — but I was not invited — It was my wish to accompany it without an invitation — but I had it not in my power for this Gov't had protested my drafts on account of the group which I am now executing for the Capitol — drafts made in conformity with my contract — accompanied by *consular* certificates of the state of my work. When my brother Alfred Greenough of Boston applied to the then Sec'y of State to know whether I should be paid, he was answered that Mr Petrick was absent from Washington and that only from *his* inspection of my credentials could it be decided if the state of my work warranted a farther advance.[1] Mr Petrick returned to Washington at length and my drafts were protested. Up to this hour I have received neither explanation or justice of any kind — The receipt of the Statue of Washington was never acknowledged to me an omission under the circumstances uncourteous & mortifying to me.

May I ask Dear Sir what steps may be in your opinion most proper for me to take to insure a proper placing of the monument to Washington and to elicit a decided mark of determination to set me aside with reference to the group, if such there be?[2]

I have always been and am still of opinion that Art should address itself to the mass of men like eloquence and poetry — If my utmost endeavor to make a statue of Washington is considered a failure and it is therefore thought unsafe to trust me with the monument for the Eastern front, I hope that such opinion will take a palpable form and I shall hear it as I may best — cherishing the consciousness that I have wrought diligently — that my whole heart was with my work and that if I have failed it has been in a different manner from other and greater artists who have before me undertaken the same godlike subject.

I shall not conceal from you that I am anxious to finish the work on which I am at present employed — I am too well acquainted with the history of Art and of artists to feel either surprise or anger at the misunderstandings and the intrigues which beset every sculptor who works for a government — I shall neither countermine nor attack any man and if I cannot succeed in establishing my claim to what *I have asked,* I shall leave the enviable task of completing the ornament of the Front to more fortunate competitors —

Asking your indulgence for so long a letter on this subject I am Dear Sir

Respectfully yours
Horatio Greenough

Endorsed: 1842 / Greenough Horatio 12 Dec'r / His Statue of Washington

NOTES

John Quincy Adams (1767–1848) was a member of Congress from 1831 to his death.
Manuscript: Adams Papers, MHS.
1. Thomas Ewing to Thomas Denny, 9 April 1841, quoted in Henry Greenough to D. Fletcher Webster, 15 April 1841, RG 59, General Records of the Department of State, Miscellaneous Letters Received, NA.

2. Presumably on the advice of Adams, Greenough prepared a petition to Congress to have the statue moved (U.S. Congress, Senate, *Memorial of Horatio Greenough, Praying The removal of the Statue of Washington from its present position in the Rotundo, to the grounds in front of the western façade of the Capitol,* 27th Cong., 3d sess., 1843, S. Doc. no. 57).

172.   To William Campbell Preston
16 December 1842

[Washington]

. . . I knew that I owed it to you that my statue of Washington had not been sacrificed in every way. . . .[1] I have some hope that the kindness of many gentlemen in both houses may effect for my sake a change in the position of the Statue. As for the *proprieties* of the matter as connected with the seat of Govt., they seem not to be aware of their existence as a body. . . .

NOTES

William Campbell Preston (1794–1860), statesman and educator, was a U.S. Senator from South Carolina from 1833 to 1842.
    Source: C. F. Libbie, *Catalogue of Autograph Letters and Historical Documents . . . April 26, 27, 1904* (Boston, [1904]), item 340. The *Catalogue* gives the place and date of the letter.
1. On Preston's motion, a joint committee on the Statue of Washington was formed in December 1841, with Preston as chairman, to arrange for the placing of the statue. The committee had it moved to a spot between the center of the rotunda and the entrance to the library and abandoned the arrangements made by Secretary of the Navy A. P. Ushur to have Pettrich ornament the pedestal (*Congressional Globe,* 22 December 1841, p. 47; Upshur to Preston, 10 June 1842, RG 45, Records of the Department of the Navy, Miscellaneous Letters, NA; Preston to Powers, 10 March 1842, Powers Papers, National Collection of Fine Arts, Smithsonian Institution; information furnished by Clara L. Dentler, Florence).

173. To Robert Maskell Patterson
        30 December 1842

Washington. D.C. Dec 30th '42

Dear Sir

Your welcome letter of the 28th inst reached me this morning.[1] I am truly happy to learn that though you despair of making any use of the designs which I enclosed, you were not displeased with them, apart from their incompatibility with existing regulations.

I have always considered the matter as one of great difficulty and the objections which you state to the several devices are very natural and I think might easily be made.

I should certainly prefer the eagle of the great seal to that which now appears on the coin and though it is impossible to make it other than a conventional image, it might be rendered more imposing by modifying the forms yet adhering to the posture and attributes.

I regard that clause of the law which requires that "Liberty" should not only be present but labelled also as fatal to that side of the coin. Liberty representing a negative idea does not easily take form or attributes — The fact that her own children require that her name be written upon her to prevent mistakes proves it. "The barbarous age of art" says a Greek historian "produced images so vague and imperfect that their authors feared to trust the public discernment and wrote under what they intended to pass for a tree τουτο δενδρον εστιν."[2]

They who fancy that real freedom depends in any way upon such puerile adhesion to an antiquated and childish conception, might get a different notion from a glance at the tower in the Grand Duke's Square in Florence, where that magic word inscribed by republican hands,[3] has been allowed to remain in pure contempt by twenty successive princes; while the bayonets that glimmer below as the guard is relieved by day and night and the rattle of arms presented on the passing of each decorated minion, shews the difference between words written and things done.

That the coinage is actually a good one for practical purposes there can be no doubt — perhaps it is unwise to endeavor to change it unless step by step with the advance of taste in the country; that such advance is making, I should want no better proof than the actual coin as compared with that of the commencement of this century.

I remain Dear Sir
Very respectfully Yours
Horatio Greenough

R. M. Patterson Esqr / U.S. Mint / Philadelphia

Addressed: R. M. Patterson Esqr / U.S. Mint / Philadelphia —
Endorsed: From / Horatio Greenough, Esq / Washington / Dec. 30 42. / Recd. Jan. 3 43.

NOTES

Manuscript: RG 104, Records of the Bureau of the Mint, U.S. Mint at Philadelphia, General Correspondence, NA.

1. In this letter (copy in RG 104, Records of the Bureau of the Mint, U.S. Mint at Philadelphia, General Correspondence, NA) Patterson wrote that although he admired Greenough's designs, he felt sure Congress would not approve them. He conjectured that a member of Congress would say of the first of one: "*Liberty* is put down, — rejected. Our fathers fought and died to obtain it, and now their degenerate sons reject even its emblem: &c &c. An eagle is, indeed, retained, but it is the imperial eagle of Rome, not our own bald-head: &c." Of Greenough's design of Indian corn he pointed out that on the reverse the goddess of liberty was kneeling before the imperial eagle. As for Greenough's "truly classical figure sowing grain" he thought it "would be attacked as a Virginia field-hand, and that our slanderers might assert that we had substituted a victim of slavery, for the goddess of Liberty." He concluded by urging Greenough to consider other designs more consistent with the law and copied out for him Section 13 of the Mint Act.
2. "This is a tree."
3. One of the nine coats of arms of the Republic and the city of Florence which are painted below the arches on which the gallery of the Palazzo Vecchio rests is a shield bearing the word "Libertas."

174.   To Joseph Leonard Tillinghast
         3 February 1843

Friday, February 3, 1843.

Dear Sir:

Though the convictions which gave rise to the statements made by me in a memorial recently presented to Congress are unchanged, yet I am induced to offer to the consideration of the committee[1] a modification of the proposition therein contained — a modification, however, only temporary, and one forced upon me by the actual state of the Treasury. I propose, then, to remove the statue to the spot which shall be deemed on the whole best to receive it; to lay the foundations, construct and finish the pedestal, and place the statue upon it, where it may be covered by a *temporary shelter,* at a *small expense,* and await the action of Congress at some future and more propitious moment. I beg that, if this plan meets the approval of your committee, you will arrange the matter in such a way as to give me the control of the operations; for the steps taken hitherto, in the face of my instructions, and the sums expended in spite of the example given in the note of my expenses for similar objects, make me despair that the matter can be safely intrusted to the usual routine.[2]

I think that the above objects can be effected for the sum of five thousand dollars. I cannot offer to contract for that amount, until I shall have learned the cost of granite and transport. If you approve of my plan, I can at once forward to Boston a draught of the pedestal, and have an estimate of the expense in the course of a few days.

I am the more anxious that this step should be taken, as I am about to return to Europe, and should wish to remove from the statue the props and stanchions of marble which obstruct the view of the arm.

I am confident that this statute will sooner or later be placed elsewhere; I am anxious that it should be done while I have it in my power to oversee the operation, and put the last touch of the chisel to my work.

I am, dear sir, with the highest respect, your obedient servant,

Horatio Greenough

Hon. Joseph L. Tillinghast.

NOTES

Joseph Leonard Tillinghast (1791–1844), was a member of Congress from 1837 to 1843.

Source: U.S. Congress, House, *Removal of Greenough's Statute [sic] of Washington,* 27th Cong., 3d sess., 1843, H. Rept. no. 219, p. 2.

1. Tillinghast was chairman of the Joint Committee on the Library, to which Greenough's *Memorial* (see Letter 171, n. 2) had been referred.
2. On 22 February 1843, Tillinghast presented a joint resolution (H.R. no. 43) providing for the removal of the statue under Greenough's direction (U.S. Congress, House, *Removal of Greenough's Statute [sic] of Washington*).

175. To Charles Folsom
2 June 1843

Boston. June 2nd 1843

Dear Sir

I have received with much pleasure your letter of the 29th May enclosing the official announcement of my election as Fellow of the American Academy of Arts and Sciences.

I beg that you will express to the Academy my sense of the honor thus conferred upon me.

Whenever as resident in Florence, my services can be useful to that body, I shall esteem myself happy in exerting myself in its behalf.

I am Dear Sir
With respect
Your Ob't Serv't
Horatio Greenough

Addressed: Charles Folsom Esqr / Corresponding Secretary of the / American Academy of Arts and / Sciences.

NOTE

Charles Folsom (1794–1872), Boston librarian, teacher, and editor, became a Fellow of the American Academy of Arts and Sciences in 1827 (see Theophilus Parsons, "Memoir of Charles Folsom," *ProcMHS* 13 [1875]: 26–42).

Manuscript: Editor's collection.

176. To John Canfield Spencer
3 July 1843

Hon. J. C. Spencer / Secretary of the Treasury / of the U. States
Sir.

Being about to embark for Europe and wishing to make preparation for the payment of the dues incurred in conformity to an act of Congress passed at the late Session,[1] I hereby respectfully request that you will place at my disposal the remaining sum of 2,500 Dollars appropriated by the above act.

> I am Sir
> With respect
> Your Ob't Serv't
> Horatio Greenough

Washington July 3d. '43.

NOTES

John Canfield Spencer (1788–1855), jurist and statesman, became secretary of the treasury in 1843, but resigned the same year because he opposed the annexation of Texas.

  Manuscript: RG 217, Records of the General Accounting Office, Fiscal Section, Report no. 87.977, NA.

  1. For the text of the act, see U.S., *Statutes at Large*, vol. 5, pt. 1, p. 642. See also Glen Brown, *History of the United States Capitol* (Washingon, D.C., 1900), 1:110.

177. To John Canfield Spencer
3 July 1843

Hon. J. C. Spencer / Secretary of the Treasury of the U States.
Sir

I enclose herewith an account of my expenditures, connected with the removal of the Statue of Washington, up to this date.

Having laid the foundations which are destined to receive the Statue and its pedestal, having constructed the temporary shelter for the same and arranged the light in a manner that will serve as a guide to the architect of the permanent structure, if such structure should be hereafter erected, I have called upon Mr Isaiah Rogers[1] Architect and engineer to perform the remaining task, that of erecting the pedestal and placing the statue thereon.

The scientific attainments and the great experience of Mr Rogers in moving large masses of wrought stone have decided my selection of him for this purpose. I have full confidence in his care and ability.

Circumstances which I am ready to state to you if I can have the honor of an interview with you,[2] oblige me either to embark immediately for Europe or to remain in this country until the next Spring. My object in asking the remaining $2,500 was to prepare means to meet the demands of the several contractors as their tasks are completed. I had intended to charge Mr John James Greenough[3] of this city with that duty, but I shall be most happy to leave the duty in the care of any person whom you may indicate as possessed of your confidence.

It would give me a material assistance in my actual position if you would indicate what steps I should take to secure a compensation for my journey hither and the time occupied in this task; as also if you would state to me whether the laws of the disbursement of the Public moneys are such as to refuse me all indemnity for the protest of my drafts in 1840, payment of which was made in Dec 1842, on the faith of the identical documents before deemed insufficient.

> I remain Sir
> With the highest respect
> Your Ob't Serv't
> Horatio Greenough.

July 3d 1843.

Expenditures for the Removal of the Statue of Washington.

Postage of letters to Quincy Mass	1,50	cts
Do enclosing drawing . . . . $	,50	
Journey to Baltimore to inspect stone & work[4]	19,	
Experiment made by Mr Emery,[5] joint'g Balt'e granite .	2,50	
Letters from agent at Boston relating to contract . . .	,50	

Do giving explanation of the mode of cutting letters . .   2,37½
Advance made to Mr J. Downer[6] contractor   200,
Paid on account as the work has proceeded   800,
To experiments in the Rotunda with lamps[7]   52,
Journey to Quincy to inspect the pedestal   47,
Letter from Mr Mills[8] relating to building . . . . . .   ,12½
Do from J. J. Greenough do . . . .   ,12½
Do from Isaiah Rogers concerning shipment . . . . .   ,25.
Paid to Rob't Mills for working plans and overseeing
   the foundations and construction of the building . .   100,
                                    $1,225,87½ cts

                                  Horatio Greenough
July 3d 1843.

NOTES

Manuscript: RG 56, General Records of the Treasury Department, Letters from Executive Officers, AB Series, 1843, vol. 1, NA.
1. Isaiah Rogers (1800–1869), Boston architect of the Greek Revival movement, had recently completed the Merchants' Exchange in Boston, the granite for which had come from the quarries at Quincy.
2. Apparently Greenough's wife was pregnant.
3. Greenough's first cousin (see note to Letter 181).
4. The purpose of this trip was to see if granite from the quarries near Baltimore would satisfy Greenough's desires respecting the pedestal; it did not.
5. John B. Emery of the firm of Emery and Gault, granite cutters, Baltimore (*The Baltimore Directory for 1845*).
6. Joel Downer, house carpenter (*The Washington Directory and National Register, for 1846*).
7. This experiment was performed on 11 January 1843. For a vivid account, see Ralph Waldo Emerson, *The Letters of Ralph Waldo Emerson*, ed. Ralph L. Rusk (New York, 1939), 3:120–22.
8. Robert Mills (1781–1855), architect, was at this time commissioner of public buildings.

178. To John Canfield Spencer
ca. 3 July 1843

Hon. J. C. Spencer / Secretary of the Treasury of the / U. States.
Sir.

The Pedestal for the Statue of Washington having been finished and set up in the grounds on the East front of the Capitol agreeably to the contract entered into between Mr Isaiah Rogers and myself I hereby request that you will place at the disposal of Mr John J. Greenough the sum of 1,700 Dollars — One Thousand and seven hundred dollars to enable him to meet the lawful demands of the said Rogers agreeably to the stipulations of the said contract.

I am Sir
With the highest respect
Your Ob't Serv't
Horatio Greenough

Washington 31 August 1843[1]

NOTES

Greenough sailed for England on 13 July. He probably wrote this letter and the following one before then, and left them with J. J. Greenough.

    Manuscript: RG 217, Records of the General Accounting Office, Fiscal Section, Report no. 87.480, NA.

    1. "Washington . . . 1843" is in another hand.

179. To John Canfield Spencer
ca. 3 July 1843

Hon. J. C. Spencer / Secretary of the Treasury of the / U. States
Sir

The Statue of Washington being now removed to the Building erected in the grounds on the East Front of the Capitol agreeably to the act of Congress passed at the close of the late session, I hereby request that you will place at the disposal of Mr John James Greenough the following sums to meet the following contingent expences incurred in the performance of that duty — For the enlargement of the windows as stipulated in the contract and for the addition of two other lateral windows the sum of Fifty two Dollars.[1] For the travelling expences and the pr diem allowance of Mr Isaiah Rogers at the rate of five dollars pr diem the sum of[2] For the colour washing the plastering of the interiour the coating of the inner surface of the glass to exclude the sunlight — the furnishing window curtains in order that each may be darkened if necessary the sum of forty eight dollars.[3]

I remain Sir with respect
Your Ob't Serv't
Horatio Greenough

Washington 31 August 1843[4]

NOTES

Manuscript: RG 217, Records of the General Accounting Office, Fiscal Section, Report no. 87.480, NA.

1. "Fifty two Dollars" is in another hand.
2. "For the travelling . . . sum of" has been canceled, presumably by another hand.
3. "Forty eight dollars" is in another hand.
4. "Washington . . . 1843" is in another hand.

180.   To Charles Folsom
8 July 1843

Wilmington Del.[1] July 8th 4[3] [*page torn*]

Dear Sir

I have delayed forwarding the enclosed[2] wi[th] [*page torn*] a hope that I should be able to meet you before leaving the States once more. The extreme press of my engagements since my arrival in the country has kept me always at Washington and when I have been able to visit

Boston, it has been for so short a time, that I have been necessarily engrossed by my agenda and my family —

It would have given me the greatest pleasure to have met you once more and to have spoken with you not only of the past, but of the present and of the *mighty* future — When I look at this country, methinks that I see in every *man* the basis on which a future mass is to stand — If this view of our relation to posterity is almost alarming by the responsibility it involves, it is also gratifying to our pride and cheering to our toils.

I yet cherish the hope of being able to visit Boston before I sail — if I should be disappointed I pray you to accept this assurance of the respect and affection which I have always cherished for your character and person and I pray you to believe that my heart is with you in your labors & that I [will?] [a]lways [*page torn*] regard as a chief pleasure the opportunity [*page torn*] [w]ay [?] serving you or any friend of yours.

I leave my country once more cheered in [the?] [*page torn*] belief that its institutions are working in the main agreeably to the intentions of their founders and eager in my humble walk to leave some trace [of] my birth right as a citizen.

Very respectfully Dear Sir
Your friend & Serv't
Horatio Greenough

Charles Folsom Esqr

Addressed: Charles Folsom Esqr. / Boston, Mass.

NOTES

Manuscript: Folsom Manuscripts, BPL. Previous publication: Nathalia Wright, ed., "Letters of Horatio Greenough in the Library," *Boston Public Library Quarterly* 11 (1959): 87.
1. The Greenoughs moved to Wilmington from Washington late in April, partly for economic reasons and partly to see more of the countryside. They remained here for the most part until they left America.
2. Greenough's letter to Folsom of 2 June 1843 (Letter 175).

181. To John James Greenough
9 July 1843

Wilmington Del. July 9th '43.

J. J. Greenough Esqr
Dear Sir

The contract with Mr Downer entitles him to receive when the stipulations contained in Schedule A are complied with the sum of 1689 Dollars — Having already advanced on account
1000 Dollars — there will fall due $689.
For enlarging the windows and making 2
more as pr bill which you hold — 52

$741
50[1]

The contract with Isaiah Rogers intitles him to the sum of 1900 Dollars when the pedestal is placed in the Building ready to receive the statue.

I have also agreed with Mr Rogers that he is to remove the statue of Washington and put it upon the pedestal and that he is to receive for so doing the sum of 5 dollars pr diem and his expences from the time of his leaving Boston until his return thither. I mean his travelling expenses and board while in Washington. To meet these demands and those below enumerated I leave with you the sum of $850.$\frac{12\frac{1}{2}[2]}{100}$

furthermore requisitions on Treasury 2500

3,350.12 cts
The sums above mentioned being 2,641.

There remains a Balance of $709.12 cts

with which to meet the contingent expences of removal of the statue, of curtains to windows and of colour washing the interiour of the Building. Should it be in your power as I doubt not it will be, I request that you will cover the interiour of the glass of windows with a composition to prevent the sun's rays from penetrating — Mr Mills will give information on this head —

Should Mr Rogers arrive before I sail, I hereby request that you will endeavour to get from him as near an estimate of his charge for contingences as he can make, that my mind may be easy on this head — he will do what is fair.

Mr Mills must be made to acknowledge the receipt of 100$ for drawing plans — and inspecting masons' and carpenters' work. To present as voucher I have the rec't given at [the] Bank.

Horatio Greenough

NOTES

John James Greenough (b. 1812), son of Horatio's uncle William Greenough, was an engraver, editor, and inventor.

    Manuscript: RG 217, Records of the General Accounting Office, Fiscal Section, Report no. 87.480, NA.

    1. "50" is in another hand.

    2. To the right of this number there appears, in another hand, "Error $15.12."

182. To Elizabeth Bender Greenough
[August 1843?]

. . . My fathers in England were by fortune and by lot of those who used the sword and not of those who felt it. They were driven out in the wars of the White and Red Roses. They fought for Lancaster and now Greenough Castle[1] is only one solitary fragment of a Tower forming a pretty Vignette for many a sketch book and little do they think, who sketched it, that blood is stronger than stone and that the race who lived there once, now lives in a distant land and thinks more of the next month than all the past. This ruin and an old Bridge, a few years ago passable, are all that now bear the name of Greenough in England. . . .

NOTES

Elizabeth Bender Greenough (1776–1866) was born in Marlborough, Massachusetts. She and David Greenough were married on 4 October 1799 (*Colonial Families of America* [New York, n.d.] 6:122).

Source: Laura Wagniére-Huntington, *From Dawn to Dusk* (Vevey, Switzerland, n.d.), p. 12. According to Laura Wagniére-Huntington, a granddaughter of Elizabeth Greenough, this letter was written in England. Greenough probably visited Greenhalgh Castle in August 1843, shortly after the *Great Western,* on which he and Louisa sailed from America, docked at Liverpool late in July. The Greenoughs remained in England until the middle of September.

   1. Greenhalgh Castle, on the Wye near Garstang, had been garrisoned for Charles I by the Earl of Derby in 1643, but was subsequently dismantled by Parliament (*Black's Picturesque Tourist and Road-Book of England and Wales* [Edinburgh, 1843], p. 212).

     Greenough is mistaken in assuming Greenough and Greenhalgh to be the same word, since the first (in another form Greenhow) means "green hill" and the second "green hollow." Genealogists have commonly assumed, however, that the families bearing these names are the same and given the meaning of both as "green hollow."

183.   To Richard Henry Dana
21 September 1843

Paris.[1] Sept'r 21st '43.

My Dear Sir

   Your letter of the 13th Ult'o has just now reached me and has been a great relief to me. The thought of having been so near Alston at the time of his death, yet not with him distressed me[2] — I longed for a voice from one of you to hear what you have now told me. What would I not have borne to have the memory which your daughter will ever retain of having listened to the last breathings of his blessed spirit![3] When Legare[4] whom I knew well and highly prized was taken away, I felt an accusing sense of not having fully appreciated him; but I knew all that I was enjoying when Alston lived —I can truly say that I heard him as an angel and that when far from him he exercised over me a power no other man ever did.

   In my eagerness to do something, I wrote to Mr Quincy and to Mr Gray to beg that they would use their influence to prevent tampering with the unfinished works which Alston has left. I tried to make them *feel* that works like his are always finished because the first lines that declared his *intention* were a *whole,* and never finished, because the last agony of elaboration was but an approximation to his thought. I wished them to understand that instead of endeavouring to help him, our task is but to receive gratefully and cherish as it is, all that came from him.

I can fully realize the anxiety with which you shrink from undertaking his biography. As a man you can record him — I know you will do it worthily! — as an artist you cannot record him! You will see that the news of his decease will elicit from England from Italy and Germany tributes to his genius — Neither can these record Alston the artist. It is to the *men* who will be born *of him* that I look for a fit monument of his career; and hence my sense of the duty of collecting and preserving his unfinished works, because they are full of invaluable instruction to kindred minds.

In whatever walk of culture a Genius now labors he is a Scourge. To the superficial — to the heartless, to the timeserving — to the false, he must be a scourge! In the early ages of art a genius threw open new sources of light and stood in a blaze of his own creation a demi-god; — but now the false prophets throw their rods on the ground and they become serpents; — The rod of the genius like that of Moses, devours them — In this sense it is that even the artist whose mission seems so peaceful, bears a two-edged sword.

America has always acted toward her artists like a hen who has hatched ducklings — She cannot understand why they run to the water instead of thriving upon the dunghill — which only asks to be scratched in order to feed them all! She will know better, but not yet.

I will write to you what I have treasured of remembrance of Alston — I cannot do it now — I cannot bring myself to think calmly enough — but when I am once more in my own home I will write — not much, because I think that all should be recorded but only a reserved biography as yet given. I know that it was impossible in America for Alston's career to be other than it was — I blame no one — but I think that we should withhold our testimony until the nation awakes to a sense of the worth of her noble child, until she begs to hear of this man who doing more for thought and truth and love than all these of the ignorant present entered not into the account of her treasures! Mr Dana you will remember how much of esteem and affection was lavished upon Alston by the higher minds of America and you will perhaps feel surprize that I speak thus. If you could but see the career of a high artist here or in Germany or even in poor Italy you would understand why I grieve.

Wherever I have been I have found some one or two persons who owed to Alston the birth of their souls and with these I have always found that what I had imbibed from him was a chain of sympathy, a bond of affection even. To look back to those hours when he was with us, to recall his words his looks, to cherish the memory of his virtues, these must henceforth take the place of his presence — Is it not thus that our father weans us from earth and prepares us also to lie down by our departed friend?

I pray you to present me kindly to Mr Edmund and to the family — Why will not the Master come to us in Italy? It is but a month's voyage? For me I know not when I shall return to the States — I am about to leave this for Italy & perhaps shall pass through Germany on my way.

If Mr Edmund will come to us he shall have a huge apartment all to himself and shall smoke his cigar every evening in full sight of Fiesole and Vallombrosa[5] — I hope to write you again before December — Very truly and affectionately yours

Horatio Greenough

NOTES

Richard Henry Dana (1787–1879), poet and essayist, was known to Greenough from his college days, chiefly through their common friendship with Allston.

Manuscript: Dana Papers, MHS. Previous publication (in part): Flagg, pp. 383–85.

1. The Greenoughs were in Paris from about the middle to the twenty-sixth of September (*Letters*, p. 161).
2. Allston died in Cambridge on 9 July, at which time Greenough was out of the city, probably in Wilmington, Delaware.
3. The last persons to whom Allston spoke before his death were his wife and his niece, Charlotte Dana (Flagg, p. 330).
4. Hugh Swinton Legaré (1797–1843), South Carolina lawyer and statesman, travelled in Italy in 1829 or 1830 in the company of Cooper (review of *The Bravo, Southern Review* 16 [1832]: 397). He died on 20 June 1843, his poor health having been overtaxed by his attendance at the unveiling of the Bunker Hill Monument three days earlier.
5. These places could be seen from Greenough's studio on the slope of Fiesole hill.

184. To Richard Henry Dana
11 June 1844

Florence, June 11th '44.

R. H. Dana Esqr
Dear Sir:

Many times since the receipt of your sad letter have I sat down to write to you of Alston. Many times have I covered my paper with reminiscences and opinions of him — As often have I destroyed them after a few days, from a belief that I can say nothing worthy your attention, nothing worthy his memory. This fear, this diffidence alas! has only come to me with gray hairs, accept it dear Sir as the only fruit of a life of sincere devotion to Art.

The few words which I shall say will be very general in their character and I feel the more reconciled to this forced silence of mine, from the reflection that Alston as a man will be fully recorded, while his works must ever be his monument as a poet.

We have seen that a living Lawrence or David exerts an influence upon co[n]temporary art which the example of a dead Raffaello cannot counterbalance. The crowd of aspirants naturally seek to reflect the qualities of the favorite of the age. This but shows that painting shares the fate of all human pursuits. What a deluge of would-be misanthropy has not been poured forth by the imitators of Byron? But if this be true of the mass, the reverse is [the] case with the man of Genius. Raffaello first absorbed the masters who had preceded him and then became their counterpart. M Angelo carried on a double war with the meagre imitation of the early Florentine sculptors and the measured and scientific grace of the antique. Caravaggio's fierce chiaro scuro was born of the emasculate gradations of Guido and in our day Canova turned to the Greeks, satiated by the extravagance of Bernini's school.[1] In some of these instances there would seem to have been as much of malice aforethought in the choice of style, as of sincere bias of the heart and of taste, but this we may venture to affirm that we have not seen two men of strong decided genius, work the same vein of thought in Painting.

Alston[2] began the study of Art in Rome at a time when a Revolution

in taste had just been effected throughout the continent. The works
of Winkelman and Visconti³ were but symptoms of the reaction which
pervaded the cultivated classes, a reaction whose first wave swept
away the puny relics of Bernini and whose second placed Canova on
the pedestal of Phidias and David on the throne of painting. To do
justice to Alston one should be familiar with the history of Art at that
epoch. He should see the colour with which David achieved his fame
to appreciate Alston's worship of the Venetians. He should know how
exclusively Roman history occupied public attention as a subject of
Art, to feel Alston's unwavering adherence to the then neglected
poetry of the Bible — He should be aware how fully M. Angelo had
fallen into disrepute, how the simpler and earlier masters were
laughed to scorn, in order to do justice to the mind of the American
painter, who without once failing to pay his tribute of admiration to
the cleverness and executive vigor of the reigning artists, kept his eye
and his heart unenthralled; daily absorbing from all that had gone before, its most varied and precious results.

Like all artists who have received a literary education Alston began
his studies by theory by books and amateur effort. Like all artists
who so begin he was forced to unlearn what he had thus acquired —
"When I first went abroad I groped for 5 years in the dark." These
were his words to me. They shew his sense of what was wanting in
his earlier means of instruction. In Rome Alston mastered painting
as a language, formed his idea of the scope and object of his art,
planned his processes and marked out his career. The Germans who
have raised so noble a school upon philosophic study of the early
painters and who are said to owe to Alston their first clear idea of the
means as well as the end of a modern school of Art, they and they
alone can do justice to that portion of his career.⁴

No artist ever felt the beautiful more keenly than Alston — none
ever gave it more exactly its due place in his heart. It was with him
always a means never an end — Moral beauty was his idol if so it
can be called; religious truth his main inspiration. Through all his
higher efforts there breathes the same spirit and a voice comes from
thence that fills the mind with awe. Whether in Jeremiah in Miriam
in Saul or in Belshazzar⁵ we hear the same dreadful words, "I will
repay."

Alston's style was extremely varied — as were the subjects he treated
— his was no formed manner operating with the regularity fecundity

and swiftness of a machine. Who would assign to the same hand the landskapes at Boston and the Desert purchased by Mr Labouchere?[6]

When I reflect upon the character of his works and the immense labor bestowed upon them, I am surprised that this age, so prone to regard Art as the handmaid of Luxury, should have employed him as it did. When I remember the astonishing rapidity of his execution, the ease with which his hand & eye mirrored the beauty before him, when I remember that his will alone stood between his poverty and the most prolific outpouring of production, with all the renown and emolument that accompany it, then I form a clear idea of the character of his genius.

His was truly a great and a noble example. Was such ever thrown away? Surely never. More even than in his works do I believe that he will live in the awaken'd mind of American art — and who shall say where the Republic will carry the achievements of painting with him for her first born poet painter.

Alas! I will not speak of the void left in your circle a void which I feel even here — for was not my heart daily with you? Did I not daily live over again those hours of my boyhood? daily warm my heart with the remembrance of that smile of heaven? daily console my absence and my sorrow with the hope of enjoying it once more?

I cannot say to you how sweet is the remembrance of those last hours which I passed with Alston and when I reflect how nearly I lost the opportunity of hearing, I may say his last words, it seems to me as if Providence had so ordered it that I should enjoy once more the benefit of that light which had guided my youth and was about to be removed from hence.

I pray you to present me respectfully to dear Mr Edmund Dana and to the family.

Very truly yours
Horatio Greenough

NOTES

Manuscript: Dana Papers, MHS. Previous publication (in part): Flagg, pp. 385–88.

1. Michelangelo Amerighi da Caravaggio (1565–1609) was noted for his extreme contrasts of light and shade. Guido Reni (1575–1642) gave his best

works a golden or silvery tone. Giovanni Lorenzo Bernini (1598–1680), architect and sculptor, was a major proponent of the baroque school.

2. In the left-hand margin Dana wrote: "See my minutes on A. as a poet, p. 30, No. 1."
3. Johan Joachim Winckelmann (1717–68), German archeologist and art historian, was largely responsible for the neoclassical revival. Ennio Quirino Visconti (1751–1818), Italian archeologist, was conservator of the Capitoline Museum in Rome and later curator of antiquities at the Louvre.
4. Greenough refers to the group of painters called the Nazarenes (see Letter 4, n. 7).
5. *Miriam the Prophetess* is owned by Richard D. Sears, Boston; *Belshazzar's Feast* is in the Dana Collection, Cambridge, Massachusetts. For the location of the *Jeremiah* and the *Saul*, see Letter 153, n. 4.
6. Allston painted a number of landscapes. His *Elijah in the Desert,* purchased in 1832 by Henry Labouchere, later Lord Taulton, is now in the Museum of Fine Arts, Boston.

185. To Robert Charles Winthrop
1 August 1844

My Dear Sir

I have learned with much pleasure that I am indebted to you for a zealous effort to prevent the statue of Washington from becoming part of a National Gothic Monument.[1] There was a time when the proposition to erect such a monument would have grieved and mortified me; but I now regard all such attempts with calm. If we have a system worthy of life, it will live, if it live, it will clothe itself in a garb harmonious with its fundamental principles; and in that case our Architecture will no more be Gothic than our policy will be English.

That the English should have adopted the Norman Style for their new Parliament house, I can understand. They have many proud remembrances connected with the people and the epoch which gave birth to that style; and though I believe that the Spirit of the Gothic is no more with them and that this attempt will therefore prove a failure, I can sympathise with their desire and see a meaning in it.

We often hear an Architecture spoken of as wanting character and with justice but a style of building is always an incarnation of a part of the intellectual character of a people and a Gothic National Monument at Washington would be most characteristic. It would shew the American people incapable of forming an opinion of their own and blindly subservient to English example, without one tie of sympathy with the style thus adopted. Mortifying as it is to remark our provincial relation to G Britain in what relates to literature, I hold that a dependance upon her in art is still more disgraceful; because that with the resources of the world at her command and rich in the knowledge of what has been effected by more elegant nations, she has, with all her lavish expenditure, never equalled either of the petty Italian Republics in this branch of culture.

Allow me dear Sir to recommend to your notice the plan for a building destined to receive the statue of Washington prepared by Mr Rogers.[2] I think it appropriate and elegant, not discordant with the buildings near which it is to stand and worthy alike of the nation and of Washington.

I am for the second time visiting this most remarkable establishment of Gräfenberg.[3] I have been the means of sending many desperate people here and I have the pleasure of seeing wan and wretched faces exchanged in a short time for radiant and healthy countenances. I am sorry to see that medical men are seizing upon this *cold water cure* not to spread its use by practise but to analyze and explain it scientifically, which I believe to be just as possible as to explain how a tree grows or whence the law of gravitation takes its rise. That all curable diseases are here cured by cold water alone we have the daily and hourly assurance of; for there are at this moment 800 sick people here mostly of the higher class from all parts of Europe, but how it is done is to my mind just as much a mystery as the conversion of bread and meat into men and women.

This I will say after what I have here witnessed that I would rather have the most dangerous fever here or the small pox in its worst form, than the slightest illness that requires medical aid elsewhere; for here all both young and old are promptly cured of all acute ailments, while I have yet to see one who in cases of chronic disease denies that he has been solaced and strengthened.

I cannot close this letter without requesting that in case my request for a farther instalment on my group should be brought before congress it may have your support. For several years I was denied the second instalment and when called to Washington, I obtained it on the same grounds before disallowed — and I find myself not compensated for my journey and in danger of being seriously embarrassed in the performance of my task. I remain Dear Sir

> With the highest respect
> Yours
> Horatio Greenough

Gräfenberg in Silesia / August 1st 1884.

Addressed: Hon. Rob't Winthrop / Care of Mess Edwards & Co / Rue de Cluny No 9. / À Paris

NOTES

Robert Charles Winthrop (1809–94), Boston lawyer and statesman, was a member of Congress, 1840–50 and a U.S. senator, 1850–51.
   Manuscript: Winthrop Papers, MHS.
1. Probably the Smithsonian Institution, begun in 1846 from plans drawn in the Gothic style by James Renwick. No proposal to move the statue at this time has been identified.
2. This building was to be an octagon forty feet in diameter and twenty-five feet high, with a skylight in the roof. Each of the two entrances was to have a small Greek doric portico with two columns. The statue was to occupy the east section of the salon, raised on a pedestal eight feet above the floor (*Niles' Weekly Register*, 22 July 1843).
3. This village in Austrian Silesia was the location of the hydropathic establishment of Vincenz Priessnitz. The Greenoughs became interested in the watercure while in England in 1843, chiefly on Louisa's account. They first went to Gräfenberg in April 1844, at which time they stayed about a month. They returned in August, remaining there through Louisa's then pregnancy.

186. To Richard Henry Dana
        23 September 1844

> Freywaldau Aust'n Silesia. Sept'r 23d 44.

Dear Mr Dana

Your letter acknowledging the receipt of mine from Florence reached me several days since and gave me much pleasure. Were I in Italy, I might obtain some details for you from the brothers Riepenhausen, who occupy a prominent position in the German

School, both as painters and as writers on Art. I am not personally acquainted with them, but know that Alston was well known to them and that they still possess a work of his hand. If Mr Leslie would consult Mr Severn who knew Alston when in London and who afterward [was] intimate with his German friends in Italy, he could scarce fail to get valuable information on the subject that interests you. I am the more certain of this as I had a long conversation about Alston at Mr Severn's house in London a year since; and he spoke of Alston's influence on the German school as a thing well known to him.

Many persons conversant with Art have been surprised that Alston's labours should have been so imperfectly known, so partially appreciated. Alston was an Idealist, and as the Ideal is a criticism of the actual, he shared the fate of those who in whatever branch of culture, rise where the mass cannot follow. From the landskape to the embodying of the highest religion, Alston's pictures were lofty, noble poetry. He owed the sympathy he won rather to the sweetness of his language than to his thought, rather to his vehicle than his substance. I believe that his influence would have been much greater, could his works have stood before the body of the people in the interior. I know how necessary is a certain familiarity with the language of Art to a full appreciation of the artist, but the wants of the country folk in this respect, are more than balanced by their freedom from the cant, the false taste and the friv[oli]ty [*page torn*] of self sufficient society.

In England we have seen portr[ait] [*page torn*] painting constantly lead to the highest honors in the gift of Gov't. After portrait comes the illustration of the Literature in vogue and the various ornamental branches of painting. High art leads straight to debt and jail. We are told that Benj Haydon[1] etc were men of bad temper and exorbitant pretensions and this they say was the cause of their ruin — What pride of English painter ever approached that of Mich Angelo who at a harsh word from the Pope turned his back on the man and that too in the palmy days of popedom?[2]

In America we have seen Copley, Stewart and Trumbull absorb a large portion of the public attention and large sums of money. We have seen Alston struggle with absolute poverty and almost unnoticed by the nation. Thus far these facts are a command to quit the paths of high art and to ornament and amuse society.

There is a battle then — There is a battle between what is and what might be, between poetry and fact — between the passions and the tastes of the day and the eternal beauty of nature. Napoleon's feeling toward what he called *"Idealogie"* Johnson's feeling toward Milton,[3] this is the feeling with which practical social life listens to the voice of genius. The conclusion is not very original — The battle is not merely in Art God knows. It is everywhere.

Alston is the head the chief — the Adam of American Idealists. He is the first of that noble Spartan band — sure to fall because the hosts of the Persian are overwhelming, but sure to carry with them to the ground whereon they fall not only the sense but the proof of having acted the noblest part that God grants to a man, that of sacrificing body to mind — expediency to right — fact to truth — now to hereafter.

Let no man think the influence of these efforts are as small as the attention he gives to them. If the gifted minds of a country like ours are to join the current, echo the cry of the street and hammer out their gold to bedizen the every day life of the many, what will be the consequence? The course will be downward and when the gifted travel in that direction they travel fast. I hope that in your biography of Alston you will lay due stress on one feature of his artistical character — He never wrought but upon subjects capable of wholly absorbing his mind and he never let his work go from him until that mind was reflected back from his canvass. To give an idea of his views of the objects of Art would be to name all his subjects. To impress one with his sense of what was due to technical execution would be to shew labors and studies which I am not able to follow him through, to appreciate the force of his genius one must have seen how deaf was his ear to the promise of gain and of newspaper renown through poverty and illness — to feel what a heart he had one must have seen him in all these struggles generous, loving, forgetful of self — living in the life of others.

[No signature]

NOTES

Manuscript: Dana Papers, MHS. Previous publication (in part): Flagg, pp. 380–82.

1. Benjamin Robert Haydon, a difficult person to get along with, was plagued by constant financial difficulties and committed suicide.
2. Early in 1506 Michelangelo left Rome and went to Florence, partly because Pope Julius II refused to furnish funds for the execution of a tomb for himself.
3. Napoleon thought ideology and ideologues were unrealistic. See J. Christopher Herold, ed., *The Mind of Napoleon* (New York, 1955), pp. 68–71, 84–104, 264 ff. Samuel Johnson disapproved of Milton chiefly on political and religious grounds but also because of what he regarded as unreconciled elements of the material and the spiritual in *Paradise Lost*.

187. To Hiram Powers
17 November 1844

Gräfenberg Aust'n Silesia. Nov. 17th [1844]

My Dear Powers

The accounts which have reached me through the German papers of the late inundation of Florence[1] have made me very anxious. If you could spare the time to tell me succinctly what has happened I should be much obliged to you. At this distance it is not easy by mere effort of memory to calculate elevations but it seems to me that the water must have been near your house and mine though I scarce fear for my studio.[2] Is it true that this disaster has been the simple consequence of rain or has there been some blunder at the bottom of it?

You will easily imagine my content and joyful anticipations when I tell you that my wife is now near her confinement and that without one threatening symptom — She has enjoyed robust health through the whole cure, though her comfort was long interfered with by a frightful eruption. When I reflect how few persons have a knowledge of this system at home and the most suspicious and quackery-looking physiognomy which the whole affair presents to a superficial observer, I feel that I have run a risk — I cannot say how soon Mrs G will be able to travel though I have hopes that Jan'y will see us on our way home. There have been 800 patients and upwards, since April, when I arrived. I have seen them come and have seen them go, and I can speak with confidence of the results of this system.

There have been 2 deaths out of 800! You can form no idea of the strange anomalous and complicated maladies which I have seen cured here.

I sent 150 £ St'g to my banker some time since and have heard nothing of the same — Not doubting that all is right, I would still thank you if you would in your walk just ask Philipson[3] if the money came duly to hand.

It is amusing to remark the underhand animosity of these Germ Gov'ts to our country — I saw the other day a cock & bull story of a woman a native of Baden having been sold for a slave in the West and the honest Editor goes on to declare to these poor German peasants that they form no idea of the perfidy and cruelty of the American quakers.

That whole townships of these poor devils go to the States is true, still they should try to lighten their taxes & relieve them of their degrading burthens of all kinds instead of telling such wholesale lies.

The weather here is as mild as it usually is in Tuscany at this season. Remember me I beg you to Skottowe[4] and all friends —

> Yours truly
> H Greenough

Mrs G sends her love to Mrs Powers. Tell her that my wife will overwhelm her with her accounts of what is done here when they meet!

Addressed: Monsieur H. Powers / Sculpteur Americain / À Florence G'd Duché de Toscane / Poste Restante.

NOTES

Manuscript: Editor's collection.
1. On 3 November 1844 the Arno River overflowed its banks, causing one of the worst floods in Florence in modern times.
2. At this time the Greenoughs lived in the Palazzo Pucci and Powers in the Via dei Serragli, both not far from the river; Greenough's studio was on the slope of the hill of Fiesole, over a mile away.
3. P. Philipson was an English banker in Florence.
4. Charles Skottowe (b. 1793) was an Irish portrait painter living in Florence.

188. To Henry Kirke Brown
1 January 1845

Florence[1] 1st Jan'y 1845—

My Dear Sir

Allow me to introduce to your acquaintance and to recommend to your good offices, my friend Capt. John Codman of Boston[2] — who makes a hasty visit to Rome and will be much obliged by a few hints from you to direct his attention to what is most desirable.

We have heard here of your beautiful statue of Ruth[3] — the accounts of which have given me great pleasure; I dare not ask for a sketch, but if an outline of it should be engraved, pray remember my desire to see the composition.

You will find in Capt'n Codman a warm admirer of the fine arts —

Very truly yours
Horatio Greenough

Henry K Brown Esq / Rome

NOTES

Henry Kirke Brown (1814–86), sculptor, a native of Massachusetts, who began the practice of sculpture in Cincinnati in 1837, lived in Rome from 1842 to 1846.
    Manuscript: Gratz Collection, American Painters, Sculptors, Engravers, HSP.
 1. Greenough made a hurried trip to Florence from Gräfenberg about this time, probably to see how the blocking out of his group for the Capitol was progressing.
 2. John Codman (1814–1900), of Massachusetts, went to sea as a young man; in later years he was an exporter and importer.
 3. Brown's statue of the subject of the Biblical book *Ruth* is now in the New-York Historical Society.

189. To Robert Cassie Waterston
       25 March 1845

Gräfenberg, 25th March, '45.

My Dear Sir

We were very much gratified by a letter from Mrs Waterston[1] of the 30th Jan'y and as Mrs G is now forbidden to write I take advantage of an indirect permission from your wife to answer her. And first let me inform you that though she does not write Mrs G is perfectly well. She goes out every day and is as hearty and as blooming as in the days of her teens and quite as saucy also.

The sketch of Mr Adams was made at Washington from a Daguerreotype[2] — That head was always the object of much interest and study to me and I have often wished that my age and acquirements could have opened to me a full communication with it — It is the only head that I have seen which has conciliated body and Soul, brought the wisdom of retirement into life and keenly lived in time without forgetting where time leads us.

You may suppose that I see the approach of a successful issue of my experiment here with much joy. I say experiment, but in fact I had given 10 months' study and experiment to this system before I came here, and I felt as strong a conviction of its soundness then as I do now. Still many accidents unconnected with the water-cure might have dashed my hopes and I felt the responsibility of risking a life against the general opinion — The fact is simply this. Seven years' experience had shown me that I had but to go on consulting "the most eminent physicians" in order to see my wife go down to an untimely grave. I was sure that her body had been injured by impertinent and ignorant and presumptuous interference. I resolved instead of letting the plant stay in the green house and calling botany, chemistry &c to explain its drooping, to transplant it to the open field of Nature. It is true that her present health and strength are a mystery to me — But thank God I have a joyful and not a mournful mystery to deal with. If the botanist and the gardener or the farmer compare *ignorances,* I am afraid that neither will have much to boast of, but I, as a plant, should rather fall into the hands — not of the botanist.

These convictions which seem at first sight very humbling to our man's pride after all only remove the crown of wisdom from the schools to place it on the collective head of the race — And it is scarce more than fair — for did not the plough and the spindle — the corn grasses and the alphabet, laws and saws come to us out of darkness? What have we done since records were made to balance what had been done before?

If physicians were right and medicine necessary the classes who most need health and strength would have least of it, and the inhabitants of London and Paris would be as superiour to the untutored millions (who live without science,) in health as they are in self sufficiency. For my part I am convinced that cities, — large capitals, are a natural developement of human society — but I also believe that noisome and poisonous accumulations and obstructions are the necessary consequences of such bodies. I believe that doctors and physic are only another means which nature adopts to disperse such tumors as large cities.

Let us hope that steam and rail roads without steam will ere long enable us to organise a civilization which shall give us neighbours without being stifled smoked and poisoned.

I have lived in various lands. I have seen many of the great men and things of my time, but what I have here seen surpasses far away in importance all that I have witnessed.

The truths laid bare by the Water Cure are not merely an admirable system of *hygiene.* They are the basis of a new philosophy — nay the germ of a new civilization — If you ask me what I think will come of it — I must remember how long the Romans stood *inside* the threshold of printing yet never knew where they were. Man steps and steps slowly, he does not fly — If I have read history aright he has always made faces at his food — nor has he ever digested a system till many years after he has swallowed it. Had I written a few days later I might have announced events instead of spinning mere talk, but I beg you to excuse me — I have been now one year divorced from civilization and have had scarce a look but the sky and the forests — We have had the mercury playing round o for 2 months but it is now warm once more. Mrs G joins me in kind remembrance to your wife and the family — we look forward to the possibility of

our being ere long in America with much happiness — I remain Dear
Sir respectfully yours

Horatio Greenough

Addressed: Rev. R. Waterston / Care of Hon Josiah Quincy Jun'r[3] /
Boston — Mass. / Steamer

NOTES

Robert Cassie Waterston (1814–93), a graduate of the Harvard Divinity School,
was a minister, writer, and public speaker (J. P. Quincy, "Memoir of Rev. R. C.
Waterston," *ProcMHS,* 2d ser., 8 [1893]: 292–302).
    Manuscript: Waterston Papers, MHS.
  1. Anna Cabot Lowell Quincy Waterston (b. 1812) and Louisa G. Greenough
     had been brought up together.
  2. Greenough refers to a study he made in 1828 for his bust of John Adams,
     but since the daguerreotype process was not made public until 1839, he
     must have made use of a drawing or painting by John Trumbull, Mather
     Brown, or Gilbert Stuart.
  3. Josiah Quincy, Jr. (1802–82) was mayor of Boston from 1845 to 1849
     (Justin Winsor, ed., *The Memorial History of Boston* [Boston, 1880–81],
     3:251).

190.   To Hiram Powers
13 May 1845

Gräfenberg 13th May. '45 —

My Dear Powers

    Mrs Greenough was delivered of a fine healthy male child[1] on the
11th. The infant weighs a little under eleven pounds — I have been
very anxious on account of the evident size of the child and my wife's
fleshy condition of body — Mr Priessnitz[2] was in the next room during
the confinement and carried out the system of stimulation by cold to
the last moment — The infant was immediately washed in cold water
— My wife is very happy and very busy with her new occupation.
Knowing how many dangers beset the first weeks of life I am pre-

pared, I hope, for any thing — The main object of my journey hither is attained. My wife has gone through 42 weeks of pregnancy without a day during which she has not taken active exercise and at least 3 baths of some kind, often 4. 5. & 6. She never looked heartier than the day before her confinement.

Tell your wife that my boy has very dark blue eyes (which he says he means shall change by and by as soon as he can get a little leisure) a famous chest and much more hair on his head than his papa — He has already changed his notes from an even wail to savage yells which are worthy of a young Mohawk — He fights like a devil in the water and seems not to share our belief in Priessnitz at all.

I should take it very kindly of you if you would see my groupe with your own eyes and tell me something of the marble and its progress — I regretted very much that the prolongation of my stay here and the failure of the consul at Leghorn to transmit a certificate as he had promised to do forced me to suspend the operations of the studio — I have no debts and wish to avoid them but if it be true that Poldo[3] is sacrificed by this step — and you could help him through till I come it would be doing me a real favor — Mr Greene has evidently made up his mind that I shall whistle for my money[4] — perhaps he may not like the sound when he hears it near him.

My dear Powers I regret that I cannot transfer to your mind the convictions which a year of careful observation have fastened upon me relative to this system — I know that you are not enthusiastic about nothing and I believe that evidence such as I have seen would both move & convince you — Mrs Mackenzie[5] who has been growling all winter like a bear with a sore head now feels the result of her campaign — Her stomach and bowels have learned to do without medicine — for twenty years her pills were mixed with her daily bread and for 10 months water has taken their place — She is strong cheerful and means to stay here through the summer at least — She has sent for her sick brother — She cried the other day in speaking of her daughter who died in Florence — Oh said she when I remember how that poor girl used to plead with me to keep Dr H.[6] away from her how she used to tell me that I was infatuated! If I had brought her here she would be now alive — If my poor old body is so strengthened what would she have effected with youth and a good constitution?

I remain Dear Powers H G——gh

Pray address me at Vienna care of J. G. Schwartz Esqr⁷ U.S. Consul
— for I shall leave this probably by the time my letter reaches you.
Mrs G will remain here during the summer with my brother's family.⁸

NOTES

Manuscript: Editor's collection.
1. Henry (after his father's death called Horatio) Saltonstall Greenough (1845–
   1916) was educated in France and lived, in his later years, in Neuilly on
   the outskirts of Paris. According to an obituary, "His pursuits . . . were
   along scientific lines" (*Boston Transcript,* 3 April 1916). He never married.
2. Vincenz Priessnitz (1799–1851), founder of the *Kaltwassercur,* opened his
   establishment at Gräfenberg in 1826. In a short time it became phenomenally
   popular.
3. One of Greenough's workmen (see Letter 133).
4. Presumably a reference to money which Greenough loaned Greene.
5. Emma Landseer McKenzie (b. 1770), English painter of animals.
6. The doctor had not been identified.
7. John George Schwarz was U.S. consul in Vienna from 1829 to 1853.
8. Henry Greenough, his wife Frances, and their two children. They arrived
   in Florence in October 1845, later than expected.

191.   To John Louis O'Sullivan?
         26 May 1845

Gräfenberg 26th May '45 —

My Dear Sir
    If the system of Hydrotherapeutics has awakened public attention
in the U States to a degree proportioned to the pretensions of its be-
lievers in Europe a few words on the subject may have an interest
for your readers — In presuming to write on such a topic I count upon
the authority which a year's residence at Gräfenberg has given me; a
sense of incapacity to do justice to the subject alone prevents me from
writing a book instead of a letter and that as a matter of sheer duty.
    Many very many books have been written upon the system of Preis-
snitz and having read them nearly all I am bound to say that though
some are the productions of very able men and all or nearly all seem

to have been dictated by high and pure motives none give me the notion of the water cure as I have here seen it.

I have seen upwards of a thousand patients treated for very various — complicated and severe maladies with water. From Plica Polonica[1] and leprosy to croupe and common colds, I have seen almost all sorts of illness here treated — The whole syphilitic family — small pox of the worst and most virulent character included — Of the thousand and upwards 4 have died — hundreds have gone hence strong active and happy — scores still remain of whom some are slowly recovering; a few seem stationary, and I declare that I have yet to see one who does not confess that he is better. Of the 4 who died one came here already in a dying state — a second an American sank under the crisis but had a softened brain of many months date — a third perished from disregard to the injunctions of the water doctor —

I have read that "severe pain is almost unknown at Gräfenberg." I have heard more growling and groaning here in one week than I have heard in months that I passed in the hospitals of Italy — I know no greater contrast than between the files of pallid, silent, people who lie in hospitals and these loud voiced sufferers — There is something almost comical in hearing a man who stands on his legs 2 or 3 miles from his lodgings with a good dinner under his jacket telling you that human nature is not equal to what he is called to endure.

The cold bath is very disagreeable at first but habit reconciles one to it — As regards danger I can only say that I have never known any bad consequences result from it here and I have seen a new born babe — my own child, plunged at once into water so cold that I cannot drink a full glass of it without stopping.

To describe the most interesting cases that I have seen — from beginning to end would be to write a book and not a letter. I have seen the bedridden victims of chronic disease on their arrival here lifted out of their carriages like infants — I have seen them gradually advancing like the hour hand of a clock and without a perceptible difference between yesterday and today rising at last with the lark and as merry as he.

There arrived here during the past winter a book writen by a Doctor Graham[2] — a book written with ability against Priessnitz — I can understand that Dr Graham should have made himself obnoxious to the hydropathist and that he should have met with a rebuff that left him sore but I cannot understand how any man pretending to decency should have signed his name to such impudent falsehoods as that book is filled with. The work occasioned here a general cry of indignation — Dr Graham states among other things that the Prince Lichtenstein after seeing his poor wife sink under the ignorant cruelty of Priessnitz went away filled with horror and disgust — Now it is notorious that the Princess was never a patient of Priessnitz at all — She died in childbed, here it is true but surrounded by the first accoucheurs of Vienna — Her husband was the patient and he continued the cure many months after the death of the princess and went away whole — Nay at the moment when that bare faced calumny reached Gräfenberg it found the infant son and heir of that fortune and title — the nephew of the lady said to have died under such circumstances — the young prince Lichtenstein — here — sent hither in mid winter from Vienna — because his sisters had taken the scarlet fever and the father was anxious to save the child from the contagion[3] — I saw that boy arrive — the seeds of the fever were in him — he was almost immediately taken ill and for 24 hours his life was despaired of — Priessnitz never left him until the danger was past and I saw that boy in one week's time living literally in the open air with the thermometer nearly at o of Fahrenheit. For myself I have here seen my own wife an invalid of many years suffering throw off all her ailments — I have learned to prefer these frosty hills to the *muggy* warmth of Italy — During 2 years since I adopted water as my drink and exchanged my former occasional tepid baths for daily cold ones I have enjoyed a health and spirits which I had supposed the privilege only of boyhood.

I conceive this stystem great and valuable as it is to the sick and the suffering to be still more important to the sound and healthy. A system which enjoins labour — which makes it clear that idleness is decay and excess and vice suicide must have important moral results — perhaps the day will come when cleanliness will be preached when decency will consist in showing a wholesome clean and well developed body instead of hiding a dirty sick one — Perhaps the day will come when some eloquent man will prove that to grasp more than you can hold is greediness — to get more than you can digest is to insure a surfeit — Perhaps it would then be clear that [not] only the soul but the body also is of God and we should learn like the brutes whom we despise to make our passions harmonize with his providence — not like the botanist worrying dissecting and peeping through lenses but like the gardner planting watering and grubbing about letting what some wise ones call Nature have his own way a little and putting trust in him — a real trust that will not believe in a fever whose cure requires navigation astronomy — and a thorough knowledge of what is beyond man's comprehension —

I do not so much respect hydropathy as a system of medical treatment as I wonder at and love it as a system of living — Society is concerned with the living but Nature as they call him makes great use of dead men. I should say after a year's residence here that water is something very different something more to us than we have supposed and that it were worth while to try it upon ourselves as it has always been tried upon our planet thus far with success.

On reading this over there is a tone of dictation and impudence about it which I should prefer to have castrated — If you can do that I am willing to let it be printed if your readers will be interested by it. You will find it enthusiastic. Respect an enthusiasm which has survived a winter at Gräfenberg! with my habits & tastes too. Remember me to Mc Cracken[4] and to Mr Bryant.

Yours

H G——gh

NOTES

John Louis O'Sullivan (1813–95), journalist and diplomat, established the *United States Magazine and Democratic Review* in 1837 with S. D. Langtree. Greenough's two essays "Remarks on American Art" and "American Architecture" appeared in it in July and August 1841.

Manuscript: Henry G. Nickerson, Dedham, Massachusetts.

1. A disorder of the scalp in which the hair becomes matted and twisted, reputed to be endemic in Poland.
2. Robert Hay Graham, *Graefenberg; or, a True Report of the Water-Cure with an Account of its Antiquity* (London, 1844).
3. Presumably Greenough refers to two of the four brother princes of Liechtenstein: Charles Jean Népomuc Antoine, whose wife was Rosalie, countess of Grünne and dowager countess of Schœnfeld; and Alois Joseph, prince of the realm, whose only son was Jean Marie François Placide and who had also six daughters.
4. John L. H. McCracken (d. 1853), New York merchant, contributed to several American magazines and also wrote plays.

192.   To Hiram Powers
          16 June 1845

Gräfenberg 16th June 45

My Dear Powers

I have been detained here from day to day and your letter no doubt waits for me at Vienna — Fearing that some accident or other may retard my arrival in Florence I remit 50£ St'g which I request you to pay to the marble merchants at Seravezza[1] as an instalment upon the price of my group —

My wife and child go on very prosperously — so much so that I think of taking them home at once instead of going without them — I am unwilling to do this without vaccinating the boy — tho' Mr Priessnitz prefers their having it in the natural way — but as I am not quite up to treating small pox on the high way I shall choose the best of two evils. Mrs G sends love to your wife — Yours faithfully

Horatio Greenough

NOTES

Manuscript: Editor's collection.
1. At this quarry near Carrara Greenough's group *The Rescue* was blocked out.

193.   To Robert Cassie Waterston
          7 July 1845

Freiwaldau[1] July 7th '45 —

My Dear Sir

You will have learned ere this that our boy was born just 5 days after your own; we wish you joy and trust that all your anticipations may be realized — Our little fellow is getting quite fat now having exchanged his mother for a peasant nurse — Mrs G though well could not give him all the nourishment he required and I have a prejudice against animals' milk for human creatures in infancy.

With all my conviction of the sublime truths on which the practice of Mr Priessnitz is founded I cannot anticipate any great result from it for society — How long is it that temperance industry and cleanliness were discovered yet we see that men are rather forced to those virtues than won by their loveliness — I have however a great consolation in this my opinion — I remark that God's care for the mass of men is constant and unwearied — I remark that famine and pestilence and even the sword and the ball have never touched the body of the human family — I remark that luxury and vice are kept away from ¾ths of mankind. I remark that the vitality with which we are endowed is strong enough to carry the mass through every blunder and mistake to a reproduction of their kind — I remark that science operates directly on very few human lives and with my principle that God's will is always done I am forced to see in the destruction that does occur only a necessary balance to the production that is effected — That three blossoms should open where one cherry ripens — that 2 babes should die where one man attains the age of maturity seems at first rather a puzzling fact but I am forced to admit that what I call abortive may not really be so & that when the blossom perishes to my eye it but travels a road which I cannot see — When I look upon the heavens at night and imagine the existences moral and intellectual that are burning there, I cannot escape the feeling that intense darkness and ignorance is our portion here; I thank my God that he has given me one ray of soul. I am conscious of but one and that ray is *trust* a loving trust.

I can imagine a world where wrong and woe and pain — should go on accumulating — a world where death should be unknown and accumulating millions should suffer all the pangs of death and of despair without being able to die — and when I see into what peaceful sweet sleep even a triumphant army sinks at last, fattening the fields it boasted to have won I am filled with admiration at so simple a balance wheel, which keeps the race ever young and the forest ever fresh —

It is clear to my mind that our race would long since have committed suicide *en masse* if its hands had not been held — They have been held by physical want — If it be true that no civilization has yet been discovered which has united the culture of the individual and the conservation of the stock, then it seems to me clear that our race may be looked on as a sort of plant whose roots are animal whose branches are moral and social whose fruit is intellectual, for no great civilization has appeared which has not added to the stock of truth in science; a kernel capable of surviving the pulp that enveloped it whose fate is destruction or rottenness. To my mind this singular discrepancy of lot is the distinguishing feature of our race — when I compare the serf with Newton or with Buonaparte I am overwhelmed with the difference of their being. It is only when I see culture end in exhaustion and ignorance come in to supply vigor to the worn out soil that I can realize a common origin and a common destiny for 2 beings apparently so different —

I love to look upon the mind of man not as an individual ever [?] repeated in slightly varying patterns, but as one as the waters of the globe are one, one as the air that weighs on the bosom of the planet is one. The fractional portions are nothing apparently — for what portion of existing science can an individual absorb? I find a consolation in thus belonging to a great whole; it saves me from my nothingness and of all annihilation a conscious one is the most humbling. I can take of *the sea* in the hollow of my hand the moon herself can not move him much — Napoleon thought he governed the mind of Europe — He merely took up a handful of it and how soon it ran through his fingers to follow its God's law of evaporation and condensation and fall!

Show me a christianity that shall not be a moral and intellectual and spiritual aristocracy — show me a christianity that can do for the souls of the mass of men, what the *wants* of nature and the apparent niggardness of nature does for their bodies and I will be baptized again into that church — I cannot conceive that such a system can be found, unless it begin with making its peace with the animal nature of man — Otherwise you will ever have over again the old story of a believing flock and a disbelieving shepherd for mark you your shepherd is an animal — has his wife in London — his concubine in Rome and his gold coat every where sooner or later — I do not mean to be profane, but I do not think those men believe for instance as the sailor believes in his compass — when his ship pitches in the midnight waters of the Atlantic — his light is trimmed then — it is not dark there! His eye is on it — fatigued no doubt. Won't you sleep a little — it will do you good — Not I — I *won't* sleep! That sailor believes —

Do not suppose that I am an enemy of Christianity — I see in it

the strongest yearning of man after the truth and the most successful — but I cannot see perfection in it because I judge it by its fruits
agreeably to the precept of its founder — I think its fundamental im-
perfection is the admission of the existence of evil — evil in God's
sight. I cannot reconcile the existence of evil with God's character
and attributes nor would any man have ever done so but for *social*
phenomena. Now Society is a natural production in my mind as
natural as a concert or a treatise on astronomy or as an oak tree but
like them it is a partial, individual, perishable existence — There is a
power in man stronger than any society because he has outlived
them all, there is a power in nature stronger than any of his fruits —
Man is like a stream which has been taught that to run seaward is
sinful — he has thrown a dam across his nature and what is the result?
He goes over it and falls instead of gliding — Only there is a mill
pond above it where human beavers live and breed. This dam gets
fatigued at last — it is man! (The stream never tires. It is God!)
away it goes and then they make another.

I feel safer therefore in hugging to Mother Earth than in theories
— I hear God's voice plainer from the clod than from the pulpit —
The clod says to me thou art my child! My blood flows in thy veins,
my bosom shall be thy last pillow. Shall I mistrust God because he
will not talk English? Fully do I believe that he will never be less
kind to me than he is now, for he is the same yesterday today and
forever. What I call silence as I look upon the ground is only a
foreign tongue; when I am transferred to that region I shall learn
its tongue and who knows that ears of corn as they grow have not an
intellectual consciousness? Who knows that this searching thought is
not destined to *feel* all that it now admires — Excuse my gabbling
and give me your views of my feeling with regard to nature — it is a
solitary elaboration and may be therefore a crazy sort of one — Look
upon me as teachable though I speak incoherently and believe me
very sincerely your friend

H G——gh

NOTES

Manuscript: Henry G. Nickerson, Dedham, Massachusetts.
1. Freiwaldau was the village at the foot of the hill of Gräfenberg. When the
Greenoughs returned in July they evidently took apartments there.

194. To Hiram Powers
    30 July 1845

Freiwaldau 30th July '45

My Dear Powers —

I received your letter at Vienna when on my way to Florence — I was obliged however to return here on account of a difficulty about Mrs Greenough's maid — China is not more completely tied up with regulations and formalities than this empire — however I think all is now ready for a start[1] — Had I had no difficulty about a passport for that servant I should have been in Florence before this. Mrs G and boy are right well. She desires to send her love to Mrs P.

I hear of Florence occasionally but only in a general way and now hardly hope to hear again until I arrive. There are now 716 names on the sick list here which when you remember that Mr Priessnitz usually receives at least 1 dollar per week without counting the large presents he gets from princes etc will give you a notion of the sort of business he is doing — Mrs Mackenzie whom you may remember as being lugged up and down stairs at her house — walked upwards of a mile yesterday — The old lady squealed horribly during the winter — said she was mad when she undertook such a cure etc — She crows now most manfully — The human race may generally be divided into old children and young children those who believe without evidence and those whom no evidence can convince. Mr Colvin[2] of New York who came here booked by the N.Y. faculty for paralysis *and* consumption (one would say that either was enough) has gone home after 8 months sousing — and though for the first 6 months of the time he could never get from his house to mine, he walked 6 miles before breakfast during the last fortnight that he stayed — I found him in tears one afternoon last winter and he told me that they were tears of joy for he had been able that day to draw his foot up and to bend and extend his toes. For 3 years he had been unable to write with his right hand until May of this year.

Should you see either of the gentlemen of the Seravezza establishment I beg you to use your influence with them to induce them to remain quiet until my arrival — I have every reason to hope that I shall be able hereafter to remain at Florence — I have paid dear for my wife's recovery but not too dear — not too dear, I am sure you justify me — Yours

H G——gh

Addressed: Hiram Powers Esqr / Sculptor / Florence —

NOTES

Manuscript: Editor's collection.
1. The Greenoughs left Gräfenberg early in August.
2. Five Colvins are listed in the New York city directory for this time; which one Greenough refers to is not known.

195.   To Hiram Powers
        19 June 1846

Freiwaldau,[1] 19th June '46.

My Dear Powers.

We have just received yours enclosing an Acc't from Philipson — I am sorry to find that you have been obliged to pay postage on Louisa's letter — I had expected that it would come to you *franco.*[2] We are much pleased to hear that Mrs P bathes her baby in cold water and doubt not but that if the practice is begun prudently, followed perseveringly and accompanied by the necessary "appliances and means to boot" viz pure air plain food and light clothing, the child [will] gain in strength and even good humor.

Harry has after looking round with his own eyes for a few days, plunged into it and his wife has followed him — I hope much advantage to both —

Mrs Mackenzie who is now 76 years of age confesses that she is now in better health than she ever enjoyed though she still grumbles fearfully at the slightest symptom of crisis.

This Mexico business[3] is a strange one and I should think with you that England was about to run a great risk, if I had a better opinion of Mexican prudence and Mexican councils — Those people have little to lose — and they count perhaps upon our aversion to begin a war which may *end* in a general fight. I heard Mr Calhoun[4] predict all this long long ago — I only hope that the sequel will be equally as he foresaw it.

I cannot believe that Mr Lester[5] meant you harm, though I presume his main object was to make a good thing in the way of Sale — He is a trumpeter by trade and those fellows' mouths soon get brassy — Perhaps he did no more than he would be glad to have done for himself — In our country there are thousands literally thousands of these busybodies employed in manufacturing *public opinion* when they want the first elements necessary to form one for themselves. A good rap upon the knuckles may teach this individual but alas there is the breed! I hope you will be satisfied with one kick and not be drawn into a fisty cuffs battle, because you know many, perhaps a majority of the bystanders feel more pleasure in the fight than sympathy with the just side.

I was quite surprised to find not less than 9 Italians here — of whom several are gone away quite well — We are now about 500. Only 8 americans —

I understand that after the slaughter of Tarnow[6] many children of noble polish houses were found crying in the streets too young to know their own names! — When asked who they were they could only cry papa! Mama! What a blessing it is to have a country where *all* are interested to see fair play or something like it! What are the defects of our system to the overwhelming horrors that from time [to time] devastate these countries governed by the grace of God? Yours —

[No signature]

Addressed: Monsieur Hiram Powers / Sculpteur / À Florence — En Toscane.

NOTES

Manuscript: Editor's collection.
1. Early in May 1846 the Horatio and the Henry Greenoughs left Florence for Gräfenberg, where they arrived by the end of that month.

2. Franked.
3. For several years England had been attempting to get Mexico to recognize Texan independence in return for guarantees against American aggression. On 25 April 1846 Mexican troops crossed the Rio Grande, and on 13 May Congress declared that a state of war existed between the two countries.
4. John C. Calhoun (1782–1850), U.S. senator from 1832 to his death. Greenough presumably refers to a statement he heard Calhoun make in 1836.
5. Charles Edwards Lester (1815–90), Connecticut-born writer, lawyer, and minister, was U.S. consul at Genoa from 1842 to 1847. He described Powers as "the artist" in his book *The Artist the Prince and the Merchant*, 2 vols. (New York, 1845). Powers approved the manuscript, but later Lester changed it, attributing to Powers statements he did not make. The case was taken to court, and Powers won a judgment (information furnished by Clara L. Dentler, Florence).
6. Tarnow, Poland, was seized by Austria in 1772.

196. To Henry Theodore Tuckerman?
[Fall 1846?]

. . . I am not aware that any American has, until now, risked the placing before his countrymen a representation of Our Saviour.[1] The strong prejudice, or rather conviction of the Protestant mind has, perhaps, deterred many. Not behind the most jealous in deprecating the abuse of images in places of public worship, I think, nevertheless, that the person and face of Our Saviour is a legitimate subject of art, because, although our conception must fall short of what the heart of the Christian looks for, yet you will allow that we may offer to many an imperfect instead of a mean or grovelling idea which they have drawn from other sources. The prayers and hymns of the most pious are as far unworthy the perfection to which they are addressed, as the lights and shadows of the artist; yet both may be accepted as fervent aspirations after the good and beautiful. It is a mistake to suppose that the artist, because he stops working, thinks his task perfect; he says only — behold the subject proposed to me as the art which is in me can give it. . . .

NOTES

Henry Theodore Tuckerman (1813–71), a native of Boston, miscellaneous writer, spent the years 1833–34 and 1836–38 mostly in Italy and on both occasions saw Greenough in Florence. He wrote about Greenough in his *Italian Sketch Book* (1835) and in *Artist-Life* (1847), expanded to *Book of the Artists* (1867). His *Memorial of Horatio Greenough* contains the first extended biographical account of Greenough and also several of his essays, edited by Tuckerman.

    Source: Henry T. Tuckerman, *A Memorial of Horatio Greenough* (New York, 1853), pp. 33–34.

    The date is conjectured on the basis of internal evidence; see n. 1, below.

  1. Greenough modelled two busts of Christ. The first was done in the fall of 1846 and is now in the Boston Public Library.

197.   To George Bancroft
       9 January 1847

                               Florence. 9th Jan'y. 1847.

Dear Sir

    I am induced to ask your assistance in a matter which though it mainly interests myself, concerns also the Gov't of the U—— States — I have been for three years past the coeditor of the Gov't for a work on which I am employed and though I have fulfilled every stipulation of the contract and though Congress has actually appropriated 8000$[1] for satisfying my demands yet it would seem that the state of the Treasury at this time makes all hope of immediae payment out of the question —

    On a former like occasion, I had recourse to Mr Everett whose good word with Mess's Rothschilds induced them to advance me 2000$ which sum I punctually paid as soon as it was furnished me by Gov't.[2] Now though I have a great horror of acting upon the usual distorted and perverted version of the maxim that One good turn deserves another, yet I cannot refrain from begging you to do me a similar favor — I have no great hopes of success — because my request is out of the course of regular business already once departed from in my behalf.

I have even requested the U.S. Gov't in case it be impossible to pay me — to grant me freedom from my contract, which as it at present stands, ties my hands by preventing my entering into other engagements and empties my pockets by the unavoidable expence of keeping a great work suspended for years while rent and service and taxes are consuming my means. My ambition to serve the country is such that nothing but my duty to my family has induced me to seek to be relieved from a connection so gratifying to my feelings and my pride as an artist — so useful and advantageous to my reputation — If the war in which the country is engaged³ calls upon the *employe's* of Gov't to sacrifice a portion of their salaries I believe I shall be ready to give as large a portion of mine as any one — and cheerfully to help to "teach" our quarrelsome neighbour *"the law"* but if as I have reason to believe I am the only one thus called on, and that not for a part, but for the whole of my supply and that indefinitely — I must be most ruinously embarrassed; situated as I am in a foreign distant land, among folk who have no sympathy for republican attempts at high art —

I have a bare hope that Mess's Rothschild being assured that 8000$ are already appropriated by Congress will advance 2 or 3000. and I ask of your kindness to propose the transaction to them — Even success in this attempt will only relieve me from embarrassment & enable me to go on — till I become one of those unhappy men who knock every year at the national door to ask a hearing for individual griefs and forgotten or intricate claims of arrears.

I am Dear Sir
With the highest respect
Your friend & Serv't
Horatio Greenough
Sculptor

George Bancroft Esqr / U.S. Envoy Extraordinary / & Minister Plenip'y to the / Court of St James's

NOTES

George Bancroft (1800–1891), historian and statesman, was U.S. minister to Great Britain from 1846 to 1849. He was a tutor in Greek at Harvard when Greenough was a student there.

Manuscript: George Bancroft Papers, MHS.

1. The sum of the third and fourth installments for *The Rescue.*
2. Late in December 1841 N. M. Rothschild & Sons advanced Greenough
   £400, at the request of Everett, which represented half the sum of his
   second installment.
3. The Mexican War, 1846–48.

198.   To George Bancroft
16 January 1847

Florence Jan'y 16th 1847.

George Bancroft Esqr.

Dear Sir   I hasten to inform you that I have just received from
the Sec'y of the Treasury the remittance so long delayed — A letter
from Mr Young[1] explains the difficulty which has arisen from mislay-
ing first the documents forwarded by me and afterward the notarial
copy furnished by my agent in Boston. The number of clerks employed being calculated for more quiet times is no doubt insufficient
to meet all calls upon the Dep't in case of war.

Hoping that this may reach you in time to prevent sacrificing your
leisure on my account and assuring you that my critical position
alone induced me to intrude upon it, I remain with the highest respect

Your friend & Serv't
Horatio Greenough
Sculptor.

NOTES

Manuscript: George Bancroft Papers, MHS.
1. McClintock Young, chief clerk and acting secretary of the Treasury Department.

199. To Robert Charles Winthrop
25 January 1847

Florence Jan'y 25th '47

My Dear Sir

I had much pleasure from your letter announcing that the statue of Washington has at length been made visible[1] — I have struggled a little as you know, against this consummation — but only in the belief that marble is destined to a short life in the open air; — as far as my own personal interest is concerned I have surely reason to be happy at what has been done.

I thank you from my heart for your exertions in this matter as also for the able and timely assistance you have rendered me when the question of my payment was before the house — I can fully comprehend the situation of Mr Young and am only too happy that after all the difficulty has been surmounted and has left no soreness in any quarter.

I return for a moment to the statue of Washington — A colossal statue of a man whose career makes an epoch in the world's history is an immense undertaking — To fail in it is only to prove that one is not as great in art as the hero himself was in life — Had my work shown a presumptuous opinion that I had an easy task before me — had it betrayed a yearning rather after the wages of art than the honest fame of it, I should have deserved the bitterest things that have been said of it and of me — But containing as it certainly *must* internal proofs of being the *utmost effort* of my mind at the time it was wrought, its failure fell not on me but on those who called me to the task. The fame of an artist is the highest boon that can be granted to me but it is not necessary to my self respect. I sat down the less disconsolate at my failure because I felt and feel that Canova and Chantry had both never passed the fatal line of *mediocre* in their images of Washington. Allow me to exult a little that during the months I passed at Washington while my statue was the butt of wiseacres and witlings, I never in word or thought swerved from my principle that the general mind is alone a quorum to judge a great work. I began the study of sculpture at 20 years of age — at 30 the model of the Wash[ing]ton was compleated — It was too little preparation I own — nay had my attempt threatened to close the door for others I should not have dared it. As it is — where is the harm? — 30000$ have been in one way or another wasted on that stone — But is not the example — the warning if you will worth the money? The relievos of the Rotunda were too good to excite the indignation of the country at wanton expenditure. The statue of Washington produced that effect. Sir when in future time the true sculptors of America have filled the metropolis with beauty and grandeur will it not be worth 30000$ to be able to point to that figure and say. Here was the first struggle of our infant art?

Accept my renewed thanks for all your kindness and my assurance of the pleasure it would afford me could I in any way serve you or yours.

I remain Dear Sir
Your friend & Servant
Horatio Greenough

Endorsed: Horatio Greenough / to R. C. Winthrop.

NOTES

Manuscript: Winthrop Papers, MHS.
1. In the fall of 1846, pursuant to the congressional resolution of May 1844, the temporary wooden shelter over the *Washington* was removed.

200.   To John Gadsby Chapman
7 July 1848

My Dear Chapman

I have just now received yours of the 25th Ult'o and hasten to answer it. I am fully persuaded that there is not another spot in Europe as quiet and as likely to remain so as this very one where I am writing. We are at war — but the seat of war is Lombardy and

Tuscany will follow the fate of that country.[1] We expect to drive the Austrians beyond the Isonzo[2] & then perhaps Italy may become the scene of internal strife and dissension. However I do not expect any thing other than quiet here.

The Italians though very resolute in regard to Austria have a most enviable conviction of the value of peace and the necessity of order. The Catholic religion whatever mischief it may have done has done this good that *all men* stand recognized before it as worthy of a place above the brutes — Hence the condition of the lowest class here is superior to that of England & Ireland and the poor *never starving* have not learned the cursed alphabet of *communism*.

I can hardly venture to speak of the journey through France though I should undertake it if necessary without real anxiety.[3] I believe the worst is over — and even at the worst you might have been safe enough at Paris by keeping in doors. Steamers ply now between England & Leghorn as you probably are aware —

I will not fail to address the Keeper of the Gallery — (Pitti) about permission for you.[4] I am not sanguine as to the result for I know that young painters here generally despair of getting it. I will put in the request at once.

I am sorry to hear that you have had reason to complain of your health and hope that the journey and sojourn will effect your entire recovery — It will be a sincere pleasure to talk with you once more & if I can be of service to you & your family I shall be most happy.

> Yours faithfully
> Horatio Greenough

Florence 7th July '48.

NOTES

John Gadsby Chapman (1808–89), painter and etcher whose *Baptism of Pocahontas* is in the Capitol rotunda, went to Rome in 1849 and there spent the rest of his life.

   Manuscript: Rare Book Collection, Wellesley College Library.

1. The Revolution of 1848 in Italy was fought chiefly in Lombardia and Venetia, between the Austrians and an army of Piedmontese, Tuscans, Neapolitans, and others under Charles Albert, king of Sardinia. The Italians were defeated in July and August.

2. This river, flowing into the Bay of Trieste, marks the eastern border of Italy and Austria.

3. Greenough is referring to the Revolution of February 1848 in France.
4. Antonio Ramirez di Montalvo was at this time conservator of the Galleria Palatina and other objects of art in the royal palaces and villas (*Almanacco Toscano* [Florence, 1848]). Chapman was probably seeking permission to copy a painting.

201.   To Hiram Powers
[25?] July 1848

My Dear Powers

My wife is in labor and will probably be delivered in the course of 2 hours[1] — It is highly important for reasons connected with the Estate, that there should be proof of the child's being born alive if such should be the case — May I ask of you the favor to hold yourself in readiness to come to me when I shall send for you? Don't leave your work but send a verbal answer.

Yours in haste
H Greenough

½ past one — P. M.

Addressed: Hiram Powers — Esqr

NOTES

Manuscript: Editor's collection.
1. On 25 July 1848, Mrs. Greenough gave birth to a daughter, Mary Louise (1848–54).

202. To Gino Capponi
18 April 1849

Pregiatissimo Sig Marchese

Ho ricevuto oggi medesimo una lettera dal Sig Prescott, recatami dal di lui figlio[1] — il quale e qua di passaggio. Il Sig Prescott esprime il desiderio che il suo figlio profitti di questa occasione per venire ed ossequiarla — Non sapendo in questi momenti, quale sabebbe per lei un ora meno incommoda, ignorando pure se ella puo disporre del proprio tempo, mi prendo la libertà di esporre il desiderio del mio compatriotto pregandola di farmelo sapere nel caso che ella ci potra ricevere.

Suo Servitore ed amico
Horatio Greenough

Dallo Studio in Barbano[2] / Adi 18. Aprile '49.

TRANSLATION

Most esteemed Signor Marchese

Today I received a letter from Mr Prescott, brought by his son,[1] who is passing this way — Mr Prescott expresses the wish that his son avail himself of this opportunity to pay his respects to you — Not knowing at this moment, what would be the most convenient hour for you, being ignorant, moreover, whether you have time at your disposal, I take the liberty to make known the wish of my compatriot, begging you to let me know in case you can receive us.

Your servant and friend
Horatio Greenough

From the studio in Barbano[2] / 18 April '49.

Addressed: Al Ill'mo Signore / Il Sig Marchese Gino Capponi / Via S. Sebastiano / SS. RR. MM.

NOTES

 Manuscript: Carteggi Capponi, Biblioteca Nazionale.
1. Presumably William Gardner Prescott (1826–95), son of William Hickling Prescott, and a lawyer who traveled in Europe in 1849–50.
2. In 1847 Greenough built a studio on the Piazza Maria Antonio (now Independenza), in an area called de Barbano.

203. To Ogden Haggerty
  [1 January 1850?]

O Haggerty Esqr
Dear Sir
 I regret very much that it will not be in my power to meet you this evening and the more so as I should have had the opportunity of becoming acquainted with so distinguished an artist as Mr Leutze[1] — I leave this for you that you may avoid that unsightly object an empty space where hearts are full.

       Yours faithfully
       Horatio Greenough
        Sculptor.

NOTES

Ogden Haggerty was a New York merchant and auctioneer. He is listed in city directories from 1832/33 to 1875/76. According to Margaret Fuller Ossoli, Haggerty was in Florence on 1 January 1850 (Ossoli to S. G. Ward, 8 January 1850, Papers of Samuel Gray and Anna Hazard Barker Ward, Houghton).
 Manuscript: Editor's collection.
1. Emanuel Leutze (1816–68), German-born American historical and portrait painter, who was in Dusseldorf for most of the period from 1841 to 1859, made a trip to the Alps and to Italy in 1849–50.

204.   To Joseph Green Cogswell
26 September 1850

Florence. Sept'r 26. 1850.

My Dear Mr Cogswell

I have received your letter enclosing that of Mr Belmanno[1] — and have immediately taken steps to secure what he wishes. In the meanwhile I write to inform him that I am busy for him —

A difficulty presents itself. Bartolini never made but one statue for the Duke of Devonshire which was a Bacchante lying prone, with her head raised a tambourine in her hand and a serpent twined around her arm[2] — This figure you will remark corresponds in some respects with that described by Mr Belmanno but it has occurred to me that at Chatsworth there may be a *Psyche abbandonata* in a somewhat similar position — However this may be I will send an outline of the only statue made by Bartolini for the Duke.

As regards the groupe of the 3 graces after Raffaelo[3] — I am almost certain that Goupil in Broadway can furnish Forster's print of it published in 42 or 43 and which is really a lovely print.[4]

Mrs Greenough gave birth to a daughter[5] about 15 days since and both she and her infant are doing well. I have now 3 children —

I confess to you that I look forward with anxiety to the future partly on account of the complications of European politics and partly from the fear that my being so long out of sight will put me equally out of mind with the public of America. My groupe is nearly done after the most tormenting delays for marble owing to contracts with the Emperor of Russia[6] — I have made a Venus which I am anxious to put into marble and I have also 2 or 3 bas reliefs which I intend to get done in the course of a few months.[7]

I have made all the studies for an equestrian Statue of Washington and hope when my groupe is seen to obtain an order for that work —

After being so long employed on works of a high order it is not possible for me to play the shopman and cut fancy work for furniture or cultivate the vogue of the day — I have chosen my path and if the state of the national taste does not afford me support I must wait and arm myself with courage for the consequences.

I am happy to learn that you are busy in congenial occupations and I am sure that wherever you are your influence tends to expand and elevate the tastes and to give a good direction to the rapid growth of that American mind which for good or for evil is destined to shape the future of civilization —

Begging to be kindly remembered to our common friends

> I am Dear Mr Cogswell
> Ever truly yours
> Horatio Greenough

NOTES

Manuscript: Mellen Chamberlain Autograph Collection, BPL. Previous publication: Nathalia Wright, ed., "Letters by Horatio Greenough in the Library," *Boston Public Library Quarterly* 11 (1959): 88.

1. Robert Balmanno was living in America at this time (see note to Letter 205).
2. Bartolini executed *La Baccante Giacente* about 1824 for William George Spencer, sixth duke of Devonshire. It is still at the family mansion, Chatsworth House, Derbyshire. See Mario Tinti, *Lorenzo Bartolini* (Rome, 1936), 1:74.
3. Raphael's painting is in the Musée Condé, Chantilly, France.
4. François Forster (1790–1872), Swiss engraver, made a famous print of Raphael's *Three Graces*. Goupil, Vibert, and Co. were printsellers and artists' colormen, located at 289 Broadway (*Doggett's New York City Directory, for 1849–50*).
5. Charlotte Greenough (1850–ca. 1919) married Hervoches du Quilliou and, in her later years, lived at Vevey, Switzerland. She had no children.
6. In 1845 Nicholas I engaged all the marble from the quarries of Serravezza for the construction of a church in St. Petersburg. Greenough did not get the second of the two blocks for *The Rescue* until 1849.
7. Greenough's statue *Venus Victrix* was not put in marble and was broken beyond repair while being transported to America in 1853. *Bacchante and Faun, The Genius of Italy*, and *The Genius of Poesy* apparently were not put into marble and have been destroyed. Photographs of the first two and possibly a sketch of the third are in the editor's collection.

205. To Robert Balmanno
29 October 1850

Florence. Oct'r 29th 1850.

My Dear Mr Belmanno

I enclose herewith the drawing of the statue executed by Bartolini for the Duke of Devonshire and which is now at Chatsworth. Our mutual friend Mr Cogswell will have communicated to you my misgivings respecting it. I have thought as the expence was small that you would rather that I would send it forward at all hazards rather than verify the matter by letter which would cost nearly as much in postage. This drawing is by Mr Nocchi[1] a young engraver of promise and costs you 5$ which you can remit at your convenience to my brother in law Mr Thos. B. Curtis of Boston.

What you say of the difficulty of procuring a drawing at Chatsworth does not surprize me. You are aware that the English idea of property is very exclusive and perhaps in regard to nothing more than in this matter of rarities and curiosities.

I am about to finish a colossal work for the Gov't which has almost exclusively occupied me for thirteen years past and shall probably come to America the ensuing year — I shall make bold to present my claim to your acquaintance and that of your gifted lady[2] and if in the mean while I can as resident here be of service to you or your friends, you will do me a real pleasure by commanding me.

Very respectfully
Your friend & Serv't
Horatio Greenough

NOTES

Robert Balmanno (b. 1780), Scottish writer, contributed articles to London periodicals and to the *Knickerbocker Magazine,* the *New York Evening Post,* and *Graham's Magazine* in the United States (Austin Allibone, *A Critical Dictionary of English Literature and British and American Authors* [Philadelphia, 1874]).

Manuscript: Mellen Chamberlain Autograph Collection, BPL. Previous publication: Nathalia Wright, ed., "Letters of Horatio Greenough in the Library," *Boston Public Library Quarterly* 11 (1959): 89.

1. Possibly Giorgio Battista Nocchi, dealer in pictures and prints (*Guida per la Città di Firenze e suoi Contorni* [Florence, 1852], p. 264).
2. Mrs. Mary Balmanno was the author of *Poems* (London, 1830) and *Pen and Pencil* (New York, 1858).

206.   To Charles Eliot Norton
November or December 1850

My Dear Mr Norton

Will you do us the favor to dine with us tomorrow at 5 P.M. You will meet Mr & Mrs Brown[1] of Baltimore and Mr Boott.[2]

As you might find some difficulty in coming to us I will call for you at ½ past four, if your engagements allow us this pleasure.

Yours truly
Hor Greenough

Tuesday Mor'g

Addressed: Monsieur Norton / Piazza Ste. M. Nouvelle

NOTES

Charles Eliot Norton (1827–1908), writer and educator, was in Florence during November and December 1850. Later, he edited the *North American Review* and helped found *The Nation.* His father, Andrews Norton, was professor of sacred literature at Harvard when Greenough was a student there.

Manuscript: Charles Eliot Norton Papers, Houghton.

1. Possibly George Brown (1787–1859), member of the banking firm of Alexander Brown & Sons and railroad promoter, and his wife.
2. Francis Boott (1813–85), amateur singer and composer, established residence in Florence with his infant daughter Elizabeth after the death of his wife in 1847. He was the brother of Frances Boott Greenough (see Francis Boott, *Recollections of Francis Boott for his grandson F. B. D.* [Boston, 1912]).

207. To the Prefect of Florence
9 January 1851

Il Sottoscritto Cittadino degli Stati Uniti d'America, Stabilito a Firenze, ossequiando rispettosamente il Sig[nor]e Prefetto di Firenze, gli fa noto che egli abita con sua famiglia la Villa detta Brichieri[1] a Bellosguardo.

1mo Che lo scopo suo principale nell'allontanarsi dalla citta, quello cioe di assicurare alla sua famiglia l'aria e l'esercizio salubre della passeggiata, gli viene frustrato da una folla quasi continua di persone, che giuocano con dischi di legno, detti Ruzzole, che pesano da una a tre libbre, la quale folla specialmente nei giorni festivi, rende il passo assai pericoloso.

2ndo Che queste persone sembrano credere un tale giuoco sulla strada maestra, un sacrosanto loro diritto e che chiunque si azzarda di voler passare di la, lo fa a proprio rischio.

3zo Che le potenza di questi projettitori e tale da andare a ferire gente non in vista dei giuocatori per via della scesa della strada e il serpeggiare di essa, ed in tale guisa due di casa sono stati colti ed hanno avuto la trista soddisfazione di sentire dai giuocatori che ne erano dolenti sinceramente.

3zo [sic] Che i cavalli del sottoscritto hanno piu volte avuto paura di queste ruzzole che gli sono passate tra le gambe ed in tale maniera messo a grave periglio quanti si trovavano in carrozza.

4to Che ogni volta che i bambini sono mandati fuori della casa, bisogna mandare un servitore di sopra e di sotto, per esplorare come farebbe una avanguardia in paese ostile.

5to Che una rappresentanza fatta al picchetto fuori della Porta S. Frediano non ha avuto altro resultato che la comparsa dei carabinieri una sola volta e la conseguente pace durante quella ora nella quale essi costa si trovavano —

6to Che l'uniforme di questi guardiani dell'ordine e visto da lontano dai giocatori ed impedisce effettualmente una sorpresa in flagrante.

Il sotto scritto dichiara pure che sua consorte ed egli pure per due volte sono stati interpellati da uomini in calzoni di brutto aspetto, i quali hanno domandato soccorso in denaro, perche come dicevano non volevano *fare del male* ed avevano gran bisogno. Il sottoscritto pacificamente disposto non ha saputo rispondere a tale minaccia, che con un corrispondente rifiuto e minaccia, e cosi si trova in stato di guerra con tale gente. Questi fatti hanno avuto luogo alle 24 ore e vicino alla Villa Nuti.[2]

7mo   Che la casa del sottoscritto e stata visitata da ladri i quali hanno portato via il pollame e diversi altri oggetti dalla rimessa — e che un rapporto fatto alla stazione fuori della Porta S. Frediano, non ha avuto resultato veruno.

In tale situazione, il sottoscritto che da venti e piu anni abita a Firenze, conformandosi alle leggi del paese, si trova nel caso di dovere a sacrifizio sloggiare onde cercare una abitazione piu propinqua a chi vuole una legge attiva e vigente[3] —

Il sottoscritto umilmente prega il Signo Prefetto, a scusare ad uno straniero che scrive in lingua non sua, tutto cio in questo rapporto che non sia conforme al rispetto che egli professa per il di lui grado.

Horatio Greenough
Console degli Stati Uniti a Porto S. Stefano[4]
Professore dell I. e R. Accademia di B. Arti

Firenze a di 9. Gennaio / 1851.
Piazza di Barbano al Canto di Via S. Caterina / e di Via S. Francesco Poverino.

TRANSLATION

The undersigned citizen of the United States, a resident of Florence, pays his respects to the Prefect of Florence and informs him that he lives with his family at the Villa Brichieri[1] in Bellosguardo.

1st   That his principal aim in withdrawing from the city was to assure his family the benefits of fresh air and the healthy exercise of walking, that this is frustrated by an almost continuous crowd of people who play with disks of wood called Ruzzole, that weigh from one to three pounds, which especially on feast days renders walking very dangerous.

2nd   That these persons seem to think such a game on the main street their sacred right and that anyone who dares to walk through it, does so at his own risk.

3rd   That the force of these projectiles is such as to injure persons not in sight of the game because of the steepness and the winding of the street and in such a manner two of the household have been hurt and have had the sad satisfaction of being told by the players that they were sincerely sorry.

3rd [sic]   That the horses of the undersigned have more than once been frightened by these ruzzole which passed between their legs and in such manner put in grave danger those who were in the carriage.

4th   That every time my children go outside the house it is necessary to send a servant before and after to look about as the advance guard of an army might do in hostile territory.

5th   That a report made to the sentry outside the Gate of San Frediano has had no results other than the appearance at one time of the carabinieri and the consequent peace during the hour in which they were there.

6th   That the uniforms of these guardians of order are spied from afar by the players and effectually prevent any surprise *in flagrante*.

The undersigned further declares that he and his wife have twice been accosted by men of bad aspect who, demanding money, said they did not want *to resort to violence* and were in great need. The undersigned being of peaceful disposition, did not know how to answer such a menace, but refused and menaced in turn, and thus has found himself in a state of war with such people. This occurred at midnight, near the the Villa Nuti.[2]

7th   That the house of the undersigned has been visited by thieves who carried away the chickens, as well as several other objects from the coach house — and that a report made to the guard outside the Gate of San Frediano has had no result.

In such a situation, the undersigned, who has lived in Florence for more than twenty years, conforming to the laws of the country, finds it necessary to move away, at a sacrifice, to find a place to live where the laws are more actively enforced[3] —

The undersigned humbly begs his honor the Prefect to excuse, in one who writes in a language not his own, anything in this report which has not conformed to the respect due his high degree.

Horatio Greenough
Consul of the United States of Porto S. Stefano[4]
Professor of the I[nstitute] and R[oyal] Academy of Fine Arts
Florence on 9 January / 1851

Piazza di Barbano on the Corner of Via S. Caterina / and of Via
S. Francesco Poverino.

NOTES

The prefect of Florence in 1851 was Cavaliere Donato Sanminiatelli (*Almanach
de Gotha* [1851]).
    Manuscript: Archivio del Stato, no. 323, file 59 (police records), Florence.
  1. The Greenoughs moved to the Villa Brichieri Colombi, which dates from the
     fifteenth century, in the fall of 1849.
  2. The Villa Lo Strozzino, on the hill of Bellosguardo, had been inherited from
     the Strozzi family by Digerini Nuti (Giulio Lensi Orlandi Cardini, *Le Ville
     di Firenze di la' d'Arno* [Florence, 1955], p. 247).
  3. There is no evidence that the Greenoughs moved before leaving Florence
     permanently in July 1851.
  4. In the summer of 1849, having had Austrian troops quartered in his stables,
     Greenough applied to the U.S. consul at Leghorn for a diplomatic post
     which would spare him such impositions. He was accordingly appointed
     vice-consul of Porta San Stefano, near Florence, though without duties.

208.   To Walter Savage Landor
28 March 1851

Florence, March 28th, 1851.

   . . . I cannot but think that such stolid impertinence as this calls for
justice at your hand.[1] I know no one else who unites the knowledge
and feeling necessary to judge them, with the vigor and mastery required for their execution. I pray you, sir, as you look upon that table,[2]
to reflect upon the size of the Grand Duchy, the aptitude of its
children for its nobler development of art, the numbers devoted to
its cultivation here, their pitiable poverty; and I am sure that you
will deal with the wrong according to its deserts. The classic scourge
of your Latin hexameters,[3] or the English whip bequeathed you by the
Dean,[4] either of these, or both, may do somewhat, as well in your
country as in mine, to check ostentatious barbarism; may show that
genius and sentiment can convert all stone to precious stone; while

the obscure diligence of years, uninformed by art, makes but a monument of laborious idleness.

. . . Perhaps Emerson is greedy in this way sometimes, but still "they be prave 'ords."[5] I am sure that the Greek statues, though they are not tormented by an ambition to say all, yet include all; and I remember having heard you remark, in my workroom, that their writers, too, were as profound in fixing the limits of their art.[6]

NOTES

Walter Savage Landor (1775–1864), English poet and prose writer, lived in Italy during 1815–35 and 1858–64; from 1821 to 1835, and during the latter period, he was in Florence.

Source (excerpts only): John Forster, *Walter Savage Landor* (Boston, 1869), pp. 472–73. The place and date are given by Forster.

1. According to Forster, this passage was prefaced by Greenough's reminding Landor of a conversation with Ralph Waldo Emerson, whom Greenough had introduced to Landor in Florence in the spring of 1833. The conversation had revolved around the unfortunate preference of Florentine rulers for highly ornamentive art, "all whose ornaments were the products of . . . Chinese industry and Turkish taste." Forster continues: "Mr. Greenough reminded Landor of a remark he had made upon their having with such gewgaws brushed the very beard of the sculptor of Moses, that it was 'as if a fellow in a laced coat should start up to claim attention where Caesar was and was speaking'; and what now would he say to the production that had been sent over from Florence to represent the birthplace of Buonarotti at the world's fair [the Exhibition of 1851, London], which was neither more nor less than a table in pietra dura that had cost a hundred thousand francesconi." Forster then quotes the passage from Greenough's letter.
2. The "table in pietra dura" mentioned by Forster (see n. 1). A circular mosaic table on a ground of lapis lazuli depicting Apollo surrounded by elaborate designs of flowers and leaves, it was the property of the Grand Duke of Tuscany (*Official Catalogue of the Great Exhibition of the Works of Industry of all Nations, 1851* [London, 1851], p. 320).
3. Greenough probably refers to Landor's poem "English Hexameters," printed in *Frazer's Magazine* 42 (1850): 62–63, in which he criticizes several English poets.
4. Jonathan Swift (1667–1745) was Dean of St. Patrick's Cathedral, Dublin, from 1713 to his death.
5. Forster indicates that this passage is from the last paragraph of Greenough's letter, in which Greenough "spoke of the fame which Emerson had justly won since the days in which they had met at Fiesole, and hinted at the only disadvantage under which the wealth of his genius placed him, of using often language so weighted with meaning as necessarily to express of any given thing more than he could by any possibility see in it." Forster then quotes the passage from Greenough's letter.

"They be prave 'ords" is from Shakespeare's *Henry V*, III, vi, 66.

6. Landor replied to this letter from Bath on 11 April 1851 (collection of David Richardson, Washington, D.C.), referring in a complimentary way to Greenough's *Washington,* saying he was avoiding the exposition at the Crystal Palace as though it were the plague, calling Greenough's remarks on Emerson admirable, and promising that Greenough's remarks on the table sent by Tuscany to the exposition would not be lost.

209.   To Hiram Powers
         3 May 1851

My Dear Powers

In the uncertainty whether Congress during the actual busy session can be brought to vote me money, I have concluded to part with the beautiful bust of J. Q. Adams.[1] I think the city of Boston or Harvard College would give a thousand dollars for it — I am prevented by my idea of what is proper and fair from offering it at other than the sum which I paid for it —

In this I may be wrong or right but I wish you might at length get the full value of your work and I offer it therefore to you, should you feel disposed to take it.

Very truly yours
Horatio Greenough

Sat'y Morn'g. / 3d. '51.

Addressed: Hiram Powers Esqr / Present.

NOTES

May was the only month in 1851 in which the third fell on a Saturday before Greenough left Florence.
    Manuscript: Editor's collection.
    1. Powers' bust is now in the Pennsylvania Academy of Fine Arts.

210. To William Cullen Bryant
7 May 1851

Florence May 7th 1851.

Dear Bryant

I am much obliged by the introduction of Mr Sedgwick,[1] whose conversation highly interested me. His family also have shown a sympathy for my artistic efforts, quite refreshing in these days of stern politics and superficial curiosity. I am about to ship to America the group you saw commenced in my studio — Its completion has been provokingly delayed. I hope that you will see in this work proof that I have kept my allegiance to [the] public since the disappointment produced by my first large work — and I now feel a certain complacency that in these years of silent and humble study, I have never been shaken from my theory that the public and the whole public is the judge of all works of art of this class; without appeal unless to a future public.

There is a right however which I believe a sacred one and which may be interfered with by a strong disapproval on the part of the present generation. I mean the right to subsist and go before a future public. You whose winged words defy the present and are sure of a future audience can scarce think how bitter is a wanton mutilation of our works to us. The thinkers of former times when their heresies were burned by the hangman smiled inwardly because copies of their works were saved — Galileo forced to recant added doggedly "eppur si muove!"[2] But once we poor fellows are broken on the wheel of practical criticism which attacks not by demonstration nor by silence nor by paragraphs but by stones or stabs we are in part annihilated. It is not fair to us to deface our works, nor is it just to those who are to come after us. Giotto was all the more esteemed that the works of Cimabue had been safely kept — they were the measure of his stride. Perugino gives lustre to Raffaello nor should it be forgotten that philosophic criticism finds in each development of art qualities peculiar to itself and valuable as distinct articulations of the human soul. As the Savage shines with certain qualities that may well excite the emulation of polytechnic culture, so the ripe fruit of art has not attained its fullness without losing a somewhat of poetry and hope and promise that was fragrant in the blossom.

I have an idea of a monument which I wish to engage your thoughts upon. I would have you turn it over in your mind that I may get your notion of it when we meet in August or July. I wish to erect a monument which shall record on the same spot — The treason of Arnold — the capture and death of Andre and the fate of Capt'n N. Hale. I believe this idea may take a form exceedingly significant of our system highly expressive of our democratic ethics — & a caution to egotistical intrigue. Arnold's figure should be represented veiled down to the waist — Under the statues of Andre and of Hale would be written their last words[3] while the [*illegible*] work would consist of the arrest of the British Adj Genl. by the 3 rangers —

If when I shall have mastered this conception it shall seem to yourself to Paulding and Cooper to be worth the while I shall go straight to the people for the means to do it and lecture and stump it, till I get the wherewithal.

I beg in the meanwhile that you will ponder upon the consequences to our struggle if Andre had not been caught or had bribed those 3 men and I believe you will join me in thinking that whatever imperfections they may have had, it was highly necessary that they should be no *worse* than they *were.*

Asking indulgence for this invasion of your leisure believe me Dear Bryant

Very sincerely yours
Hor Greenough

Addressed: William C. Bryant Esqr / New York / Care of Mess Baring Brothers & Co / Bankers / London / Forwd. by H. Greenough / for Steamer

NOTES

William Cullen Bryant (1794–1878), the poet, was also editor and part owner of the *New York Evening Post.*
    Manuscript: Bryant-Godwin Collection, NYPL.
    1. Theodore Sedgwick (1811–59), New York author, lawyer, and diplomat, traveled in several European countries, including Italy. He was a nephew of Catherine Maria Sedgwick (Benjamin Dwight, *The History of the*

> *Descendants of John Dwight of Dedham, Mass.* [New York, 1874], 2:744–45).
>
> 2. At the end of his forced recantation of the Copernican theory, Galileo is reputed to have whispered, "E pur si muove" ("Nevertheless, it does move").
>
> 3. André's last words were, "It will be but a momentary pang." Hale's were the famous "I only regret that I have but one life to lose for my country."

211. To the editor of the *Boston Daily Evening Transcript* [3?] November 1851

Mr. Editor:

The sympathy with Hungarian patriotism pales and dwindles. Kossuth,[1] whose apotheosis had been proposed while he was a prisoner, is now to be kicked out of the borders of civilization. A letter from somebody's correspondent in Marseilles, without the name of a man subscribed, attacks this fallen hero, and words which *may be* but hireling slander, circulate and are backed by editorial disparagement of him whom we had taken under our protection.[2] Sir, let us not do things by halves. Let us send a deputation to General Gorgey and Haynau,[3] and invite them to our shores. The former, who did so much for law and order by leading his trusting troops into the Tartar trap, now hides his head in a suburban villa at Graetz.[4] The latter, red to the skin with the blood of the wives and children of rebels, is kicked for daring to write his glorious name in democratic London. These, sir, are the real demigods of this century. Let us give a lesson to the *ignorant present* by showing Europe that, by doing for these men, we know where to find merit and how to reward it.

Yours truly,

H. G.

NOTES

Greenough and his family arrived in Boston from Europe on 17 October 1851. The letter is dated on the basis of internal evidence (see n. 2, below) and on the basis of its date of publication.

Source: *Boston Daily Evening Transcript,* 4 November 1851, p. 2.

1. Major Louis Kossuth (1802–94), one of the principal figures of the Hungarian uprising of 1848, fled after the Austrian victory to Turkey. In September 1851 he embarked on the U.S. man-of-war *Mississippi* for America, but interrupted his voyage with a three-week visit in England in October and November.
2. Presumably Greenough refers to an article in the *Transcript* for 3 November 1851, "Kossuth and the *Mississippi*." It reprinted from the *Newark Daily Advertiser* a letter from a former U.S. congressman who reported that Kossuth had expressed offensive revolutionary sentiments and had refused to cooperate with American officials in Marseilles.
3. Arthur Görgey (1818–1916), Hungarian military leader under Kossuth, capitulated to the Russians.
   Julius Jakob Haynau, Baron von Haynau (1786–1853), Austrian general, ordered the execution of the vanquished Hungarian chiefs.
4. Or Grätz, then in Poland.

212.   To William Cullen Bryant
   4 November 1851

Boston Nov'r 4th 1851.

Wm C. Bryant Esqr
Dear Sir

I had hoped to have seen you in person ere this — but my ties here are so many and so strong that some days, must yet elapse before I leave this neighbourhood.

The death of my dear friend & early patron Mr Cooper[1] has afflicted me with the greater grief, as I had promised myself so soon to look once more into that blue eye where I never saw ought less than goodness and nobleness. I propose to erect a monument to him — to consist of a seated portrait of himself, the base to be flanked by 2 figures which I think will recall his greatest triumphs as a writer of fiction — Leather Stocking & Long Tom Coffin — This will be a monument for a colossal niche either in a façade or in the court of some literary institution — I do not wish to interfere with any other monument which his friends may erect, and if they do it in New York, I shall try to place mine in Philadelphia or Baltimore — I intend also to commence almost immediately a colossal equestrian Statue of Andrew Jackson, and wish you would let the matter occupy your thoughts a

little, with reference to the adjuncts, which I desire should be com-
memorative of his military civil and private career. I propose to collect
25 cents a head from those [who] are able and willing to spare it for
this object and I ask if there be any means of doing this without opening the door to imposture and thieving. I propose to be accountable
to a committee for the outlay on the work.[2]

I thank God from the bottom of my heart that I have once more
put foot on my own, my native soil and I hope though now arrived
to the "mezzo del cammin di nostra vita"[3] to be of some use here
both in illustrative art and in structure for here I mean now to stay.
Begging that you will present me kindly to Mrs Bryant I remain Dear
Sir Yours faithfully

> H Greenough
> Sculptor.

Addressed: Wm C Bryant Esqr / Editor of the Evening Post / New-
York.

NOTES

Manuscript: Collection of American Literature, Beinecke.
1. On 14 September 1851.
2. Nothing further came of the Jackson project.
3. Dante, *Inferno*, I, 1.

213. To the editor of the *Boston Daily Evening Transcript* [4?] November 1851

Mr. Editor:

In the New York Herald of Nov 3d, I find, under the head of "Our
Marseilles Correspondence," a long account of Kossuth's alleged mis-
behavior at Spezzia and afterwards at Marseilles. We are told, sir,
that this man and his hangers-on have forced Commodore Morgan[1]
to order away the Mississippi from the Gulf of Spezzia, on account
of their insubordination and exciting speeches. Why was not Kossuth

set on shore? Does "our correspondent" not know that Spezzia is in the kingdom of Sardinia, and that thousands of Austrian rebels are at this moment protected by that Government, nay pensioned from Turin? If, however, the Hungarian patriots were demagogues at Spezzia, they had become somewhat worse at Marseilles. Hear "our correspondent:"

"I have been told by a gentleman, who was personally acquainted with Capt Long,[2] that all these Hungarian heroes (with the exception of two or three, who behaved themselves like gentlemen) gave him great trouble. They complain of their accommodations, find fault with their food, and, last not least, do all in their power to create disturbance on board of the man of war."

Now, sir, I am not intimate with Capt Long, though I can claim the honor of his acquaintance, and I much doubt, if he would suffer in any harbor the presence of any heroes whatever, who were doing all in their power to create disturbance on board of the man-of-war under his orders. But our correspondent evidently has been probing pretty deeply for reliable information. Hear him once more: "Kossuth is surrounded by spies, who are paid by the Austrian Government. I am told by good authority that there is a Jew with his wife and seven children who are with him in this capacity." One of these seven is doubtless an *enfant terrible.* Really, this is "piling it up rather too mountainous."

That Austria pays spies is no secret; but she knows how to choose them and correspondents also. The haughty house[3] that, after centuries of domination, was forced by the arm and the skill of Kossuth, to break down the dyke that held back the greedy muscovite — that house that perjured itself in Tuscany, butchered in Brescia, cannonaded Prague, and made the fusillade familiar to every denizen of the Vienna Bastions — that house, sir, will not spare gold to blacken the man whose boast it is and ever will be that he brought it to the brink of destruction — nay, unless I read the symptoms amiss, yet further than the brink.

Whither are we allowing ourselves to be cajoled or hurried, or deceived? Cast your eye back, sir; read the appreciations of Austrian policy and Austrian tyranny that have dropped, like rain from the press of England and America, since 1820 — not incoherent and puerile tattle of "our correspondents," but sober reasonings and historical verdicts, by the first minds and best hearts of Britain and

America. Are we now to turn our backs on the foe of Austria, and this after taking him under our guns and our flag, because a paper, infamous from the day it first polluted this land with its hireling venom, takes up the yelp, of which the bull-dog Times[4] barks the key note, and shall we do this, without asking if "our correspondent" be a man or a woman — an American or a stranger, a protestant or one who confesses to a Romish priest?

H. G.

NOTES

Source: *Boston Daily Evening Transcript,* 5 November 1851, p. 2.
1. Charles W. Morgan, commander of the U.S. squadron in the Mediterranean.
2. John C. Long was captain of the *Mississippi.*
3. Of Hapsburg.
4. The *New York Daily Times* for 3 November 1851 contained a violent attack on Kossuth in an article headlined "Kossuth. Letter from an American Attache. Alleged Misconduct of Kossuth and his Suite." The paper also ran an editorial entitled "Kossuth Again," regretting the tone of the article and defending Kossuth.

214. To Rufus Wilmot Griswold
19 November 1851

Wednesday. 19th Nov — 1851.
Washington D C.

Rev. Rufus. W. Griswold. / New-York.
Dear Sir

Instead of writing you I should have today left this in order to meet the committe tomorrow evening, but that I am detained by business commenced at the Treasury Dep't and not yet finished.[1]

It has occurred to me that your committe may wish before taking other steps about the Monument, to get rid of any embarrassing debts that may annoy the family of Mr Cooper. If so and you see no impropriety in my so doing, I would wish to subscribe $50 in the name of "A friend to the family" for that object.

I have seen the operations of Mr Mills[2] in bronze and have no doubt, after what I have there seen that your committe may decide upon that material without danger, and without going out of the country for workmen.

I notice in the Nat'l Intellig'er an article recommending this city as the proper site of a monument to Mr Cooper.[3] I think Sir that there is an insuperable objection to Washington as the site of any monument of which the *preservation* is important. There is neither respect for such objects as public property — nor interest in them as works of art.

The Mannekin-Pis of Brussells[4] which I take to be the lowest example of a European monument has more care and more efficient care taken of it than all the works at Washington on which so much money has been expended. I make no complaint of any one — I know not who is to blame — I suspect that this is an example of duties which are said to be every bodies' business.

I find the Capitol with its pictures & its statuary under the safe keeping of an Irishman one Easby,[5] whom I should not trust for one hour in the *presence* of any work of art without having him watched — I speak only in reference to his total ignorance, which in matters relating to art, is Vandalism.

Begging Dear Sir that this letter may remain a confidential communication to yourself and through you to the committee I am

Yours faithfully
Horatio Greenough

Addressed: Recommended to Mr Stetson's[6] care / Rev. Rufus. W. Griswold. / Sec'y of the Committee of the friends / of Mr Fenimore Cooper / Astor House. / New-York —

NOTES

Rufus Wilmot Griswold (1815–57) was an author, editor, and minister. He was an admirer but not a very close friend of Cooper's. A committee to arrange for a monument to Cooper held its first meeting on 25 September 1851. Griswold was made secretary of the Cooper Monument Association, constituted on 25 March 1852. See *Memorial of James Fenimore Cooper* (New York, 1852).

   Manuscript: Griswold Manuscripts, BPL. Previous publication: Nathalia Wright, ed., "Letters of Horatio Greenough in the Library," *Boston Public Library Quarterly* 11 (1959): 89–90.

   1. Greenough went to Washington at this time to investigate the government's

delay in paying the remaining sum for the removal of the *Washington* and the last installment on *The Rescue.*

2. Clark Mills (1810–83), self-taught sculptor, cast in bronze his statue of Andrew Jackson for Lafayette Square in Washington in 1852. At that time it was the largest work to be put in bronze in America.

3. "Monument to Cooper, the Novelist," *Washington Daily National Intelligencer,* 17 November 1851. The suggestion that it be erected in Washington was made by Judge W. A. Duer.

4. Executed by François Desquesnoy and erected in 1819.

5. William Easby, formerly a ship contractor, became superintendent of public buildings on 12 March 1851 (*The Washington Directory and National Register, for 1846*).

6. Charles Augustus Stetson (1810–88) was proprietor of the Astor House.

215. To the editors of the *Washington Daily National Intelligencer*
13 December 1851

Gentlemen:

I remark in the Home Journal of to-day a Profile of Washington from one by Samuel Folwell,[1] of Philadelphia, which was commended by Mr. Watson, in the Annals of New York, as an "off-hand, happy hit."[2] It is interesting, as every thing of the kind relating to Washington must be, and I am grateful for a sight of it.

This profile has that unmistakable type which no sign-painter ever yet missed. As a correct manuscript of the man, a comparison with the head by Houdon, wrought geometrically from a plaster mask, will reduce its pretensions to zero. The length from the frontal sinus to the tip of the nose is preposterous. The marking of the eyelash gives equal proof of "off-hand" handiwork. The mouth is feeble; it wants that firm reserve which John Adams is said wittily to have envied.

Washington's face was scarce all lost in any limner's hands. It held too much for any "off-hand" grasp. Compare the impressions of your own friends with regard to any portrait of the day, and you may measure the value of an individual *ipse dixit* in these matters.

The correspondent "L.," who seems to have given attention to the portraits of Washington, and who deals with them summarily, speaks of the statue by Chantry as a colossal one in "classic drapery." Chantry's statue is not colossal; its dress is as classical as that worn by Dr. Johnson every day; no more so. It is the same! L. speaks also of the statue by Greenough, as "seated like the Jupiter Tonans[3] of Phidias." The Jupiter of Phidias held a sceptre in his right hand, a winged victory in his left, and was not Tonans. Greenough's statue is seated as the Giuliano of Buonarotti is seated, as the Copernicus of Thorwaldsen, the Maximilian of Rauch, the Rousseau of Pradier, the Galileo of Demi are seated,[4] as people must be seated who do not loll. The colossal granite figures of Egypt are the earliest types of this posture, and their authors probably regarded it not as a stretch of invention. This fling is "off-hand," like the profile it accompanies. Like the profile, it shows more readiness than preparation.

If the treatment of a high and noble subject in art, as in letters, contain proof that its author has made a careful and conscientious study of the analogous works of his predecessors, shall this be made a matter of reproach? If Bancroft remind us of the models of Greece in writing the history of our land, has he sinned? Was not Dante, the most original of modern poets, so imbued with classic lore as to let slip the title of Jove applied to the Saviour?[5] Did Milton cull on British ground the flowers that perfume the stern theology of his epic? There is a class of critics which would fain effect in the world of art and of letters what Gen. Cass (nobly, I think) recommended in our relations with Austria — "cut the string."[6] What makes this intolerance of example ludicrous is the fact that we build at this moment in all the styles elsewhere invented, and stick up our shirt-collars because that arrangement is becoming to some scrofulous prince of the blood royal.

I am, sir, respectfully yours,

H. Greenough, Sculptor.

Washington, Dec. 13, 1851.

NOTES

Source: *Washington Daily National Intelligencer*, 19 December 1851, p. 2.
1. Samuel Folwell (*ca.* 1765–1813), miniaturist, silhouettist, and engraver, did a silhouette of Washington, supposedly from life, which is his chief claim to fame; it is now in the New-York Historical Society.
2. John Fanning Watson, *Annals and Occurrences of New York City and State in the Olden Time* (Philadelphia, 1846), p. 334, declared that Folwell's profile "was a happy hit."

3. "Thundering."
4. Michelangelo's statue is in the new sacristy of the church of S. Lorenzo, Florence; Thorvaldsen's is in Warsaw; Rauch's is in the Max-Joseph Platz, Munich; Pradier's is on Rousseau Island, Geneva; and Demi's is in the University of Pisa.
5. *Purgatorio* 6. 118–20.
6. On 24 December 1849, Lewis Cass presented resolutions to the Senate urging the suspension of diplomatic relations with Austria as a means of encouraging the Hungarian revolution (W. L. G. Smith, *The Life and Times of Lewis Cass* [New York, 1856], pp. 639–42).

216. To William Cullen Bryant
27 December 1851

Washington D.C. Dec. 27th [1851]

W. C. Bryant Esqr
Dear Sir —

I have since my arrival in this city prepared a paper on Structure & Ornament[1] — in which I seek to show — 1st that we have many dialects in our buildings, but no language — 2nd that we have developed in our ships, our carriages and engines a new style. 3d that this style, which I call the Yankee Doric, is strictly in harmony with the great primal law of God's own structures, and is in these partial exhibitions of it, as near perfection, as our knowledge is to pure science — 4th that it is high time to rouse the country to introduce in structures of a civil character, the sound logical doctrine embodied in the engine; and thus by demonstrating practically its beauty as well as utility, to check the influx of foreign & *hostile* aesthetics — Can you and Mr Godwin[2] spare time to hear me read this paper and give me your suggestions? One hour will suffice — I pray you to address an answer[3] to the Astor house — "to be kept till called for" —

Very faithfully yours
H. Greenough
Sculptor.

NOTES

Manuscript: Editor's collection.

1. Greenough evidently refers to his pamphlet *Æsthetics at Washington,* published in Washington in 1851, presumably in December, by John T. Towers. Apparently, in this letter he is asking for suggestions about the architectural theory expressed in the pamphlet, not about the pamphlet itself.

2. Parke Godwin (1816–1904), editor and author, was employed by Bryant on the *New York Evening Post* in 1836 and remained with the paper for forty-five years.

3. Apparently Bryant replied to this letter on 30 December 1851 (Carnegie Book Shop Catalogue, no. 157, March 1851).

217.   To Ralph Waldo Emerson
28 December 1851

Washington D.C. Dec. 28th '51

R. W. Emerson Esqr

My Dear Sir —

I ask permission to occupy your attention for a moment — I am unwilling to invade your leisure — But I find the men who are capable of such investigation as I require, are so busy in holding each other's hands and watching each other's eyes, that I can't effect a lodgment of my whim-wham —

I broached a theory 10 years since (1843) in the Democratic Review[1] — a theory of structure — My occupations since that time have prevented my doing more than to confirm myself in that theory and to ripen it. I find this country in sad want of an application, practical, immediate and thorough-going of that theory — I find also in the ships — the carriages and engines, a partial illustration of the doctrine and a *glorious* foretaste of what structure can be in this country in 10 years' time — if men of science and speech will come to the rescue of a population struggling amid gewgaws and extravagance after a *beauty* which will never obey other than the call of genius — The men are not wanting — if they can be made to see the soundness of the basis.

Here is my theory of structure. A scientific arrangement of spaces

and forms to functions and to site — An emphasis of features proportioned to their *gradated* importance in function — Colour and ornament to be decided and arranged and varied by strictly organic laws
— having a distinct reason for each decision — The entire and immediate banishment of all make-shift and make believe —

Now I wish you to hear me read what I have prepared on this
subject and I beg you in the interim to reflect that this godlike human
body has no ornament for the same reason that men do not gild gold
— That the painted flowers are tinted to enable them to take their
respective doses of sunlight, and that even the mottled and pearly
shells are stained for the myriads of the deep — not to charm the idle
eye as they are here & there are tossed in ruin on the shore.

This theory is too lovely not to be hated by those who are not loving and strong — It is a true theory — and will do for all structure
from a bedstead to a cathedral what the Doric law did for the Parthenon — It will produce harmony — for all machines have a family
likeness & are blood relations — It will not be monotonous for the
wants on which it will wait are varied. It will be expressive — for a
guillotine and a rocking chair both speak English — It will be as much
more beautiful, than what we now possess as a naked Apollo is more
beautiful than a tattooed and feathered and blanketed savage —

I wish to strike a blow for this style now because the aesthetical
world abhors a vacuum, and ours is fast sucking in hostile elements. I
mean the excremental corruptions of foreign and hostile systems. —
Pray let me know if I can find you at Concord when I come to Boston.

Will you favor me with a few words addressed to care of Henry
Greenough Cambridge Mass — I had a letter from Landor[2] not long
since but missed seeing him in London by a strange chance — I found
your "representative men"[3] in the hands of a *dame* du Palais at Vienna
in '48 and have learned that she has been exiled — having made herself politically obnoxious —

> Very respectfully yours
> H Greenough.
> Sculptor.

Addressed: R. W. Emerson Esqr / Care of Geo. B. Emerson Esq.[4] /
Boston. Mass.

NOTES

Ralph Waldo Emerson (1803–82) first met Greenough in Florence in 1833. As a result of their association, Emerson apparently incorporated Greenough's functional concept into his own theory of architecture.

Emerson replied to this letter on 7 January 1852. He expressed pleasure at hearing from Greenough, agreed with his architectural theory, and invited him to come to Concord (Nathalia Wright, ed., "Ralph Waldo Emerson and Horatio Greenough," *Harvard Library Bulletin* 12 [1958]: 100–101).

Manuscript: Emerson Family Papers, Houghton. Previous publication: Wright, "Ralph Waldo Emerson and Horatio Greenough," pp. 98–100.

1. "American Architecture," *United States Magazine and Democratic Review* 13 (1843): 206–10.
2. Possibly that of 11 April 1851 (see Letter 208, n. 4).
3. Emerson's *Representative Men* (1850). Greenough read it in Switzerland in the summer of 1851 and commented to his brother: "There is a deal of talent in it. It is both ambitious and captivating; but I cannot entirely accept it" (*Letters,* p. 236).
4. George Barrell Emerson (1797–1881) was principal of the academy at Lancaster, Massachusetts, when Greenough attended.

218. To William Cullen Bryant
5 February 1852

Cambridge. Mass. Feb'y. 5th '52.

Dear Mr Bryant

When I left you in the hope of soon joining you on the Brooklyn side, I hastened to apologize to a friend for not dining with him on Sunday as I had engaged — This was strictly necessary, because I had begged off once before — I did not find him and was forced therefore to remain and meet the bill when due. I regretted this much, because I had hoped to speak at length on the Cooper monument and had promised myself to hear at least a part of the "Apple Tree"[1] from your own lips.

I had a letter from Mrs G the next day which brought me hither in hot haste. There was *entre nous* an appearance of much danger to all that we possess, from the embarrassment of J. Quincy Ju'r[2] who has held our prop'y in trust — The danger seems now quite averted and I am happy to say, leaves the character of the trustee in a fair light.

I here fell in with the Ja[nuar]y thaw and took a real Yankee cold — one of those colds that make the marrow of your bones ache and burn — I have starved in bed for a week.

I have concocted a plan for the Cooper Monument — It is intended to occupy the centre of one of your noble squares — (University³ for instance). It is an oblong simple building lighted from above. It will be raised on 3 high steps running quite around it, at the corners of these steps will stand 4 characteristic creations of Cooper's. The frieze (exterior) will be carved with illustrations of the poetry of the forest and the flood and together with the 4 statues will take possession of the spectator as he approaches and announce the character and purposes of the building — On entering will be seen at the further extremity the colossal portrait of Cooper raised on a shaft of polished granite — The walls will be adorned with compositions from his works — The ceilings of blue with stars — The pavement of reticulated iron hexagons, defying the chewing race for 24 hours and movable for cleanliness —

I propose that, with the exception of the actual imitative art of the highest class, this building contain no unmeaning flourish or foliage or girigogoli⁴ whatever & I pretend that *the art* can only be heard with such a silence for its basis — I am free to admit that this structure as I propose to carry it out, will cost double as much as one 2ce as large, covered all over with 3rd rate carving and fretted into lace by the ignorant repetition of petty detail — I am free to own that they who see only with their eyes will prefer a shawl shop or a jeweller's window to all that I can, or am willing to, effect in this monument — I am willing notwithstanding to attempt the model in detail of the whole monument — because filled as I am with a sense of Cooper's genius and of his action upon the soul of this people; and upon the world as holding up the abstract type of the *American ideal man* I count fearlessly upon that sense to get utterance in the stone — Thoughts mould stone, even as earth quakes knead the rocks and when the stone gets the upper hand it is because the *faith* was wanting.

I have preferred a building to a monument in the open air for several reasons — 1st Because the size of your larger squares would require an enormous mass; while a small square would be unworthy the subject — perhaps — 2d because 4 months of our year make an out of door statue look painfully exposed unless of a certain character — 3d I feel that the painters have a just claim to compete with us of the chisel in this truly American task — while some of its requirements can only be fully met by them.

Now my Dear Mr Bryant, remember that of all men poets and artists least *need* monuments — *We* need those monuments. They are the occasions which mark our progress in high culture — I declare solemnly that I find in N. York, the pictorial power capable of making the monument I propose a bright and enduring *national gem* — But it cannot be done either quick or cheaply — It may be done in 4 or 5 years but it will require immense study to do it faithfully. I believe that some of the ablest landskape painters could be induced [to] join with the historical artists in creating 2 or 3 illustrations.

I am very anxious to know how Mr Cooper's family is now situated as regards their means — and whether the possession of the paternal estate is secured to them. Begging you to remember me respectfully to Mrs Bryant I am Dear Sir

Yours very faithfully
Horatio Greenough

NOTES

Manuscript: Bryant-Godwin Collection, NYPL.
1. "The Planting of the Apple-Tree" was written in 1849 and first published in the *Atlantic Monthly* 13 (1864): 17–18.
2. Josiah Quincy, Jr., who succeeded his father as trustee of Louisa G. Greenough's estate, had been relieved of his position as treasurer of the Vermont Central Railroad in November 1851 because he had used bonds of the company for his private debts, though it was alleged that these debts were incurred for the company's benefit (*Boston Daily Evening Transcript,* 22 March 1852).
3. Presumably Greenough means Washington Square. The street bounding it on the east was formerly called University Place, from the location of New York University nearby.
4. "Scrawls," "unintelligible abbreviations."

219. To Henry Wadsworth Longfellow
21 February 1852

My Dear Sir

Will you do me the favor to come and pass an hour or two with me this evening? I am to have the company of Mr Story and my brother — also of Mr Pierce if I can persuade him[1] — We shall eat oysters at 8. I was delighted with L Bridgman's gratitude to you for your poem.[2] It was worth two laurel crowns such as are to be had in the market —

Yours very respectfully
Horatio Greenough

Saturday morning

NOTES

Henry Wadsworth Longfellow (1807–82) met Greenough shortly after he arrived home in the fall of 1851.

The date appears on the last line of the manuscript in Longfellow's hand.

Manuscript: Longfellow Correspondence, Houghton.

1. William Wetmore Story (1819–95) was a lawyer, sculptor, and writer. Presumably the brother to whom Greenough refers was Henry. The third member of the proposed company was probably Benjamin Peirce (1809–80), mathematician and astronomer, who was librarian of Harvard from 1826 to his death.

2. Laura Dewey Bridgman (1829–89), a native of Hanover, New Hampshire, was made deaf and blind by scarlet fever at the age of two. She learned to read and write at the Perkins Institute in Boston. Longfellow's diary for 14 February 1852 quotes a letter from her in which she said of his Evangeline, "I should love to meet her with my soul in heaven when I die on earth" (Samuel Longfellow, ed., *Life of Henry Wadsworth Longfellow* [Boston, 1886], 2:217).

220.   To Richard Henry Dana
         23 February 1852

Boston, 23d February, 1852

My dear Sir,

I have several times sat for an hour in the same room where Mr.
Brackett's group of the "Wrecked Mother and Child"¹ is exhibited,
and always with a new sense of the power which has made that block
of stone the vehicle of so many sad and tender thoughts, expressed
in the language of beauty.

I have admired the art by which he so placed the head, that a
glance tells us her sufferings are passed, and so swept every limb and
tress, that we see the surge has lodge her there, and there left her.

To have told all [this] at the first glance even to the indifferent
eye, is a triumph. The action of her left arm, or rather, its *record* of
her last act, is most happy — that babe has been hugged to her heart,
and borne out of harm's way to the last moment of consciousness, and
there is visible in the posture of her limbs, the decency and dignity of
womanhood.

I was a little puzzled at the eagerness of many spectators to get so
near this work that it was impossible for them to see it, and I venture
to suggest to those who wish to enjoy it, that they s[i]t quietly on the
several sides of the room, and even there survey it with half closed
eyes. The work is of marble — it is vain that you will seek aught else
by crowding upon it. By remaining at a proper distance, you will find
that it is no longer marble, but poetry. To hope to enjoy a higher
illusion by scrutiny, is like going to Milton to enjoy the *blue* of the
Blue Hills.²

I was somewhat pained by the reflection that this work — wrought
with all the fervor and self-sacrifice of an earnest mind — was almost
overlooked in the hurry of busy life, amid the crowd of competitors
for the spare time of the public; but I took comfort from the remembrance that works of this class must be before the world for a season,
before they are fully seen and valued. I felt sure that others, too, must
feel toward the author of it as I felt, and that something might be
effected to secure it a permanent place in one of our public buildings.

As the work of one who has studied here *at home,* I must think this group worthy of an enduring position somewhere. I cannot but feel also that the artist has a claim on his fellow citizens for the means to go on in the path he has chosen, and for which he seems so well fitted.

If any one will read the gratulatory and exulting notices with which the press and the leading men of the country have from time to time cheered the efforts of American artists, he must feel that such stimuli are as the sound of a trumpet to a youth conscious of artistic power, and I think that when at the public call he starts thus *full grown* to the race, he should have fair play.

I can only say that if a subscription is organized to purchase this work for some public institution, I shall be happy to contribute my mite for the object.

I am, dear sir, your obed't serv't,

Horatio Greenough.

Richard H. Dana, Esq.

NOTES

Source: *Boston Daily Advertiser,* 25 February 1852. Also published in the *Boston Daily Evening Transcript,* 27 February 1852; *New York Evening Post,* 27 March 1852; *Home Journal,* 3 April 1852; *Catalogue of the Twenty-Fifth Exhibition of Paintings and Statuary at the Athenaeum Gallery* (Boston, 1852), p. 15.
1. *The Shipwrecked Mother and Child,* by Edward Augustus Brackett (1818–1908), is now at the Worcester (Massachusetts) Art Museum.
2. The Blue Hills are in the township of Milton, about seven miles south of Boston.

221. To Charles Sumner
30 March 1852

New York. March 30th 1852.

My Dear Sumner

I think I mentioned to you that the Sec'y of the Navy assured me at the opening of the session that orders had been sent to Com Morgan to ship my group home. I waited 6 weeks at Washington in expectation of it and then had it *whispered* to me that the ship was not coming.[1] I came away.

I wish to obtain the balance due on this work[2] — I must think it fair that I receive it. I am debt in Florence — and the mishap which has befallen Mr Quincy who was our trustee though it did not occasion we hope any ultimate loss has pinched us for the moment.

I know very well that there is no one officially cognizant of this matter — could you not see Mr Appleton and Mr Davis[3] and ask if I can be helped.

I count upon your regard to receive with pleasure the news I am nearly ready to begin a colossal equestrian Statue for Union square here.[4] I beg you not to mention it yet.

You will remark that Lola Montez inspects our schools.[5] Ou diable tant *d inspection* va t'elle se nicher?[6]

> Yours faithfully
> Horatio Greenough

Hon Chas Sumner U S Senate. / N 98 Chambers St.

NOTES

Manuscript: Editor's collection.
1. The Secretary of the Navy at this time was John Pendleton Kennedy. Orders were sent Morgan in May and October 1851 instructing him to ship Greenough's group *The Rescue,* but he received them too late to obey until the spring of 1852, at which time it was discovered that the cases were too large to be taken on his vessel.
2. The final sum of $3500 owed Greenough by the government for *The Rescue* was paid in 1853, after his death, to his estate.
3. William Appleton (1786–1862), Boston merchant, and George Thomas Davis (1810–77), Boston lawyer, were both members of Congress.
4. Greenough and Henry Kirke Brown were to execute an esquestrian statue of Washington for this location (see Letter 229).
5. Lola Montez was the stage name of Marie Dolores Eliza Rosanna Gilbert (1818–61), Irish adventuress and dancer who, as the mistress of Louis I of Bavaria, virtually ruled that country until the Revolution of 1848. In the course of a tour of the United States she visited three schools in Boston, but disapproval based on her questionable reputation was expressed in the *Boston Daily Evening Transcript* for 27 March 1852, and a brief controversy about the matter followed.
6. "Where the devil will so much inspection wind up?"

222. To ?
Between March and September 1852

My Dear Sir
    I was most occupied during the morning in arranging matters for an attempt at a colossal equestrian statue of Washington for this city[1] — I learned from Mr Stiles[2] that you had been to look for me and got unto an omnibus to come to you at Mr Bellows';[3] but when I had reached Canal street I found that I could barely speak with you; being engaged at 7. I will make an effort to see you this evening between 10 & 11 P.M. If I fail I will try again in the morning.

Very faithfully yours
Hor Greenough

Friday Ev'g.

NOTES

The dating of this letter and the next three is based upon internal evidence and upon the fact that Greenough was in New York City most of the time from March to September 1852.
    Manuscript: Editor's collection.
    1. See Letter 229.
    2. Probably William Henry Stiles (1808–65), who was a member of Congress in 1843–45 and chargé d'affaires to Austria in 1845–48, at which time Greenough apparently met him.
    3. Possibly Henry Whitney Bellows (1814–82), minister of the First Unitarian Church of New York from 1839 to his death, and an active participant in numerous civic enterprises during this time.

223.   To Charles Gould
Between March and September 1852

Chas Gould Esqr
Dear Sir
I received your kind invitation to dine with you today from Mr Brown[1] and regret very much that my engagement must deprive me of that pleasure — I promise myself an early visit to you in the evening. Accept my thanks and believe me dear Sir — respectfully

Yours
Hor'o Greenough

Thursday Mor'g.

NOTES

Charles Gould was a New York broker. He is listed in city directories from 1833/34 to 1870/71.
    Manuscript: Autograph File, Houghton.
    1. Presumably Henry Kirke Brown.

224.   To Henry Kirke Brown?
Between March and September 1852

My Dear Sir
I send herewith the letter of Dr Gage[1] — I find him assert (page 3d) that M Angelo was *sent fuori 2 or 3 times* by the Signoria while *passim* he seeks to show that he was *sent* only *once* — to Ferrara[2] — He gives as Michel Angelo's *own* account Busini's letter[3] which he at the same time confesses exists in many forms the one different from the others & he *chooses* to consider most satisfactory that account which accuses M Angelo of *paura.*[4] It is possible that M Ang might

choose to appear to have fled lest falling into the hands of the enemy he might capitar male[5] —

If Dr Gage thinks that capir un carrattere storico e un guistificando[6] why does he maintain such an invidious silence on the subject of the money carried away by Michel Ang? The question here is not of *paura* but whether that immortal man was a thief or not — Either he went to Venice in the service of his country or he went there a felon — Non vi e' punto di mezzo[7] — as I see the matter. Perhaps you can tell me something of Busini and whether he was a man to whom Michel Ang might trust the real nature of his mission — I find so few traces of paura in his life & character that I must suspend my belief of this charge thus far —

Yours truly with many thanks

H G——gh

NOTES

Manuscript: E. Maurice Bloch, Los Angeles, California.

1. Probably Charles Pinckney Gage (1811–94), surgeon, of Concord, New Hampshire, who was a classmate of Henry Kirke Brown (Granville P. Conn, *New Hampshire Surgeons in the Rebellion* [Concord, 1906], pp. 396–400).
2. During the seige of Florence in 1529, Michelangelo, who was in charge of the city's fortifications, was sent to Ferrara to consult the Duke Alfonso about fortifying San Miniato. After his return he suddenly left for Venice, carrying 3,000 ducats, presumably because he was overcome by a temporary panic; subsequently he returned (Michelangelo Buonarroti, *The Letters of Michelangelo*, trans. E. H. Ramsden [Stanford, Calif., 1963], 2:290–94.)
3. According to a letter by the writer Giovanbattista Busini to the historian Benedetto Varchi, 31 January 1549, Michelangelo told Busini that he fled Florence after being informed that Malatesta Baglioni, one of the generals in charge of its defense, would betray it.
4. "Fright."
5. "Fare badly."
6. "To understand a historical character is a justification."
7. "There is no middle point."

225.   To Abner Dumont Jones
       Between March and September 1852

Confidential

My Dear Sir

I enclose an outline of my artistic career[1] — which contains I believe every thing of importance in it — If I might venture to make a request — it would be that you will limit yourself as nearly as possible to this outline — I speak of the facts merely and of course do not undertake either to make or to direct opinions.

I believe that more harm than good is done to artists by lugging them forward before an indifferent public — We must win our place in the hearts of men before we can live as Shakespear says *"in their mouths."*[2]

With many thanks for the honor you do me by admitting me to a niche in your Temple of renown I am dear sir

Yours very respectfully
Horatio Greenough.

Friday Mor'g.

NOTES

Abner Dumont Jones (1807–72) was a clergyman, editor, and author (Abiel Abbott Livermore and Sewall Putman, *History of the Town of Wilton, Hillsborough County, New Hampshire* [Lowell, 1888], p. 133). His most ambitious literary undertaking was this proposed six-volume *Illustrated American Biography*, consisting of portraits and brief accounts of the most prominent Americans from Columbus to his own day; only three volumes appeared (New York, 1853–55).
     Manuscript: Collection of American Literature, Beinecke.
  1. Presumably for Jones' *Illustrated American Biography*, 2:283–84. The engraving on p. 283 was from the daguerreotype made a few weeks before Greenough's death.
  2. Presumably an allusion to *Henry IV*, pt. 1, 3. 2. 50–53.

226. To the editor of the *Home Journal*
After 3 April 1852

Dear Sir: —

I see reprinted in the *Home Journal* of the 3rd inst., a letter of mine to Mr. Dana, in which I ventured to call the attention of the public to Mr. Brackett's group.[1] I should be happy if what I have said should obtain a hearing in New-York.

You have mentioned me as an authority.[2] In my capacity of citizen, I am one of the jury — as an artist, I am myself on trial. We all look to the constituency for employment and for reputation; nor is there any appeal from the public of to-day, but to their children. My earlier efforts were noticed by Alston and Morse, and many distinguished men of letters, in a manner that gave me *work*. I felt that I owed my voice to a man like Mr. Brackett.

Work, sir, is what young artists need, and the American public, thus far, has discovered the workers, and kept them employed; not indeed confirming the high-sounding claims of injudicious partisans — for these are often harmful.

We all want sunshine; but even sunshine can be drawn to a focus too hot for any living thing.

If any one will examine the reviews of the Italian exhibitions, for the last twenty years, he will see that a shower of hyperbole is as good a leveller as can be found. A man will often seek and enjoy a meritorious work, who would shrink from the most "astounding genius of the age." These large drafts at sight are always in danger of being protested. No one likes even to seem a dupe.

Let us hope, sir, that Mr. Brackett's work will win for him all that I believe he asks — a right to go on. I am, Dear Sir, faithfully yours.

H. Greenough,
Sculptor.

George P. Morris, Esq.[3]

NOTES

Source: *The Home Journal,* 10 April 1852.
1. It was at this time being exhibited at the Stuyvesant Institute in New York.
2. The article in the *Home Journal* referred to Greenough as the "highest artistic authority" in the United States.
3. George Pope Morris (1802–64), coeditor, with Nathaniel P. Willis, of the *Home Journal.*

227.   To Charles Sumner
       7 April 1852

98 Chambers Street.
7th April 1852.

My Dear Mr Sumner
I thank you for the speech of Mr Soule[1] which I think covers the whole ground. Never was a more dastardly selfishness than that which has dictated the foreign policy of England since '48[2] and to follow her as our prosperity worshippers wish, would be doubly base.

It should never be forgotten that the English aristocracy, though not averse to all the liberty necessary for trade and manufactures still would prefer despotism to democracy — There is no aristocracy in history that has not preferred a master who would make them safe to a struggle with the masses.

I think it rather small in us in 1852 to reason so much about what Washington meant. In the name of God what do *we mean?* That's the question. Are we going to make of Washington a Confucius and so act by formulas quoted from the last century? If so a statesman hereafter is unnecessary — We only require skilful grammerians to understand the political gospel.

Yours faithfully
Hor Greenough

NOTES

Manuscript: Sumner Correspondence, Houghton.
1. Pierre Soulé (1801–70), U.S. Senator from Louisiana, delivered a speech in the Senate on 22 March 1852 in which he argued that Washington had advocated neutrality as a temporary measure only. He also criticized England for her hostile maneuvers around Cuba. See U.S. Congress, Senate, *The Congressional Globe,* 32d Cong., 1st sess., 1852, appendix, pp. 349–54.
2. The English foreign minister at the time of the revolutionary uprisings of 1848 was Lord Palmerston, who was dismissed in 1851, largely because of his friendliness toward the revolutionaries.

228.   To Alfred Pell
17 [April 1852]

Brooklyn. Sat'y — 17th [April 1852]

My Dear Friend

I have reflected long and seriously upon the course you kindly advised me to take and though I believe you are right in thinking it the best way to forestall enmity and keep my claim in sight, I feel an unconquerable aversion to it.

Neither my habits or my temperament adapt me for managing an undertaking of this kind[1] without the presence of 2 data — 1st a desire for the success of the enterprise on the part of the constituency — 2nd a preference of my work on other grounds than those of personal influence and electioneering — I have done all that I think I can do without pushing — I beg you to remember me in all kindness to Mr Bryant & Mr Sedgwick —

Very faithfully
Yours
Horatio Greenough

A. Pell — Esqr

NOTES

Alfred Pell was a lawyer and insurance broker in New York. He is listed in city directories from 1840/41 to 1894/95. In 1844 he was a trustee of the National Academy of Design.

This letter is dated on internal evidence; see n. 1, below. The seventeenth of April 1852 was a Saturday.

Manuscript: Bryant-Godwin Collection, NYPL.

1. Presumably Greenough refers to the project for a monument to Cooper, from which he apparently dissociated himself about this time. The project was never carried out.

229.   To the editor of the New York Evening Post
[29?] April 1852

Dear Sir:

Fifty-four citizens[1] of New York have associated to ensure the erection of an equestrian statue of Washington, in the military costume of the revolution, in this city. This statue is to be of bronze, fourteen feet in height, exclusive of the pedestal,[2] and is to be erected by Henry Kirke Brown and myself.[3] The list, which I inclose, is one of which any city may well be proud. It has been suggested to me that there is a numerous class whose right to assist in this undertaking is sacred, and to whom an opportunity should be afforded of recording their names in connection with this object. I shall be most happy to aid in any effort for this object, which shall shut the door to imposture and importunity.

                              Very respectfully yours,
                                        H. Greenough

NOTES

Source: New York Evening Post, 30 April 1852.

1. The names of the final fifty-two subscribers to the project are appended to Letter 232.

2. On 7 April 1852, Henry Greenough wrote Horatio urging him to make the

statue smaller. Horatio's reply, dated 12 April 1852, appears in *Letters,* pp. 238–39.

3. According to the contract drawn up, the sixty-eight original subscribers pledged $34,000. When they were called on, however, sixteen of them withdrew. During the summer the contract was canceled by mutual consent, but in September another was made with Brown alone. At this juncture seven more subscribers withdrew, leaving forty-five, who pledged $27,000. The statue, which Brown executed alone, was set up in 1856. See [James Lee], *The Equestrian Statue of Washington* (New York, 1864); see also Agnes Miller, "Centenary of a New York Statue," *New York History* 28 (1957): 167–76.

230.   To Fitz-Greene Halleck
       4 May 1852

Dear Mr Halleck

I have made arrangement[s] with Mr Brady[1] for tomorrow morn'g as soon after 10 A.M. as will suit your convenience and I will wait upon you at that hour.

Very respectfully
Yours
H Greenough —

May 4th 1852

NOTES

Fitz-Greene Halleck (1790–1867), poet and editor, spent most of his career in New York City. Greenough drew a profile of his head, probably in the spring of 1852, from which an engraving was made and reproduced in *Putnam's Magazine* 11 (1868): opp. p. 137.

Manuscript: Morristown-Edison National Historical Park, Morristown, New Jersey.

1. Mathew B. Brady (*ca.* 1823–96), the distinguished Civil War photographer, had a studio at this time in New York. Apparently Greenough was arranging for Brady to photograph Halleck, of whom Brady made two photographs (Nelson Frederick Adkins, *Fitz-Greene-Halleck* [New Haven, 1930], frontispiece and pp. 386–87, 417). Greenough had met both men in connection with the project of erecting a monument to Cooper.

231. To George Bancroft
7 May 1852

No. 850. Broadway — May 7th 1852

Confidential

Geo. Bancroft Esqr

Dear Sir

I count upon the interest you have manifested in my artistic efforts, to excuse my invasion of your leisure. I wish to consult you on a question of Historical propriety.

In designing the colossal statue of Washington for Union Square, I desire to place at the angles of the pedestal, 4 statues of subordinate Generals and I would fain place in the rear, Arnold with a veil thrown over the upper portion of his figure.

The talents and services of Arnold were great. His crime made him for several months our chief danger and obstacle — His infamy can only add lustre to the faith of his fellows and the fame of his captors.

"It is written that evil shall come — but woe unto him by whom it cometh!"[1]

I have never seen any ground for American sympathy with Andre.[2] For his king he staked his head at a foul game and fairly lost it — he has received at the hands of his masters such compensation as his devotion and manhood had earned.

I find a certain squeamish aversion to drag Arnold forth. To my sense it is as if Judas were excluded from the *Cenacolo*,[3] when our constellation of patriots appear shorn of this damned contrast. May I ask your views of this matter?

Very respectfully yours
Hor'o Greenough
Sculptor.

NOTES

Manuscript: Editor's collection.

1. See Matthew 18:7 and Luke 17:1.

2. André's fate excited sympathy both in England and in America because of his courage, military talent, and personal charm.

3. "Last Supper."

232. To the editor of the *New York Evening Post*
9 May 1852

Dear Sir:

I send herewith the list of subscribers for the statue of Washington, which was handed to the sculptors by James Lee, Esq.,[1] to whose zealous action we are indebted for this great opportunity thus nobly offered.[2] I shall send another list on the first of June.

Yours, respectfully,
H. Greenough.

New York, May 9th, 1852.

Aspinwall, Wm. H.	$500	Hunt, W. G.	$500
Astor, W. B.	500	Knapp, Shep'd	500
Belmont, Auguste	500	Lee, James	500
Bridge, John	500	Leupp, C. M.	500
Brown, James	500	Lenox, Jas.	500
Boorman, James	500	Little, E. B.	500
Carman, R. J.	500	Little, Jacob	500
Chamberlain, Wm.	500	Lorillard, P.	500
Coit, H. A.	500	Marshall, Chas. H.	500
De Forrest, W. W.	500	Miller, D. S.	500
Doremus, Thos. C.	500	Minturn, Robt. B.	500
Field, Benj. A.	500	Mitchil, Sam'l L.	500
Fish, Ham'n	500	Miller, D. J.	500
Graves, E. R.	500	Morgan, M.	500
Green, T. C.	500	Mount, And'w	500
Grinnell, Moses H.	500	Parrish, Dan'l	500
Grosvenor, T.	500	Phalen, James	500
Grosvenor, Seth	500	Rhinelander, W. C.	500
Howland, S. S.	500	Robinson, Nelson	500

Smith, Corn's	$500	Wetmore, W. S.	$500
Smith, U. J.	500	Ward, Aug. H.	500
Stuyvesant, G.	500	Whitewright, W.	500
Schermerhorn, P.	500	Wilmerding, W. E.	500
Sturgis, John	500	Winthrop, B. R.	500
Suydam, James	500	Williams, Robt. N.	500
Taylor, Moses	500	Wolfe, John D.	500

NOTES

Source: *New York Evening Post,* 10 May 1852.
1. James Lee was a member of the firm of James Lee and Co., importers.
2. Most of these subscribers may be identified in the New York city directory for 1852.

233.   To George Washington Greene
        27 July 1852

151. Atlantic Street[1]
27th July '52.

G. W. Greene Esqr / 16 Bond Street. New York
Dear Sir —

It was only this morning that I received your note of Monday and I hasten to express to you my satisfaction at the terms in which you speak of the debt you owe me[2] and of your readiness to renew the note now outlawed by the lapse of time. I regret that your talents and acquirements should lack a proper field for their exercise and trust that in a land like this, such will not long be the case. You err in supposing that I was under the impression that you had spoken ill of me or had acted in any hostile manner toward me. I never had any such misgiving — My total complaint was owing to what seemed to me a culpable negligence of my claim upon you — a claim which my circumstances make it a duty to use all proper & gentle means of getting recognized by you & satisfied — Whenever I shall see reason to suppose that you sincerely desire and intend to pay me in whole or in part the money loaned you in friendship & not as a matter of business, I shall feel a satisfaction such as they only feel who return to confidence after having had it shaken away from them.

I receive my letters at Delmonico's[3] because they thus reach me 24 hours earlier than by passing through the Brooklyn P. office.

Very truly
Yours
Horatio Greenough

NOTES

Manuscript: Joseph Downs Collection, Henry Francis du Pont Winterthur Museum.
  1. According to *Hearnes' Brooklyn City Directory, 1852–53,* Greenough's address was 115 Atlantic. Presumably he established a studio here in which he worked on the statue of Washington for Union Square.
  2. Possibly the money referred to in Letter 190.
  3. The Delmonico Hotel at 21–25 Broadway, New York.

234. To Susan Augusta Fenimore Cooper
11 August 1852

Newport. R.I. Aug't 11th [1852]

My Dear Miss Susan
    Your letter introducing Mr De Lancey[1] has come to me here — where my family are residing, and where I am forced to remain for a few days, during Mrs Greenough's absence. She has gone to Bos—— on a visit to my family there. I shall address Mr De Lancey by today's mail and send my letter to Dr Francis who seems to me more likely to ensure its reaching him, than any other person I know. I shall explain to Mr De Lancey my forced detention here and place myself at his service as soon as Mrs Greenough returns — which I think will be in a few days, four days at most.

    I need not say to you that my utmost exertions in any way that can serve you and yours will be my pleasure.

I should have addressed you earlier, nay I should have come to you to join my tears to your own grief,[2] but that I have been overwhelmed with the necessity of doing my own duty and that of others.

We are here for the health of an invalid child[3] and have the happiness of seeing her slowly recover. I should be so happy if fate would allow you and my wife to know each other and to live nearer together!

Dear Miss Susan your father was my instructor — he finished my education and he was my ideal of an American gentleman as was your sainted mother my pattern of a Christian lady — You know not how I have grieved that I was forced to live so separated from him, or what a blow I received in the news of his death. Let me I pray you learn what are your own plans and in all things and at all times regard me as a brother, insofar as my sincere attachment to your house can make me such.

I write with a noisy boy at my elbow and beg you to excuse my incoherence — I had almost forgotten to say to you that the colossal model of your father's portrait is finished. It will be cast in bronze in a few weeks.[4] Let me hope that I shall hear again and at length that I may also tell you what I have done what attempted and what I feel called now to undertake — I am Miss Susan

Most sincerely yours
Horatio Greenough

Addressed: Miss Susan Fenimore Cooper / Cooperstown—Otsego cy / New-York-State.

NOTES

Susan Augusta Fenimore Cooper (1813–94) was a painter, musician, and writer (see Anna K. Cunningham, "Susan Fenimore Cooper: Child of Genius," *New York History* 25 [1944]: 339–50).
     The year is assigned to this letter on the basis of internal evidence.
     Manuscript: Cooper Collection, Beinecke.
1. Possibly Edward Floyd De Lancey (1821–1905), one of Mrs. Cooper's nephews, who was a lawyer in Albany and New York. She had two other De Lancey nephews: John Peter II (1828–70) and Thomas James, Jr. (1822–59). See Cooper, 5:295, 3:231.
2. Cooper's wife died on 20 January 1852.
3. Mary Louise Greenough. The Greenoughs went to Newport about the middle of May.
4. The model was not cast and has evidently been destroyed.

235.   To Ralph Waldo Emerson
2 September 1852

Brooklyn L.I.
Sept 2nd 1852.

Dear Sir

I send you herewith my newspaper articles in a book form[1] and ask of your kindness to read the chapters headed Stone cutter's creed and Relative & Independent beauty — I am quite sure that they are not fit for publication now that I see them again — but I believe the views are sound — Still are they in a shape to make thinkers think — I care not for the slovenly *opus* but I am sensitive about the *materia* — I am sure I shall have your candid opinion — I publish nothing as yet — I wait your answer[2]

Yours very faithfully
Horatio Greenough

Addressed: R. W. Emerson Esqr

NOTES

Manuscript: Emerson Family Papers, Houghton. Previous publication: Nathalia Wright, ed., "Ralph Waldo Emerson and Horatio Greenough," *Harvard Library Bulletin* 12 (1958): 103.
  1. Greenough's book *The Travels, Observations, and Experience of a Yankee Stonecutter,* written under the pseudonym of "Horace Bender," was printed by G. P. Putnam about September 1852. It was apparently unbound at this time, and the issue was small, there being only two copies located in this century. It included three articles which had appeared in the *Home Journal* in June 1852.
  2. Emerson replied to this letter on 6 September. He praised Greenough's book, but predicted that its aggressive and hasty tone might prevent its becoming popular and objected to its anti-Negro sentiment (Wright, ed., "Emerson and Greenough," pp. 103–4).

236.   To Ralph Waldo Emerson
11 September 1852

Newport. R.I. Sept'r 11th [1852]

My Dear Sir

I was prepared for a much severer criticism of my performance than you have inflicted and not prepared for the favorable judgments you have pronounced — perhaps too favorable — I believe the better way will be to let this edition lie and only issue a few copies to individuals in order to get light and help.

If you will ponder at leisure the bearing and tendency of the doctrine I have set up you will, I think, agree with me that it contemplates changes too vast for one life time and a subversion of interests too powerful to yield to any mere logic — If it were possible to get your marks against the objectionable passages and your hints even such as could be given in one word — I should attempt the expurgation and extension of what I have written, with a better chance of becoming presentable[1] —

My adhesion to the South is political and is based on a belief that once a ship is *at sea* whatever else we may do we must let her timbers alone — I believe that the example of the north and the growth of the Irish and German additions to our population will put an end to slavery sooner than any war made upon the south upon moral and scriptural grounds — Precisely because northern morality coexists peaceably with greater woes than the woe of Slavery — The South drives negroes not by *motu-proprio* but as the agent and servant of the North and of Europe — In vain shall we preach abstractions and perfection to the south while we offer *gold* for their tobacco cotton and sugar. If we are to act upon the south fairly, we must begin by withdrawing the demand for Slave products — England has tried this and found that Jehovah was against such coercion[2] —

I am a staunch believer in free discussion & have no objection to hear any amount of abuse of slavery and slave holders — provided there be also a fair hearing for the defense — So far as the negro himself is concerned I fully believe & roundly declare that I believe he *can exist here* only as a bondsman — Are we not a little rash in asserting our own freedom? We are parts of an organization — and being such can have no *freedom* as I understand that term but by the dissolution of the system of which we are fractional and functional components. Now I believe that our law *is not* in harmony with God's law and that therefore the result of our action will be a reductio ad absurdum — We seek not *the law* — we ask for relative success and say one and all — *après moi le deluge*. The Homo has yet to seek his mission — He has condemned his own nature and at the same breath asserted godship — One of these dogmas must give way if we are to have other than the see-saw of anarchy and despotism.

[No signature]

Addressed: R. W. Emerson Esqr / Concord Mass.

NOTES

Manuscript: Emerson Family Papers, Houghton. Previous publication: Nathalia Wright, ed., "Ralph Waldo Emerson and Horatio Greenough," *Harvard Library Bulletin* 12 (1958): 105–6.
1. For Emerson's reply to this letter, dated 25 September 1852, see Wright, ed., "Emerson and Greenough," pp. 106–7.
2. Slavery in the British Empire was abolished in 1833, but England continued to import the products which Greenough named.

237.   To John Pendleton Kennedy
22 September 1852

John P. Kennedy / Secretary of the Navy
Sir —

Having learned that Congress during its recent session appropriated monies for the transshipment of the group of Statuary executed by me, under contract with the President of the United States and designed to complete the illustration of the Eastern stairway of the Capitol, I respectfully ask your attention to some considerations which seem to me important for the due performance of the transshipment in question.[1]

I have caused the various blocks which form the group to be faithfully secured in frames of timber. This apparatus has in travelling from the interior of Tuscany to the sea-board, been put to tests more severe than any that may be anticipated in sailing hither, provided the work be shored up securely in the hold of the vessel that bears it.

If it be permitted me to make a suggestion, I would recommend that the Engineer[2] employed by me for the packing of this work and its transportation to Leghorn, be allowed also to controul its movement until its actual delivery on board; that his action then cease and that the engineer of the United States Service take charge of its shipment and its secure and stable position in the hold.

It cannot be doubted that the transfer of the work in a states vessel would be safer than in a chartered merchantman, particularly in case the voyage be deferred to a late season of the year; still it is to be remembered that such an arrangement would involve the necessity of carrying it out to the Leghorn Roads and consequently of an additional transshipment; whereas the chartered bottom can receive it at the pier of the inner harbour, as was done in the shipment of the colossal statue of Washington.

I would recommend that the engineer be instructed to secure the work from the drip of water from above, as the iron unavoidably situated near the marble, may by its oxidation seriously injure the effect of the sculpture.

I respectfully ask of the Government the permission to ship together with this work, my library and such portion of my personal effects as can be put on board without occasioning delay.

If remarks upon the position of this group be not out of season, I should wish to address to you some observations upon the anomalous site now occupied by the Group of Columbus and the Indian to which my work is destined to form a *pendant* and my reasons for strenuously advocating a lower and more appropriate situation for both works.[3]

Allow me Sir to express my satisfaction that in making these last arrangements to deliver my work, as in its first inception, I find myself in relation with a gentleman whose fame in the kindred pursuit of letters insures an appreciation of the significance and value of Art, and a sense of the peculiar difficulties under which its cultivation must yet awhile labor amid the more imperative and sterner demands of our national requirement.

I am Sir with the highest respect
Your Obedient Servant
Horatio Greenough
Sculptor.

22nd Septr. 1852 / National Hotel / Washington D.C.[4]

NOTES

John Pendleton Kennedy (1795–1870), author and statesman, was secretary of the navy in 1852–53.
 Manuscript: RG 45, General Records of the Department of the Navy, Office of the Secretary of the Navy, Miscellaneous Letters Received, NA.
 1. In August 1852 Congress appropriated the sum of $7000 for the transportation and erection of Greenough's group *The Rescue*. For various reasons, however, it did not reach Washington until August 1853; it was erected within the next few weeks.
 2. The Florentine engineer O. Batelli.
 3. He had presented his argument for a lower location of Persico's group in his *Æsthetics at Washington*.
 4. Kennedy replied to this letter on 23 September 1852 that instructions had been sent Com. S. H. Stringham, then commander of the Mediterranean Squadron (copy, RG 45, General Records of the Department of the Navy, NA).

238.   To Ralph Waldo Emerson
20 October 1852

Cambridge 20th Oct'r 1852

R. W. Emerson Esq
Dear Sir
 I am anxious to speak with you once more about my pamphlet[1] — particularly since I have developed somewhat farther my views of structure and of organization.
 If you can give me an hour or two more of your leisure I believe

that I am better prepared to profit by them than before — I beg you to
present me respectfully to Mrs E² —

Very faithfully yours
Hor Greenough
Sculptor.

NOTES

Manuscript: Emerson Family Papers, Houghton. Previous publication:
Nathalia Wright, ed., "Ralph Waldo Emerson and Horatio Greenough," *Harvard
Library Bulletin* 12 (1958): 107.
1. *The Travels . . . of a Yankee Stonecutter.*
2. Emerson replied to this letter on 21 October 1852, inviting Greenough to
   Concord on the following Tuesday, 25 October (Wright, ed., "Emerson and
   Greenough," p. 108).

239. To Ralph Waldo Emerson
22 October 1852

Cambridge 22nd Oct'r 1852.

Dear Sir

I will come to you on Tuesday next as you indicate and will take
the 12 o'clock train.

I only wait to get rid of certain not important or rather impertinent
parts in order to obey you and publish — I write amid an immense
row — a discussion of spiritual rappings¹ and must say au revoir!

Very gratefully
Yours
Horatio Greenough

NOTES

Manuscript: Emerson Family Papers, Houghton. Previous publication:
Nathalia Wright, ed., "Ralph Waldo Emerson and Horatio Greenough," *Harvard
Library Bulletin* 12 (1958): 108.

1. At this time, and for several years after Greenough's death, his wife was interested in spiritualism, a current vogue.

240.   To Ralph Waldo Emerson
   4 November 1852

Newport. R.I.
Nov 4th

Dear Mr Emerson

A thousand thanks for your suggestions,[1] I will avail myself of them one and all — I enclose more words "in behalf of this Falstaff."[2] I wish you to tell me its weak point — since you are the man midwife of my babe. I will fight this fight to the end of all time for I believe we are after all together —

I thought you would be puzzled to trim my style — it's like washing dirt and only makes mud of it — A clown is never so clownish as when he tries to behave — Perhaps I shall do better as I go on — Here is a missive from G P Putnam — are you in the list?[3]

I wish you would run your pen through what offends you as you read. I fear you may get used to it as I have to tobacco. I beg, my respects to Mrs Emerson and to Edith & Emma.[4]

Yours faithfully
Hor'o Greenough

P.S.   Dusseldorf can neither make nor mar a man[5] — he might do worse —

Addressed: R. W. Emerson Esqr / Concord. Mass'tts

NOTES

Manuscript: Emerson Family Papers, Houghton. Previous publication: Nathalia Wright, ed., "Ralph Waldo Emerson and Horatio Greenough," *Harvard Library Bulletin* 12 (1958): 110.
1. Emerson had written Greenough on 1 November 1852, pointing out several

weak chapters in his book, but again urging him to publish it soon (Wright, ed., "Emerson and Greenough," p. 109).

2. See *The Merry Wives of Windsor* 2. 4. 532.

3. Possibly a list of persons to receive complimentary copies of Greenough's book.

4. Edith (1841–1929) and Ellen Tucker (1839–1909) were Emerson's daughters.

5. In his letter of 1 November 1852, Emerson had asked Greenough's opinion of the instruction at the Academy of Painting at Dusseldorf. Emerson had learned that young W. H. Furness, Jr., portrait painter, was going there.

241.   To Ralph Waldo Emerson
         10 November 1852

                                        Cambridge Mass. Nov 10th 52.

My Dear Mr Emerson

I am going to undertake the reading of 2 lectures[1] and have no copy of my pamphlet. Will you send me your copy by mail? If you should still hold the Addenda about Slavery I shall beg you to send that with them.[2]

I am anxious to do some thing in order to get the means to print and mean to make my theory live according to the strictest rule of demand & supply.

I have written a criticism of Mr Parker's sermon[3] —

                                        Yours faithfully
                                        H. Greenough
                                        Sculptor

Addressed: R. W. Emerson Esqr / Concord. Mass.

NOTES

Manuscript: Emerson Family Papers, Houghton. Previous publication: Nathalia Wright, ed., "Ralph Waldo Emerson and Horatio Greenough," *Harvard Library Bulletin* 12 (1958): 110.

1. On 24 and 29 November 1852, Greenough read two lectures, entitled "Art as Related to Life," in the lecture room of the New Music Hall, Winter

Street, Boston. As he read the second, he gave evidence of being deranged. A few weeks later he died of what was diagnosed as brain fever.

2. Emerson replied to this letter on 11 November 1852, saying that he had sent both Greenough's book and "the chapter"—apparently Greenough's "Addenda"—and he again took Greenough to task for his attitude on slavery (Wright, ed., "Emerson and Greenough," pp. 110–11).

3. Theodore Parker (1810–60), Unitarian clergyman, was at this time minister of the new Twenty-Eighth Congregational Society of Boston. Presumably Greenough refers to the sermon which Parker preached on 31 October 1852, a week after Webster's death, in which he criticized Webster's opposition to secession.

Unrecovered Letters / Index

Unrecovered Letters

1826   *ca.* April, to Edmund Dana (Greenough to Allston, 9 May 1826).
Spring?, to Robert Weir. Formerly in possession of Mrs. James De Wolf Perry, Charleston, South Carolina.

1828   *ca.* May, to John Ludlow Morton (Greenough to Morse, 15 May 1828).

1829   After 31 July 1829, to "My dear Sir" (fragment of draft, editor's collection).
ca. 1–15 September, to James Fenimore Cooper (Cooper, 1:389–91).
ca. October, to James Fenimore Cooper (Cooper, 1:394–97).
ca. mid-November, to James Fenimore Cooper (Cooper, 1:398–99).

1830   January, to James Fenimore Cooper (Cooper, 1:403).
ca. February, to Robert Gilmor, Jr. (Greenough to Gilmor, 7 September 1830). Apparently lost in transit.
ca. February, to John? Grant (Greenough to Gilmor, 7 September 1830).
ca. late March, to James Fenimore Cooper (Cooper, 1:406–7).
Before 5 May, to James Fenimore Cooper (Cooper, 1:412–13).
ca. 25 October, to James Fenimore Cooper (Greenough to Cooper, 6 December 1830). Apparently lost in transit.
To Robert Gilmor, Jr. (C. F. Libbie, *Catalogue of the Autograph Letters and Manuscripts of the Late Col. Brantz Mayer . . . Nov. 11, 12, 13, 1879*).

1831   *ca.* 9 February, to James Fenimore Cooper (Greenough to Cooper, 17 February 1831).
ca. August, to Robert Weir (*Letters*, p. 75).
ca. 8 December, to Samuel F. B. Morse (Greenough to Morse, 5 January 1832).

1832   30 May, to Edward Everett (Everett to Greenough, 29 July 1832).
Before June, to Robert Gilmor, Jr. (Greenough to Gilmor, 10 June 1832).

1833   29 January–10 April, to James Fenimore Cooper (Greenough to Cooper, 10 April 1833).
30 September, to Edward Everett (Everett to Greenough, 13 January 1834).

1 December, to ? (Bickford Cooper, "Sculpture in America," *Journal of American History* 1 [1907]: 164).

ca. 16 December, to Felix Cicognari (Greenough to Winslow Lewis, 16 December 1833).

1835   15 March, to Edward Everett (Everett to Greenough, 8 June 1835).

1836   17 March, to Richard Henry Wilde (C. F. Libbie, *Catalogue of the Collection of Autographs of the late Rev. W. S. Alexander, of Cambridge, Mass. . . . Dec. 4–5, 1902*).

Before 14 June, to James Fenimore Cooper (Cooper, 3:219).

Summer?, to Hiram Powers (Powers to Everett, 28 May 1859, Letter Book, Powers Papers, National Collection of the Fine Arts, Smithsonian Institution, Washington, D.C.).

1837   10 October, to Nathan Mayer Rothschild and Sons (Rothschild to Greenough, 24 October 1837).

16 October, to John Forsyth (RG 59, General Records of the Department of State, Index of Letters Received by the Secretary of State, NA).

1838   *ca.* spring, to President Martin Van Buren (John Forsyth to Greenough, 11 July 1838).

1839   29 March, to Edward Everett (Everett to Greenough, 20 May 1839).

ca. September, to James Kirke Paulding (Greenough to Greene, 15 September 1839).

1840   7 June, to Edward Everett (Everett to Greenough, 8 July 1840).

28 July, to Edward Everett (Everett to Greenough, 4 August 1940).

1841   10 or 11 March, to Isaac Hull (Greenough to Daniel Webster, 16 March 1841).

ca. June, to Charles Sumner (Edward L. Pierce, *Memoir and Letters of Charles Sumner* [Boston, 1878–93], 2:184).

20 November, to Edward Everett (Everett to Greenough, 3 December 1841).

14 December, to Edward Everett (Everett to Greenough, 23 December 1841).

1842   26 January, to Edward Everett (Everett to Greenough, 7 February 1842).

2 February, to Edward Everett (Everett to Greenough, 23 February 1842).

17 June, to Edward Everett (Everett to Greenough, 20 June 1842).

16 December, to William Hickling Prescott (Prescott to Greenough, 29 December 1842).

1843   10 December, to Edward Everett (Everett to Greenough, 26 February 1844).

1846   22 July, to James Buchanan (RG 59, General Records of the Department of State, Register of Letters Received by the Secretary of State, NA).

Summer?, to James Fenimore Cooper (Cooper to Greenough, 6 May 1847). Apparently lost in transit.

1847   24 February, to George William Curtis (Anderson Galleries, *Library of the Late Adrian H. Joline, Part VIII: American Autograph Letters and Documents, Nov. 22, 23, 24, 1915*).

1848   3 January, to Robert Charles Winthrop (Winthrop to Frances Boott Greenough, 28 May 1887, collection of Henry G. Nickerson, Dedham, Massachusetts).

1849   20 January, to Edward Everett (Everett to Greenough, 21 May 1849).

17 June, to Edward Everett (Everett to Greenough, 17 July 1849).

15 August, to Edward Everett (Everett to Greenough, 10 September 1849).

1850   *ca.* 26 September, to Robert Balmanno (Greenough to Joseph Green Cogswell, 26 September 1850; George A. Leavitt & Co., *Catalogue of an Exceedingly interesting Collection of Autograph Letters . . . (being a third portion of the Magnificent Private Library now on sale by J. R. Bouton . . . May 20, 1868 and following*).

1852   1 January, to William Appleton (RG 42, Edward Stubbs to B. B. French, November 1853, NA).

ca. 1 April to Henry Greenough (Henry to Horatio, 7 April 1852).

3 April, to George Ticknor (Ticknor to Greenough, 6 April 1852).

17 June, to President Millard Fillmore (RG 42, Edward Stubbs to B. B. French, November 1853, NA).

25 June, to Edward Everett (RG 59, General Records of the Department of State, Register of Letters Received by the Secretary of State, NA).

12 July, to Edward Everett (RG 42, Edward Stubbs to B. B. French, November 1853, NA).

27 July, to Edward Everett (RG 59, General Records of the Department of State, Register of Letters Received by the Secretary of State, NA).

Undated   To James Fenimore Cooper, 3 letters (Louisa G. Greenough to Thomas R. Lounsbury, 17 April 1852, Beinecke).

To Robert Gilmor, Jr. (Gilmor to Brantz Mayer, 29 August 1848, NYHS).

To ?, referring to a duty laid on plaster models by the Duke of Modena (C. F. Libbie, *Catalogue of the Autograph Collection of the Late Mrs. J. S. F. Fogg, March 20, 21, 1906*).

Index

Abercrombie, Ralph, 212n, 219, 220n
Académie de France à Rome, 63, 64n
Académie des Beaux Arts, Paris, 38, 43n
Accademia di Belle Arti, Florence, 18, 22n, 24, 36, 130, 292, 295, 296, 299, 384
Adami, Lorenzo, 72–73, 74n
Adams, John, 354, 397. *See also* Greenough, Horatio, sculpture of
Adams, John Quincy, 265, 269, 326n, 327n; letter to, 325–26. *See also* Greenough, Horatio, sculpture of
Albani, Francesco, 77, 79n, 105, 107n, 165
Albany, N.Y., 119
Alexander I, Tsar of Russia, 54, 55n
Alexander the Great, 174
Alexander, Francis, 110, 111n, 122, 123n, 130, 142, 143n, 303, 306n
Alfieri, Vittorio, 86, 92n, 187
Allori, Alessandro, 164, 165n
Allori, Angiolo, 164, 165n
Allori, Christofano, 164, 165n
Allston, Martha Remington (Dana), 92, 93n, 171, 188, 207
Allston, Washington, 9n, 10n, 12, 13n, 22n, 42n, 44n, 79–80, 93n, 110, 144, 146, 168, 172n, 188n, 189n, 287, 297, 297n, 340–42, 342n, 343–45, 346n, 349–50, 413; letters to, 7–9, 17–21, 28–30, 36–42, 45–48, 86–92, 169–71, 185–88, 207–8, 228–30
Alps, 86
Alverez, Don Jose de Pereira y Cubero, 9, 10n
America. *See* Greenough, Horatio, on American culture; Greenough, Horatio, on art and artists in America

American Academy of Arts and Sciences, Boston, 331
American Academy of the Fine Arts, New York, 101n, 104n, 110n, 135n, 295
American Revolution. *See* Greenough, Horatio, proposed works of
Amory, James Sullivan, 242, 243n
Amory, Mary Copley (Greene), 242, 242–43n
André, Maj. John, 390, 391n, 418, 419n
Andrei, Giovanni, 44n
Andreini, Dr. Vincenzo, 231, 231n, 233, 245
Andryane, Alexandre Phillippe: *Memoires d'un Prissonier d'Etat*, 315, 316n
Antinuoüs, The Braschi, 103, 104n
Antonio, workman, 262
Apollo di Belvedere, 11, 13n, 20, 23n, 168, 169n, 229, 230n, 401
Appleton, Thomas, 39, 44n, 184, 280, 281n, 282, 285, 291
Appleton, William, 408, 408n
Arcspedale di Santa Maria Nuova, Florence, 124, 126n
Argus, 120
Arno, dog, 200, 201n
Arnold, Gen. Benedict, 390, 418
Arno River, 30n, 115, 352n
Aspinwall, Col. Thomas, 27n, 131; letter to, 27
Aspinwall, William Henry, 419
Astor, William Backhouse, 419
Astor House, New York, 399
Atlantic Ocean, 86, 127, 364
Atlantic Street, Brooklyn, N.Y., 420
Auchmuty, Lt. Henry J., 158, 158n

7   6